WARRIOR DREAMS

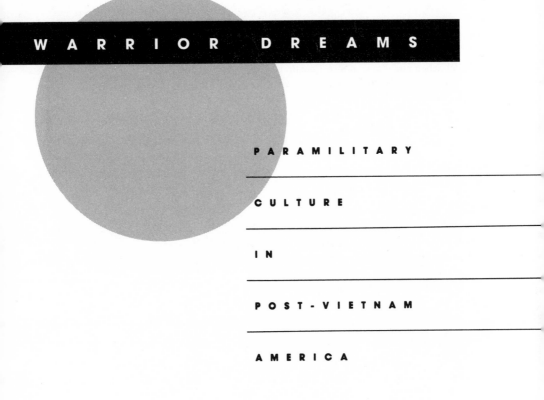

WARRIOR DREAMS

PARAMILITARY

CULTURE

IN

POST-VIETNAM

AMERICA

JAMES WILLIAM GIBSON

HILL AND WANG

A DIVISION OF FARRAR, STRAUS AND GIROUX / NEW YORK

A version of "Becoming the Armed Man" appeared in *Public Culture* © 1991 by Center for Transnational Cultural Studies, Vol. IV, no. 1, Fall, 1991. Reprinted by courtesy of the University of Chicago Press.

LIBRARY OF CONGRESS CATALOGING-IN-PUBLICATION DATA
Gibson, James William.
Warrior dreams : paramilitary culture in post-Vietnam America / James William Gibson.—1st ed.
p.   cm.
Includes bibliographical references and index.
1. Popular culture—United States—History—20th century.
2. Militarism—United States—History—20th century. 3. United States—Social life and customs—1971–   I. Title.
E169.04G53   1994   306'.0973—dc20   93-29960 CIP

ACKNOWLEDGMENTS

The research for *Warrior Dreams* started back in the early 1980s. During those years I was aided by grants from Carol Bernstein Ferry and W. H. Ferry, the Kaltenborn Foundation, the Dick Goldensohn Foundation for Investigative Reporting, and the American Council of Learned Societies. In the late 1980s the Harry Frank Guggenheim Foundation and the John D. and Catherine T. MacArthur Foundation provided significant funding to allow me to devote all my time to research and writing. A fellowship from Cornell University's Society for the Humanities in 1990–91 provided additional assistance.

When I taught at Southern Methodist University in the mid-1980s, two students, Deanna Deck and Joseph Ginto, helped me with my research. The office manager of the sociology department, Barbara Babcock, deserves special recognition for transcribing taped interviews. My literary agent, Diane Cleaver, found a good publisher.

Several people read drafts of the manuscript and offered comments—thank you, Barbara Zheutlin, Bernice Martin, and Charles Noble. My editor at Hill and Wang, Sara Bershtel, gave this project much attention and had many suggestions for improving the book. My thanks as well to Sally Singer and Ariel Kaminer.

Most of all, though, I want to thank my wife, Carol Lynn Mithers. She heard all my ideas long before they were ever written down; she saw drafts that never got out the door to anyone else. Carol gave me her time, her energy, and her loving support—all this while she had her own book to write.

An earlier version of chapter 9—"Becoming the Armed Man"— appeared in the journal *Public Culture*. My thanks to the Center for Transnational Cultural Studies and the University of Chicago Press for allowing me to use parts of that essay.

J.W.G.

CONTENTS

WARRIOR DREAMS

We couldn't see them, but we could hear their bugles sound the call. The Communist battalions were organizing for a predawn assault. Captain Kokalis smiled wickedly; he'd been through this before. A "human wave" assault composed of thousands of enemy soldiers was headed our way. The captain ordered the remaining soldiers in his command to check their .30- and .50-caliber machine guns. Earlier in the night, the demolitions squad attached to our unit had planted mines and explosive charges for hundreds of meters in front of our position.

And then it began. At a thousand meters, the soldiers emerged screaming from the gray-blue fog. "Fire!" yelled Captain Kokalis. The gun crews opened up with short bursts of three to seven rounds; their bullets struck meat. Everywhere I could see, clusters of Communist troops were falling by the second. But the wave still surged forward. At five hundred meters, Kokalis passed the word to his gunners to increase their rate of fire to longer strings of ten to twenty rounds. Sergeant Donovan, the demolitions squad leader, began to reap the harvest from the night's planting. Massive explosions ripped through the Communist troops. Fire and smoke blasted into the dawn sky. It was as if the human wave had hit a submerged reef; as the dying fell, wide gaps appeared in the line where casualties could no longer be replaced.

But still they kept coming, hundreds of men, each and every one bent on taking the American position and wiping us out. As the Communists reached one hundred meters, Kokalis gave one more command. Every machine gun in our platoon went to its maximum rate of sustained full-automatic frenzy, sounding like chain saws that just keep cutting and cutting.

And then it was over. The attack subsided into a flat sea of Communist dead. No Americans had been killed or wounded. We were happy to be alive, proud of our victory. We only wondered if our ears would ever stop ringing and if we would ever again smell anything other than the bittersweet aroma of burning gunpowder . . .

Although an astonishing triumph was achieved that day, no historian will ever find a record of this battle in the hundreds of volumes and thousands of official reports written about the Korean or Vietnam war. Nor was the blood spilt part of a covert operation in Afghanistan or some unnamed country in Africa, Asia, or Latin America.

No, this battle was fought inside the United States, a few miles north of Las Vegas, in September 1986. It was a purely *imaginary* battle, a dream of victory staged as part of the *Soldier of Fortune* magazine's annual convention. The audience of several hundred men, women, and children, together with reporters and a camera crew from CBS News, sat in bleachers behind half a dozen medium and heavy machine guns owned by civilians. Peter G. Kokalis, *SOF*'s firearms editor, set the scene for the audience and asked them to imagine that the sandy brushland of the Desert Sportsman Rifle and Pistol Club was really a killing zone for incoming Communist troops. Kokalis was a seasoned storyteller; he'd given this performance before. When the fantasy battle was over, the fans went wild with applause. Kokalis picked up a microphone, praised Donovan (another *SOF* staff member)—"He was responsible for that whole damn Communist bunker that went up"—and told the parents in the audience to buy "claymores [antipersonnel land mines] and other good shit for the kids." A marvelous actor who knew what his audience wanted, Kokalis sneered, "Did you get that, CBS, on your videocam? Screw you knee-jerk liberals."[1]

The shoot-out and victory over Communist forces conducted at the Desert Sportsman Rifle and Pistol Club was but one battle in a cultural or imaginary "New War" that had been going on since the late 1960s and early 1970s. The bitter controversies surrounding the Vietnam War had discredited the old American ideal of the masculine warrior hero for much of the public. But in 1971, when Clint Eastwood made the transition from playing cowboys in old *Rawhide* reruns and spaghetti westerns to portraying San Francisco police detective Harry Callahan in *Dirty Harry*, the warrior hero returned in full force. His backup arrived in 1974 when Charles Bronson appeared in *Death Wish*, the story of a mild-mannered, middle-aged architect in New York City who, after his wife is murdered and his daughter is raped and driven insane, finds new meaning in life through an endless war of revenge against street punks.

In the 1980s, Rambo and his friends made their assault. The experience of John Rambo, a former Green Beret, was the paradigmatic story of the decade. In *First Blood* (1982), he burns down a small Oregon town while suffering hallucinatory flashbacks to his service in Vietnam. Three years later, in *Rambo: First Blood, Part 2*, he is taken off a prison chain gang by his former commanding officer in Vietnam and asked to perform a special reconnaissance mission to find suspected American POWs in Laos, in exchange for a Presidential pardon. His only question: "Do we get to win this time?" And indeed, Rambo does win. Betrayed by the CIA bureaucrat in charge of the mission, Rambo fights the Russians and Vietnamese by himself and brings the POWs back home.

Hundreds of similar films celebrating the victory of good men over bad through armed combat were made during the late 1970s and 1980s. Many were directed by major Hollywood directors and starred well-known actors. Elaborate special effects and exotic film locations added tens of millions to production costs. And for every large-budget film, there were scores of cheaper formula films employing lesser-known actors and production crews. Often these "action-adventure" films had only brief theatrical releases in major markets. Instead, they made their money in smaller cities and towns, in sales to Europe and the Third World, and most of all, in the sale of videocassettes to rental stores. Movie producers could even turn a profit on "video-only" releases; action-adventure films were the largest category of video rentals in the 1980s.

At the same time, Tom Clancy became a star in the publishing world. His book *The Hunt for Red October* (1984) told the story of the Soviet Navy's most erudite submarine commander, Captain Markus Ramius, and his effort to defect to the United States with the Soviets' premier missile-firing submarine. *Red Storm Rising* (1986) followed, an epic of World War III framed as a high-tech conventional war against the Soviet Union. Clancy's novels all featured Jack Ryan, Ph.D., a former Marine captain in Vietnam turned academic naval historian who returns to duty as a CIA analyst and repeatedly stumbles into life-and-death struggles in which the fate of the world rests on his prowess. All were bestsellers.

President Reagan, Secretary of the Navy John Lehman, and many other high officials applauded Clancy and his hero. Soon the author had a multimillion-dollar contract for a whole series of novels, movie deals with Paramount, and a new part-time job as a foreign-policy expert writing op-ed pieces for the *Washington Post*, the *Los Angeles Times*, and other influential newspapers around the country. His success motivated dozens of authors, mostly active-duty or retired military men, to take up the genre. The "techno-thriller" was born.

At a slightly lower level in the literary establishment, the same publishing houses that marketed women's romance novels on grocery and drugstore paperback racks rapidly expanded their collections of pulp fiction for men. Most were written like hard-core pornography, except that inch-by-inch descriptions of penises entering vaginas were replaced by equally graphic portrayals of bullets, grenade fragments, and knives shredding flesh: "He tried to grab the handle of the commando knife, but the terrorist pushed down on the butt, raised the point and yanked the knife upward through the muscle tissue and guts. It ripped intestines, spilling blood and gore."[2] A minimum of 20 but sometimes as many as 120 such graphically described killings occurred in each 200-to-250-page paperback. Most series came out four times a year with domestic print runs of 60,000 to 250,000 copies. More than a dozen different comic books with titles like *Punisher, Vigilante*, and *Scout* followed suit with clones of the novels.

Along with the novels and comics came a new kind of periodical which replaced the older adventure magazines for men, such as *True* and *Argosy*, that had folded in the 1960s. Robert K. Brown, a former captain in the U.S. Army Special Forces during the Vietnam War, founded *Soldier of Fortune: The Journal of Professional Adventurers* in the spring of 1975, just before the fall of Saigon. *SOF*'s position was explicit from the start: the independent warrior must step in to fill the dangerous void created by the American failure in Vietnam. By the mid-1980s *SOF* was reaching 35,000 subscribers, had newsstand sales of another 150,000, and was being passed around to at least twice as many readers.[3]

Half a dozen new warrior magazines soon entered the market. Some, like *Eagle, New Breed*, and *Gung-Ho*, tried to copy the *SOF* editorial package—a strategy that ultimately failed. But most developed their own particular pitch. *Combat Handguns* focused on pistols for would-be gunfighters. *American Survival Guide* advertised and reviewed everything needed for "the good life" after the end of civilization (except birth control devices—too many Mormon subscribers, the editor said), while *S.W.A.T.* found its way to men who idealized these elite police teams and who were worried about home defense against "multiple intruders."

During the same period, sales of military weapons took off. Colt offered two semiautomatic versions of the M16 used by U.S. soldiers in Vietnam (a full-size rifle and a shorter-barreled carbine with collapsible stock). European armories exported their latest products, accompanied by sophisticated advertising campaigns in *SOF* and the more mainstream gun magazines. Israeli Defense Industries put a longer, 16-inch barrel on the Uzi submachine gun (to make it legal) and sold it as a semiautomatic carbine. And the Communist countries of Eastern Europe, together with the People's Republic of China, jumped into the market with the devil's own favorite hardware, the infamous AK47. The AK sold in the United States was the semiautomatic version of the assault rifle used by the victorious Communists

in Vietnam and by all kinds of radical movements and terrorist organizations around the world. It retailed for $300 to $400, half the
price of an Uzi or an AR-15; complete with three 30-round magazines,
cleaning kit, and bayonet, it was truly a bargain.

To feed these hungry guns, munitions manufacturers packaged new
"generic" brands of military ammo at discount prices, often selling
them in cases of 500 or 1,000 rounds. New lines of aftermarket
accessories offered parts for full-automatic conversions, improved
flash-hiders, scopes, folding stocks, and scores of other goodies. In
1989, the U.S. Bureau of Alcohol, Tobacco and Firearms (ATF)
estimated that two to three million military-style rifles had been sold
in this country since the Vietnam War. The Bureau released these
figures in response to the public outcry over a series of mass murders
committed by psychotics armed with assault rifles.

But the Bureau's statistics tell only part of the story. In less than
two decades, millions of American men had purchased combat rifles,
pistols, and shotguns and begun training to fight their own personal
wars. Elite combat shooting schools teaching the most modern techniques and often costing $500 to over $1,000 in tuition alone were
attended not only by soldiers and police but by increasing numbers
of civilians as well. Hundreds of new indoor pistol-shooting ranges
opened for business in old warehouses and shopping malls around
the country, locations ideal for city dwellers and suburbanites.

A new game of "tag" blurred the line between play and actual
violence: men got the opportunity to hunt and shoot other men without
killing them or risking death themselves. The National Survival Game
was invented in 1981 by two old friends, one a screenwriter for the
weight-lifting sagas that gave Arnold Schwarzenegger his first starring
roles, and the other a former member of the Army's Long Range
Reconnaissance Patrol (LRRP) in Vietnam.[4] Later called paintball
because it utilized guns firing balls of watercolor paint, by 1987 the
game was being played by at least fifty thousand people (mostly men)
each weekend on both outdoor and indoor battlefields scattered across
the nation. Players wore hard-plastic face masks intended to resemble
those of ancient tribal warriors and dressed from head to toe in
camouflage clothes imported by specialty stores from military outfitters
around the world. The object of the game was to capture the opposing

team's flag, inflicting the highest possible body count along the way.

One major park out in the Mojave Desert seventy miles southeast of Los Angeles was named Sat Cong Village. *Sat Cong* is a slang Vietnamese phrase meaning "Kill Communists" that had been popularized by the CIA as part of its psychological-warfare program. Sat Cong Village employed an attractive Asian woman to rent the guns, sell the paintballs, and collect the twenty-dollar entrance fee. Players had their choice of playing fields: Vietnam, Cambodia, or Nicaragua. On the Nicaragua field, the owner built a full-size facsimile of the crashed C-47 cargo plane contracted by Lieutenant Colonel Oliver North to supply the contras. The scene even had three parachutes hanging from trees; the only thing missing was the sole survivor of the crash, Eugene Hasenfus.

The 1980s, then, saw the emergence of a highly energized culture of war and the warrior. For all its varied manifestations, a few common features stood out. The New War culture was not so much military as paramilitary. The new warrior hero was only occasionally portrayed as a member of a conventional military or law enforcement unit; typically, he fought alone or with a small, elite group of fellow warriors. Moreover, by separating the warrior from his traditional state-sanctioned occupations—policeman or soldier—the New War culture presented the warrior role as the ideal identity for *all* men. Bankers, professors, factory workers, and postal clerks could all transcend their regular stations in life and prepare for heroic battle against the enemies of society.

To many people, this new fascination with warriors and weapons seemed a terribly bad joke. The major newspapers and magazines that arbitrate what is to be taken seriously in American society scoffed at the attempts to resurrect the warrior hero. Movie critics were particularly disdainful of Stallone's Rambo films. *Rambo: First Blood, Part 2* was called "narcissistic jingoism" by *The New Yorker* and "hare-brained" by the *Wall Street Journal*. The *Washington Post* even intoned that "Sly's body looks fine. Now can't you come up with a workout for his soul?"

But in dismissing Rambo so quickly and contemptuously, commentators failed to notice the true significance of the emerging paramilitary culture. They missed the fact that quite a few people were not writing Rambo off as a complete joke; behind the Indian bandanna, necklace, and bulging muscles, a new culture hero affirmed such traditional American values as self-reliance, honesty, courage, and concern for fellow citizens. Rambo was a worker and a former enlisted man, not a smooth-talking professional. That so many seemingly well-to-do, sophisticated liberals hated him for both his politics and his uncouthness only added to his glory. Further, in their emphasis on Stallone's clownishness the commentators failed to see not only how widespread paramilitary culture had become but also its relation to the historical moment in which it arose.

Indeed, paramilitary culture can be understood only when it is placed in relation to the Vietnam War. America's failure to win that war was a truly profound blow. The nation's long, proud tradition of military victories, from the Revolutionary War through the century-long battles against the Indians to World Wars I and II, had finally come to an end. Politically, the defeat in Vietnam meant that the post-World War II era of overwhelming American political and military power in international affairs, the era that in 1945 *Time* magazine publisher Henry Luce had prophesied would be the "American Century," was over after only thirty years. No longer could U.S. diplomacy wield the big stick of military intervention as a ready threat—a significant part of the American public would no longer support such interventions, and the rest of the world knew it.

Moreover, besides eroding U.S. influence internationally, the defeat had subtle but serious effects on the American psyche. America has always celebrated war and the warrior. Our long, unbroken record of military victories has been crucially important both to the national identity and to the personal identity of many Americans—particularly men. The historian Richard Slotkin locates a primary "cultural archetype" of the nation in the story of a heroic warrior whose victories over the enemy symbolically affirm the country's fundamental goodness and power; we win our wars because, morally, we deserve to win. Clearly, the archetypical pattern Slotkin calls "regeneration through violence" was broken with the defeat in Vietnam.[5] The result was a massive disjunction in American culture, a crisis of self-image: If Americans were no longer winners, then who were they?

This disruption of cultural identity was amplified by other social transformations. During the 1960s, the civil rights and ethnic pride movements won many victories in their challenges to racial oppression. Also, during the 1970s and 1980s, the United States experienced massive waves of immigration from Mexico, Central America, Vietnam, Cambodia, Korea, and Taiwan. Whites, no longer secure in their power abroad, also lost their unquestionable dominance at home; for the first time, many began to feel that they too were just another hyphenated ethnic group, the Anglo-Americans.

Extraordinary economic changes also marked the 1970s and 1980s. U.S. manufacturing strength declined substantially; staggering trade deficits with other countries and the chronic federal budget deficits shifted the United States from creditor to debtor nation. The post-World War II American Dream—which promised a combination of technological progress and social reforms, together with high employment rates, rising wages, widespread home ownership, and ever increasing consumer options—no longer seemed a likely prospect for the great majority. At the same time, the rise in crime rates, particularly because of drug abuse and its accompanying violence, made people feel more powerless than ever.

While the public world dominated by men seemed to come apart, the private world of family life also felt the shocks. The feminist movement challenged formerly exclusive male domains, not only in the labor market and in many areas of political and social life but in the home as well. Customary male behavior was no longer acceptable in either private relationships or public policy. Feminism was widely experienced by men as a profound threat to their identity. Men had to change, but to what? No one knew for sure what a "good man" was anymore.

It is hardly surprising, then, that American men—lacking confidence in the government and the economy, troubled by the changing relations between the sexes, uncertain of their identity or their future—began to *dream*, to fantasize about the powers and features of another kind of man who could retake and reorder the world. And the hero of all these dreams was the paramilitary warrior. In the New War he fights the battles of Vietnam a thousand times, each time winning decisively. Terrorists and drug dealers are blasted into oblivion. Illegal aliens inside the United States and the hordes of non-whites in the Third World are returned by force to their proper place. Women are revealed as dangerous temptresses who have to be mastered, avoided, or terminated.

Obviously these dreams represented a flight from the present and a rejection and denial of events of the preceding twenty years. But they also indicated a more profound and severe distress. The whole modern world was damned as unacceptable. Unable to find a rational way to face the tasks of rebuilding society and reinventing themselves, men instead sought refuge in myths from both America's frontier past and ancient times. Indeed, the fundamental narratives that shape paramilitary culture and its New War fantasies are often nothing but reinterpretations or reworkings of archaic warrior myths.

In ancient societies, the most important stories a people told about themselves concerned how the physical universe came into existence, how their ancestors first came to live in this universe, and how the gods, the universe, and society were related to one another. These cosmogonic, or creation, myths frequently posit a violent conflict between the good forces of order and the evil forces dedicated to the perpetuation of primordial chaos.[6] After the war in which the gods defeat the evil ones, they establish the "sacred order," in which all of the society's most important values are fully embodied. Some creation myths focus primarily on the sacred order and on the deeds of the gods and goddesses in paradise. Other myths, however, focus on the battles between the heroes and villains that lead up to the founding.[7] In these myths it is war and the warrior that are most sacred. American paramilitary culture borrows from both kinds of stories, but mostly from this second, more violent, type.

In either case, the presence, if not the outright predominance, of archaic male myths at the moment of crisis indicates just how far American men jumped psychically when faced with the declining power of their identities and organizations. The always-precarious balance in modern society between secular institutions and ways of thinking on the one hand and older patterns of belief informed by myth and ritual on the other tilted decisively in the direction of myth. The crisis revealed that at some deep, unconscious level these ancient male creation myths live on in the psyche of many men and that the images and tales from this mythic world of warriors and war still shape men's fantasies about who they are as men, their commitments to each other and to women, and their relationships to society and the state.

The imaginary New War that men created is a coherent mythical universe, formed by the repetition of key features in thousands of novels, magazines, films, and advertisements. As the sociologist Will Wright points out, the component elements of myth work to create a common "theoretical idea of a social order."[8] These New War stories about heroic warriors and their evil adversaries are ways of arguing about what is wrong with the modern world and what needs to be done to make society well again. The organization of this mythic universe is analyzed in Part I, "Stories from the New War."

War games took these fantasies one step further and allowed men to act on their desires in paramilitary games and theme parks that one would-be warrior described as "better than Disneyland" (Part II). Here, away from the ordinary routines of world and family life, men could meet, mingle, and share their warrior dreams. Three major types of imaginary war zones developed: the National Survival Game, or paintball; the annual *Soldier of Fortune* convention in Las Vegas; and combat shooting schools and firing ranges. In these special environments, the gods of war could be summoned for games played along the edges of violence.

Finally, the imaginary New War turned into the real nightmares of "War Zone America" (Part III). Since the 1970s, a number of racist groups, religious sects, mercenaries, and madmen have literally lived their own versions of the New War. At the same time, as hundreds of thousands of military-style rifles have entered the domestic gun market and become the weapon of choice for some killers, the gun-control debate has escalated to a new level. And not surprisingly, the myths of the New War have profoundly influenced several presidential administrations, affecting both those leaders who make military policy decisions and the lower-ranking personnel who carry out covert and overt operations.

Only at the surface level, then, has paramilitary culture been merely a matter of the "stupid" movies and novels consumed by the great unwashed lower-middle and working classes, or of the murderous actions of a few demented, "deviant" men. In truth, there is nothing superficial or marginal about the New War that has been fought in American popular culture since the 1970s. It is a war about basics: power, sex, race, and alienation. Contrary to the *Washington Post* review, Rambo was no shallow muscle man but the emblem of a movement that at the very least wanted to reverse the previous twenty years of American history and take back all the symbolic territory that had been lost. The vast proliferation of warrior fantasies represented an attempt to reaffirm the national identity. But it was also a larger volcanic upheaval of archaic myths, an outcropping whose entire structural formation plunges into deep historical, cultural, and psychological territories. These territories have kept us chained to war as a way of life; they have infused individual men, national political and military leaders, and society with a deep attraction to both imaginary and real violence. This terrain must be explored, mapped, and understood if it is ever to be transformed.

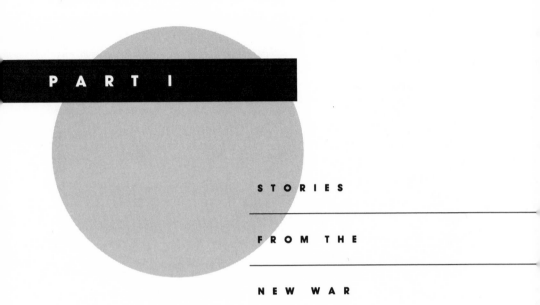

PART I

STORIES

FROM THE

NEW WAR

1

OLD WARRIORS,

NEW WARRIORS

America has always had a war culture, and that long history of martial adventures provides a crucial background for understanding the post-Vietnam warrior. This culture has two fundamental stories, one celebrating the individual gunman who acts on his own (or in loose concert with other men); the other portraying the good soldier who belongs to an official military or police unit and serves as a representative defender of national honor. And these mythologies, sometimes overlapping, sometimes competing, have at different times defined the martial mentality of the country.

The lone gunman has the longer story to tell. Many of the earliest heroes of the American Revolution, from the Minutemen to Francis Marion (the South Carolina "Swamp Fox" guerrilla fighter), were acclaimed for their independence and willingness to fight on their own. The revolutionary army was not an army in the modern sense but a militia of mobilized citizens. That a kind of paramilitary force won the Revolution is a fact of profound consequence: the story of independent gunmen defeating evil enemies and founding a new society became America's creation myth.

The frontiersman who fought in the Indian Wars from the 1600s to the 1880s had a similarly important impact on American history and culture. He was the central figure of the mythologized West, a world neatly divided between a wilderness (or primeval chaos) full of savage Indians and wild beasts—a "frontier" zone of isolated cabins, ranches, and small towns—and an established civilization back East. In the mythology of the American West, evil Indians relish the chaos of their wilderness and violently resist efforts of Anglo pioneers and townspeople to push civilization westward. The heroes of these stories—figures such as Daniel Boone and Davy Crockett—are invariably men of great bravery and virtue who live on the frontier and fight on behalf of civilization, but who themselves never desire to live in the domesticated interior of society. They either fight the Indians or outlaws by themselves or recruit more ordinary men into posses to assist them in the struggle to defend the sacred order against evil.

After the Civil War, the U.S. Army became the most important armed force in the American West. Lone gunmen and paramilitary posses began to seem like archaic relics who had more in common with the Indians and outlaws they fought than with the disciplined forces of the emerging industrial society. Indeed, the lone warrior faced a real crisis once the Indian Wars came to a close. Within a decade after Custer and a detachment of his 7th Cavalry were killed at the Little Bighorn River in 1876, the battles to avenge him had driven the surviving Indians to reservations. With the "enemy" vanquished and the United States settled from coast to coast, there were no more battles for the warrior to fight and no more wilderness for him to conquer.

Without his historical mission, the old warrior hero found himself recast in a variety of roles, imaginary and real. William F. Cody was a genuine Western scout when, in 1869, a writer named Edward Judson sought him out as a source of fresh material. Writing under the pen name Ned Buntline, Judson used only the barest traces of Cody's life to create the first Buffalo Bill novels. Published on newsprint and costing just a dime, these serial adventures were an immediate success, spawning hundreds of sequels through the 1870s and 1880s. Other authors soon took the Buffalo Bill character as their model and renamed him in their works. Cody, on his part, used the growing national and international audience for his fictionalized exploits as a market for a new kind of theater, the Wild West Show. In these performances Cody repeatedly emphasized how he, personally, represented the boundary between chaos and order: "I stood between savagery and civilization most all of my early days."[1] The confrontations he staged between cowboys and Indians received at least as much acclaim as the novels.

Cody's greatest admirer was Theodore Roosevelt. It was Roosevelt who rescued the warrior hero from the circus and reintegrated him into history. And it was Roosevelt who first understood the potency of warrior images for inspiring the nation with military fervor. The scion of a wealthy New York family, Roosevelt was enamored of the romance of the Western myth; he dreamed as early as 1886 of leading the grandest posse of all time, a cavalry troop of "harum-scarum rough riders."[2] (Rough Riders was the nickname for the cowboys in William Cody's Wild West Show.) After the battleship *Maine* exploded in Havana harbor in February 1898, Roosevelt resigned his position as assistant secretary of the Navy and asked President McKinley for an officer's commission as second-in-command of a special volunteer cavalry unit. In April 1898, McKinley called for 125,000 volunteers to fight in Cuba and authorized the formation of the First U.S. Army Volunteer Cavalry, a special unit "to be composed exclusively of frontiersmen possessing special qualifications as horsemen and marksmen."[3] Roosevelt negotiated with William Cody to enlist all of his Rough Riders in the First Cavalry.[4] Before leaving for Cuba, the First Cavalry picked up two other important recruits —a pair of photographers from Vitagraph, one of the world's first motion-picture companies.[5]

The legend of Roosevelt's victory at San Juan Hill was in large part created by Vitagraph. When the photographers shot the battle, what they captured on film was a slow, undramatic encounter in which the Rough Riders were one unit among many. To make a more exciting newsreel, the Vitagraph photographers and the Rough Riders then staged a mock-battle at Santiago Bay after the real fight was over; they gave captured Spanish troops guns whose cartridges had gunpowder but no bullets, then choreographed an American charge against them. This fake footage became part of the official record of San Juan Hill. Vitagraph also staged a number of other battles showing U.S. troops winning glorious victories, some of which included scenes of Roosevelt and the Rough Riders.[6] Partly because of the fame he gained from these choreographed battles, Roosevelt became a national hero and vice president under McKinley in 1900. After McKinley's assassination in 1901, Roosevelt became president.

In reworking the Western myth of the frontiersman fighting Indians into one of U.S. Army troops fighting Spaniards in Cuba, Roosevelt created a rough synthesis of both American martial traditions. He also encouraged the emerging film industry to follow his lead and begin the transition from the Western into what would become the war movie. In 1915, Roosevelt joined forces with the president of Vitagraph, his friend Stuart Blackton, to promote *Battle Cry of Peace*, a fictional account of a German invasion of the United States made to encourage U.S. entry into World War I.[7] *Battle Cry of Peace* was among the world's first full-length feature films and had an immense success. (Vitagraph had previously made *Birth of a Nation*, D. W. Griffith's ode to the redemptive power of the paramilitary Ku Klux Klan to save white Southerners from black savagery after the Civil War.)

The film industry quickly emerged as the central medium for creating and communicating an American war culture. By the late 1930s, both Hollywood and the U.S. government understood that creating favorable images of soldiers and combat was essential to mobilizing the American populace for war. Hollywood began working closely with the military: for example, the Army Air Corps assigned over 110 planes to Metro-Goldwyn-Mayer for the production of *Test Pilot* (1939), a story loosely based on the development of the first major U.S. strategic bomber, the B-17.[8] MGM needed the planes to make the movie convincing to audiences, while the Air Corps wanted publicity to help persuade Congress to approve money for mass production of the B-17. The plan worked: Congress granted the requested appropriations.

Besides creating interest in advanced weaponry, the films made on the eve of World War II stressed the morality of going to war and the problems civilians faced in becoming soldiers. Jesse L. Lasky of Warner Bros. personally approached Sergeant Alvin York, the World War I fighter, for the rights to make a movie of his transformation from Christian pacifist to war hero.[9] Gary Cooper, the Western star, played York; the film was the top money-maker in 1941.[10] Among the millions of young men who saw it was a poor Texas farm boy named Audie Murphy who subsequently joined the Army and became the most decorated soldier of World War II. He later had a career as an actor in Westerns and war movies.[11]

After Pearl Harbor, the film industry and the Roosevelt administration established more formal working relationships. The armed forces had to recruit and educate millions of men from very different backgrounds. Hundreds of films were produced: training films on such subjects as basic personal hygiene; complex technical films on how to use and maintain equipment; political documentaries designed to motivate the troops. Ronald Reagan spent much of World War II making films like these, while other stars—John Wayne, for example—continued to appear in feature films on military subjects. Wayne wanted to enlist, but at thirty-four, married, and apparently suffering from an old University of Southern California football injury, he was not eligible. So instead he starred in *They Were Expendable* (1945) and other war epics.

Of the 1,700 full-length feature films made from 1941 to 1945, more than one-third were war-related. Film was the government's preferred medium to mobilize support for the war effort. In the words of Elmer Davis, director of the Office of War Information (whose Hollywood branch guided scriptwriters so that films would receive official approval), "The easiest way to inject propaganda ideas into most people's minds is to let it go in through the medium of an entertainment picture when they do not realize that they are being propagandized."[12] An estimated 85 million people went to the movies each week during these years, and the war films they saw told essentially the same story again and again.[13]

First, American forces are nearly always portrayed as virtuous defenders of a just cause. Second, U.S. soldiers typically win their fights against Germans and Japanese. A few films made in the early years of World War II—such as *Wake Island* (1942) and *Bataan* (1943)—showed American troops fighting to their deaths, but even in these rare cases American casualties are portrayed as necessary sacrifices, as a way to buy time for the coming American counteroffensive that will surely lead to victory. In the World War II films, might and right go hand in hand.

Third, in these films soldiers always fight as part of a larger military organization which has clearly defined command structure, and acts on behalf of the nation. Actual combat is almost always shown as a struggle between opposing military forces—civilians rarely get killed in cross fire.

Fourth, might and maturity are also linked: In the standard combat narrative, immature youths arrive at a training camp or the base area of the combat unit to which they have been assigned, receive harsh but loving instruction from a paternal commander, and then, in the course of battle, mature into men. War is presented as a relatively benign ritual transition from boyhood to adulthood.

Fifth, in these films war seems safe, even attractive. Bullet and shrapnel wounds are relatively painless and bloodless. No one screams in agonizing pain. Even death is discreet, signified by a small red dot on the chest. Finally, American soldiers never fight for the sheer joy of fighting. They are at war to stop the enemy and to establish or preserve the sacred order.

These genre conventions outlived the war they portrayed. From 1948 to 1968, under the shadow of the Cold War and American involvement in Korea, war movies and Westerns continued to be America's most popular entertainment. Approximately 1,200 war movies were made in those years; over 200 received major assistance from the Defense Department. [14]

From the 1950s to the late 1960s, millions of American boys— the male cohort of the baby-boomer generation—watched these films. Between 1965 and 1973, about 3.5 million men went to Vietnam, most of them from this generation. Indeed, one of the strongest themes to emerge from the hundreds of Vietnam War novels and oral histories concerns the profound influence imaginary wars had on these men as youths and young men.

Ron Kovic describes his boyhood excitement in his memoir, *Born on the Fourth of July*:

> Every Saturday afternoon we'd go down to the movies in the shopping center and watch gigantic prehistoric birds breathe fire, and war movies with John Wayne and Audie Murphy. Bobbie's mother always packed us a bagful of candy. I'll never forget Audie Murphy in *To Hell and Back* [based on Murphy's book, a memoir of his World War II experiences and starring Murphy himself]. At the end he jumps on top of a flaming tank that's just about to explode and grabs the machine gun, blasting it into the German lines. He was so brave I had chills running up and down my back, wishing it were me up there. There were gasoline flames roaring around his legs, but he just kept firing that machine gun. It was the greatest movie I ever saw in my life.[15]

After Marine Corps recruiters visited his high school, Kovic enlisted. Philip Caputo entered the Marine Corps officer candidate school for a similar reason: "For me, the classroom work was mind-numbing. I wanted the romance of war, bayonet charges, and desperate battles against impossible odds. I wanted the sort of thing I had seen in *Guadalcanal Diary* and *Retreat, Hell!*"[16] Lieutenant William Calley, later court-martialed for ordering the soldiers in his unit to open fire upon—and kill—several hundred Vietnamese villagers in the 1969 "My Lai massacre," entered the Army officer candidate school with his own vision of movie glory: "We thought, we will go to Vietnam and be Audie Murphy. Kick in the door, run in the hooch, give it a big burst-kill, and get a big kill ratio in Vietnam. Get a big kill count."[17]

Once in Vietnam, some soldiers tried to reenact the film scenes they had seen or read about in war fiction. One senior sergeant at the central Military Assistance Command Vietnam (MACV) headquarters reported that in the first four months of 1968 some sixty Americans either killed themselves or killed others while playing fast-draw with their pistols.[18] Michael Herr recounts tragic cases in which soldiers acted like war-movie heroes for network television news teams during firefights with enemy forces:

I keep thinking about all the kids who got wiped out by seventeen years of war movies before coming to Vietnam to get wiped out for good. You don't know what a media freak is until you've seen the way a few of those grunts would run around during a fight when they knew there was a television camera nearby; they were actually making war movies in their heads, doing little guts-and-glory Leatherneck tap dances under fire, getting their pimples shot off for the networks.[19]

But these cases seem the exception, not the rule. For most soldiers, the realities of Vietnam led to disenchantment with war mythology. Tom Suddick, a former infantryman, discovered that "the movies lie. There are no young men in war. You're nineteen or twenty, and you become old with the first case of the Viet shits. Your youth drops purgatively out of your asshole during your first week in Vietnam."[20] Ron Kovic went into shock after he accidentally shot and killed a fellow Marine instead of the enemy. Referring to himself in third person, Kovic writes: "He'd never figured it would ever happen this way. It never did in the movies. There were always the good guys, the cowboys, and the Indians. There was always the enemy and each of them killed each other."[21] Another soldier shot a Vietcong opponent, but experienced emotional reactions very different than he expected: "I felt sorry. I don't know why I felt sorry, John Wayne never felt sorry."[22]

As the war continued, the name of John Wayne—whose war and Western films had grossed over 700 million dollars—took on many different meanings.[23] Gustav Hasford's fellow Marines found Wayne's movie on Vietnam, *The Green Berets* (1968)—the only major studio release on Vietnam made during the 1960s—hysterically funny. In the fictionalized account of his war experiences, Hasford writes:

He [John Wayne] snaps out an order to an Oriental actor who played Mr. Sulu on "Star Trek," now playing an ARVN [Army, Republic of Vietnam] officer, who delivers a line with great conviction: "First *kill* . . . all stinking Cong . . . then go home." The audience roars with laughter. This is the funniest movie we have ever seen.

Later, at the end of the movie, John Wayne walks into the sunset with a spunky little orphan. The grunts laugh and whistle and threaten to pee all over themselves. The sun is setting in the South China Sea—in the east—which makes the end of the movie as accurate as the rest of it.[24]

Others couldn't laugh at all. Charles Anderson remembers an infantry sergeant warning new soldiers against movie-style heroics: "Now, we don't want to see no John Wayne performances out here. Just do your job and listen to your fire team and squad leaders—they're the ones who'll teach you everything and help you to get through the next few months."[25] And after a few months, warning turned into invective: "There was no longer any doubt about what warfare in the modern industrial world had come to mean. The grunts—newbys, short-timers, and lifers alike—could see now that what happens to human beings in mechanized warfare has absolutely no poetic. Fuck you, John Wayne!"[26]

Some soldiers, however, clung desperately to the myth, perhaps to make their lives in the war zone more bearable. War-movie and comic-book heroes always survived their battles; identifying with these fantasy heroes may well have helped many soldiers conquer their fear of death. In his novel *Fields of Fire*, James Webb, later secretary of the Navy during the Reagan administration, describes a soldier's thoughts as he prepares to make a helicopter assault on a landing zone where the enemy is known to be waiting. Willard Polk, he writes, "was too cold and wet and angry to be scared. He sat huddled up on the metal deck of the helicopter daydreaming about John Wayne: tough, flinty-eyed, strong, quick to fight. Somehow it helped make the situation into which he was flying seem less threatening and real."[27]

Only political and military leaders far removed from the battlefield were able to go through the Vietnam War without having their movie-informed fantasies of "regeneration through violence" severely shaken. President Richard Nixon watched *Patton* several times in the spring of 1970. In the film, George C. Scott portrays the general as a charming eccentric whose brilliance and valor save an American airborne division under siege from a German offensive. According to then–Secretary of State William Rogers and White House Chief of Staff H. R. Haldeman, Nixon talked incessantly about the movie as he decided that U.S. forces should invade Cambodia.[28] Nixon even ordered American military chaplains to pray for a change in the weather, just as Patton did during the Battle of the Bulge—a modern example of what anthropologist Sir James George Frazer called the archaic practice of homeopathic or imitative magic.[29]

Henry Kissinger also resorted to movie imagery to explain why he remained popular even at the height of the Vietnam War. "I've always acted alone," said Kissinger.

> Americans admire that enormously. Americans admire the cowboy leading the caravan alone or astride his horse, the cowboy entering the village or city alone on his horse, without even a pistol maybe, because he doesn't go in for shooting! He acts, that's all: aiming at the right spot at the right time. A Wild West tale, if you like.[30]

But all these assertions of mythic grandeur and all the displays of American power, such as the massive B-52 bombing of North Vietnam in December 1972, could not sustain the myth that this was a country that always won its battles. In May 1975, Communist forces entered Saigon and television audiences watched in horror and disbelief as helicopters evacuated the last Americans from Vietnam.

At first, then, the trauma of the prolonged war in Vietnam, followed as it was by ignominious defeat, seemed to spell the end of the traditional war mythology. Both the Western and war-movie genres faded away in the late 1960s and 1970s. John Wayne's death in 1979 seemed to bring a symbolic closure to this cultural history. But paradoxically, the old mythology of American martial prowess and moral virtue instead assumed an even greater hold on the popular imagination. Why it did has much to say about the American way of looking at the world: defeat was incomprehensible, both morally and "scientifically."

Ever since World War II, it had been an article of faith of U.S. military policy that a country's technological sophistication and the sheer quantity of its war supplies were the decisive factors that would lead to victory. In this new model of warfare (which I call "technowar"), war was conceptualized as a kind of high-technology production process in which the officer corps were managers, the enlisted men were workers, and the final product was death: whoever had the biggest, most sophisticated apparatus was sure to produce the highest enemy body count and thus win.[31] The "soft" variables of war, such as the history, culture, and motivations of a people, were not seen as being important because they had none of the "hard" reality of weapons.

Not surprisingly, then, many military leaders and policy analysts were unwilling to rethink their conceptual approach as the war in Vietnam dragged on—or they were incapable of doing so. Any advance by the Vietcong and North Vietnamese Army was seen as only a temporary gain sure to be reversed by a further escalation of U.S. intervention. The basic assumptions of technowar were reasserted again and again even at the bitter end. Defeat in Vietnam came to be viewed as the result of what the Joint Chiefs of Staff called "self-imposed restraints." From this perspective, technowar would have inevitably produced victory if it hadn't been for the influences of liberals in Congress, the antiwar movement, and the news media, who together stopped the military from unleashing its full powers of destruction.*

Under the rational veneer of this conservative intellectual argument lay the classic mythology of the heroic American warrior who always won his battles and simply could not be defeated. U.S. defeat in Vietnam could only be explained by arguing that the full powers of the heroic American warriors of legend had not been unleashed. As

---

* This is of course an extraordinary argument, a rhetorical coup d'état that completely dismisses just how great an effort the United States had made. Over 3.5 million men and women served in Vietnam. At the height of the war in 1968–69, the United States deployed more than 550,000 troops, a figure that excludes at least 200,000 to 300,000 more people serving in the Seventh Fleet off Vietnam, in U.S. Air Force bases in Thailand and Guam, and in logistic, repair, and training capacities in the United States. Roughly 40 percent of all U.S. Army divisions, more than 50 percent of all Marine Corps divisions, one-third of U.S. naval forces, half of the Air Force fighter-bombers, and between 25 and 50 percent (depending upon the year) of B-52 bombers in the Strategic Air Command fought in the war. From eight to fifteen million tons of bombs (U.S. versus Vietnamese figures) were dropped on Southeast Asia—at minimum, over four times the amount the United States dropped in World War II—along with another fifteen million tons of artillery shells and other munitions.

Will Wright argues in *Sixguns and Society*, a mythology often serves to "solve" a contradiction between a people's core belief system and their experiences. Hence the appeal of a "New War," one in which traditional mythological warriors—either with or without official approval—could do what was necessary to win victory and thus affirm the fundamental truths of America's virtue and martial prowess.

Conservative politicians, syndicated columnists, and military intellectuals had offered versions of the "self-imposed restraint" argument for years, both during and after the Vietnam War. By the late 1970s and early 1980s, it was not an esoteric doctrine, but a widely accepted explanation. Among those people who accepted the conservative analysis were magazine and novel editors and film producers who intuitively understood the popular desire for narratives of victory—New War stories featuring American heroes whose triumphs in battle could somehow heal the wounds of a crippled political system. As Alexander M. S. McColl editorialized in the premier issue of *Soldier of Fortune: The Journal of Professional Adventurers*, "The disastrous events of the last month in Southeast Asia are not only an appalling human tragedy for the peoples of Cambodia and South Vietnam, they are the most serious defeat of Western Christendom in a generation, and the final requiem of the United States as a great power."[32] *SOF*, of course, was among the first to call for the private warrior's redemption of Vietnam through new battles.

Many Hollywood filmmakers explicitly set out to revise and revive the old mythology. Menahem Golan, who, as president of the Cannon Group, was responsible during the mid-1980s for cranking out scores of profitable action-adventure films, modeled his stock adventure films on Westerns. "What is a Western?" he asked. "A Western is basically a fairy tale of a hero who is supposedly good saving the town or saving the poor or fighting for something which is moralistically important to the family, to the human beings fighting for the good, fighting all the evils of the world, fighting all the demons of the world." Like fairy tales, his movies would have happy endings.[33]

Other Hollywood directors and novelists also saw themselves as modern mythologists. Joseph Zito, director of the Chuck Norris *Missing in Action* films (1984 and 1985), thought of Vietnam as an imaginary land, the perfect setting for new cowboy-and-Indian movies.[34] Lionel Chetwynd, who directed *Hanoi Hilton* (1987) for Cannon, claimed that as a director "you owe your allegiance to the mythic mold, as opposed to the war. We use [the war] as a landscape." Film, he insisted, was the direct descendant of myth.[35]

John Milius in turn referred to the warrior as an "archaic figure" and presented him as such in *Conan the Barbarian* (1982). Milius also developed the original story idea for *Dirty Harry* and later wrote and directed *Red Dawn* (1984), the World War III story of a Colorado high school football team that conducts guerrilla war against invading Russian and Central American paratroopers. He thought of war as a kind of peak experience in which men reach an "extremely vital state in order to kill each other." Even the most ordinary men, the "plodders," he observed, are "often forced to achieve great endeavors in times of war." War was men's "greatest fantasy," and its appeal was that it served as an outlet for all sorts of frustrations. Indeed, Milius was a crack shot and a passionate fan of warrior culture, an admirer of both the Japanese samurai tradition and the Western, and, like Nixon, fond of quoting lines from *Patton*. "We are lucky war is the hell it is, lest we love it so," was a particular favorite.[36]

To say that the Hollywood film industry, the editors of men's paperback novels, and the publishers of paramilitary magazines deliberately intended to create New War culture does not mean that they consciously designed every single component of that culture. On the contrary, these men, in interviews, almost uniformly denied the existence of, much less their responsibility for, any grand design. Instead, they saw themselves as "discovering" what people wanted—and giving it to them. But whether the New War was intentionally created or half-consciously discovered during the late 1970s and 1980s, it developed basic properties that distinguished it from earlier versions of American war culture.

The New War is fought principally by paramilitary warriors who are most often hostile to official legal and police authorities. Their hostility usually dates from their experience in Vietnam. For example, in *The Black Berets* (a novel series), the five main characters are used and betrayed by their CIA controllers during the war. Years later, when the team reunites to conduct contract mercenary missions, their sole client is an unnamed U.S. government agency. Still, the team keeps its distance; memories are not so easily erased. The Black Berets cannot forget that they are "despised symbols of a war that had been lost, not by them, but by the fucking politicians and the fucking undercutting CIA. Why had they ever gone to Vietnam if they weren't intended to win?"[37] Given this history, they will never become part of the system again, but will instead retain their autonomy by signing on only for individual missions on a contract basis.

These warriors fight with a savagery lacking in their predecessors. Film critic Robert Warshow once contended that the classic Western film was not really about martial ability and violence, but about moral character. John Wayne, Gary Cooper, James Stewart, and Humphrey Bogart all played virtuous men with highly developed personal codes of honor. Their fighting ability flowed from moral strength.[38] Most of the time, they did not even seem to be really angry at the men they were fighting. Nor did anyone ever seem to really get hurt—those small red dots indicating bullet wounds were just a way of keeping score. This highly abstract approach to violence was often criticized in works by Vietnam veterans. As Larry Heinemann wrote in his novel *Close Quarters*, "The war works on you until you become part of it, and then you start working on it instead of it working on you, and you get deep-down mean. Not just kidding mean; not movie-style John Wayne mean, you get mean for real."[39] Post-Vietnam mythic heroes are completely enraged when they fight, and the violence they inflict is shocking. The scores of scenes featuring dismemberment, torture, and shredded bodies oozing fluids are absolutely central to the culture and are far removed from the older, dispassionate moral accounting. The New War promotes a vicious appetite for destruction that cannot be satiated.

Indeed, so great is that hunger for killing that the New War appears to be a war without end. At one level, this means New War stories can be set in widely varying historical eras. Many refight the Vietnam War, either in imaginary battles or in rescue missions to bring POWs home. A second type of story shows the heroes fighting terrorists of one kind or another, either inside the United States or abroad on a global battlefield. The third type presents post–World War III Armageddon narratives in which the surviving Americans battle Russian invaders in the rural South and West. In this scenario, the cities are destroyed and America returns to the mythical Western frontier, only this time the Russians are bad-guy cavalry and the Anglos get to be good-guy Indians.

The most important characteristic that distinguishes the New War mythology from the old, however, concerns the warrior's relationship to mainstream society. Although the Western hero often moved on into the wilderness after defeating the Indians or the rustlers or the corrupt cattle ranchers, he always left behind a stable world. The Western myth also made it clear that the hero believed in civic values, even if as a warrior he could only live on the margins of society. And, as previously noted, the warriors in World War II movies were soldiers—members of an official military—who fought to protect the American values of freedom and democracy and to liberate others from tyranny.

In contrast, the New War has nothing at all to say about what kind of society will be created after the enemy is vanquished. The sheer intensity of the violence in these stories tends to make the warrior's victories look like a definitive restoration of a fallen America. It's as if the end of gunfire must mean something good. But the defeat of chaos is not the same thing as the re-creation of a sacred order. In other words, the New War resembles those archaic creation myths that glorify the violent struggles that precede the establishment or restoration of social order, but not those that exalt the sacred order itself.

The New War, then, developed into a distinct mythological universe that borrowed liberally for its symbolism and themes from American frontier mythology and World War II films, and even ancient cosmogonic myths. However, the New War has one other significant predecessor, a twentieth-century political movement that also drew on archaic warrior themes for its imagery and fundamental narratives. As World War I drew to a close, Germany's military forces became politically divided. Many wanted peace, and many were excited by the Bolshevik Revolution in Russia. Another part of the German Army, though, was bitterly disappointed by the armistice signed in November 1918. As they saw it, the military had done its part and defeat was the result of having been "stabbed in the back" by the liberals of Germany's new Weimar Republic. These army men were also deeply threatened and enraged by the German Left, which was organizing and demonstrating for socialism.

And the result was that part of the German Army never demobilized after the armistice. Instead, several thousand soldiers formed their own paramilitary force, the *Freikorps*. Their far-right battalions regularly attacked leftist demonstrations and hunted down and killed key organizers. To them, war was a way of life complete with its own obligations, affiliations, and psycho-sexual dynamics. The novels and memoirs written by these men permeated German culture in the 1920s and 1930s and were a central component of the rising fascist movement. As the novelist Ernst Junger wrote, describing his fellow warriors, "We were asked to believe that the war had now ended. We laughed—for we were the war. Its flame burned on within us and gathered all our actions under the glowing and mysterious spell of destruction."[40]

The flame that burns from within represents the core of fascist culture. Although post-Vietnam America was worlds away from Weimar, it shared a similar despair and search for rebirth. Two hundred years after the ratification of the Constitution, the American mythology of war and the warrior was no longer connected to any idea of founding a sacred order. Instead, the New War culture portrayed the warrior as the epitome of masculine power and self-development, and combat as the only life worth living.

2

New War warriors are special men, men whose whole being is dedicated to fighting the enemy. Although they once led normal lives and had careers and families, something has happened to change them, to transform them into warriors perpetually in search of adventure, danger, and death. More often than not, New War stories have their origin in the Vietnam War. Most of the heroes served in Vietnam. Others did not serve in Vietnam per se, but fought in limited, undeclared wars elsewhere and were similarly betrayed by leaders who sold them out. Yet others suffered some form of Vietnam-like "self-imposed restraint" at home, when major social institutions—particularly the police and the court system—failed to combat the enemies of American society.

Thus, in *Year of the Dragon* (1985) a New York police detective and Vietnam veteran (Mickey Rourke), frustrated by both Asian organized crime and the politics of his department, declares: "This is a fucking war and I'm not going to lose it, not this one. Not over politics. It's always fucking politics. This is Vietnam all over again. Nobody wants to win this thing. Just flat-out win." Later the detective will simply ignore all the rules and wage the war against crime according to his own standards. Out in Los Angeles, Sylvester Stallone, a police detective battling a satanic cult in *Cobra* (1986), has the same objections: "As long as we have to play by these bullshit rules and the killer doesn't, we've lost." Down south in Florida, the governor realizes that the terrorists who threaten the state's theme parks can never be stopped by any kind of regular, established law enforcement agency. As he explains to his new top-secret contract employees, Niles Barrabas and his mercenary team, in the novel series *SOBs: Soldiers of Barrabas*: "I need someone who can go in there and kick ass like it's never been kicked before. The rest of the guys who were here all have constitutional and other restrictions on their authority. The only limitation you have is the level of risk you're prepared to accept."[1]

When brave soldiers and policemen who are doing their best to stop dictators and criminals discover that the leaders of their organizations expect them to put their lives on the line while at the same time crippling them with regulations, they become outraged. In their righteous anger at the "system," they either ignore the law, disobey their superiors, or resign. At that moment they become paramilitary warriors. Rambo was not alone when he asked "Do we get to win this time?" Virtually all the heroes are born by questioning and rejecting the corrupt institutions that constrain them. The paramilitary warrior must fight outside the system because the official power structure is unwilling to fight even though the enemy threatens to destroy America and the values it represents.

Most New War stories further personalize this sense of danger and betrayal by showing that the official structures of military and police fail to protect not only society as a whole but, more immediately, the hero's family.

Sergeant Mack Bolan first earned his nickname, The Executioner, by killing some thirty-two high-ranking North Vietnamese officers, forty-six Vietcong guerrilla leaders, and seventeen Vietcong village officials. Bolan is suddenly called home and discovers that everything he held sacred has been taken from him in a string of tragic and criminal events. His father, who had lost his job because of heart trouble, had been forced to borrow $500 from the Mafia after his health insurance expired. When he was unable to make his loan and interest payments on schedule, he was severely beaten by mob enforcers. To earn enough to repay the debt and save her father, Bolan's sister Cindy became a prostitute. On discovering what she had done, Bolan's father, in a fit of shame and rage, killed his daughter, his wife, and then himself.

With his family dead, Bolan deserts the Army and vows to conduct a one-man "war of attrition" against the mob. He writes in his journal, "I guess it's time a war was declared on the home front. The same kind of war we've been fighting at 'Nam. The very same kind."[2] But there is one major difference between the two wars. At home Mack Bolan has no legal license to kill. When he decides to live outside of society to conduct what he calls a "holy war," he becomes a paramilitary warrior—the real Executioner. As a warrior he will do what the police and legal system failed to do. At least thirty mobsters or "hardmen" die in the first novel of the series, and hundreds more perish in the subsequent thirty-eight volumes.

In other New War tales, the hero loses his wife or children or both. In the film *Mad Max* (1980), a highway patrolman squares off against vicious motorcycle gangs in a world verging on complete economic collapse and social disintegration. After gang members burn Max's fellow patrolman "Goose" beyond recognition, kill his child, and critically injure his wife (the doctors say she is "salvageable"), Max quits the highway patrol, dons his black leather suit, revs up his V-8 patrol car, and goes to war. He becomes *The Road Warrior* (1982). These Mad Max films launched actor Mel Gibson's career as an action-adventure hero. Gibson went on to star in *Lethal Weapon* (1987) and *Lethal Weapon 2* (1989), in which the loss of loved ones is again central to the action. In these films, Gibson plays Martin Riggs, a burnt-out Los Angeles police detective who has no private life—in the first film his wife has been blown up by villains; in the second, more bad men drown his new girlfriend.

A few New War stories have the hero's family survive after nearly being killed. In Tom Clancy's novel *Patriot Games* (1987) Irish terrorists, angry at Jack Ryan for ruining their effort to kidnap Queen Elizabeth's husband, try to kidnap Ryan's wife and daughter; a high-speed chase ends in a serious though not fatal accident. After visiting his family at the hospital, Ryan sets out for Langley, Virginia, where he rejoins the CIA. After Ryan is hired back in his old position as an intelligence analyst, he uses his agency affiliation as a hunting license, a permit to operate as a lone warrior.

The trauma of having loved ones kidnapped, killed, or nearly killed, while discovering that the military and police are corrupt or otherwise ineffective, changes men. In 1988, poor John Rambo is asked to go on yet another rescue mission, in *Rambo: Part 3*. This time it is to save his surrogate father, a Green Beret colonel, being held by Russian torturers in an Afghan dungeon. When a CIA agent tells him he will not be helped by the U.S. government if he is captured in Afghanistan, Rambo shrugs sadly and says, "I'm used to it." Clearly, American political leaders have little concern for their subordinates.

At the start of these New War stories, the hero (civilian, soldier, or policeman) expects that his family will be protected by the powers that be. When his family is destroyed, a fundamental social contract is broken. Besides grieving for his family, the hero mourns the rending of the very agreement that established his place in society. He experiences a kind of psychological and social death. The hero of *Vigilante*, a former judge, explains his transformation: "The bomb that killed my family killed Adrian Chase as well."[3] Jack Ryan takes a solemn vow after the terrorists nearly kill his wife and daughter: "Seeing his wife weeping tears caused by someone else started a cold rage in him which only that someone's death could ever warm."[4] And in his rage, he abandons the old ways: "If we can do it [defeat the enemy] by civilized rules, well and good—but if not, then we have to do the best we can, and rely on our consciences to keep us from going over the edge."[5]

Thus the warrior is born, a new being, cut off from society, without family—a man apart. But for all the sadness and grief that accompany the loss of every connection—in *Lethal Weapon*, Detective Riggs is so upset over the death of his wife that he comes close to biting a

9mm slug from his own pistol—the warrior's separation from main-stream organizations and normal family life also offers him significant opportunities.

For one thing, the death of his family means that a new family can be created, one that is not simply a different version of the one killed off. Instead, the new family is typically *all male*—a warrior "tribe." In *Cherry Boy Body Bag*, volume 4 of the *Saigon Commandos* novel series, author Jonathan Cain describes a young sergeant's new intimacy with his brood of military policemen: "But the thirty-year-old buck sergeant had grown close to his enlisted men over the last few months. Vietnam did that to you. Brought you closer emotionally sometimes to your comrades than you had ever been to your wife or even parents back in The World. Girlfriends didn't even rate."[6]

These all-male warrior tribes present a radically new vision of male "reproduction" and maturation without parents and without all the conflicting feelings of dependency, love, hate, and disappointment that childhood and adolescence entail. The bonds between men result exclusively from the mutual recognition of one another's martial accomplishments. Aggressive competition rarely triggers envy or insecurity; instead, men form a harmonious order based on a natural hierarchy of ability and a necessary division of labor. As Commander Jake Grafton instructs his elite group of naval aviators in Stephen Coonts's 1988 novel, *Final Flight*: "We can't function unless every man does his job. We must all do the absolute best we can, each and every one of us. We'll each do our part. We'll stick together. We'll accept responsibility . . . You must have faith."[7]

In the war zone there is no mother at all. In the thousands of New War films, novels, magazine articles, and television shows, only two characters—Rick and A. J. Simon, the San Diego detectives in the 1980s television series *Simon and Simon*—had a mother who played an important role in their lives. They talked to Mom all the time. But *Simon and Simon* was a comedy, a sweet parody of action-adventure. In the serious world of war, Mother is gone. And this banishment extends to all older females who have a hint of nurturing power and can remember (or imagine) a time when the warrior was not an imposing figure, but a mere boy. For the same reason, older sisters, aunts, grandmothers, and even fairy godmothers simply do not exist in this mythical universe. Older women are reminders of a warrior's past weaknesses, needs, and dependency.

By banishing all traces of these women, the warrior becomes a man reborn without a mother. This separation is idealized, seen as a source of power and strength, a necessary step toward maturity. One prominent two-page magazine advertisement for the U.S. Army's National Guard in the mid-1980s captured it: two young soldiers wade knee deep in a steamy swamp, their eyes searching for the enemy. The one holding an M60 machine gun at hip level has found a target somewhere to the left. In small print, the caption reads "Kiss Your Momma Good-bye."

At the same time, young men are constantly searching for mentors or substitute fathers, and older men for sons. Frequently the bonding with a new father takes place through warrior training. Maverick, the immature fighter pilot in *Top Gun* (1986), gets help from Viper (the code name for the head instructor at Top Gun, the Navy's advanced air-to-air combat school). Viper helps Maverick in two ways. First, he tells Maverick that the old Navy stories about Maverick's father, also a naval pilot, are not true. He was not a troublemaker, not a loser. Instead, Viper confides, Maverick's father had been entrusted with a secret mission over Vietnam, during which he saved Viper's life and lost his own. Second, he nurtures the young pilot through the tragic death of his navigator and best friend. Having found a father, Maverick decides to become one in his turn. He too will become an instructor at Top Gun and help other adolescents make the transition to mature warrior.

In all these stories, sons and fathers forge filial bonds in the crucible of training and combat—an adoption by ordeal. *Soldier of Fortune* magazine writers are particularly taken with this process. Journalist Mark Warman writes of one leader's efforts to train Afghan rebels: "My basic aim is to make a real man and a tough man with confidence."[8] Other *SOF* articles take the reader through the coming-of-age of elite commando units in various U.S. and NATO armed services.

Adoption by ordeal also appears in several of the pulp serials. In *Louisiana Hellstorm*, volume 5 of *The Black Berets*, the team's Indian leader, Billy Leeps Beeker, rescues a mute sixteen-year-old Indian boy whose parents were killed by white racists: "Beeker saw in the boy the kind of son he would have chosen over all others, if fathers ever got that sort of choice. A youngster who had obvious pride and ability, who continually proved himself trustworthy and even courageous."[9] The moment of truth for this foundling comes when he is left behind at the team's Louisiana home base after the Black Berets have gone off on an overseas mission. A plot to assassinate the Berets, hatched by a former CIA operative who had earlier betrayed them in Vietnam, is thwarted when the mute teenager—alone for the first time—kills all the attackers. When the Berets return, they notice that the boy has been transformed:

> The men looked at the youth, shivering though he was wrapped in the striped blanket from the plane. They remembered similar boyish faces from Vietnam, faces much too young to bear such knowledge and experience behind the eyes. Before they went away, he had seemed a child—his emaciated body had helped that illusion. Now that they had returned, he seemed a man.[10]

Beeker gives the boy a new name, Tsali, in honor of a famous Cherokee Indian warrior. Officially reborn a warrior, he is thus adopted into both the Black Beret tribe and his ancestral Cherokee nation.

Paramilitary culture always stresses the tribal organization of males as the family type best suited for life in the war zone. Most New War books, movies, and magazines feature relatively small tribes. Either they are elite units, like the fighter pilots or commandos, within a large military bureaucracy or they are independent mercenary groups. In the techno-thriller genre, which depicts conflicts on a global scale, such elaborate institutions as NATO or Warsaw Pact forces turn out to be nothing more than extended male families or confederations of male tribes.

Intertribal adoption ceremonies occur frequently among the federated families of NATO. In Tom Clancy's World War III epic *Red Storm Rising*, Edwards (code-name Beagle), a U.S. Air Force meteorologist, is the ranking survivor of a Soviet airborne assault on an American air base in Iceland. He becomes "father" to the handful of younger Marines who escape with him. Equipped with a powerful radio, they move across Iceland providing valuable intelligence information to senior command, thus paving the way for a subsequent Allied invasion. In the process, Edwards rescues a beautiful blond Icelandic woman from the Russian soldiers who have raped her and killed her parents. On the day of the Allied invasion, Edwards is seriously wounded and awakes on a Navy assault ship with the beautiful Miss Vigdis by his side. In walks a Marine general, commander of the invasion force:

> "So, you're Beagle?"
> "Yes, General."
> "And this must be Miss Vigdis. They told me you were pretty. I have a daughter about your age."
> The General pulled a small box out of his pocket. "Well done, Marine!"
> "Sir, I'm Air Force."
> "Oh, yeah, well, this here says you're a Marine." The General pinned a Navy Cross to his pillow.
> "Miss Vigdis, would you please look after this man for us?"[11]

Transcending the distinction between Air Force and Marine tribes, the general adopts Edwards, anointing him with the Marines' most prestigious service medal. Adoptions can also take place across NATO's transnational tribes. For example, when Clancy's heroic CIA analyst, Jack Ryan, saves the Prince of Wales and Lady Diana from assassination by Irish terrorists, the Queen Mother in gratitude knights him, thus adopting him as a son of the Royal Family.[12] Ryan has no further meaningful encounters with her after the ceremony; after all, she is a mother figure. But he forms close working relationships and friendships with men in high-level British intelligence and military positions.

These stories echo archaic male initiation rites. In some of the archaic ceremonies, a boy's parents feign death to help speed their son's passage to adulthood. In others, a boy is removed from his mother's care for extended periods so that male elders may instruct him in the ways of manhood in preparation for his symbolic rebirth.[13]

It will be the adult warrior's vital task to keep society safe from real enemies, such as hostile tribes, and symbolic enemies, such as demons. Only when evil is kept "outside" can female-centered biological reproduction, infant care, and child rearing occur inside society.

The repetition of similar adoption ceremonies in New War stories suggests that contemporary American men also see war as a primary rite of passage. And, in truth, the modern world offers few ritual transitions from boyhood to manhood other than combat or combat training. Both in the classic war movies celebrating World War II and in the New War, the mature warrior is without question a man. He is so powerful that his sense of self-worth is not threatened by younger men. And he is always willing to engage in the all-male task of social reproduction by helping young men make the transition into full adulthood.

But it is at this point that the old and the new diverge. The function of the older ceremonies is to return new adult warriors to society to serve as its protectors. The same process operates in World War II movies. In most New War stories, by contrast, the "adult" male is not reintegrated into society. He may fight on behalf of society, but he is not part of it. His enemies are never fully defeated; the New War never ends. Instead, like Clint Eastwood in his starring roles in Sergio Leone's spaghetti Westerns, the new warrior remains forever "the man with no name" (without family).[14] Freed from the ambivalence and restraints of deep emotional relationships, freed from the boring tasks and burdensome responsibilities of everyday life, he is reborn into the mythic world of primeval chaos, where he can develop his full powers of destruction.

While all warriors are reborn either directly through their families' deaths or through adoption ceremonies performed by father surrogates, once they are full adults they may choose a variety of paths. Some become lone warriors. The Charles Bronson character in the *Death Wish* films, Mack Bolan in the *Executioner* series, and the many novel and comic-book heroes modeled after Bolan fight their battles with little or no help from others. But lone gunmen comprise only a minority of the New War warriors. Most men join forces with their brothers to form either two-member "couples" or larger family tribes. When New War stories feature men in couples, the plot almost inevitably turns on mutual love triumphing over individual differences. In the first *Lethal Weapon* film, actors Mel Gibson and Danny Glover portray L.A. police detectives so different in temperament and background that they can barely function as a team. But by the end of *Lethal Weapon 2*, Glover holds his comrade in his arms, their kiss averted only because Gibson is wounded and not dead.[15] The love that dare not speak its name is still silent in the New War; only life-and-death situations permit the display of affection.

In some of the novels, men really do kiss. In the *SOBs: Soldiers of Barrabas* series, two members of a five-man team have long been antagonists. But the hot-tempered Greek, Alex Nanos, and the cool Englishman, Geoff Bishop, finally make up. Shortly thereafter, their boat is blown up, leaving Alex unconscious and drowning: "Supporting Alex's torso with one arm, Geoff Bishop held the Greek's head back. Once again he kicked hard, sealing his lips around Nanos's mouth and breathing into him."[16]

Although such erotic/fraternal relations are not characteristic of warrior tribes, these commando groups are more than simply a collection of men who fight together in wartime and then disperse when the war is over. When in *Uncommon Valor* (1983) Gene Hackman seeks out the former members of his missing son's old Vietnam reconnaissance team to organize them for a rescue mission in Laos, he is at first rebuffed. "I live a good life here. I cannot save the goddamn world," says one ex-trooper who is reluctant to leave his wife and family. But ultimately men owe their deepest personal allegiances to the brotherhood of war. Everyone signs up for the mission.

Once the group has assembled, it becomes a living entity into which individual men merge their separate identities. This unity is extolled over and over again in New War stories. As Colonel Yakov Katzenelenbogen says of his comrades in *Phoenix Force*, "I know those four men as if they were parts of my own body."[17] Higher up the chain of command, Colonel John Macklin Phoenix (actually Mack Bolan, given a new identity by the federal government) has comparable feelings about Katzenelenbogen and his men together with a second group, Able Team: "Phoenix Force, like Able Team, was an extension of Mack Bolan the man, and Mack Bolan the freedom fighter. Each time that extension was thrown into combat, Mack Bolan lived, breathed and battled with them in spirit."[18] The given is that if the members of the group are all parts of one body, that body is the leader's—the acknowledged "better" man.

Service with the leader is an honor jealously guarded against incursions by other tribes. Cowboy—a member of the Black Berets—warns the Marines talking with Billy Leeps Beeker: "He may have started out as a Marine . . . But things happened to him in 'Nam that you guys can't even begin to imagine . . . And there are other things that make him a Black Beret, and now he's our leader. So look but don't touch."[19]

Commando groups also achieve a kind of organic unity through their division of labor. Following the precedents set by outfits like the U.S. Army's Special Forces A-Teams, each man is cross-trained in two or three specialties, such as demolitions, heavy weapons (machine guns and mortars), communications, scouting and sniping, and medical care.[20] In New War adventures, this technical division of labor is simultaneously ethnic, racial, and national. Not just any man can do any job. Asians are expert in Oriental martial arts; they kill with their hands, carry samurai swords and ninja *shruiken* (metal "throwing stars"). Indians in turn are master archers and knife fighters. "Devilish" people, whether "hot-tempered" Latins or "wiry" Jews, thrive as demolitions experts. American WASPs and Northern Europeans fight with cold precision; their rifle and pistol shots always find their mark. In this sense the members of a warrior tribe are not individuals; each man is but a representative of his social origin, and each race or nationality is represented by the weapons most suited to its unique character.

Conversely, when warriors fight with weapons that are not normally associated with their social origins, it is a sign that they are in some ways "half-breeds." Actors Chuck Norris (star of the *Missing in Action* films) and Steven Seagal (*Hard to Kill*, 1989) are not simply Caucasians who have mastered martial arts, but bicultural men who know the ways of the Orient: Norris has a Vietnamese wife (who is of course killed) and child in *Missing in Action 3* (1990), while Seagal wears his hair pulled back in a carefully groomed ponytail reminiscent of samurai warriors. Rambo's use of high-tech compound bows with exploding arrowheads is explained by reference to his half-German, half-Apache ancestry.

The brotherhood of war thus brings men together in ways that efface their individuality. Their parents are killed; their wives are killed. They merge themselves into the leader and become instruments of his will. And their "personal" characteristics are but the markers of group traits signified by the weapons they carry. Still, in a New War story, each member of the team does get his own individual moment of stardom when he fights the enemy. For all its extraordinary reductionism and emphasis on the group, the New War still presents the warrior as a lone hero who transcends mass society.

The unity of warrior tribes is cemented by one other important force: a common commitment to die for the group. As *SOF* author Alex McColl noted after the fall of Saigon in 1975, renewing America would require reaffirming the best values of the martial tradition, where a soldier's love for his comrades is the greatest love of all: "There is more to love than carnal lust and warm, sudsy emotion. 'Greater love hath no man than that he lay down his life for his friends.' "[21] In recent years, former Marine lieutenant William Broyles, Jr., has become the most noted interpreter of "why men love war." Writing about his six months as a platoon commander in Vietnam, he says, "War was an initiation into the power of life and death. Women touch that power at the moment of birth; men on the edge of death. It is like lifting off the corner of the universe and peeking at what's underneath."[22] What this "edge of death" means becomes clearer in another passage:

We loved war for many reasons, not all of them good. The best reason we loved war is also its most enduring memory—comradeship. A comrade in war is a man you can trust with anything, because you trust him with your life. Philip Caputo described the emotion in *A Rumor of War*: "[Comradeship] does not demand for its sustenance the reciprocity, the pledges of affection, the endless reassurances required by the love of men and women. It is, unlike marriage, a bond that cannot be broken by a word, by boredom, or by anything other than death."[23]

Paradoxically, comradeship requires that some warriors die. In archaic mythology, repeated blood sacrifices are often necessary to pacify the gods and secure their allegiance.[24] Modern warrior mythology ignores Judaism's condemnation of human sacrifice and Christianity's message that Christ's death on the cross was the last necessary sacrifice and instead reverts to this more archaic theme: ultimately, only another sacrifice can redeem the blood already spilt and secure a future for the community.

Such deaths are central to the plots of many post-Vietnam movies. In *The Deer Hunter* (1978) Robert De Niro fails to rescue his childhood friend who has remained in Vietnam, addicted to self-destruction. The friend plays one too many rounds of Russian roulette, and his death both deepens the ties among his loved ones back at home and helps them understand the sanctity of life. In *Uncommon Valor* nearly half of the private commando team dies rescuing the American POWs held in Laos; the ratio of Americans killed to Americans saved is slightly less than one to one. Even in *Platoon* (1986), a film explicitly critical of the Vietnam War, the good "father," Sergeant Elias, is murdered. His death is the precondition for the platoon members' moral awakening and the hero's transformation into a man.

This same kind of comradeship, even love, is present when one warrior asks another to kill him rather than let him be captured by the enemy. To ask for, and receive, this "gift of death" is a scene always rendered with the greatest poignancy. William Holden as "Bishop" slays his wounded fellow outlaw in one of the last great Westerns, *The Wild Bunch* (1969). Richard Burton similarly kills a fellow merc who fails to make the last plane out of an African hellhole in *The Wild Geese* (1978).

In the classic World War II war movies, it was customary for part of the group to die; their deaths bonded the survivors. Usually the male leads survived the battle—an important indicator of the way these films made war seem a relatively safe ritual transition from boyhood to manhood for the Vietnam generation. Still, those films followed ancient cosmogonic mythologies in that they portrayed death as a sad necessity in the struggle for a higher good—the creation of a sacred order. Men talked of home and family, together with their hopes that somehow their sacrifices would lead to a better world.

Most hoped that they personally would not have to die. But if they did, they would be dying for peace.

Blood sacrifice in the New War has very different intentions. The act itself is sacred, beyond any relation to a cause. The sanctification of ritual death, of course, denigrates life. No doubt, men really do care for one another in war and real sacrifices must be recognized. But in New War tales, only war and death can forge powerful bonds between men. Ordinary human relationships with their inevitable ambiguities, insecurities, and moments of boredom and disappointment are denigrated in favor of the pure feelings generated by the transcendent nature of blood sacrifice.

Moreover, blood sacrifice now has no end in sight. The New War is not like the old ones; the warriors are not fighting a limited war for specific purposes. Many of the heroes vow to fight to their deaths. They have abandoned normal society, and few have hopes of founding a new sacred order. Instead, the primeval chaos of the war zone becomes the new holy ground. The last lines of *The Executioner*, volume 1, read:

> Behind lay everything he had ever held dear. Ahead lay every-thing he had ever learned to fear. He cleared his mind of self-pity, letting go even of the image of tender Val [who had nursed him when he was wounded], and scowled into the bright glow of the setting sun. There was nothing ahead but hell. He was prepared for hell. Somebody else, he avowed, had better get prepared for it, too. Mack Bolan's last mile would be a bloody one. The Exe-cutioner was going to live life to the very end.[25]

Some New War stories intimate that their heroes will not be stopped even by death, but instead will be reincarnated as warriors in life after life. One self-described "star mercenary" recalls his feelings as his Mirage jet fighter spun out of control: "I felt no fear at all. Many times in my life when I have faced a dangerous situation for the first time, I have had the strange feeling that I have done it all before. I had that feeling now; I knew exactly how to eject and there was no need to worry about it."[26] The immortality of the warrior is the central motif in *Casca: The Eternal Mercenary*, a novel series by Barry Sadler, a former soldier and the composer of the famous "Ballad of the Green Berets" who later became an *SOF* editor. Casca, a slave turned gladiator who fought his way to freedom, ends up a Roman soldier assigned to watch Christ on the cross. Casca does not like Jesus at all: "You fool," he taunts him. "No one lives forever. Stop that whining and prepare to die like a man, and stop calling for your father."[27] He then stabs Jesus with his spear. Jesus responds by willing a drop of his blood into Casca's mouth. He says, "Soldier, you are content with what you are. Then that you shall remain until we meet again." This blood makes Casca immortal until the Second Coming. He must fight and die, only to come back to life as a fully adult warrior to fight and die again and again. While for most people this would be a curse, for Sadler's character—the New War warrior—it is a blessing.

To be reincarnated like Casca—whose self-healing body generates new flesh to repair the "fatal" damage sustained in the last fight—is to experience birth without a mother or father and to become an adult without passing through childhood and adolescence. Thus immortality, in practice, means complete autonomy. Not only is the hero not dependent on a larger organization to sustain him in his battles, he is completely removed from all normal human bonds and emotions. In many ways, Casca is but the most extreme example of the New War hero; all the new warriors are characterized by their radical autonomy. And just as Casca retains the same identity even as he is reborn into different nationalities and historical eras, so too are all the new warriors ultimately the same kind of man dedicated to the same endless war.

This particular combination of character and plot suggests that powerful psychological dynamics are operating in New War tales. Bruno Bettelheim contends that myths and fairy tales "speak to us in the language of symbols representing unconscious content." The "outward" journey of heroes on the battlefield and their relations with other men and women—the ostensible story—is at the same time a "voyage into the interior of our minds, into the realms of unawareness and the unconscious."[28] Part of myth's persuasive appeal, Bettelheim argues, derives from the connection it creates between our unconscious and our experience in the real world. This does not mean, of course, that everyone, or even all members of a specific social group—such as young men—will interpret stories in exactly the same way. Instead, myth simply indicates the presence of a set of cultural symbols that exert a strong pull on our unconscious, and that speak to our unresolved conflicts, needs, and fantasies.

From this perspective, what is so striking about New War stories is their obsession with vengeance. And vengeance is a very special kind of violence—a violence that has no end. René Girard describes it: "Vengeance professes to be an act of reprisal, and every reprisal calls for another reprisal . . . Vengeance, then, is an interminable, infinite process."[29] What is equally striking is that these wars of vengeance are typically unleashed by the death of the hero's family.

Sigmund Freud always insisted that an analyst first pay attention to a dream or myth's primary scene, and not be distracted by its complexities and secondary elaborations. In New War stories, the common motif of killing the hero's parents, wife, and children seems at first a simple plot device and genre convention, a way to set in motion the "real" story of the hero's war against the enemy. It is my sense, however, that it is precisely these killings that constitute the primary scene of these tales. During them, something happens. As the family is killed, excitement and anger explode in the hero—and in the reader/viewer. This rage is of the very essence of the new warrior and constitutes a significant part of his popular appeal.

In its all-consuming intensity as well as in its common targets, the warrior's fury seems to have more in common with a kind of infantile rage than with any adult emotion. The origins of infantile rage have been analyzed in detail. First, the trauma of separation from the mother: Infants initially experience themselves as one with their mothers; later they perceive parts of the mother's body, such as the breast, as separate, and eventually reach the stage where they can recognize their mothers as completely separate beings. During this last phase, the baby begins to experience deeply ambivalent feelings. The infant both loves the all-providing mother and hates her because she does not satisfy all demands immediately. As infancy gives way to early childhood, this ambivalence is increased by the mother's efforts to socialize and discipline the child. Children accustomed to unconditional love must now exercise self-control and obey their mother in order to win her approval. At the same time, the father is experienced as a threat to the pleasures provided by the mother—he commands her attention in a way the child cannot.[30] Hence, the young child's ambivalent relationship with the father becomes a second source generating infantile rage.

While both male and female infants and children experience this rage, there are important differences between the genders. As they mature, young girls retain their primary identification with their mothers. As a result of this sustained identification, some analysts theorize, a female's sense of self always involves connection to others.[31] This mitigates against the more extreme forms of infantile rage; rage against another person would be experienced as self-destructive. Conversely, the dynamics of the boy's emotional separation from his mother, together with the requirement that he identify with the father, intensifies his rage. This follows because the father is often emotionally remote; identifying with him does not offer the same kind of closeness it does with the mother, nor does it provide a specific kind of male closeness. To be masculine the youth must try to "stand alone" and form psychological boundaries that are always hard and intact. This attempt at radical autonomy is a source of both fearful anxiety and pride, just the mix necessary to generate and sustain rage.

As Freud demonstrated, unresolved conflicts from infancy and early childhood are unconsciously repeated throughout adulthood. It is not rare for unresolved infantile rage to find expression in adult fantasies about killing loved ones. But these fantastic killings of parents and wives and children in turn create their own problems: people feel guilty when they wish their loved ones dead. This guilt is unbearable, and to assuage the pain, blame is projected upon someone else—an "enemy."[32]

The stories of the New War are not the first to use the killing of the family as a way to help boys cope with the ambivalence of both wanting their parents dead and fearing the guilt and loneliness these deaths would bring. Back in the 1870s when Buffalo Bill became a dime-novel hero, at least one of his fictional compatriots, Edward L. Wheeler's Deadwood Dick, first sought the war path when outlaws murdered his foster parents.[33] In *Stagecoach* (1939), John Wayne played the Ringo Kid, a man searching for the Plumber brothers who had murdered his father and brother. Years later, in *The Searchers* (1956), Wayne again fought his personal war, this time against Indians who had killed his brother and sister-in-law and kidnapped his niece. Many other Western films, a group Will Wright calls the "vengeance variation," use the killing of the family to create their male hero.[34]

But for all their similarities, the New War and the Westerns differ in one crucial respect. The Ringo Kid gives up his war of vengeance against the Plumber brothers. He instead helps protect the small society of passengers on the stagecoach from Indians. In the process he falls in love with a prostitute and at the end of the film the two ride off together to marry, have a family, and run a cattle ranch in Mexico—the Ringo Kid's warrior days are over. Similarly, in *The Searchers*, Wayne finds his niece and takes her back even though she has been married to an Indian and is thus a fallen woman. At the end he returns her to Anglo society; his war against the Indians is over.

In contrast, the New War warrior never gives up his war of vengeance. After his family is killed, he leaves society and enters the primeval chaos of the war zone. There he will find new comrades— a new family—to assist him in his war of vengeance. And in time, these new family members, too, will die, triggering yet another round of regression and summoning up unresolved infantile rage for yet another rebirth as a warrior who vows yet another New War of vengeance against the enemy.

3

BLACK-WIDOW WOMEN

In April 1983, the cover of *Combat Handguns* featured a new Safari Arms .45 automatic for women. It looked like all the other clones of Colt's famous 1911 model, except for the grip. The synthetic ivory micrata sported a spiderweb with a large black-widow spider (complete with the red markings of a female) on each side. And that's what the gun was called too: "Black Widow—The Venomous Manstopper." For those who missed the 1983 debut of the Black Widow, the magazine ran a virtually identical story nine years later.

As all good schoolboys learn sometime around puberty, the female black-widow spider kills the male after mating and then eats him. At the very moment when a boy is trying harder than ever to establish his autonomy, this piece of spider lore calls up scenes of the overpowering mother from his infancy and childhood. At the same time, just when he is first beginning to feel some attraction to the girls around him, the image of dangerous female sexuality confirms his own worst fears—that no matter how he approaches one of them, the encounter will end badly. The New War never progresses beyond these adolescent fears. All women are black-widow women. To be sure, there are several different subspecies, but all are dangerous creatures, enemies of one kind or another who are to be either avoided, mastered, or killed.

The most deadly woman of all is of course the mother. Her death—or at least her permanent absence—is a prerequisite for the formation of the hero. Stable marriages and long-term relationships with women are also threatening to the warrior. "Good" women exist all right; they are women who recognize the power and wonderfulness of the hero. Sometimes they even love him deeply and are ready to make their lives and careers secondary to his. The hero, in turn, may finally be touched by a woman's loving grace and start to strip off his emotional armor. A "deep" relationship looms. But something always happens to these women.

"Ko," the Vietnamese woman who aids Rambo in his rescue of the American prisoners, is blown up by a Communist mortar round only seconds after they kiss and talk about the possibility of her returning with him to the United States. In *Lethal Weapon 2*, Mel Gibson finally recovers from his first wife's death only to have his new lover drowned by South African drug dealers—the lovers had only one night together! On *Miami Vice*, poor Sonny Crockett loses his second wife to a murderer's bullet shortly after they are married (his first wife divorced him at the beginning of the series because he was always off fighting bad men), while his buddy Enrico Tubbs sees his wife gunned down on their honeymoon.

In paramilitary novels, the suffering of good women is described in great detail. Natalia, the Russian heroine in Jerry Ahern's *The Survivalist* series, finally recognizes, around the time she falls in love with the American hero, that the Soviet invasion of the United States is morally wrong. Noticing her distraction, Vladimir, her Russian husband, begins to beat her:

> She watched the belt starting up again and tried to move aside, but his left fist crashed into her stomach and she doubled over, dropping to her knees on the carpet. Then she felt the belt across

her back, felt his hand in her hair as though it were being ripped out by the roots, her head drawn back and her neck bent back to where she could barely breathe.[1]

The chapter ends as Vladimir rapes her with a vodka bottle, taunting "If I do not please you, then perhaps this will."[2] Natalia survives. Most good women in these stories don't. Carl Lyons, a member of *Able Team*, sees his girlfriend go up in smoke as her helicopter is shot down by Soviet drug traffickers.[3] Eighteen volumes later, Lyons's new girlfriend, an FBI agent, ends up with "the front of her dress soaked—drenched—with blood" from five "cruel, craterlike entrance wounds."[4] In this way, men vicariously destroy the women who get too close to them, and at the same time avoid guilt by blaming the "enemy." Indeed, the warrior will always punish those responsible for these crimes.

The overt rage against women expressed in these works is never acknowledged by those responsible for creating them. "A permanent woman is like one long kissing scene," explained one New York paperback editor when asked why the warrior's good lovers are always killed. He was referring to the pace of "action" in the action-adventure genre. In his assessment, a story of human relationships moves much more slowly than a story about adventure and killing. To maintain the genre, then, the good woman has to die.

Formal genre conventions, however, always delineate the major contours of an ideal social world. And this particular ideal obscures perverse psychological dynamics, such as the blatant appeal to repressed anger. In the New War, "good" women represent the deep domestic interior of society, where women give birth and raise children. But the warrior is a man who can only live outside society, on the frontier, exempt from the confining laws and moral codes that regulate social life. This is where he must be to fight the enemy. And so he must throw off the good woman to fulfill his destiny.

Conversely, to have a serious relationship, a man must retire as a warrior and accept the limitations of mortal men. A small number of New War films do indeed depict the hero's last battle. Typically, he fights it in an effort to gain control over some unruly woman. The notion of the knight winning the heart of the lady through valor is an old one. In the New War, however, some damsels are not exactly waiting for Prince Charming. Many are feminists who have either divorced or separated from their warrior husbands. Some, like Aggie in *Heartbreak Ridge* (1986), can't stand the anxiety of not knowing whether their men will live or die on the battlefield and, therefore, refuse to commit themselves. Others, like Holly Genera in *Die Hard* (1988), are focused on their own careers as rising corporate managers. These are basically "good" women, but like the black widow, they have a mean streak and an agenda that sometimes differs from the hero's.

Still, their warrior-men love them and desire them despite their faults. In *Heartbreak Ridge*, Marine Corps Gunnery Sergeant Highway is near the end of his career. A Korean war hero who also served in Vietnam, Highway (Clint Eastwood) sits in his pickup truck, studying women's magazines to find out what went wrong in his marriage. "Did we nurture each other?" he asks. Meanwhile, at work, Highway "nurtures" a Marine reconnaissance platoon from childish infancy toward maturity. They deploy to Grenada, where they win a great victory over the Cuban Army and defy a foolish battalion commander who tries to control their martial progress. Highway comes home and announces his retirement, secure in the knowledge that he has reproduced himself in his protégés, and walks off with his ex-wife.

John McClane, Holly Genera's estranged husband in *Die Hard*, single-handedly fights the wicked terrorist group who hold Holly and her corporate colleagues hostage. Although he is seriously wounded by shards of skyscraper glass, he defeats the evil ones. Afterwards, Holly abandons her maiden name and again calls herself Mrs. McClane. To be sure, *Die Hard* is a parody of the New War genre, but it is a very loving parody. The point is clear: the desirable future for these men is a return to the prefeminist past.

In all the hundreds of New War stories, the handful of heroes who want their former mates back are the only men who are in any way concerned about their relationships with women. (In contrast, modern women's romance novels depict virtually all men as obsessed with their would-be lovers.)[5] And the task these warriors have set themselves is as difficult as any paramilitary mission. To win the hearts of their alienated significant others, warriors must prove that their powers and virtues are far greater than those of ordinary men. Only death-defying risks really impress the feminists; only then do these women relent in their demands and accept their roles as normal wives.

But few New War stories tell of marital reconciliation through warfare. Instead, most concentrate on the other kinds of females available to the hero if he is willing to take the risks. Just as the war zone is full of violent male demons, so too is it filled with powerfully erotic female creatures. Although good women are usually shown as attractive, even sexual beings, their sexuality is not the center of their lives. In contrast, the image of the fully erotic woman is one of unlimited wantonness, sexual hunger, and electricity so extreme that she gains the power to dominate men.

Billy Leeps Beeker, commander of the Black Berets, accepts contract assignments from a supersecret U.S. intelligence agency. His "case officer" is a voluptuous woman named Delilah. Every sexual encounter with her is a struggle for power:

> Now he stood in front of the cot and damned himself. He was angry because Delilah was there, waiting for him—waiting for him in every meaning of the term. Naked, her hands provocatively exploring herself. That, and they were egging him on, moving against the flesh he had come to desire too much—well, he thought, sometimes too much.
>
> He was naked as well. His readiness for her was as apparent as hers for him. It took all of his self-control to stop him from just pouncing, just climbing right over on top of her. But he'd learned a lot about Delilah. He knew that neither of them would leave the room before they got what they wanted. The only question was— who would show the greater need? It was a contest Delilah had no intention of losing. She was going to stay right there on the cot and enjoy this. The smile on her face showed that. She enjoyed the subtle mixture of pain and pleasure that this self-denial inflicted on Beeker.[6]

Beeker loses the battle. Delilah is, of course, the mythic biblical Delilah, who cut off the hair of the great warrior Samson and so destroyed his powers. The message is clear: sexually powerful women are "castrators" who cannot be mastered. When the warrior gives in to sexual desire and finds himself "losing control" during intercourse, he relaxes those all-important hardened boundaries. This vulnerability is a form of self-destruction that the New War hero must guard against vigilantly.

The erotic woman poses dangers to the warrior's career as well. In W. E. B. Griffin's best-selling six-volume saga, *The Brotherhood of War*, one of the principal characters is the brilliant, courageous, superlatively handsome son of an old Long Island family of wealthy investment bankers. C. W. Lowell, a young lieutenant stationed in Germany shortly after World War II, meets his wife-to-be one night when he picks up a girlish-looking blond prostitute and takes her back to his hotel. As fate would have it, she is a poor woman who just that evening has decided to trade her virginity for survival. Lowell thus finds, fucks, and then marries the virgin whore. And indeed, it's all too good to be true. She is killed in a car accident a few years later.

For the rest of his nearly thirty-year career, Lowell is plagued by women who find him irresistible. Movie stars make love to him in his tank. Wherever he goes, the wives of senior officers weaken his will by stripping and demanding sex. The wife of one powerful congressman on the House Armed Services Committee repeatedly orders him to undress and service her or risk having her tell her husband that he seduced her. Many of these transgressions become known to senior officers. Lowell's career is nearly ruined; he retires as a mere colonel, albeit a famous one, rather than with the four stars his ability warranted.

But at least Lowell survives. Often the erotic power of women threatens to kill the warrior. In the novel *Cherry Boy Body Bag*, one poor GI in Saigon "stuck his nose in a floorshow act, got cunt juice in his eyes, and woke up the next day with both eyes swollen shut, infected with VD. The medics had to slice the eyelids apart with a razor blade, only to learn the soldier had contracted one of the incurable strains of the clap."[7]

A member of the *Soldiers of Barrabas* merc team meets a mud wrestler who just can't keep her hands off him: "Liam O'Toole was under assault, and he wasn't doing anything to prevent it. He'd been shacked up with the muscular blonde for a week at the tavern and motel called The Mercenary, and she'd about worn him out . . . Every time they got into bed, she traced her fingers over the scars, driven by lust she couldn't control, worked her hands over his body."[8] Given the equation of women's sexuality with a deadly hunger, it's not surprising that war stories use female imagery to convey all kinds of threats to the hero. Thus, when Mack Bolan is caught in "an invisible undertow," the natural force is described as an insatiable water-nymph that "sucked greedily at him, eager to hold him in its deadly embrace."[9]

Sometimes just the sight of an erotic woman can kill a man weakened by desire. In an early volume of *The Survivalist*, one poor Russian soldier becomes so entranced while watching his beautiful comrade Natalia urinate that he does not notice the American redneck sneaking up to slice his throat.[10] In this scene, Natalia is not yet the good woman who loves the American hero, but is instead a reincarnation of Medusa, who turned all those who gazed upon her into stone. Natalia has the same petrifying powers; she also kills the redneck who wants to rape her.

Women who are uncontrollably driven by their erotic hunger are obviously capable of doing practically anything to get their needs met. They can readily separate sex from love, friendship, or even the most modest recognition of a common humanity. These erotic women are so emotionally removed from their partners that like the black-widow spiders they can kill a man after making love with him. And many try. Quite often the erotic woman who appears to desire the warrior so ardently is in reality an enemy agent. Beautiful enemy agents are not in themselves new. James Bond, the famous "007" of Her Majesty's Secret Service, always seemed to find one in his bed. But Bond's charm and swordsmanship inevitably won them over; these femmes fatales always wanted him warm and alive, not cold and dead.

In the New War, however, the erotic woman's desire for sex and desire to kill tend to merge into a single orgasmic death lust. In *Saigon Commandos*, the beautiful Communist "Hummingbird" women kidnap the Vietnamese policeman Jon Toi. After stripping and taking her knife out, the leader of the Hummingbirds "snatched up his limp penis roughly, jerked it out to its full length, and ran the sharp edge of the blade against the base of the shaft, drawing a trickle of blood . . . When she was firmly seated atop the *canh-sat* those same dirty hands flew forward, grabbed his throat, and began squeezing as hard as they could as she banged his head up and down on the tabletop and ground her hips feverishly against his own."[11] Toi is saved when a black American GI deserter hired to rape him instead lets him go.

The combination of lust for killing and lust for sexual pleasure is especially acute in female terrorists, who epitomize the height of erotic passion fatally conjoined with the coldest, most sadistic perversities. In *The Delta Decision*, a West German terrorist is described as "one of the big predatory cats" whose "big pointed breasts joggled tautly under the cotton of her t-shirt."[12] While hijacking a plane, "her eyes glittered with excitement and her breath was quick and short."[13] In her excitement, she shoots off a man's hand with her sawed-off shotgun. Finally, it gets to be too much: "She needed it very badly, the excitement and the blood had inflamed her."[14] While the hijacking is still going on, she and a comrade take a sex break in the pilot's cabin.

Nora, an Arab terrorist in Stephen Coonts's *Final Flight*, is equally perverse. As a young dance student in Paris, she had been disowned by her wealthy family because of a lesbian affair. Now, she sleeps with both sexes and both "sides." Insatiable, she seduces the terrorist leader—insisting on doing it even while they are hiding in the trunk of a car. At the same time, she relishes her assignment, which involves turning a kidnapped American nuclear technician into her sex slave. The American, a Jew, is easily undone by his sexual predilections; the Arabs blackmail him with pictures of him performing fellatio on a six-year-old boy. He readily shifts the object of his desires when Nora becomes his dominatrix, and soon the Jew provides all the information necessary to make an atomic bomb to destroy Tel Aviv. But even as he helps prepare the second Holocaust, Nora won't give him sexual release: "She permitted him to use only his tongue and lips."[15]

In *Ghost Train*, volume 31 of the *Able Team* novels, a young woman, Kara, describes "the sensations of pleasure that radiated warmly throughout her body" as she killed her male martial-arts instructor at a Communist training camp for terrorists. The instructor had thought he could master his student and break her hold. He was wrong.[16] Kara soon found out that she loved her work as an assassin: "Yes, I killed them. It was easy, and I enjoyed it, I enjoyed watching them die, those fascists, those oppressors, those . . . men."[17]

In the 1980s this image of the female terrorist was accepted by many as an accurate profile of actual operatives. Gayle Rivers wrote two books on fighting terrorists, *The Specialist: Revelations of a Counterterrorist* and *The War Against the Terrorists: How to Win It.*[18] Rivers claimed to have first served with the British Special Air Services and then become an elite mercenary for the United States and other NATO countries who needed secret commando services. He wrote that in his fifteen or more years of hunting and eliminating terrorists "the majority of female terrorists I've had to confront are spoiled, well-educated women from so-called good backgrounds who are turned on by aggressive acts."[19] According to Rivers, such women are also noted for their willingness to kill children.*

The clear implication is that all of these women—operatives, agents, and terrorists—generate a kind of evil sexual energy that is useful to the enemy. And when they embrace the male terrorist or criminal or Communist they fuse female erotic power with male violence into a single disease-ridden, demonic spirit. Interestingly enough, Peter G. Kokalis, the firearms editor of *Soldier of Fortune*, encountered such a constellation of threat, sex, and degeneracy in the behavior of the American press corps during one of his tours of duty in El Salvador. He is contemptuous of the journalists, who, he says, spend their days "sitting in the Camino Real bar, gloating over guerrilla spectaculars, sneering at the 'incompetence' of the Salva-

---

* Some writers in American paramilitary magazines did not think Rivers's books were legitimate. His tales of receiving assignments on his car phone while driving his Mercedes on the German Autobahn struck them as far-fetched, as did his accounts of extraordinary commando raids, assassinations, and kidnappings in Lebanon and other world hot spots. Rivers also made some major mistakes in his descriptions of weapons, ones that a real professional or even a more knowledgeable amateur would easily have avoided. Although the *Sunday Times* of London published a two-part article in 1985 that impugned Rivers's claims to have been an SAS veteran and mercenary, he succeeded in having American newspapers syndicate excerpts of his second book the following year.

doran Army officers."[20] What's worse than daytime drinking, though, is the press corps' nighttime whoremongering and their Commie-loving news articles. Kokalis contrasts his early-morning virtue in going to assist his comrades in the countryside with the antics of the liberal press in San Salvador:

> I rolled out with the relief column at 0500 [5:00 A.M.], just about the time the press corps has finished turning the FMLN's (Farabundo Marti National Liberation Front) daily propaganda into hot, smoking poop after a rough night downing Pilsners at Gloria's, the local cathouse.[21]

In one sentence, he links the news media, Communist propaganda, excrement, alcoholic excess, and fornication—presumably from nightfall until five in the morning. All of these people and actions roll into a single enemy: Communism as shit; shit as sex; sex as Communism. It is an image of crude, orgiastic excess, perversion that subverts all that is good and orderly. In this respect, Kokalis follows the *Freikorps* tradition in Germany after World War I. When Ernst Otwald described his image of the enemy in his novel about German paramilitary life, *Peace and Order*, he wrote, "For that matter, the terms 'cathouse,' 'bar,' 'criminal,' and 'communist' are inseparably connected in my mind."[22]

The division of women into the good, "pure" sister and the bad, "impure" temptress was also characteristic of *Freikorps* literature. *Freikorps* men frequently wrote about the virtues of their sisters, and the "whoring" of "red" working-class women. As Klaus Theweleit argued in his analysis of over two hundred *Freikorps* novels and memoirs, the repeated equation of erotic women with Communism meant that in some ways these men experienced both Communism and erotic women "as a direct assault on their genitals."[23] From this perspective, the "sister" is the only safe woman with whom the warrior can have a relationship—platonic, to be sure. According to Theweleit, "Anything beyond her is uncharted, dangerous territory, yet she herself is taboo."[24]

Just as his older brothers in the *Freikorps* rejected the erotic woman, the New Warrior must firmly maintain his hardened boundaries to avoid being contaminated by impure enemy women. He too must say no. And most stories in the New War contain at least one of these nay-saying scenes. Thomas Rourke, the hero of *The Survivalist* series, rejects the beautiful Soviet Natalia even though he is clearly aroused ("You are human," Natalia says when she determines his condition).[25] Although Mack Bolan frolics with delicious prostitutes twice in volume 1, he later regains self-control. In *Hell's Gate*, volume 86 of *The Executioner*, Bolan travels to Vancouver, Canada, to destroy a Mafia pornography operation. Unfortunately, another enemy—a Cuban agent—spots him and shoots him in the shoulder. Bolan is subsequently nursed by a young graduate student in social work who now works as a porn star and a prostitute to repay her Mafia loan.

Melody Megrims has blond hair, but Bolan is continually reminded that "if her hair were black and her face held some life, she would look something like his dead sister."[26] Bolan's dead sister, Cindy, had sold herself as a Mafia prostitute to help pay off her father's loan back in volume 1. Over and over again Bolan is reminded how much Melody resembles his sister—meaning that to have sex with her would be incestuous. At the same time, though, the reader is told how luscious and desirable she is. She is not just any call girl, she's a $500-a-night escort. At one point she gives Bolan, who is still gravely wounded but recovering, a sponge bath:

> When Melody gave him his sponge bath, he was more than a little aware of its thoroughness.
>
> "He's definitely feeling better," Melody told Johnny. She turned back to Bolan with a smile. "Relax, my intentions are strictly honorable." She paused to look him up and down and added, "At least they're honorable while your brother's here."[27]

A few pages later Johnny leaves and Melody, who has become genuinely fond of the Big Guy, tries to seduce Mack: "Naked, freshly showered and without her heavy makeup, Melody Megrims stood before Bolan. She was transformed from something tawdry into a fine example of the female animal. Her body was slim, her breasts small and firm, her muscles well defined. She had the body of an athlete."[28] She slides into bed with Bolan, "letting her fingernails trail tantalizingly across his lower abdomen." But again, something about Melody reminds him of his dead sister. Despite his erection, he refuses to make love with her.

The only other "safe" woman is the nurse, who, in *Freikorps* literature, is similar to the sister in that "the nurse's is a dead body, with no desires, no sexuality (no 'penis')."[29] In essence, then, Bolan transforms the dangerously erotic Melody into the safe nurse-sister. His refusal of her bodily charms is represented as his moral work— the redemption of a fallen woman.

More common than such noble and transforming refusals are the sometimes cruel scenes of men leaving women for war, a recurrent motif in *Freikorps* literature as well. Once, the comic-book hero Punisher literally has to push a woman off him while they are on a mission. "Cool it," he says. "Let's keep it business. Fate throws us together. But that doesn't mean we have to start acting like those animals down there."[30] On some occasions, a working-class warrior takes pleasure in leaving an upper-middle-class woman alone in bed, still wanting him.[31] Many men express relief when they no longer need to bear the burden of satisfying sexually insatiable women. In volume 30 of the *SOB*s, for example, two of Niles Barrabas's men nearly die on a sailboat so filled with hungry, naked women that all one can see are "buttocks and breasts in a kaleidoscope of white, black, and tan." When Niles calls the two men on the radio, they first chitchat about things. But soon the tension of waiting for the word gets to be too much. One warrior exclaims in joy, "Colonel? Thank God! Tell me you need us for a job. Please."[32]

There is obviously more than a hint of male narcissism in such scenes. The warrior considers himself so desirable to women that he can leave the one he's with and turn down new offers while preparing for war, because he is positive another woman will always want him. Niles, for example, can abandon a naked playmate, one with a "dark coffee color" tan all over, because he is bored—"His finely tuned mind and body were crying out for a challenge." Then, before he even gets to the airport, he has to turn down the advances of a sumptuous waitress—"Next time, baby. Maybe next time."[33]

In all of these instances, when men avoid or leave their women lovers, they appear to be exercising self-control. Only with their body armor fully in place can they guard the boundaries of society against all its enemies. Public duty seems to take precedence over private pleasure.

But what the New War really shows is that men are still deeply afraid of women. The erotic woman appears in so many terrible guises, in so many incarnations of projected fear and hostility: she is an insatiable animal; an evil terrorist aroused by killing and liable to destroy the warrior; a superficial, disposable playmate; a temptress who ruins careers and endangers missions. Compared to women, war is clean and good and dependable. By going off to war, then, men try to control their fears of women. War is the only means by which a man can subdue the erotic woman or avoid her dangerous entrapments. For the sad fact is that there can be no equality with black-widow women, only domination or subordination.

Finally, a few words must be said about a very rare character in the New War, the heroic woman warrior. Only three have appeared in recent years: the Sigourney Weaver character who battles space monsters in *Alien* (1979) and *Aliens* (1986); the Jodie Foster character who, as an FBI agent still training at the academy, tracks down a psychotic serial killer in *The Silence of the Lambs* (1991); and, in *Terminator 2* (1991), Linda Hamilton's character, the woman who tries to stop the future war between robots and humans. When movie directors and novel editors were asked in the late 1980s whether there would be more women warrior characters, the uniform answer was no. Some said that since there was little historical precedent for women combatants in war (which is not true), then obviously only the rare outer-space gig was possible. More frequently, though, the men interviewed seemed deeply vexed by the question. One well-known novel editor simply said, "I think women want to have men as heroes, and men want to have men as heroes."[34]

And that's exactly what they get. The women in the three films mentioned are strikingly similar to male New War heroes. If anything, they are hypermasculine. Women warriors avoid any romantic or erotic relationships with men, even more than male warriors avoid serious relationships with women. Linda Hamilton in *Terminator 2* is so obsessed with fighting the enemy that she is even distracted from caring for her son. A New Warrior, regardless of genitalia, is obviously incapable of sustaining serious relationships outside the war zone. Thus, although these films portray women as powerful, they maintain a strict gender dichotomy between those who fight the enemy and those who nurture, love, or have a distinct erotic presence. These warrior women are as one-dimensional as the men they replace. The difference is only superficial; their presence does not significantly change the basic mythology. After all, they fight the same villains, the same insatiable evil.

4

Free of the family members who remind him of childish weaknesses, and of the women who seek to entrap him, the warrior is ready to begin his mission and confront the enemy. The enemy is the most important figure in all war mythologies, because without him neither society nor its heroic defenders would exist. In ancient myths, the evil ones are first defeated by the gods. After the Great Battle, the sacred order is founded, and the dark forces are cast outside the boundaries of society. They are still there, always trying as hard as they can to penetrate society and destroy it completely. When societies undergo serious crises, the particular identity of the enemy as well as the location of the symbolic boundaries may change. As sociologist Kai T. Erikson writes, "Boundaries are never a fixed property of any community. They are always shifting as the people of the group find new ways to define the outer limits of their universe, new ways to position themselves on the larger cultural map."[1]

For many Americans in the 1970s and 1980s, the "larger cultural map" wasn't just changing, it was becoming unrecognizable. The New War represented these fears by portraying a world where all symbolic boundaries were weak. Now more than ever, the evil ones were gaining power and threatening to intrude.

In New War movies and novels, the heroes journey beyond the threatened boundaries into primeval chaos. No place embodies anarchic evil more than Vietnam. In *The Deer Hunter*, Robert De Niro finds Saigon not a city, but hell itself, a smoky dungeon in which frantic Asian crowds place bets on drug addicts' games of Russian roulette. In *The Executioner*, volume 123, the pilot who flies Mack Bolan back to Vietnam for a mission in 1989 describes it as "the end of the world, man. Right where civilization stops and the jungle begins."[2]

Soldier of Fortune also strove to take its readers to the edge of chaos. From Africa, Jeff Cooper reported on the civil war in Rhodesia during the mid-1970s; the nation's chromium deposits were so necessary for the manufacture of steel and weapons, he asserted, that "the frontier of civilization of which the United States is a part lies on the Zambezi River."[3] *SOF* also published dispatches from Beirut where "Christian soldiers man the Green Line," the boundary between Christian West Beirut and the barbaric forces of Islam to the east.[4] And from 1979 to 1989 there were literally scores of stories with titles such as "The War on Our Doorstep: *SOF*'s Front-Line Report from Central America."[5]

In these dark regions dwell the enemies of the New War. Since they do not live in civilized society, their fundamental natures are not civilized either. Far from being small-time criminals hustling a living through petty theft, these deeply savage animals are perverts who commit crimes for pleasure. At the most mundane level, the evil ones are driven by greed. In *The P.O.W. Escape* (1986) the Vietnamese camp commander exploits his American prisoners and the local populace to accumulate a treasure chest of gold bullion and jewelry. The German terrorist group in Wilbur Smith's novel *The Delta Decision* specializes in kidnapping the rich. They get a $150 million ransom for the OPEC ministers, "for the Braun brothers 25 million, for Baron Altman another 20 million—that's the defense budget for a nation."[6] But of course they want still more.

Bad men also lust after women. They always have harems at their disposal. When Mack Bolan joins the Mafia as a ploy in his war of revenge, he finds that the source of their wealth is a commercial sex operation controlled by a computerized Prostitution Program System. One of the mob's hard guys explains the fringe benefits of working for them as a gunman: "Girls. All kinds of girls. Hostess girls, party girls, call girls, house girls, street girls . . . Don't worry, my sergeant, you'll have all the female flesh you can stomach."[7] Soviet submarines preparing to launch the first missiles of World War III are said to be staffed by special KGB "relief women" who are "trained to perform the necessary services," and Greek criminals have villas "decorated with fine-looking women, in the way lesser men use plants and flowers."[8]

For bad men, additional sexual pleasures can readily be obtained through rape, torture, and killing. In Carl Yaeger's novel *A Hunger for Heroes* the Soviets send African troops into Cuba, both to receive terrorist training and to have sex with local women—such miscegenation will reduce the threat of nationalism to the Soviet Empire in future years. Soon the Ethiopians run amok, looting and raping. "One of the soldiers held a microphone to her mouth. Her screams and moans filled the room with electronic anguish."[9] In post-World War III fantasies, these attacks are even more common. In the first volume of the novel series *C.A.D.S*, a motorcycle-gang leader reflects that World War III had proved him right after all: "They had wasted their lives holding back their lusts, their evil desires, their raping, rampaging impulses. And for what?" With nothing to lose, the outlaw biker "tried to decide which one he liked best. It had been a while since he'd had a real small one. And virgins were best, for there weren't any doctors to go to if you got the clap from some slut you corncobbed."[10] The leader makes plans to kill, roast, and eat his victim afterwards.

Even when such villains hunt and kill men, the same perverted desires drive them. Pham, a Communist Vietnamese soldier, rejoices when he hears that his old adversary Mack Bolan is back in town:

"Pham could feel the death lust singing inside him as it never had before."[11] Villains are so base that they seem like animals with "wolfish features and cold, merciless eyes." They have "the smell of the beast" about them and an "air of cruelty and brutality."[12] Occasionally the evil ones are not men at all, but aliens from outer space with these same characteristics, like the four-fanged trophy hunters who skin humans for sport in *Predator* (1987) and *Predator 2* (1990).

Bad men are often so evil that they will not grant their victims the mercy of a quick death. Neofascist drug dealers in Argentina burn their victims slowly, while Colombians prefer to lower people inch by inch into vats of acid. Soviet doctors threaten one hero with excruciating torture, administered along with a drug "that will keep you awake, alert, in spite of the pain, so that you can experience it all. There will be no unconsciousness, only an endless burning hell."[13]

Villains also take great pleasure in spreading diseases and drugs. In one World War III scenario, David Alexander's *Dark Messiah*, the Soviets develop biological-warfare diseases that turn the contaminated (called "contams") into "blood-drinking subhumans practically overnight. The contams became cannibals with a voracious appetite for human flesh."[14] *RoboCop 2* (1990) presents an evil drug trafficker—named Cain—working on the most addictive drugs to date, the "Nuke" ensemble: "There's a Nuke for every mood." It isn't money Cain desires, but the thrill of destroying ordinary human feelings with his chemical trances. Frequently, the enemy is himself infected with disease: Niles Barrabas, the counterterrorist leader, looks at the face of his opponent and sees "the glowing eyes of a maniac. Foam gathered at the corner of the terrorist's mouth."[15]

What is so interesting about all these enemies—the drug dealers, the left-wing terrorists, the neo-Nazis, the Soviets, and the Mafia—is how closely they resemble one another. They all commit the same evil crimes for the same perverted reasons. And, in the New War, all of the enemies are connected to each other, no matter how different they may seem at first glance. For example, in Robert Moss and Arnaud De Borchgrave's novel *Monimbo*, the KGB plots to destroy the United States with the help of its Latin-American Communist allies. Cuban and Nicaraguan intelligence agents manipulate Colombians and right-wing Cuban exile groups in Miami to give part of the profits from the drug trade to black radical groups and the most recent wave of Cuban refugees—the ex-prisoners and mental patients known as *marielitos*. Together with various assassins and saboteurs from the Communist countries, these criminally insane radicals are supposed to launch a war inside the U.S.A. The book's first page succinctly describes their mission: "Create a scenario of chaos—ugly race riots in Miami, a panic of blackouts in New York, and everywhere a wildfire of murder and mobs running through the darkened streets."[16]

Creating chaos is the objective of the evil ones in the New War, just as it was at the beginning of time. Each criminal action furthers the spread of chaos. Every boundary they penetrate—from the geographic borders of good countries like the United States to the physical boundaries of a once-pure body ravaged by rape, torture, and death—leads to the victory of chaos and the destruction of the sacred order. And with each victory the enemies want more; they incarnate what Paul Ricoeur calls "the evil infinite of human desire."[17]

Ultimately, the evil ones can only be satisfied by the collapse of social stability and all moral values. The Mafia wants to corrupt everyone, from the highest political officials to the poorest woman selling her body to pay off her family's debt. The drug dealers want a world so addicted to drugs and the money drugs bring that people will do anything the dealers want. Luther Enoch, arch-villain of *Dark Messiah*, speaks for all the evil ones as he watches television screens on the eve of initiating World War III:

> The Dark Messiah scanned each screen in the bank, delighting in the harvest of death he had reaped.
> The Great Chaos had come.
> The New Order would begin.[18]

Since the enemies of the New War are all essentially the same, the New Order they envision looks about the same, too: a totalitarian world that resembles their criminal organizations. At the top stands the supreme leader, be he the Mafia's "boss of bosses," the head of the Soviet KGB, a local gang leader and drug lord, or Carlos the terrorist. The supreme leader is war chief of his tribe; under him are an assemblage of henchmen who do his bidding in return for a share of the spoils. And below the henchmen are the spoils themselves— slaves who labor in the evil ones' factories and drug addicts who buy their wares, men who can be hunted for sport and the women who can be taken and disposed of at will.

The New Order is a world without law or individual rights. There are neither rules nor rituals to give the world rhythm and meaning. Instead there is only the will and desire of the leader. To him, everyone is expendable, especially those who fail to carry out his orders immediately and with success. The New Order that the evil ones so fervently desire is both a form of social organization and a continuation of chaos.

Given the depth of his depravity, the enemy, one might think, poses an obvious danger to society. But oddly enough, in New War narratives this danger is not always immediately apparent. Many times his crimes at first look like ordinary killings, personal tragedies for the victims and their families but not a threat to the entire social order. In order to alert readers and viewers to the true dimensions of the problem, New War stories usually cast their enemies as reincarnations of older, more recognizable enemies of society.

The most obvious and detectable villains look somewhat like Indians. From the dangerous streets of *Death Wish* to the bloody highways of *The Road Warrior*, common street punks, their more organized motorcycle-gang brethren, and the tough leaders of the drug trade all have an Indian look about them. The men have long, wildly flowing hair or fierce Mohawk cuts or Jamaican-style dreadlocks. Either their faces are smeared with dirt and grease that looks like war paint or they actually wear war paint. They are only partially clothed, usually in leather, and their massive arms and chests are always bare. Just as Indian men traditionally wore necklaces, earrings, and other jewelry, so too do their modern-day reincarnations. These Indians can be white men, but more often they are some shade of brown or black. Finally, the new "Indians" show their teeth and shout war cries when they attack, shattering contemporary civilization with frightening echoes from an archaic past.

All of these images can in turn be summoned up by one phrase

—"Indian country." During the Vietnam War, "Indian country" showed up time and time again in the everyday language of the troops; it continued to appear in their novels and memoirs later on. In the 1970s, the Indians turned up in Rhodesia, where an American in the Rhodesian Army formed a cavalry unit to ride them down during that country's civil war.[19] A few years later they reappeared in El Salvador. Peter G. Kokalis began one of his many *SOF* reports on the Atlacatl infantry battalion whom *SOF* trainers regularly advised with the dateline: "Indian country—just east of the Rio Lempa in Usulutan Province, El Salvador. The rugged terrain is infested with Communist guerrillas, swarming gnats, tall grass, and choking heat."[20]

When villains don't resemble Indians they may be reimagined as the Nazi and Japanese enemies of World War II. For example, when Rambo returns to Vietnam in *First Blood, Part 2*, he finds Vietnamese who wear World War II Japanese caps and are led by a blond-haired Russian who wears black leather and speaks with a guttural, vaguely Germanic accent. Myth readily substitutes one enemy for another, combining them in ways that make cultural sense: If Russian white men really controlled and directed the yellow Vietnamese, then the U.S. defeat becomes more understandable and belief in white superiority is confirmed.

At the same time, if Vietnamese are only Japanese in disguise, then even the Vietnam War with its murky moral imperative was not that different from a good clean fight like the Second World War. This process of taking what America already "knows" about an old enemy and transferring it to a new enemy has infinite possibilities. If the Vietnamese are simply reincarnations of the bad Japanese, then logically any group or nationality who resemble the Vietnamese in any way (using the AK47 rifle, for instance, or wearing sandals) will have the same evil connotation. By establishing such analogies, myth creates closure, replacing doubts about present conflicts with certainties about the just wars of the past.

Given that so many of the enemies in the New War are not white, one must ask to what extent the New War is about white racism. The notion that all nonwhites are the enemy finds its strongest contemporary expression in the right-wing fundamentalism of Christian Identity theology, which claims that the Anglo-Saxons and the Teutons (Germanic peoples) are the lost tribes of Israel and the true heirs of Abel, the child of Adam and Eve. The Jews are actually the descendants of Cain, who, say Christian Identity theologians, was the son of Eve and the Devil. All nonwhites—"the mud people"—are descendants of the Jews. Hence, they are literally the children of the primordial evil one, the Devil himself.[21]

In 1978, William S. Pierce published a novel informed by this racist philosophy. *The Turner Diaries* tells the story of the white victory in a race war fought in the United States in the early 1990s.[22] The novel is presented as the lost diary of Earl Turner, a low-level white guerrilla who is killed in the war. White historians subsequently find his document and annotate it for the reader. Hence the book appears as the history of the future.

As the diary reveals, two events precipitated armed revolution by whites against the U.S. government, which is called ZOG—the "Zionist Occupational Government." First, the government's ban on guns made it impossible for white men to protect their families from the ever-increasing criminal attacks by nonwhites. At the same time, ZOG also abolished rape as a crime, on the grounds that it was sexist: men can't be raped. Consequently, nonwhite men were free to rape white women, and they did so by the tens of thousands. The last barrier against universal miscegenation had been breached. Only the white revolution could stop the devil's work.

The open contempt for nonwhites, particularly blacks, expressed in *The Turner Diaries* may be found in some pulp novels as well. But in general such blatant racism is rare. Instead, the New War uses several different rhetorical mechanisms to shift attention away from the important fact that the evil ones who cannot control their desires are predominantly nonwhite.

The process of reincarnating old enemies as new ones is one such method. Since the Indian Wars fought over a hundred years ago are presented as the struggle between civilization and savagery (rather than as the aggression of white society against Indian society), any "new" Indian is just another savage. Killing an Indian, then, seems a victory for civilization in general, not whites in particular.

A second, related rhetorical technique that diffuses the racism of the New War involves the avoidance of race as an explicit plot theme; it appears as secondary detail. Movies and novels stress the crimes in question. They give names like terrorist, Communist, and drug dealer to the people who commit these crimes. Few New War stories openly address the racial composition of the enemy, but in the telling of the tale, it emerges that most of the enemies are not white. Hence the heroes fight drug dealers who just happen to be black.

To make race appear even less of an issue, the heroic warrior tribes are usually shown as integrated. Although white heroes typically head these tribes, there are a few noteworthy exceptions. Rambo is half Apache. Danny Glover, the black costar of the first three *Lethal Weapon* movies, finally gets the star role in *Predator 2*. He leads his elite, racially integrated team of L.A. detectives against Colombian and Jamaican drug gangs and against alien predators from outer space. If the heroes transcend racial differences in their relations with one another, then surely the battles they fight against the evil ones are not racist, either.

Finally, the unity of the various enemies tends to obscure the fact that most of them are not white. Although gangs in the real world have traditionally been racially segregated and are frequently enemies, in the New War white, Latin, and black hoodlums are often bosom buddies who share the same evil pleasures. When they are not buddies, at least they can find a temporary common ground in a mutually beneficial division of labor for their criminal endeavors.

Of course, political terrorism is the greatest glue of all. Soviet KGB agents hand out drug money to black radicals. Bulgarian hangmen do the dirty work in Nicaragua. German terrorists assist their comrades around the Third World in hijackings and assassinations. Establishing links among disparate enemies also makes each one look more dangerous. The local warlord and his handful of minions are a threat to society, because they are potentially connected to all the other enemies. As the counterterrorists of *Phoenix Force* reason, "They were out there somewhere, the vermin, planning murder, plotting revolution. They were everywhere where men knew a measure of freedom. They subscribed to different political faiths, but behind the slogans and the false patriotism they were all the same."[23]

———

"Against a world infested with terror goons," heroic warriors must be ready to risk their lives to save society.[24] Yet, to their bitter frustration, they have to contend with a different kind of enemy every step of the way—"bleeding heart" liberals and complacent government officials, moral cowards who refuse to fight. Why do these leaders make themselves the enemy of courageous good men?

To answer this troubling question, New War stories point to a deep philosophical flaw in liberalism or what the religious right wing in the 1970s and 1980s called "secular humanism." Although most social and political analysts would say that post-Vietnam America has been decidedly conservative, in the New War a liberal ethos still permeates the leadership. These "practicing" liberals deny some fundamental truths; above all, they refuse to recognize the absolute reality of evil. By insisting that there are no bad men, but only bad social conditions, liberals fail to see that criminals, terrorists, and Communists commit their horrendous acts because they feel pleasure in killing, raping, and kidnapping. They are men who have lost self-control and succumbed to their desires—and their desires are infinite. Infected with evil, criminals can neither be contained nor reformed as liberalism would have it; they must be eliminated.

This fundamental split between liberalism and New War conservatism is well illustrated by *Dirty Harry*. In one of the movie's early scenes, detective Callahan is reprimanded by his boss for shooting a naked man running through the streets—a person who, in liberal eyes, is obviously mentally ill and needs help, not a .44 Magnum slug. Callahan reminds his boss that the man had an erection—and a knife. From Callahan's perspective, shooting the man was the right thing to do.

In foreign policy, liberalism's failure to understand the evil of the enemy threatens to delude politicians into thinking they can negotiate peaceful settlements to violent conflicts. But warriors know that the devil's word means nothing; he will lie, cheat, and steal to get what he wants. One newspaper cartoon reprinted in *Soldier of Fortune* shows Senator Christopher Dodd of Connecticut standing on the steps of the Capitol declaring that "any fool knows this is the time to force the government of El Salvador to the bargaining table with the leftists to . . ." As Dodd speaks, his car is stolen. He runs after the thief yelling "How 'bout a negotiated settlement?"[25] Liberals like Dodd are trying to stop the U.S. military from winning victories abroad by demanding bogus political settlements like the one that led to defeat in Vietnam.

Liberalism is also associated with serious character defects, moral corruption, and outright cowardice. (In Brian Garfield's *Death Wish*, "A liberal is a guy who walks out of the room when the fight starts."[26]) Often, corruption is linked to greed. Class, too, is a factor. Liberal elites, the graduates of Harvard and other Ivy League schools, are frequently pitted against heroic warriors with working-class origins. In his first commando film, *Good Guys Wear Black* (1978), Chuck Norris learns that the last survivors of his former Vietnam team are being assassinated because a State Department Ivy Leaguer wants a big promotion and needs them dead to protect his secret negotiations with the North Vietnamese.

The selfishness of superiors, coupled as it is with liberal cowardice, is the reason why subordinates are forced to fight the enemy with one hand tied behind their backs. "I expect you and every other man in the department to behave with restraint or turn in his resignation," the lieutenant informs Callahan in *The Enforcer* (1976) in response to Harry's having killed four bad guys, caused $14,000 in damages to a police car and a store, and injured three hostages while rescuing them from certain death (they plan to sue the police department for "excessive use of force"). The lieutenant is worried that Harry's actions will somehow reflect badly on the lieutenant and damage his career.

For the warrior, therefore, the official guardians of society are no longer legitimate. And society itself has become suspect. Liberalism has permeated the educational system, the churches, and the news media. Men who fight have been relegated to a "polluted," taboo caste—even though they risk their lives for those who despise them. Indeed, they will be condemned for their violent acts no matter what they do. The British SAS team in *The Final Option* (1982) is warned before they storm the Iranian embassy in London:

In front of worldwide television cameras and uninformed members of the press, you will have to attempt to rescue the hostages. If, during the operation, some of them are killed, you will be damned. And if somehow you manage to save them, but in doing so you kill the terrorists, you will be damned.

Sentenced to hell by the media, unappreciated by most ordinary people, and abused by the power structure, in time the New War warriors are forced to let go of their old allegiances. Instead of being part of the system, they find they have been betrayed by it. So the warriors must always fight on two fronts. They must do battle with the true evil ones and, at a minimum, avoid the representatives of the establishment. To carry on this war, they need to establish bases far removed from the mainstream of society. In *Uncommon Valor* the private commandos train on an isolated Texas ranch. *The Black Berets* have a bunker-like home on a rural Louisiana farm. Sonny Crockett has his sailboat for a retreat when things aren't going well with the CIA or the DEA or his other bosses in *Miami Vice*. Seagal and his two buddies find an abandoned warehouse in *Marked for Death* (1990) in which to plan their attack on a drug syndicate leader in Jamaica. Oddly enough, the sacred spaces of the heroes aren't very different from those of the evil ones—except that the villains fill theirs with women. Those on the enemy side also like yachts and isolated beach homes and ranch houses on large estates. They too have nondescript apartments as safe houses. They too show great fondness for dark, old warehouses. Both evil ones and heroes are men of the shadows.

In this twilight, the true nature of both the evil ones and the heroes is briefly silhouetted. In the enemy, the hero glimpses himself. The reflection is his mirror image gone bad, a vision of a man who cannot control his desires but has instead surrendered to them completely and thus become evil.

Scenes of doubling or mirror-imaging occur with some regularity in the New War. In *Mad Max*, the Mel Gibson character, Max, and the chief of his highway-patrol unit have an extraordinary conversation after Max's buddy, Goose, has been burned by the outlaws. The chief wants Max to keep fighting because the public needs heroes. Max replies that he is about to lose control. "Look, any longer on that road, then I'm one of them." The chief says it's already too late. "You're hooked, Max, and you know it."

This same idea, that the hero and the villain are equally addicted to violent excitement or killing, occurs in the *Soldiers of Barrabas* series. Niles Barrabas's girlfriend, Erika, has had a gun fired near her head, a simulated execution designed to terrorize her. But instead of hating her torturer, she sees her lover Niles more clearly: "She would not let Barrabas help her through it. She had stared into the black, howling abyss and had finally seen what her lover, the mercenary leader, was addicted to. And for the first time in their ten-year friendship, she was afraid of him."[27]

In Don Pendleton's instructions to writers of the Mack Bolan series, he first warns against reducing the enemy to a caricature: "Do not indulge in some juvenile misunderstanding of the forces that move and shake this world. These people are dangerous, not because a gun is in their hands, but because something cold and deadly is in their heart."[28] Yet, only a few pages later, he also characterizes someone else as equally cold: "Bolan is, as it were, dead inside. He has to be in order to operate in the way he does. It is an essential aspect of his popularity."[29]

Sometimes heroes find their increasing identification with the evil ones to be unbearable. Vigilante, one of the many comic-book avengers of the 1980s, finally admits that "instead of stopping crime I became the criminal. I was supposed to rid the streets of killers and madmen, wasn't I? I didn't want to die. I couldn't continue to live."[30] To end his pain, he kills himself. Not all heroes have this option— Catholics, for example. At the beginning of *Marked for Death*, a distraught undercover narcotics detective confesses his sins to a priest: "I did whatever I had to do to get the bad guys. I realize that I have become what I once despised. I have lied, slept with informants, done drugs."

But in the end there is really only one way to stop the mirror-imaging of hero and villain. The mirror must be shattered; someone must die. Hence, the mythology of the New War always involves a radical reduction of social conflict to one basic scene: the duel. To create this duel, myth reduces the Indians, the Vietnamese, the Soviets, the Arabs, and all the other collective enemies to a handful of men. Never do these enemies have any political or social or moral reasons for fighting; they have no real historical existence. How they came to be the enemies of America and what they want is never mentioned. As Roland Barthes once said, "*myth is depoliticized speech*"; by depoliticizing the enemy, it avoids "the whole of human relations in their real, social structure, in their power of making the world."[31]

Removed from history, the enemy is transformed by myth into the embodiment of evil: a man who cannot control his desires. Once evil is defined in this way, the struggle between hero and villain can be represented as a psychological conflict within the hero; the villain is but a phantasm, a projection of the hero's own desires, rages, and frustrations. Thus, like most mythological tales, New War stories function on at least two levels: they are simultaneously a vision of a social world—the battlefield—and a journey into the psyche.[32] At the psychological level, the New War narrative appears to be a story about male self-control.

Warriors are men of nearly impeccable self-control, with enemies as well as with women. They begin killing only because they must —to avenge a loved one or to see justice done—and not because they like it. As Pendleton points out, Mack Bolan feels no joy in his killings; only the "psychopathic" villain "wants to go out and slay and see blood flow."[33]

Everyone who has lost self-control, from the American political elite to rapists and murderers, is the warrior's enemy. Since in the New War all human desire is seen as insatiable and thus evil, without self-control every man would rape, murder, and try to become dictator of the world. Hence the hero's recognition of himself in the villain. When Dirty Harry shoots the naked man running wild in the streets with his knife and erection, he in effect shoots every man (including himself).

In the New War, criminal actions appear wonderfully exciting. In doing exactly what he wants to do, the villain moves freely from one kind of pleasure to another; he suffers under no restraints and his only responsibilities are to sustain and increase his pleasure. Upon inspection, though, it becomes clear that the enemy's gratification is derived from a single source—from transgression, from breaking all laws and acting contrary to all moral codes. Even the standard image of hedonism and sensuality—the villain surrounded by his harem—reveals this same pattern. The villain's pleasure comes from neither heightened love nor lust, but from having more than one woman, thus breaking the rule that says a good man gets just one.

In her study of Marquis de Sade, Angela Carter illuminates the nature of this transgressive impulse. Sade's pornography, she argues, has little to do with sexual pleasure per se and everything to do with a compulsive need to defy authority. Hence the characteristic combination in his work of endless scenes of anal, oral, genital, and group sex with incest, abortion, prostitution, patricide, and other more mundane murders—and of course domination and submission. For Sade, Carter says, sex is essentially a criminal act and the libertine's "entire pleasure" is "the cerebral, not sensual one, of knowing he is engaging in forbidden activity."[34]

By presenting sexuality as a constant and inescapable alternation of domination and submission, Sade removes it from the realm of mutual human relations; since there is no experience of pleasure with equal others, the individual is left alone. At the same time, by presenting sexual desire as "cerebral insatiability," in Carter's words, Sade denies that it can ever be fulfilled: each act of defiance of authority requires yet a greater transgression to provide the same rush of excitement. Eventually, in Sade's works, this compulsive need to break all rules leads the libertines to regress from adulthood to infancy:

> Transgression becomes regression and, like a baby, they play with their own excrement . . . The shamelessness and violence of the libertines is that of little children who are easily cruel because they have not learned the capacity for pity which the libertines dismiss as "childish" because the libertines themselves have not grown up enough to acknowledge the presence of others in their solipsistic world.[35]

The New War portrays human desire in much the same way. The evil one always wants more, because what he ultimately desires is to defy the laws of society, and seeking that solitary pleasure takes him down the road of cerebral insatiability toward childish regression. When the hero and his mirror-image villain face off, their confrontation may be seen as the hero's attempt as an adult to control his own regressive child-like nature.

But that isn't what happens. There is tragedy here, not psychological development. The New War, like Sade, eliminates the reality of other people and the good companionship and satisfaction they can give. If the villain in effect is a needy, enraged child who must have everything and everyone at his disposal, the hero is still another kind of child. He is the narcissistic, omnipotent child, the one who says "I need nothing and no one to sustain me." The villain must transgress the parental law to feel that he is alive, while the hero must deny that he ever had parents at all. Both the villain and the hero live in completely self-referential worlds.

The villain's murderous rage is a natural part of his pleasure in transgression, in violating all boundaries—both those of the body and those of society. In contrast, the hero's rage comes from his constant self-denial and personal sacrifice. This rage and self-denial is easy to see on the face of the hero. All the major male stars wear that same hard, mean look of controlled power. The heroic warrior lives for the final confrontation with the evil one. Only his prowess in combat, a form of impeccable self-control, enables him to protect the boundaries of society against threatening intrusions by the insatiable enemy. At the same time, only by killing the enemy can he release the rage accumulated from a life of emotional self-denial.

5

The old Hollywood warriors did not have tremendous physiques or special guns to signify their powers. Their martial prowess was grounded in their moral character. Although they were skilled in the use of weapons, their guns were not in themselves important. John Wayne carried an ordinary Colt .45 revolver in all his Western adventures. Humphrey Bogart likewise had but a plain .38 Special police revolver when he played detective Sam Spade. And in the war movies, heroes were equipped with standard U.S. government issue firearms. Robert Taylor and his comrades fought to the death in *Bataan* because they were brave men, not because they had big guns.

In the New War, the hero's weapons are central, potent symbols with important connotations. The modern hero carries very elaborate or customized weapons; they are *his* particular tools for inflicting death, "signatures" of sorts. In addition, the weapons are so powerful that they readily mark the hero's independence from other people.

With them, one man or a small group can hold the whole world at bay; the heroes never need reinforcements from the corrupt power structure. At the same time, weapons are also consumer goods that are routinely evaluated and advertised in paramilitary magazines. Until more restrictive federal and state gun laws were passed in 1989, almost all modern semiautomatic rifles could be purchased legally. And even with these laws, virtually all "combat" pistols and shotguns are still legal, as are most of the so-called assault rifles. The fact that guns and knives used by New War heroes are readily available for purchase is an important aspect of the myth's appeal. The sheer physical existence of steel combat weapons makes the mythology seem more realistic. It is as if the myth can be touched and held in the hand. In turn, the war stories make the rifles and pistols seem especially alluring. As one scholar of material culture, Adrian Forty, writes:

> Every product, to be successful, must incorporate the ideas that will make it marketable, and the particular task of design is to bring about the conjunction between such ideas and the available means of production. The result of this process is that manufactured goods embody innumerable myths about the world, myths which in time come to seem as real as the products in which they are embedded.[1]

When Clint Eastwood's *Dirty Harry* started the cinematic New War, he brought along a special weapon, a huge Smith and Wesson .44 Magnum. John Milius, the *Dirty Harry* screenwriter, owned a .44 Magnum and thought that "it seemed like an interesting concept that a cop would carry a gun like that."[2] The revolver was over a foot long and weighed over three pounds, making it nearly impossible for even a big man wearing a baggy coat to conceal. In low light or at night, the flame which shot out the barrel temporarily blinded the shooter. The gun had so much muzzle blast that it deafened the pistolero, leaving him with ringing ears for days. When the cartridge was loaded to full power, its recoil was so pronounced that no gunman could recover in time for a quick second shot. These features made it totally unacceptable as a combat pistol in the real world.

But Eastwood's Dirty Harry was not fighting in the real world. He fought inside an America gone bad, a place of almost primeval chaos. Harry was "dirty" because he alone recognized the absolute reality of evil, and what had to be done to stop it. He fought alone, and for that fight he needed "the most powerful handgun in the world." A truly dangerous enemy might recover from the wound of a .38 Special (a liberal way of "containing" rather than eradicating evil). Only a .44 Magnum could destroy the enemy's body beyond any hope of recovery. Scene after scene focused on villains' terror as they faced that big .44. The hero's power thus shifted from his virtue to a combination of virtue and a weapon so powerful, so advanced that it was, in effect, "magical."

After *Dirty Harry*'s great success, other film and pulp-novel warriors followed Eastwood's lead in going to war with spectacular weapons. Mack Bolan carried a custom-made .44 Automag, a pistol far more powerful than the .44 Magnum revolver, along with a small Beretta submachine gun. Sylvester Stallone's Rambo developed modern versions of ancient armaments—a huge custom knife (virtually a short sword) and a special bow with exploding fire arrows. In *Commando* (1985) Arnold Schwarzenegger started on his rescue mission with an enormous combat shotgun called a SPAS, an Uzi 9mm submachine gun, a .45 automatic pistol (with laser sight), and a giant knife.

As the guns and knives and bows got bigger and bigger, the hero's ability to gracefully swing them around and fight with them became even more impressive. (Weapons began to seem like parts of the hero's body.) But only the hero's powerful warrior will and ability allowed him to use these weapons so well. Since this fusion with the weapon was so difficult to master, warrior heroes judged men with lesser weapons to be lesser men. In one of the *Dirty Harry* films, Inspector Callahan looks at another detective's puny snub-nosed .38 and advises him to stay in the station house: "A man should know his limitations." When Mel Gibson and Danny Glover prepare for their first assignment together in *Lethal Weapon*, Gibson checks the

15-round magazine in his Beretta 9mm semiautomatic and picks up another four magazines as spares. When he sees his new partner pull out a plain six-shot .38 revolver, he smirks and says incredulously, "I heard a few old-timers still carried those things."

The heavily armed warrior is the man of the future; only he can fight the evil ones and counter the breakdown of society. As Dale Dye, a former *Soldier of Fortune* editor and technical adviser to Hollywood once remarked, the tremendous escalation of weaponry "allows the characters to do what they want to do. If they've got superweaponry, they can pull it off."[3] At the same time, the increased use of military weapons by both heroes and villains meant that cinematic body counts went higher and higher. The previous distinction between cop pictures and war films disappeared. War abroad found a companion in war in the streets.

Once the weapons escalation began, moviemakers quickly began to focus on the hero's guns. Mark Lester, director of *Commando*, looked at more than three hundred guns in choosing Arnold Schwarzenegger's arsenal. To determine the most photogenic weapons, Lester's production crew took pictures of the actor posing with different guns. Lester explained the dynamics of firearm modeling: "I might say to Arnold, 'You look great with that big powerful gun, you know.' And Arnold might say back, 'This one feels great, I like this.' "[4] A whole industry of firearm consultants and gun dealers arose to help Hollywood find esoteric firearms for its stars.

And, just as a superweapon could help make a movie superhero, a successful movie could make a best-selling weapon. Smith and Wesson originally introduced the .44 Magnum in 1964 for a relatively small market of hunters. After *Dirty Harry*, gun dealers reported that they had customers calling and walking in who had never owned a gun, and didn't even know what to ask for other than to say that they wanted the "Dirty Harry gun," together with a shoulder holster just like Clint had.

Rambo's knife also hit big. Jimmy Lile, an Arkansas custom-knife maker, found himself overwhelmed with orders. Within a year, scores of manufacturers were turning out copies of Rambo's knife. Some were expensive custom items, others "quality" machine-made knives, but most were cheap imitations. Stallone subsequently formed special licensing agreements to produce the knives and bows used in his later films. After noticing how well the Hollywood tie-in weapons sold, manufacturers began lobbying filmmakers to have their latest offerings adopted.

For the consumer and would-be warrior, it is important in choosing a gun to find a model that has already been used to win victories over the evil ones. As Mircea Eliade says, awareness of the tales of primordial victories gives the warrior strength. He derives confidence from the knowledge "that what he is about to do has already been done before." The aura of myth "helps him to overcome doubts as to the result of his undertaking. There is no reason to hesitate before setting out on a sea voyage, because the mythical Hero has already made it in a fabulous time."[5]

Over the years, a few weapons have achieved such symbolic power by association—for example, the Colt single-action .45 revolver. Although many different revolvers were used in the old West, the Colt .45 was adopted by the United States Army in 1873, and subsequently became the weapon of choice in Western movies—a true hero's gun. Jeff Cooper, founder of the prestigious combat-shooting school, Gunsite Ranch, once described what holding an old .45 single-action revolver means: "Just to hold one in your hands produces a feeling of kinship with our Western heritage—an appreciation of things like courage and the sanctity of man's word."[6] To own a Colt .45 revolver is to possess a "time-travel" machine, an object so laden with rich historical associations that it can transport its owner back to the mythic frontier.

In 1911 the U.S. Army adopted another Colt .45—a semiautomatic pistol. The Army and the Marine Corps used this model in World War I, World War II, Korea, Vietnam, and all other U.S. conflicts until the adoption of the 9mm Beretta in 1986. To own and shoot a Colt .45 automatic opens a tremendous historical domain for an imaginary traveler. He too can fight with the Marines at Belleau Wood, or with their descendants at Iwo Jima, or with the third generation at the Inchon Reservoir in Korea, or with the great-grandchildren at Khe Sanh in Vietnam. This weapon's mythic status bestows strength on the modern paramilitary adventurer. Armed with a .45, the warrior is confident in the knowledge that thousands before him have slain their enemies with the same gun. He becomes one with his weapon: tough as steel, reliable under the worst conditions, a hard hitter.

Movies and novels provide one kind of mythic validation to a weapon. A second, related kind of magical aura is generated by the way gun magazines and advertisements talk about the firearms used by military and police forces. Gun manufacturers are fully aware of how important historical fantasies are to the marketing of their products. Springfield Armory's advertisement for a .45 clone said that it was the "affordable legend." The American Historical Foundation offers a special "commemorative" edition of each major U.S. firearm and knife. Its advertisement for an engraved .45 proclaimed: "If you were born between the late 1880s and 1968, it is the symbol of your time, your day, your age. And future Americans will look back on our time, with reverence, as the '.45 Era.' "[7]

Those companies offering relatively new firearms and knives must invent a fantasy domain for their products. Heckler and Koch, a German manufacturer, advertised its Model 94 9mm carbine in a still-life composition, also featuring a knife, a pistol belt with an H&K pistol, loose cartridges, several ammunition magazines, and most important, a *map* and a *compass*. The carbine was framed as a key to adventure; it would take its owner beyond conventional society into the primordial wilderness. Similarly, a pistol of a radically new design is presented by another manufacturer as "Aiming for the 21st century . . . At GLOCK, we've looked beyond the status quo to respond to the growing security needs of the coming century."[8]

Firearms made and used by the enemy must be marketed with special care. More than thirty-five million Kalashnikov AK47 assault rifles were produced in Communist-bloc countries; thousands of American troops in Vietnam were killed by men (and women) using them. The AK has also been popular with the Nicaraguan and Salvadoran revolutionaries, with the African National Congress in its militant years, and with "terrorist" groups. Scores of newspaper photographs, television news clips, fictional movies, and novels have acquainted the American public with this weapon. The American man who owns one is obviously a truly bad hombre, one who can wrest power from the enemy and claim it as his own. Advertising must sell the gun as powerfully "bad" without explicitly referring to its history, lest someone question the ethics of marketing enemy guns. When the AK47 (semiautomatic version) was first introduced to America, the ad simply mentioned how "arousing" it was:

> The AKM burst on the international firearms scene almost three decades ago. Since then, no automatic rifle has aroused so much curiosity among collectors and shooters for its toughness and versatility. No automatic rifle has aroused so much envy among firearm designers for its simplicity of operation and absolute reliability . . . Satisfy your curiosity about this new beauty. See it at your sporting arms dealer. Snap one up. Then *you'll* be the envy of your fellow shooters and collectors.[9]

John Berger once observed that envy is a central emotional dynamic in advanced capitalism; the person who wants to be envied tries to buy self-confidence and happiness by making others feel inadequate.[10] Mercedes and Porsches and other expensive automobiles are clearly purchased and valued as signs of class membership and consumed for the purpose of creating envy. With combat weapons, membership dynamics are somewhat different. It isn't entrée to any particular social class in the modern world that's being bought but access to the mythic world of combat. Buying a combat weapon is like joining a tribe; each weapon is a specific tribal totem. Men can belong to more than one tribe, however. The more weapons the warrior owns, the more power he can appropriate from their histories, and the more fantasy adventures he can pursue.

Since paramilitary culture projects a world in which the male warrior is left alone to defend himself and his loved ones—or to avenge their deaths—the boundaries of the "society" he has to protect become synonymous with the farthest distance he can secure against a potential enemy.

Of course, by changing weapons a man can also change his personal boundaries. A paramilitary warrior lives inside what I call the "concentric rings of power," each ring measuring how big he can become and how close his enemies are. Both paramilitary magazines and mainstream gun magazines teach men the lethal range of available weapons and evaluate a consumer's choices at each threshold.

The first ring of power is arm's reach—an arm extended by the length of a knife. Since 1987, various knife makers and soldiers have debated in *Soldier of Fortune* just how long a knife blade should be. One school suggests that men should carry modern Bowie knives with heavy blades from nine to twelve inches long, since these were the best weapons developed before reliable firearms: "Frontier America in the 1830s and '40s was a rough and tumble place, a harsh environment of raging rivers and vast forests full of wild animals and wilder men. Towns and outposts were as bad if not worse . . ."[11] Others consider six inches sufficient—long enough to cut a throat, slice an arm, or pierce the enemy's heart.

The second ring of power is about thirty-five yards from the warrior, the farthest distance most competent shooters can fire a full-size combat pistol quickly and accurately. Thirty-five yards is also the maximum range that most models of "social" or combat shotguns can group at least one-fourth of their buckshot on a human chest. Within this second ring, gun writers debate whether semiautomatics are better than revolvers, which calibers are best, whether one should use a shotgun instead of a pistol, and how many pistols a gunman should carry. Most novels and movies of the New War feature their armed confrontations between heroes and villains at very close range, well within this second ring.

At a hundred yards the shooter enters the third ring. "Good" shotguns firing solid slugs are accurate at this range. Civilian models of submachine guns (carbines firing pistol cartridges) also reach their limit at around one hundred yards. Gun writers frequently say that this distance is about the maximum range for combat inside a city. Shotguns and small carbines are thus often referred to as "urban" weapons.

The M16s used by Americans and the AK47s used by the Communists both shoot accurately out to 200–250 yards, perhaps a bit further for M16s and other rifles firing 5.56mm shells. Here, then, is the fourth ring. These weapons are considered to be "general purpose" combat arms. A paramilitary warrior's arsenal must include one of them to be "respectable." The warrior need not buy weapons with longer ranges to secure solid membership in the culture.

Beyond 250 yards, the fourth ring of power, just how far a warrior can extend his reach is a matter of much dispute. Some gun writers advocate the adoption of heavy-barreled sniper rifles with high-resolution scopes that are accurate to 800–1,000 yards. T-shirts favoring this approach parody AT&T television commercials with a picture of a sniper captioned "Reach out and touch someone." Other gun writers say the military "battle rifles" of the 1950s that fired 7.62 × 51mm NATO cartridges with a 400-to-500-yard range are all a warrior really needs. Of course, the true "professional" owns all the weapons, and can pick an appropriate arm for every occasion.

At one level, moving through the rings represents aggression. A warrior claims more "personal space" at each ring; his self expands to fill the limits of this space. In mastering combat arms of longer range, the warrior prepares to kill more and more people. And face-to-face combat disappears as the ranges increase; the warrior can enforce his deadly will upon victims before they have a chance to react. Indeed, at the longer ranges, the warrior is often not responding to a threat against himself; he is on the attack.

There is a terrible contradiction in the way the New War presents the ownership of combat weapons as the solution to a hostile world full of enemies. Combat weapons and the concentric rings of power they create are not only a means of aggressive self-expansion; they also function as "body armor."[12] But the enemy is always imagined to be more dangerous than the body armor developed to keep him away. Thus, the gun magazines' obsession with weapons and their lethal ranges can also be read as a discussion of fear—fear of an unbeatable, unstoppable enemy. The warrior is deeply afraid that no matter how many weapons he has, the enemy will penetrate each and every ring. No matter how many enemies he kills with his sniper rifle, carbine, and pistol, he will still be left alone to face just one more with his knife. This fear of being killed is so great that the warrior cannot even risk using a urinal in a public rest room:

> Standing at a urinal, you are very near helpless. Any mugger knows that a public john is a great place to take wallets. The solution? Don't use the urinals. Use the stalls with doors on them. Sitting down, facing outward, with a door protecting you, you are in a much more tactically sound position, particularly if you use the

technique brought back from Rhodesia by Jeff Cooper. Your pistol rests in your shorts between your knees. In that position it is instantly accessible if someone comes crashing through the door, and is unavailable to the person in the next stall.[13]

Combat weapons and the ammunition they fire are designed to kill people, but magazines frequently transform killing into a technical discussion about firearms and ammunition. Articles place each new weapon in relation to all its predecessors and contemporaries. *Combat Handguns* magazine introduces each monthly issue with phrases like, "In this issue we find three different interpretations of the Combat Handgun." Guns are texts to be interpreted in relation to the established wisdom.

In his monthly features, Peter G. Kokalis, *SOF*'s firearms editor and one of the world's foremost firearm experts, masterfully discusses aesthetic and technical properties of weapons while only discreetly touching upon their deadly use. Frequently this displacement is conducted through writing about killing as if it was a purely mechanical process involving machine operators "producing" hits—a form of skilled, yet impersonal, industrial labor. Here, he reviews the MAC-10 submachine gun (a drug-dealer favorite):

One could live with all of the MAC's minor idiosyncracies were it not for its major flaw: The cyclic rate in every version is close to 1,200 rpm [rounds per minute]. Submachine guns should ideally fire between 500–600 rpm. A bullet hose serves only the ends defined by movie producers. Only the most highly trained operators can muster the trigger discipline required to produce consistent two-to-three-shot bursts with a MAC submachine gun. Hit probability decreases as the length of the burst increases.[14]

Kokalis has also mastered the technique of letting the reader vicariously experience killing without making the thrill too blatant. The Italian Red Brigades, along with several other terrorist groups, sometimes used a small .32-caliber submachine gun manufactured in what were formerly Yugoslavia and Czechoslovakia. A small submachine gun is called a "machine pistol." Kokalis's review begins:

It's Ulster, or maybe Beirut, or even Paris. A young assassin waits nervously in the shadows, eyes following a black Mercedes limousine that pulls up to the curb. His victim steps out onto the sidewalk, two bodyguards hovering about him. The terrorist steps out away from the dark wall, fires a three-round burst into his enemy's chest, whirls, and pumps short bursts into the upper torsos of the bodyguards before they can react. All three drop, never knowing they have been felled by a pipsqueak cartridge—the supposedly impotent .32 ACP. The assailant slides back into the night, his commitment to Allah or Marx ended for the evening. His instrument of death? A small black machine pistol with a most appropriate name: the Skorpian.[15]

The small man from the small group armed with the small "impotent" .32 can kill or "pump" the big, rich, powerful man in his Mercedes, along with his expensive bodyguards. But the rest of the three-page article concerns where the gun is made, how it works, how to take it apart, and how well it shoots. Kokalis concludes by placing the Skorpian text in relation to its genre:

Machine pistols are highly specialized instruments and fill a very small niche in the modern small arms arsenal. Rugged, reliable and efficient, the Skorpian is one of the very few successful weapons in its genre—despite its use by some unsavory characters.[16]

Good technical qualities overcome association with the "bad" enemy, and displace the reality of assassination. The reader is left more technically competent; he has "learned" more about weapons. This kind of textual play also occurs in discussions about ammunition. Warriors are concerned about the damage various bullets can do. Military rifle bullets travel from 2,400 to 3,200 feet per second and almost always completely penetrate the body. Some bullets, especially the M16's 5.56mm bullet, have a strong tendency to tumble upon impact, causing further damage. Consequently, discussions on rifle cartridges only rarely focus on raw killing power, instead favoring talk about reliability, accuracy, and range.

But pistols fire far less powerful ammunition than do rifles. Their bullets travel from 750 to 1,400 feet per second, depending upon the cartridge's capacity for gunpowder and bullet weight. Shooters have a choice between smaller .38 or 9mm pistols which fire bullets at 1,000 to 1,400 feet per second or larger .44 Special or .45 automatics firing much bigger bullets around 850 feet per second. Ammunition manufacturers have designed "hollow-point" bullets for pistol cartridges that expand upon impact. Only the smaller, lighter bullets fired by .357 Magnums, .38s, and 9mms travel fast enough (over 1,000 fps) for the bullets to expand with some consistency. An expanded bullet has its shaft intact, but the head is folded back into a mushroom. (A perfectly expanded bullet bears some resemblance to an erect penis.) Those pistoleros who favor the .45 automatic say that its 230-grain bullet makes such a big hole that it does not need to expand. They favor military-type ammunition with a full metal jacket called "hardball."

Almost every gun magazine has reports and pictures of bullets that did or did not expand. Bullets are fired into a simulation of human flesh called "ballistic gelatin." Sophisticated magazines show graphs contrasting bullet expansion and penetration, often accompanied by drawings of wound channels that look very much like vaginas. They also calculate how many cubic inches of ballistic gelatin each bullet displaces. Field statistics for most of the better 9mm, .38, and .45 loads, however, show that their chances of stopping the "adversary" with one shot are all about the same, and all quite high—62–80%. Given that these figures are by no means secret, the seemingly compulsive repetition of penetration tests suggests they carry a strong psycho-sexual charge.

Despite the wonders of combat weapons, most are produced with serious flaws. Identifying the flaws and learning how to correct them is a major task facing any potential warrior. Gun discourse establishes the standards of gun perfection, the ways guns fail to meet these standards, and how they can be redeemed. For example, magazine writers insist that a good pistol must have a smooth trigger pull to be fired accurately. But such guns are hard to find—to reduce labor costs, gun manufacturers no longer hand polish the metal parts of a gun's trigger and firing mechanisms. As a result, the trigger pulls on many weapons are often heavy and irregular. To fix a gun like this, a warrior must take it to a gunsmith who will polish the trigger mechanisms to make them function smoothly and shoot accurately.

Modifying a firearm is not only technical performance, however. Modern weapons are mass-produced; customizing means a gun is no longer a commodity available to anyone, but a work of art that symbolizes its owner. Since the work of art is unique, it now "fits" the warrior's hands and becomes part of him. Said another way, customizing transforms metal into flesh. Customizing enables the warrior to make a dramatic statement about who he is and what he can do.

Changing the appearance of a weapon is one way of performing this transformation. With its wooden stock and five-round magazine, Ruger's Mini-14 looks like an old World War II rifle, not a modern combat arm. To correct this flaw, companies began marketing black plastic stocks, folding stocks, longer magazines that hold more cartridges, muzzle-flash hiders, and other deadly-looking accessories. An advertisement for the "Maxi-14" folding stock reads, "Our new Maxi-14 was designed for the man who is really serious about his weapon. Now you can upgrade your Ruger Mini-14's classic WW II design and make it look and function like a modern combat weapon should."[17] To be a modern man requires having a modern weapon. Ironically, the "classic" wooden stock of the Mini-14 saved it from being outlawed in 1989 when California and several other states banned "assault" rifles.

Converting a semiautomatic military rifle or submachine gun back to full automatic capacity is another way to create a powerful self. A semiautomatic can be fired almost as fast as a full automatic weapon, but it does not have the same deadly aura. Until the late 1980s, converting a weapon to full automatic was legal so long as it was then registered with the Bureau of Alcohol, Tobacco and Firearms. After that time the Bureau did not grant permits for new machine guns. To own an illegal machine gun (and an estimated 500,000 men do) is to constantly assert one's willingness to defy authority and live beyond the law. Yet very few men actually use these automatic weapons in criminal acts. Owning an illegal weapon is simply a very good way to appear "bad."

When movie and novel heroes modify their weapons, they inevitably succeed—as when Steven Seagal in *Marked for Death* gleefully test-fires his homemade sound-suppressed submachine gun into a hanging beef carcass. However, gun publications stress that since modifications do not follow firmly established standards, there is always a significant risk that the modifications will fail and the owner will look like a fool to "real" warriors. One writer draws a contrast between fancy, elaborately customized handguns and the more straightforward Gunsite Service Pistol (a modified Colt .45 semi-automatic marketed by Jeff Cooper):

There are no fancy stocks. There are no holes drilled in the trigger. There are no chrome-plated mudflaps, no foxtails on the antenna, and no flames painted on the sides . . . This is a gun for saving your life, not impressing your friends. If you wear $95 jeans embroidered with the names of Italian designers of indeterminate sex, then you won't like the GSP. Let me suggest something in a shiny two-tone, with sharp corners and lovely pearl stocks; if you want a gun that goes bang when it should and hits where it should; if you want a hard-hitting, heavy-duty pistol to carry for the serious business of self-defense, check out the Gunsite Service Pistol. [18]

Finally, there is the danger that an unqualified gunsmith will completely ruin the weapon. The publisher of *Handgun Tests* warns his readers:

Gunsmith is a term that many people who drop out of shoemaker school apply to themselves. Currently, many of these "gunsmiths" are telling everyone to take out the firing pin lock on the series '80 guns . . . Do not let your so-called "gunsmith" leave the parts out. These "gunsmiths" are the guys who are now out of work since abortion was legalized! Keep them away from your nice Colt. [19]

Modifying a weapon, then, is not without risk for the would-be warrior. If he succeeds, he gains immense power, since the customized firearm is no longer a mass-produced commodity but a powerful extension of his body. Moreover, men who own customized weapons considered "serious" by fellow warriors are highly respected. But if the newly customized weapon is viewed as foppish by other gun owners, then he will be ridiculed and rejected.

At the same time that gun magazines establish the standards of "serious" weaponry for shooters, they also contrast what firearms can "really" do and how they should be held with the way they are handled in Hollywood movies. Paramilitary magazines are particularly fond of proving that their authors have much more of the right stuff than film heroes. For example, *Gung-Ho* took a strong stand against holding a pistol up near one's head when charging into a room full of terrorists. The caption underneath the picture of a SWAT team member doing it the wrong way reads: "Looks great in the movies, but: (A) He could shoot himself in the head; (B) He can easily be shot through the door."[20]

Along the same lines, gun magazines regularly publish stories critical of Hollywood's practice of showing men being knocked off their feet by a single shot. As gun manufacturer Paris Theodore writes in *Combat Handguns*, "It has been understood for many years among the cognoscenti that there has never been a pistol caliber capable of delivering 'knock-down' power. It is a figment of the collective imagination of all Hollywood scriptwriters."[21] Thus, anyone who reads this article or one like it becomes one of the elite cognoscenti—a man truly prepared for combat—as opposed to all the fools whose ideas about gunfights come from Hollywood.

By the mid-1980s publishing-industry executives and movie directors had learned that a significant portion of their audience read these gun magazines. One editor responsible for men's action-adventure novels said that whenever there was the slightest error in describing the capabilities of a weapon, her publishing house would receive a torrent of complaints. She called the correct portrayal of what combat weapons could realistically do a "code of death" that publishers dare not violate. Readers seemed to consider gun descriptions a powerful measure of a story's truth or falsity.[22]

Within this world of words about guns, sexual references are common. In line with their powers of penetration, combat weapons are sometimes described as penises. Jay Mallin describes how U.S. Army Special Forces advisers addressed Honduran troops in "Heating Up Honduras: U.S. Troops Train for Nicaraguan Threat":

> Members of a 140-man Honduran Army unit lie prone on canvas or palm fronds. Special Forces trainers lean close, giving guidance. One trainer cautions: "Don't yank the trigger. Caress it as if you were playing with yourself." They are receiving training in firing the M16s with which they have recently been equipped.[23]

Sexual references, though, are usually more subtle. John Bianchi manufactures pistol holsters. In one of his long-running magazine ads from the 1980s, Bianchi appears dressed in a tuxedo. Next to him stands a beautiful blond woman, wearing a low-cut black evening dress slit up to her hip bone. This picture follows the standard codes of sexual display: the man conceals his body and the woman reveals hers. In the next two photos, he takes off his coat and rolls his pants up to his knees. One photo shows him facing front and the other shows his back, revealing seventeen pistols, each in a different model holster. Men conceal their sex organs and their armaments; they are both hidden powers and delights.

Holsters are always erotically charged. They both protect the weapon and attach it to the man's body; he feels the gun through the medium of the holster. Even the process of making a leather holster has sexual overtones. To make a holster, leather is "wet-worked," meaning that wet leather is stretched over a particular model of gun and then dried to give the holster its shape. Some custom-holster makers request that a consumer mail them his gun, so that a holster can be made so tight it will only accept that particular gun—not just any Colt 5-inch .45 automatic, but his .45 automatic. Such a holster is the ideal vagina, since it firmly grips its owner and rejects all other suitors.

Phallic guns and vaginal holsters do not exhaust the sexuality of weaponry. J. B. Woods writes about his attraction to a customized Smith and Wesson .45 revolver he bought at a gun show:

I am really delighted with my new Smith and Wesson .45 combat revolver. With a little luck I'll talk the Cobra Gunskin people into building me a super shoulder holster in which to carry it. It could be a constant companion for years to come, but then again we gun lovers are somewhat fickle . . . are we not?[24]

Is J. B. Woods a man wooing his female lover? Or is Woods a typical "fickle" woman who can't make up her mind? Other men write proclamations of their undying love to their female weapons. Robert Lange begins his review of Spanish-made Star pistols in *Special Weapons and Tactics* magazine with a warning:

I would, though, beg your indulgence this time around, as the primary gun reviewed here is, and has been for years, my personal carry gun. This is a love story. Passion, then, must overrule a certain degree of objectivity . . . I am in love with Star pistols and I must admit that it is love in the extreme, for all the members of the family.[25]

Lange loves most the Star 9mm BM—"simple, traditional fare." She readily became part of him: "Unlike the comfort of, say, an old leather jacket, or a pair of well-worn Levi's, I do not merely wear this pistol; it is as much a part of me as the hand that holds it." The Star BM is like a woman: "Apart from the fact that the thing works every time, the BM's most enduring quality is its feel. Like a woman's, the Star's design was gotten right for the first time." Only once was he tempted to leave her: "At one time, I flirted with its otherwise identical twin sister, the alloy framed 8KM which weighs but a mere 25.59 ounces." Lange finally decides he liked the older, heavier woman, because he favors her "more reassuring feel in the hand."

If a man is "firing" a woman-weapon, then controlling the recoil of the weapon is like controlling a woman's body as she moves in orgasm. Graphic demonstrations equating combat weapons with women's sexuality began to appear during the late 1970s. Posters and videotapes featured naked women with guns and knives. A few years later, Chuck Traynor, the former manager of pornography stars Linda Lovelace and Marilyn Chambers, moved to Las Vegas and opened

"The Survival Store."[26] The Survival Store specializes in selling and renting combat weapons; the store has an indoor range. Traynor staffs his store with beautiful models.

His first major poster, entitled "Bo," shows a half-naked woman with a dangerous look on her face, standing in a swamp with one hand resting on an Uzi submachine gun and the other on a huge knife. She is so "hot" that the swamp behind her is steaming. This poster sold 50,000 copies by 1987. Traynor then made a videotape featuring "Bo" firing an M60 machine gun in the desert. She is naked except for a belt and knife on her waist. As she fires the machine gun, the camera shifts to a slow-motion sequence of her body (particularly her breasts), moving from the recoil.

In the mid-1980s other companies began marketing posters and videos of women firing guns. Each model is introduced along with the weapon she will fire. A graph shows the gun's technical features on one side, with the model's height, weight, and breast, hip, and waist measurements on the other. As in the "Bo" film, the camera shows each model's body moving from recoil as she fires long bursts of 20 to 40 rounds. Models hold the weapon at their waists so that the camera can focus on their breasts. As Traynor explained, "Guns and tits and ass all mix."[27]

Sometimes warriors view their weapons not as lovers, but rather as elders or children. Peter G. Kokalis laments the approaching death of the Fusil Automatique Léger, the famous Belgian assault rifle, used by Western European and Third World armies from the 1950s through the mid-1980s: "Although its death will be many years coming, anyone who wants a FAL should buy a LAR [the current model] now. The FN FAL, one of the 20th century's grandest dogs of war, will be remembered fondly and mourned mightily by all those who used it in the flame and sweat of battle."[28]

While the old perish, the young are held tenderly. When Mack Bolan returns to Vietnam in *The Executioner #123: War Born*, jungle rain worries him. First he covers his Galil assault rifle with a poncho and then looks down at his waist. Much to his relief, "The AutoMag and the Beretta were safely snuggled in leather."[29]

A weapon can shift from being an extension of man to an extension of woman, to an elder or to an infant. In all cases it is a living being, an exciting and precious family member who can play virtually any sexual or family role the warrior desires. The combat weapon represents life that responds to the warrior's will.

As consumer goods, combat weapons have one other charm that distinguishes them from cars or stereos or new clothes. Advertising for these "civilian" items stresses that they will transform the life of the customer, making him or her a more exciting, desirable person. Paramilitary culture presents weapons as offering an even more radical transformation. Buying weapons helps transform the ordinary man into a warrior. Guns are absolute necessities for the warrior to avoid death; guns are the means to life itself. In the post-nuclear-war novel *The Survivalist #3: The Quest*, hero John Rourke and his sidekick Paul Rubenstein finally arrive at Rourke's hidden survival retreat in the Stone Mountains of North Georgia after a perilous journey from Arizona. Like Batman and Robin, they wheel their Harley-Davidson motorcycles inside a granite mountain to a secret cave. When the wall closes down and the lights come on, Rourke guides Rubenstein through rooms filled with supplies he has bought in preparation for World War III. The last room they visit contains the gun case, the contents of which he describes with great precision:

"Smith and Wesson Model 29 six-inch, Metalifed and Mag-Na-Ported; Smith and Wesson Model 60 two-inch stainless Chiefs .38 Special; Colt Mk IV, Series '70 Government Model, Metalifed with a Deutonics Competition Recoil system installed and Pachmayr Colt Medallion grips. That little thing is an FIE .38 Special chrome Derringer, and the little tubes on the shelf down here are .22 Long Rifle and .25 ACP barrel inserts made by Harry Owens of Sport Specialties. Makes the little gun able to fire .38 Special, .22 rimfire, or .25 ACP. I've got more of those insert barrels for my Deutonics, for my shotguns, et cetera." Rourke pointed back up to the cabinet. "That gun is a Colt Official Police .38 Special five-inch-Metalifed with Pachmayr grips. Same frame essentially as a Python, so I had it reamed out to .357 to increase its versatility." Then Rourke moved to his right to the long guns, racked one over the other. "That's standard AR-15, no scope. That's a Mossberg 500ATP6P

Parkerized riot shotgun, Safariland sling on it. That's an original Armalite AR-7 .22 Long Rifle. Take it apart and it stows in the buttstock, even floats. Had enough?"

Rourke turned, smiling at Rubenstein. Rubenstein asked, "How much—I mean it's rude, John, I know that but how"—Rourke replied, "Every cent I could scrape together for the last six years, after the cost of the property itself. I gambled. I'm sorry I won, but I guess it paid off."[30]

In the primeval chaos of dark worlds where violence rules, money is worthless. In post–World War III America, Rourke is a wealthy man. Weapons and ammunition are themselves the true currencies, since with them the warrior can obtain everything else and without them his life is worth nothing. When the warrior goes shopping he is not like a frivolous woman shopping for clothes and other vanities. Instead he is preparing to defend himself and his family against mortal dangers. To refuse a purchase means that he values money more than he does his own life. Every new item, from a speed-loader for his revolver to a flash-hider for his carbine, gives him a tiny edge over the enemy. Each purchase will help him face what gun writer and combat-shooting instructor Massad Ayoob calls "The Moment of Truth," when he must kill or be killed. The warrior buys and buys, waiting for The Moment to come. Only after killing the enemy will he be fully affirmed as a man.

6

All the exciting escapades that characterize paramilitary movies and novels—helicopter sweeps over office buildings and enemy camps, parachute jumps into green jungles and blue oceans, manhunts up and down stairs and fire escapes—are only part of the action to which the genre title "action-adventure" refers. The true essence of paramilitary mythology lies in one particular action—killing.

Killing, of course, has long been a central component of much dramatic fiction. All kinds of human conflicts can readily be symbolized as a struggle between armed protagonists; even complex moral questions may be reduced to "good" versus "evil." In this sense, the New War is just a continuation of the same old morality play. However, the *act* of killing has traditionally not been very important. For the most part, the dead Indians in the Westerns, and dead Germans or Japanese in the World War II films, simply fell down and vanished from the screen. Killing in these films signified moral progress, a means to an end, not an end in itself.

In the New War, though, both the physical action of killing and its moral repercussions are radically changed. Killing is shown in detailed scenes as part of an elaborate ritual process with archaic overtones. In the modern world, when someone is killed, it is understood that his life force is no longer present on earth—whether in the Christian view of the spirit ascending to heaven or descending to hell after death, or in the atheist view of death as the final dissolution of the person.

However, the older notion of killing as "taking life" more accurately captures the New War meaning. When Dirty Harry draws his .44 Magnum down on three street punks and invites them to "make my day!" more is going on than a clever little joke. By shooting them, he absorbs their life force. It isn't just Harry's "day" that's being made; Dirty Harry himself—the warrior demigod—is being created through his kills. Similarly, when Bruce Willis in *Die Hard* manages to strangle one of the terrorists holding his wife hostage, it is the energy he absorbs from his victim that gives him the audacity to send the corpse back to his comrades with a sign attached, "Now I've got a machine gun, too. Ho! Ho! Ho!" Referred to as "incorporation" in psychoanalytic theory, this fantastic appropriation of another's life force has ancient roots. As the religious-studies scholar E. O. James says, "To the primitive mind good and evil, life and death, are in the nature of materialistic entities capable of transference or expulsion by quasi-mechanical operations."[1] Of course, at its most extreme this is the logic of cannibalism: by eating the enemy's body, the warrior completes the incorporation that began with killing.

But even in less literal forms, "taking life," with its associations of transference and incorporation, is essentially a sacred act. And this is perhaps the most useful way to understand New War killings. When Dirty Harry shoots down those three punks, he does more than uphold the secular law of the modern world. He becomes a "primitive" man performing a sacred action; when the good warrior kills an evil one, he effectively transforms evil power into good power. The converse is also true: when an evil villain kills a virtuous victim, evil gains strength. Hence, no matter how secular the New War warrior may appear with his high-tech weapons and tremendous "efficient" kills, he is essentially a religious figure.

The "rites" of killing follow very specific rules. Although New War heroes like Rambo and Mack Bolan sometimes fight and kill scores of enemies in a movie or novel, not all of these killings fully qualify as sacred acts. Often the enemies simply fall down and vanish, as they do in World War II movies. There are always some scenes, though, in which the hero and villain fight face-to-face. Only through such personal combat can there be a transfer of energy from the vanquished to the victor.

When the hero and villain face each other in their final confrontation, they often engage in a short conversation or series of pronouncements before the fighting begins. Although few words are exchanged, these conversations are very important. At one level, they affirm that the fight about to take place is both personal and to the death, as when John Steele, a Vietnam veteran, addresses a drug lord in *Steele Justice* (1987): "This isn't Nam, Quan. This time only one of us is coming back. Quan, just you and me." At a second level, the verbal exchanges between hero and villain also indicate that the men in question represent two different visions of the ideal society. Quan, the leader of a Vietnamese gang in Southern California, responds to Steele's challenge by quoting the gang's totalitarian motto, "The only law is Black Tiger law." Thus, although the hero is an ex-policeman conducting his own personal war outside the corrupt establishment, he still serves as the true representative of justice.

Quan and Steele actually do have a gentlemanly duel to the death after their conversation. In many New War stories, however, there is no fair fight at all. Instead, the final confrontation between hero and villain is a scene in which the hero ceremonially executes the bad guy. Although readers and viewers already know the heinous crimes that have been committed, pronouncing sentence serves to distinguish the hero's act of murder from the villain's violent deeds. Tom Clancy develops one of the most elaborate such ceremonies in *Red Storm Rising* when Lieutenant Edwards judges three captured Russian soldiers: "Gentlemen, you are charged under Uniform Code of Military Justice with one specification of rape and two specifications of murder. These are capital crimes . . . Do you have anything to say in your defense? No? You are found guilty. Your sentence is death.' "[2] Edwards subsequently crushes the larynx of one man, causing him to suffocate ("unable to breathe, his torso bucked from side to side as his face darkened"), while a young Marine slits the throats of the other two.

In less elaborate execution ceremonies, pronouncing sentence simply indicates that the hero is in full control of himself. To kill impulsively, or to kill after yelling a savage, Indian-like war cry, would mean that the warrior has succumbed to base desires. But by uttering "Make my day!" as a warning to the villains or "Because we live here!" as the good teenage boys say before they kill their traitorous friend in *Red Dawn*, the heroes prove they are guided by a sense of justice. Sometimes the hero does not have to speak to the villain, so long as he addresses him in some way. Paul Benjamin, the hero of *Death Wish*, first fires his gun to get the attention of a culprit, then says to himself, "Well, that wasn't a miss. You son of a bitch. It was just to turn you around so you can watch me shoot you." When the suspect turns around and shows his "vicious, sneering face"—a confession of his guilt—Benjamin "steps into the light" so the intruder can see him and executes the man.[3] Thus the hero's words—even his internal monologues—establish the justice of his acts. His killings are morally sanctioned.

The hero's words are as much weapons as they are legitimation for his conduct. When he speaks to the villain, there is no real communication. Hero and villain do not come to "understand" each other better through their dialogue and so resolve their conflict. Instead, the heroic warrior's speech partially paralyzes the bad guy, rendering him more vulnerable to the next phase of the attack. In some of the ancient warrior myths, Joseph Campbell says, the most powerful man was one who "would require no physical weapon at all; the power of his magic word would suffice."[4] In the modern secular world, no hero can fight with magic words alone. Yet no contemporary warrior could win his battles without them.

Either slightly before, during, or after the death verdict has been articulated by the hero, his body hardens. At one level, there is a kind of erotic anticipation of the kill. This blending of sex and violence is most clearly expressed in Mickey Spillane's extremely popular novel, *I, the Jury*, first published in 1947. In it, detective Mike Hammer swears to find the killer of his World War II buddy, Jack Williams. (Jack had saved Mike from death at Guadalcanal and lost his right arm in the process.) Hammer finds that the killer is none other than his own beautiful blond fiancée Charlotte. When he confronts her, she takes off her clothes in an effort to save her life. Charlotte's sensuous striptease to her transparent panties—done while Hammer is accusing her of murder—is described in minute detail. Hammer's penis is undoubtedly erect when he pulls the trigger of his .45 automatic. Killing her, then, blends self-control and sadism. When, with her dying gasp, she asks, "How c-could you?," he can flatly say, "It was easy."[5]

In the New War, though, it isn't just the warrior's penis that hardens, but his whole body. Whereas the actors who played the old war and Western heros were usually big men, their flesh was only rarely exposed on the cinematic battlefield. Their bodies were not weapons. New War heroes, in contrast, must be men of steel, and the stars who portray them buffed and chiseled. Arnold Schwarzenegger was a world-class bodybuilder, while Chuck Norris and Steven Seagal were renowned martial-arts experts. Almost all of the other top male action-adventure stars have muscled physiques as well.

When movie directors and novel editors were asked why hard-bodied warriors came into fashion, some replied simply that America was on a fitness binge and the warrior of course had to be ahead of the pack. Others, like Dale Dye (a former *SOF* editor and technical adviser to *Platoon*), explained that the warrior's extraordinary body was necessary to make extraordinary deeds seem that more plausible:

The "Rambo" films could not do what they wanted unless the heroes appeared superhuman. It would have been too great a stretch of the imagination otherwise. They needed a larger than life character. Well, look at the guy! Of course he could do that shit! Of course he could fire a machine gun from the hip! Of course he could lift a helicopter or haul an armored personnel carrier out of the sand with nothing but his own incredible strength![6]

Frequently the bodies of New War heroes are so strong and co-ordinated that they are referred to as "machines." Colonel Trautman, the Green Beret leader who serves as Rambo's father figure, calls him "a pure fighting machine." In *War Born*, Mack Bolan (often referred to as "Stony Man One"), becomes so excited when he returns to his "home" in the jungles of Vietnam that he no longer needs to eat or sleep. He is transformed into a god-like perpetual-motion machine "that feeds on the energy involved to create new energy," with eyes and ears so mechanized that whenever he spots an enemy soldier, he "locks into target acquisition" like a radar- or infrared-controlled missile.[7]

Some warriors kill with their hard bodies. In *Lethal Weapon* Mel Gibson strangles a villain with his thighs. Norris and Seagal break necks and backs with simple karate moves, their muscles bulging as they summon the strength for the executions. Other heroes have actual metal implants in their bodies to replace broken or lost limbs. Mad Max, the road warrior, has a metal brace to strengthen a wounded leg. Colonel Yukov Katzenelenbogen, of *Phoenix Force*, chooses a flesh-colored stainless-steel hand to replace the one he lost when terrorists blew up his car and killed his wife and child:

> The hand's steel fingers were slightly curled, resting naturally. When the fingers were locked straight, the hand was a two-pound sledge, capable of smashing any wood-paneled door. A glancing side blow could tear off a man's ear. A forward chop, against the sternum, could paralyze heart and lungs, kill.[8]

In techno-thriller and fighter-pilot movies such as *Top Gun* and *Iron Eagle* (1985), the steel of tanks, planes, and submarines becomes part of the bodies of the men who control them; the steel weapons become flesh. Harold Coyle describes this fusion between Folk, the gunner, and his tank in *Team Yankee*: "Folk, the loader, the cannon, and the fire control system were one complete machine, functioning automatically, efficiently, effectively."[9]

In other futuristic battle scenarios individual warriors simply don armored suits to gain tremendous power. *RoboCop* details how the brain of a critically wounded Detroit policeman is transplanted into a computerized robot to create the ideal patrol officer. In the *C.A.D.S.* novel series, the U.S. fighting men who survive the Soviet nuclear assault wear "immense black suits of destruction covering their bodies in protective cocoons." The "Computerized Attack Defense System" warriors were "gods of the Technological Age. Within their battle suits, their mortal bodies possessed the power of whole armies of the past."[10]

Bulging muscles and armored suits represent what psychologists call "exoskeletal defense" mechanisms, efforts to reconstruct the human body. Although bones are the hardest part of the body, they lie under layers of softer fleshy tissue and relatively fragile skin. By projecting the hard skeleton outward to the surface of the skin, the body is in fantasy made far stronger and better able to ward off threats and attacks.

The hardened bodies discussed so far fall into one of two categories. When a powerfully muscled warrior fights half-naked, his hard flesh marks his transformation into a kind of "minotaur," the legendary half-man, half-animal. He gains both the animal's power and its ability to hide. Rambo once immerses himself completely in a muddy riverbank. The entire bluff seems to move when he steps out to knife an unsuspecting Vietnamese soldier.[11] Later in the movie, he hides underwater and then leaps up in the air, like a powerful killer whale, to capture a Russian helicopter. *Soldier of Fortune* once ran a cover photograph of a man with a completely blackened face and an animal-skin bandanna over his forehead—clearly a beast of the jungle.

The second form of exoskeletal projection overcomes human weakness by transforming all human flesh into metal. The tank crews, fighter pilots, and "battle suit" wearers all fall into this second category; they, like RoboCop, are "cyborgs." Their cousins are heroes like Mack Bolan, warriors who always go into battle dressed completely in black. Black clothes are a kind of body armor: black is the color of steel, of death. At night, black hides the warrior from his many enemies. On top of these black clothes warriors wear layer upon layer of weapons and supplies. Even the head and face are frequently hidden, either by masks or by black face paint. Cyborgs often look like modern versions of medieval knights with their visors down. The body seems far away.

Either as minotaur or as cyborg, the warrior can no longer feel his skin as battle approaches. It has been transformed into nearly impenetrable body armor. At times, the hero's body armor also can make him nearly invisible to his enemies. At the very minimum, the helmet and face mask mean that the eyes of the hero cannot be seen—he has become an executioner. The enemy is thus seen and sentenced to die, but he cannot look back and establish human contact to tacitly appeal the verdict. It is a combination that can create "disbelieving horror" in even the most evil of the evil ones.[12]

For decades the standard Hollywood gunfight ended with the victim collapsing with one small red dot on his chest. Rarely was there much blood. And while some old detective novels, particularly those by Mickey Spillane, featured more blood, they did not contain prolonged, graphic descriptions of killing and dying. Most New War stories, in contrast, require that the enemy body be torn open so completely that it lose human form. At minimum, the small red holes have been replaced by much larger splashes of blood, both where the bullet enters and where it exits the body.

But usually the enemy's death is much more spectacular. In *No Mercy* (1986) the mercenary hero employed as a contract agent for the CIA captures a terrorist, puts a grenade in his mouth, and then blows him apart in a ball of fire. In *Commando*, Arnold Schwarzenegger takes care of his last opponent by ramming him through the chest with a pipe that is a good four inches in diameter. Both Clint Eastwood and Chuck Norris have used antitank rockets to open up the chests of their adversaries.

In paramilitary novels, the violence is especially striking. In volume 123 of *The Executioner*, a North Vietnamese gunman fires at a woman who discovers his position: "The glass planes shattered, spearing her hands. Her face dissolved into crimson pulp and she fell out of sight."[13] In volume 39, *The New War*, Bolan shoots so that he can "feel the quick kick of the recoil in his shoulder while he watched the guy's head explode like a ripe cantaloupe smashed by a hammer."[14] Magnus Trench, the hero of *Dark Messiah*, volume 1 of *Phoenix*, has a body so hard that it kills post–World War III plague germs—the "contam" disease—upon contact. He really knows how to open up a bad guy:

> A hail of 9mm zappers destroyed the shotgunner from the waist down, tearing away his stomach, bladder, genitals, small intestines, kneecaps, and all the arteries and muscle tissue over, under and in between. Death reflexes triggered a burst, the pumpgun discharging into Badass One's own ugly face and leaving a raw, bloody mess behind as the headless, legless, faceless torso jerked forward, fountaining redly from both ends.[15]

Thus, at the moment of dying, an opponent is so thoroughly penetrated by the bullets, knives, and grenade fragments, that he completely loses control of his body. Victims are flooded with bodily fluids; they drown in their own blood, making gurgling noises as they die. It is as if violent death is a special kind of sexual release. When this orgasm comes, the body always moves uncontrollably. Legs twitch, sphincter muscles open, blood spurts from ears, noses, and mouths. Men fall to their knees, screaming, and "collapse into a heap" of shapeless flesh.[16]

Often the dead are referred to as "meat." Occasionally, though, excremental overtones are discernible. For example, the heroes frequently take special pains not to be contaminated by their victims. Jerry Ahern's protagonist in *The Defender* kills the terrorist leader (who was responsible for his family's death) with a 13½-inch knife, but the "blood spraying toward Holden's eyes" was stopped by his gas mask.[17] In *The Black Berets*, "Cowboy" kills an enemy disguised as a seductive airline stewardess in an airplane bathroom: "Cowboy then held her up till he saw that her eyes had glazed over. Then he shoved her down onto the toilet seat and returned to the first-class cabin, leaving an Out of Order sign prominently on the door."[18]

In contrast, the hero always maintains control of his body during combat. Rambo easily and comfortably fires a modified M60 machine gun with one hand while running at full speed. Dirty Harry gracefully rolls with the recoil of his .44 Magnum. Martial arts stars such as Norris and Seagal are essentially performing male dances with their victims as they kill them with their hands and legs. In the novels, this sexual connection between victor and vanquished is rendered explicitly. Tom Clancy describes Air Force Lieutenant Edwards's knifing a Russian in *Red Storm Rising* as a virtual act of rape: "Edwards rammed the knife under the man's ribs, turning his right hand within the brass-knuckled grip as he pushed the blade all the way in. The man screamed and lifted himself on his toes before falling backward, trying to get himself off the knife. Edwards withdrew and stabbed again, falling atop the man in a grotesquely sexual position."[19] Afterwards, the young Marines accompanying Edwards in their retreat across Iceland affirm his potency and call him "skipper" for the first time.

This use of sexual language and imagery to describe killing is not accidental. Editors of men's action-adventure novels acknowledge that the development of the genre was influenced by pornography. Don Pendleton actually began his career writing soft-porn novels. One editor indicated that some writers hired to write commando sagas had previous experience writing gay sadomasochistic stories. A second said that a '70s genre of pornographic novels set in the Old West became the model for action-adventure. Another editor theorized that the publishing industry had been influenced by the slow-motion killings portrayed in director Sam Peckinpah's films, such as *The Wild Bunch* and *Straw Dogs*. In his view, writers and editors said to themselves "Whoa, we can slow this down—and we can write violence like we write sex."[20]

The linkage of violence to sex also surfaced when editors speculated on why male readers enjoyed these books. The publisher of Zebra books believes these novels help men deal with their "frustrations."[21] Another editor says, "I'm not a psychologist or psychiatrist, but I always thought their basic function was to vent or sublimate feelings of violence."[22] From the editorial perspective, the "realistic" portrayal of the hero is an important piece of this dynamic. For example, Pendleton's guidebook to writers for *The Executioner* series says, "Bolan is not Flash Gordon. He is an idealized man, yes, but such men are certainly to be found beyond the comic strips. There is nothing super about Bolan except his command of self and I have known such men in real life."[23] Several other editors also mentioned their disdain of the older comic-book superheroes. The man who theorized that "we can write violence like we write sex" best described the type of hero that all the industry seemed to want. That hero is someone within reach of the male audience, someone with whom they can identify:

> I think that one of the important things about the books is that the hero always be somebody that the reader can say, "Well, if I just worked out a little bit, you know, and if I thought a little harder, if I concentrated, I could do this."[24]

Readers want to identify with the hero because "they feel like some piece of their turf is being threatened," the editor explained. The problem isn't that motorcycle gangs or terrorists are camping outside the reader's front door, but that many men feel "symbolically threatened" in some way by the world. "I think it is a symbolic need and that's why the books sell—because they give the opportunity for a cathartic release."[25] The editors insist that this process of reader identification with the hero for a climatic "catharsis" is either harmless or a positive social good, but certainly other interpretations are possible.

While the paramilitary warrior's body remains hard and intact, the ruptured body of the enemy confesses its evil by exposing all its rotten spilled fluids. This pattern has an important historical precedent in the *Freikorps*. As Klaus Theweleit points out, there, too, sexuality is placed in the service of destruction as the hard, metallic bodies of heroic warriors "open up" the enemy. The *Freikorps* man's body is "poised to penetrate other bodies and mangle them in its embrace."[26] The final one-on-one duel is also a sexual climax:

> The nearest thing this man will enjoy to the utopian encounter of the lover and beloved is at the same time the most distant from it: a collision between the unbending wills of two peoples, embodied in two men in armed confrontation. They meet to kill; and the only one to "flow" is the man who dies. The holes bored in him are a signal of the murderer's own transcendence of self. His self dissipates as he melts into the blood of the man of his own kind.[27]

When the evil one's body is broken open and he "flows," the victor experiences two sensations. First, the hero notes that the other's death means that his own insecure boundaries are intact and those hardened boundaries are interpreted by him as a sign of his virtue and self-control. At the same time, the hero also experiences the pleasure—never otherwise permitted him—of merging with another as he begins to absorb the villain's life force.

The final act necessary for the heroic warrior to fully appropriate the life force of the evil ones and to transform evil into good is to burn their corpses. He must create a cleansing fire to remove the pollution created by their spilled fluids. There are so many fires in the New War that it often seems the whole world is ablaze. The very first Rambo film, *First Blood*, ends when John Rambo blows up electrical transformers and a filling station to set the small Oregon town on fire. Chuck Norris in his turn burns down the prisoner-of-war camp in *Missing in Action*. Sigourney Weaver uses a flamethrower to destroy the nest and eggs of the monster in *Aliens*. And in *Die Hard 2* (1990), Bruce Willis even manages to kill all the terrorists (who have ruined his Christmas vacation) by burning their jet airplane when it takes off.

The heat of all these fires pales next to the infernos of World War III. General Sir John Hackett sensuously describes the great conflagration of Minsk after NATO forces launch four nuclear missiles in retaliation for the Soviet destruction of Birmingham, England. Above the city "what seemed about to form huge mushrooms was now writhing in promethean patterns, turning, twisting, and whirling" while below at ground zero, "up to 5 kilometers from the former Communist Party headquarters, everything combustible was immediately set on fire."[28] And so the putrid filth of Communism is erased.

Back in the United States, Frank Sturgis, commander of C.A.D.S., enters a post–World War III city to find "a carpet of corpses." The dead are all brown-tinted because "an army of roaches was crawling through the mouths, the eyes, the opened chests and stomachs of uncountable corpses." Worse yet, feasting rats are also celebrating victory over mankind. Sturgis orders "flame on" and his men open up with flamethrowers: "The rats were ignited instantly by the burning stream of liquid plastic that caught onto fur and claws and burned until there was nothing left."[29]

All of these New War infernos seem to be part of an archaic rite. Mircea Eliade says that in the ancient world men often used fire in their religious ceremonies for the purpose of communal purification: "The sins and faults of the individual and the community as a whole are annulled, consumed as by fire."[30] In Eliade's terms, when the New Warriors burn enemy corpses and the enemy's headquarters, they are metaphorically removing evil from the world.

But such purification rites always fail. When heroes die in the brotherhood of war, it is clear that their deaths are in the name of the "good." But when the modern-day evil ones are killed and their corpses burned, just where their spirits go is less clear. Undoubtedly the constant victory of the heroes over the enemy in the New War means that at least some of the enemy's power is transformed (incorporated) into good. But at the same time it must be remembered that in New War stories the hero's victory never results in the creation of a better society or the restoration of the original sacred order. Instead the power structure of society is still corrupt, and the hero is left living in the border zones on the frontier. Nor is he redeemed or purified by his victories. He is still a warrior who is ready for—indeed, wants—more war.

So if all the killing and burning does not empower the good gods of virtuous order, whom does it empower? There is a dark possibility here. In one of the last scenes of Sylvester Stallone's *Cobra* (1986), Stallone picks up the bad guy and rams a huge industrial hook hanging from a crane through his chest. The impaled body is then carried off into the mouth of a massive steel furnace in which fire is blazing—hell itself. It looks as if Stallone is *returning* a member of a devil-worshipping cult to the devil. The anthropologists Henri Hubert and Marcel Mauss indicate that some ancient societies made sacrifices to evil deities:

Sacrifices of this kind were usually addressed to the infernal deities or to evil spirits. As they were charged with evil influences, it was necessary to drive them away, to cut them off from reality. It was vaguely implied that the soul of the victim, with all the maleficent powers it contained, departed to return to the world of the maleficent powers.[31]

The New War explains the persistence of evil in a similar way. If the spirit of a modern-day evil one returns to the primordial hell, then it can be reincarnated on earth in yet another form. Thus the drug dealer can come back as a Communist, the terrorist as an outlaw biker, the beastly motorcycle man can return as an angry black radical.

This makes psychological sense, of course. If the function of the enemy is to represent uncontrollable human desire, then he must be constantly reincarnated in some form or another. The mercenary leader Niles Barrabas complains that Karl Heiss, the Harvard-educated former CIA case officer who betrayed him in Vietnam, simply will not die: "Too many times in the past he had viewed the bullet-ridden or burned bodies believed to be Karl Heiss. And every time it had turned out to be a hoax; every time the man had resurfaced to do more evil."[32] Without his mirror-image—the evil one who is out of control—the hero cannot exist as the embodiment of self-control and moral purity. Without the evil one, the hero would have to acknowledge his own conflicting desires and rages and his own capacity to act immorally. Without the evil one, the hero would have to confront people who are different from him—in spirit, concerns, and values.

But such recognition is exactly what the New War warrior tries to avoid. Hero and devil are but fragments of the same human psyche, dependent upon each other for their very identity. Hence, the victory of the heroes is in large part an illusion. The New War never moves forward, never transforms society into a morally better place, never propels the hero into maturity. Killing simply makes it possible for another violent cycle to begin.

After the cleansing fires have consumed the carnal remains of the enemy and his headquarters, the hero is left alone. Sometimes he watches the fire from a distance; in other cases, he rises from the wasted ruins, covered with ashes. These fires usually destroy most if not all the evidence that good and evil confronted each other in battle. But when the heroic warrior finally leaves the battleground, the story of the struggle is indelibly inscribed in his flesh. Bullets, knives, and other weapons all leave "grazing wounds" or scars on his skin as signs of battle. American mythic heroes have always suffered these injuries but what is new here is that the hero displays his scars much more prominently than did his predecessors.

Since contemporary heroes fight wars that the power structure cannot or will not fight, they take on the public responsibilities for combating evil. Consequently, when they suffer, they suffer for all men. When the Russians capture and torture Rambo with electricity, they tie him down to a steel bed frame and spread his arms like Christ on the cross. Both Chuck Norris and Mel Gibson are captured and hung up in torture scenes. By the end of *Die Hard* (1988), Bruce Willis's bare chest is covered with blood and he limps on bare, bloody feet completely lacerated from broken glass. The symbolism in all these cases is obvious.

Yet a hero always manages to overcome his pain and transform pain into power. In the most extreme cases the hero even cauterizes his own bleeding flesh. By applying the cleansing fire to himself, the warrior stops the flow of bodily fluids and reconstructs the inviolate surface of his body armor. In *Rambo: Part 3*, for example, Rambo is shot in the shoulder while attempting to rescue Colonel Trautman from Russians in Afghanistan. He breaks open some rifle cartridges, pours gun powder into the wound channel, and lights it with a match. Flame shoots through his shoulder, sealing both the entry and exit holes with charred flesh. Although Rambo writhes on the ground in pain during the night, by dawn his full powers are regenerated. (Both the chief monsters in the *Predator* movies also have similarly good experiences with cauterization after being wounded by humans.) A scar is a small price for fixing the armor—and moreover, the warriors did it themselves, with no reliance on a doctor or nurse.

These scars function as tattoos. They are a special kind of exo-skeletal defense, namely a type of "heraldry" that in sociologist Clinton Sanders's words allows men "to symbolize their membership and indelible commitment to the group."[33] As tattoos, the scars of warriors become ways of gaining individual recognition from their peers, who know how to read the secret codes. Although the movie dialogue says nothing about scars on Rambo's breasts, Stallone (a collector of American Indian art) gave his famous character sun-dance scars. In one version of the sun dance, a ritual of the Plains Indian tribes, young men place barbed hooks under their nipples; the hooks are attached by long leather ropes to a tall pole. When the spirit reaches him after days of dancing and numbs him to pain, a man pulls back on the rope and the barbs rip open his chest. Having endured and learned to transcend pain, having written this lesson on his body and completed an important rite of passage, he can now face the world as a more powerful man.[34]

All of the great warriors are covered with such marks. Mack Bolan's body looks "like he's been hit with damn near anything that will fire or cut."[35] When the doctors in Vietnam examine Casca, the eternal mercenary, they see so many scars that "it was impossible to tell which is the oldest wound."[36] Mark Hazzard, the comic-book mercenary, has a vertical scar running both above and below the center of his right eye; the whole eye looks like a cross-haired rifle scope.[37] With these scars, the warrior proves the veracity of his war story. If and when he returns to the world, his body, emblazoned with the blood tattoos of battle, testifies to the strengths of his boundaries and the glory of his martial deeds.

At first glance, then, the warrior's state-of-the-art weaponry, hard body, and battle scars radiate male power. He is the embodiment of the masculine ideals of autonomy, integrity, physical courage, and competence. While ordinary men succumb to fear and watch from afar, he acts. He is not trapped by forces beyond his control, but instead meets and masters all challenges. His violence changes the world far more than the words and deeds of others do; his individual existence counts and he knows it.

But at second glance, a far different man appears in the hardened shell of the warrior's body. In fact, he is not really a man at all, but instead a little boy whose anger, fear, and desire are all totally beyond his control. His journey away from the family and into the war zone has not made him a man. To the contrary, far from being a path toward personal empowerment and maturity, the New War promotes psychological regression and the retreat into a solipsistic world; the New War is a playpen for men, a special one without the drag of a supervising mother.

Just as the New War warrior never grows up, so too does he prefer the play of imaginary battle that lets rage run wild to the moment when battle ends and a new sacred order is founded. The films and novels and magazine articles of paramilitary culture do not say what kind of society will be created after the enemy is vanquished. The sheer intensity of the violence in these stories tends to make the warrior's victories look like a definitive restoration of a fallen America. It's as if the end of gunfire must mean something good. But the temporary defeat of chaos is not the same thing as the recreation of a sacred order.

As in the *Freikorps* literature, nothing is created other than the pleasures of battle and the renewal of the warrior. The New War does not affirm any virtues other than warrior virtues and the nobility of male groups. Beyond that, just what the paramilitary warrior really believes in remains a mystery; many stories tell of the warriors' contempt both for the power structure and for ordinary people. Most important, there is no vision of a new society. The warriors do not go home. The war never ends.

Mythologies are created in historical contexts and no mythology can completely transcend those contexts. In the aftermath of Vietnam, the failure of the New War to imagine what a new or restored America might look like beyond the battlefield indicates a profound lack of consensus about what the United States should become. Victory over an enemy, any enemy, substitutes for the effort to establish a better society. Rambo and all his friends are fighting a death-filled holding action, and making that fight seem like the best of all possible worlds. It is truly a dark, tragic vision. Social stagnation masquerades as restoration and social progress. Psychological regression wears an armored suit of maturity. Undeveloped and emotionally dead personalities appear as the height of individualism. An aesthetic of sexual violence is presented as realism. These inversions create powerful traps. There's no easy exit from the New War.

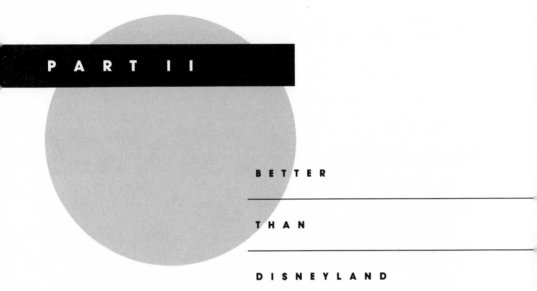

PART II

BETTER

THAN

DISNEYLAND

7

In ancient societies, religious festivals were vitally important occasions during which people left their ordinary lives behind them and "lived" the myths of their society. They did not just celebrate the memory of the gods, but instead saw themselves as voyagers into a sacred realm. In modern America, religious festivals have lost much of their magical aura. But other ritual spectacles have arisen in their place. In 1955 Walt Disney opened Disneyland in Anaheim, California, and the modern theme park was born. Disneyland was created by the same set of designers who worked on Disney's films. Each "village"—such as "Frontierland," "Mainstreet USA," and "Tomorrowland"—was built like a three-quarters-scale movie set to give the place a more intimate feel. Visitors entered a "Magic Kingdom," a space where all of Disney's mythological universes came to life. "I don't want the public to see the world they live in while they are in the park," Disney said. "I want them to feel they are in another

world."[1] Decades later, it was a principle the entrepreneurs of paramilitary culture took seriously.

Big Navy had served aboard an aircraft carrier in the early 1980s, a
member of a squadron that flew helicopters in search of enemy submarines. He was a good six-two, and he carried a lean, mean 220
pounds on his hardened frame. In his massive steel-like hands he
carried a big gun to match, a real smooth piece equipped with extended 16″ barrel, a 12″ noise suppressor, state of the art "red dot"
optic scope, and folding metal stock. The CO_2 tank powering this
baby rode high on the back of his bulging shoulders in its own special
olive-drab nylon harness, while the black neoprene high-pressure
hose connecting the tank to the gun looped under his armpit. Black
Cordura nylon and elastic bandoliers crisscrossed his chest, holding
100–150 rounds of ammo. The bandoliers perfectly matched the tiger
stripes on his camouflage fatigues, Big Navy's third outfit of the day.
An olive-drab bandanna, pulled tight against his forehead and
wrapped over his hair with the corners tied in back, completed his
fashion ensemble. He definitely knew what he was about, and what
was going down. His assignment was to lead a group of men deep
into enemy-held territory, capture their flag, and return to home base.
Along the way they would face their opponents, each armed with
heavy-duty guns firing gelatin capsules filled with bright red, yellow,
green, or blue paint. Big Navy and his men would have to "kill" as
many of these bad guys as possible to win victory; they would also
have to protect their own flag against enemy attacks.

All in all, the mission didn't look good. In front of him in the dusty
parking lot stood his men, a motley assortment of ragtag pickup
players. Cowboy's headgear, a genuine U.S. military Kevlar helmet,
was an eye-catcher. He'd been badly hurt in a motorcycle accident
not long before, and thought the $300 for the helmet well worth the
price to protect himself. A complete set of U.S. military web gear—
equipment belt, ammo pouches, canteen, and suspenders—wrapped
around his waist and over his shoulders. He carried a big gun, too,
and said that he liked full-scale firefights, no matter what the odds;
they didn't call him Cowboy for nothing. Burnt-orange goggles ob-

scured his eyes; a Darth Vader-type *Star Wars* mask hid the rest of his face.

Next to him was a former professional football player with seven years of experience on the Minnesota Vikings. It was his very first game, and he wore brand-new camouflage fatigues that fit skin tight (not exactly the military concept). Although he was the largest man on the field that day, far bigger than Big Navy, the ex-pro was nervous. He'd been forced to retire from football because of a leg injury. "There's still a lot of nerve damage down there," the big man said anxiously to his friend. His buddy nodded in sympathy. He, like Cowboy, had been the victim of a motorcycle accident. Sometime before his accident, he had bought walkie-talkie radios with earplugs and mikes mounted on headsets, similar to the kind worn by police SWAT teams and counterterrorist units. He brought them along today for the fight ahead.

The youngest members of Big Navy's squad of ten were two high-school kids from a San Diego military academy. Although they normally were allowed to fire M14 rifles, Colt .45 automatics, and the new Beretta 9mm's at least twice a month at school, recently the academy had rented out its entire arsenal to a movie production company. They needed to keep their shooting reflexes honed if they were going to make it to Annapolis and then move on to F-14 fighter-pilot training. One said he was aiming for Top Gun, the Navy's elite air-to-air combat instruction school at Miramar Naval Air Station near San Diego. Of course they'd seen the movie. Big Navy tried to discourage them. There weren't enough port calls and "things happen out there the Navy doesn't tell you about," he warned, referring to murders and thefts and accidents aboard ship. But the kids didn't want to listen, and besides, it was time.

With his squad collected, Big Navy led his men across the parking lot, past the gunmetal-blue Jaguar V-12 sedan with the "Whoever Dies with the Most Toys Wins" bumper sticker, on toward the gate. Overhead a Los Angeles County Sheriff's Department Bell Jetranger helicopter just cleared the tops of the Conquest playing field's palm trees as it approached the landing zone next door at the Malibu substation. As the thump-thump-thump of the rotors faded away, Big

Navy fired his gun through the chronograph, checking to make sure it was shooting just under 300 feet per second, the field limit. He finally turned and faced his team, pulled his full-length plastic face mask down, and gave the battle cry, "Okay, boys, it's time to rock and roll."

When they passed beneath the old wooden beams that arched over the gateway, the men found themselves in what looked like a ghost town, something out of the American West. And sure enough, some thirty to thirty-five yards down the dusty street lined by Old West style buildings that made up this former movie set, the enemy stood, spread out and waiting. They were a Latino team from the San Fernando Valley, just north of Los Angeles. Their leader, owner of a machine shop that made parts for air-to-air missiles, had bought team shoulder patches for all his employees who wanted in on the game: the three corners of the inverted triangle were labeled Judge, Jury, Executioner, while in the middle in full caps stood the unit name— VIGILANTE.

Each player wore full camouflage, and each held an advanced "constant-air" gun with extended barrel and silencer like those used by their Anglo and black opponents. All of them carried a long 16″ brush (used to clear gun barrels) in camouflage sheaths that hung from their waists. It gave them a special Central American jungle-fighter look, as if they were packing machetes and had just hacked their way through the underbrush into town for a rendezvous with destiny.

David, the man who ran Conquest, explained the rules for today's battle. He pointed to a line of banana trees that marked one of the boundaries; it wasn't legal to sneak past it. He described where each team's flag was, so that no one would be confused about where the key action was going to take place. He made sure every man was wearing a red or yellow strip of cloth on his arm and explained that a man who was hit was supposed to wave this cloth over his head as he marched off the field to keep from getting shot again. Any man seen with his eye goggles off would be instantly disqualified. Two referees were supervising the players to enforce these rules. Everybody looked bored; most had heard this story scores of times before, and even the new guys knew what to expect. Besides, it was a hot, dry August afternoon, a time when the Pacific breeze couldn't make it past the beach a half-mile away. At last David gave the countdown—3–2–1—and blew his whistle. An instant later twenty or more shots filled the air as players ran for cover, firing from the hip. The fight was on.

David couldn't afford to stay and watch. New players were driving up all the time. He got from 20 to 120 customers on each weekend day, and each paid $20 to get in, and another $20 to $35 to rent one of the modern guns with the big air tanks. Everybody needed extra tubes of paintballs, and that ran a couple of bucks for a tube of ten. He still kept a finger in his old office supply business, but he liked doing this a lot more. It was ironic, David chuckled. His mother had always been against his playing war as a kid. "Now I make my living playing war," he said to me. He was especially busy this Saturday because on Sunday he was playing with his own "expert" team. With so much to do, he couldn't talk much more. "You know," David added, "the *A-Team* used to film here all the time. Really."

By now the battle of the Vigilantes versus Big Navy's walk-on players had been going on nearly half an hour. Casualties had been taken on both sides. The first victims waited at the gate to minister to their more recently fallen teammates, using a garden hose to wash the bright yellow or red or blue or green water-color splotches off their uniforms. No one seemed to take getting hit personally; no angry words were spoken. In fact, no one said anything at all to the other side that afternoon.

Off the battlefield, each group partied by themselves. The men popped open cans of beer—Corona, Coors, and an occasional Bud. They lit up Marlboros and sucked in that first heavy drag of smoke. Girlfriends woke up from tanning naps taken on lounge chairs in the back of spotlessly clean four-wheel-drive pickups. Some listened dutifully to war stories, while others just wanted to know when they were leaving. But the men were all willing to hear another teammate's war story of a good shot or a shot missed, and of course how they came to get hit; in exchange they told their own. Some blamed their woes on their guns, first cursing them, then taking them apart for cleaning. After reassembling the guns, the men twisted knobs and valves, test fired the guns, and then cursed some more to start the cycle again.

As the last shots were being fired between Big Navy, his team's last holdout, and the surviving (and victorious) Latino machinists, two fresh groups got ready for their battle. One new guy had just stumbled upon paintball the day before, having found *Action Pursuit Games* on the newsstand next to his magazine of choice, the *Hollywood Reporter*. The Conquest advertisements showed a handful of male players being held prisoner at gunpoint by long-legged, big-bosomed women wearing shorts and tight-fitting camouflage tank tops. "Another typical day at Conquest" read the caption.[2] So he came looking for some action. When a teammate tied a red ribbon to his arm he quipped, "Does this mean we're Communists? Do we have to read Marx?"[3]

The development of mock-combat war games in the United States a few short years after the Vietnam War is not in itself surprising. One scholar of games and sports, Brian Sutton-Smith, argues that historically what he calls "games of strategy" are developed as "models of problems in adaptation. They exist to simulate some adaptive problem that the group is having . . . Players are not hunting real tigers, or taking a chance with angry gods or trying to outwit diabolical adversaries. The dangers that go with these excitements in real life are largely curtailed and can therefore be studied within manageable levels of anxiety."[4] As suggested by its original name, the National Survival Game, paintball in effect transformed the cultural and political crisis of defeat in Vietnam into a game that combined elements of both combat and play.

What is surprising, though, is how quickly the emphasis in paintball shifted from play to combat. This was not the intention of those who founded the National Survival Game in the New Hampshire woods in 1981. They were inspired by a more archaic vision of the lone hunter-woodsman sneaking through the forests, killing an opponent only when absolutely necessary to capture the flag. The game was to be a test of cunning and stealth. As Lionel Atwill writes in *The New, Official Survival Game Manual*, published in 1987: "There will be no machine guns on Game fields. No tanks. No helicopters. And the Game will always be played in the spirit in which it was conceived. In a spirit of fun and play. There will be no Viet Cong villages, no mock mutilations. No bogus wars."[5] But all these things would come to pass.

According to Mike Jasperson, publisher and editor of *Front Line*, the first paintball magazine, it was the coming of the New War movies in the mid-1980s that both helped the sport gain popularity and moved it in a paramilitary direction. In his words, "What they have done, more than saying war is good, they're saying that it is okay to wear camouflage, okay to play war." Paintball offered men the opportunity to participate in a film-fantasy world rather than just watch it. "You drive a forklift eight hours a day," says Jasperson. "You work a cash register eight hours a day or whatever; you watch television and here's *Magnum P.I.* and he's running around with his gun and here's Don Johnson running around with his gun on *Miami Vice*."[6] Compared to the stultifying routines of work and family responsibilities, the lives of these warriors were exciting and glamorous. Paintball provided a way for average men—and the game was played mainly by men—to get in on the action. Some players even watched action-adventure films the night before a game as a way to get "psyched up" and shouted lines from movies as they played.

The popularity of these movies and television shows was in turn noticed by new entrepreneurs who were opening new playing fields. Denis Bulowski, the Los Angeles policeman who built the famous Sat Cong Village with its bamboo compound flying a Vietnamese National Liberation Front flag, and the Nicaragua playing field with its facsimile of a downed cargo plane used for resupplying the contras, said that before he constructed his mock battlefields the idea of playing war "was already in people's minds. People see it in the movies. They think 'I wish I was out there doing that kind of stuff.' "[7] Paintball offered "better toys" to play with, and attractive theme parks like the Vietnam and Nicaragua playing fields to enrich the fantasy. That movies such as *Platoon* were in part filmed at Sat Cong Village added to the magic aura of the place.

Similarly, the manager of War Zone in Fountain Valley, California, said that although the game first hit California in 1983–1984, playing areas did not change from plain old marked fields to full-scale warrior theme parks until the fall of 1985, after *Rambo: First Blood, Part 2* and some of the other New War movies appeared. War Zone was the first playing field to develop mock tanks, hire helicopters, and provide teams with walkie-talkies and special "Heavy Fire Machine Guns" with 800-shot capability.[8] Not surprisingly, the bases on War Zone's playing fields were named after recent movies—the Hanoi Hilton, for example, and the Temple of Doom, and the Rambo Hotel.

At the same time that the fields became transformed, blue jeans and old shirts stopped being acceptable clothing. Increasingly, full camouflage outfits were perceived by all players, even novices, as a fashion necessity, not just better for hiding in the brush. Mike Jasperson described the transition as one that "makes the fantasy a little more complete. You know, now it's gone from imaginary to visual."[9] Indeed, magazine articles such as Frank Hughes's "Picking Your Paintball Persona" began to appear regularly to help players interpret the outfits worn by others and thus choose the ensemble best for them. The foremost fashion rule, writes Hughes, is to "keep in mind that while everyone knows 'dressing up' is one of paintball's enduring charms, it is considered bad form to admit it. Your clothes must have a rough utilitarian look to them (like you stopped to play paintball on your way to Nicaragua), and must never seem to be a costume."[10] Said another way, the "good" player always stays in character; he does his best to help himself and others maintain their "joint engrossment," as sociologist Erving Goffman calls it, in a fantasy world.[11]

On the other hand, the new player should avoid purchasing the cheapest, most readily accessible kind of camouflage clothing, the standard-issue U.S. military BDUs [Battle Dress Utilities] in the common "woodland" camouflage pattern. Although such clothing can give newcomers a comfortable "anonymous look" for a while, they will be seen by others as "players who lack confidence." Instead the ideal fashion statement is that of the "Special Forces" soldier. According to Hughes, "this is more of a concept than a specific outfit. The basic idea is to look military, but not regular military. You're a specialist, a dangerous individual . . . With the right patches and equipment, you'll leave them guessing as to whether or not you really were a SEAL."[12] As this paramilitary ideal spread, mixing and matching pieces of very expensive, exotic surplus outfits from Rhodesia, South Africa, and the Soviet Union became popular.

With the body now enclosed in full military camouflage, all that remained visible of the old self was the face. Although the advent of full-length plastic face masks was in some ways a "functional" improvement—paintballs sting painfully when they hit sensitive skin—more is at issue. In an effort to discourage aiming for the head, the overwhelming majority of field owners in the mid- and late-1980s declared that "head shots" did not count as legitimate hits. Still the masks became a regular accessory. As players hand painted fierce animal faces on them, and companies began marketing prepainted masks of wolves' heads or savage "wild men," the archaic elements of this ostensibly functional accessory became clear.

Anthropologist J. C. Crocker writes that the "ornamented body" is a mode of "communicating at once to society and to the self a specific identity." Ceremonial masks in particular have potentially transformative powers: "By donning a mask one becomes what otherwise one could never be. Men into women, old into young, human into animal, mortals into gods, dead into living (and vice versa)."[13] In paintball, masks facilitate a particular transformation: they help the civilian with no military experience "conjure up the spirit" and change into an imaginary warrior.[14]

Many players and paintball businessmen speak of the appeal of these costumes. One store manager alluded to the "military mystique" of "dressing up in cammies." His assistant manager put it plainly: "You dress bad to be bad."[15] But there are limits, as Mike Jasperson insists: "You know, the timid people are still timid on the field. The rest of the people—for example, salesmen—are aggressive. The underlying personality, well, I don't know if that changes. I don't think it does."[16]

Whether or not real personality changes occur through donning military fatigues, paintball certainly provides men the opportunity to gain the *appearance* of warrior power through playing dress-up. Ironically, then, an image of manhood is obtained by violating the social norms according to which playing with clothes is an exclusively feminine activity that real men disdain. As Brian Sutton-Smith says in his *Toys as Culture*, much of the appeal of games and sports comes from their openness and fluidity; games permit us "to express our desires and our contradictions in ways that are not possible within the conventional boundaries of society."[17]

The last material component of paintball to become radically militarized in the mid- and late-1980s was the basic paintball gun. The founders of the National Survival Game had from the beginning expressed some ambivalence concerning the role of the gun in the sport. An early page of Lionel Atwill's *New, Official Survival Game Manual* refers to it as a "long-range paintbrush" that is a gun "only in the semantic sense."[18] Later on, though, Atwill says this: "That the gun looks like *a gun* adds great weight to the Game. The gun is a tool that mimics a weapon. In its mimicry it becomes symbolic, and that symbolism, with its element of real or imagined fear, heightens the fantasy of the Game. The gun makes the Game work on several levels."[19]

In the beginning, the physical limitations of the first paintball pistols gave some credence to the assertion that these were simply long-range paintbrushes. Built by the Daisy Manufacturing Company for a firm called Nel-Spot, these "guns" were initially intended for use by farmers and ranchers to mark trees and animals with watercolor paint contained in gelatin capsules. Powered by a small 12-gram CO_2 cartridge, the Nel-Spot had an accurate range of fifty feet and a maximum range of seventy-five feet. Each CO_2 cartridge could propel only twenty or so paintballs, and the last few shots didn't have much velocity. The pistol's magazine only held around ten paintballs, and loading a paintball from the magazine into the firing chamber required several slow hand movements. Changing CO_2 cartridges also took time. Although these features were perfectly adequate given its intended farm use, from a warrior's perspective the Nel-Spot wasn't much of a statement.

For several years the National Survival Game founders wanted to keep the weaponry relatively low-tech. In late 1985 NSG, Inc., the corporation which developed and franchised the Game, introduced its own official paintball pistol, the Splatmaster. Made completely from plastic, the gun was relatively cheap (about $100 list price when first introduced). Easy to clean and maintain, the Splatmaster had a bit more range, held a few more paintballs, and was somewhat faster to operate than its predecessor. It was merely an improvement, though, and not a generational advance.

Meanwhile, back in Southern California, things were headed in a very different direction. Beginning in 1985, more and more paintball devotees became entrepreneurs. One group persuaded Benjamin-Sheridan, a manufacturer of BB and pellet air guns, to begin production of paintball pistols and *rifles*. Several brand-new companies entered the gun market as well. Scores of men went into business as "airsmiths," specializing in customized modifications of Nel-Spots and other paintball guns. Stock-issue gun barrels were replaced by smoother, more carefully machined and polished substitutes to increase accuracy and range. Shotgun-like "pump" actions were added to radically increase the speed of loading a paintball from the magazine into the firing chamber, and the whole feeding mechanism was changed to make it faster and more reliable. Long pipes were welded onto the gun magazines, giving them at least a 20-shot capacity, easily replenished with a 10-shot tube. A modestly coordinated shooter could now fire well over a shot per second.

But he couldn't keep firing very long. The old 12-gram CO_2 canisters remained a real bottleneck in the whole paint-pumping process. They couldn't power much more than 20 shots, and changing the cartridges still took a long time, especially when the shooter was suffering from the debilitating stress of an on-going firefight. Then, one day in November 1985, the game's most eminent airsmith, 46-year-old Lou Grubbs (or "Gramps" as he's known in the trade) finally ran out of air one time too many. "This is bullshit," Gramps declared. He'd been raised in a machine shop and had spent seventeen years teaching industrial arts and loved "to tinker and play and design stuff."

And so he went to work. At first he tried connecting three standard 12-gram CO_2 cartridges in a "tray system," a gambit that didn't quite work. Then he found some steel tanks similar to, but smaller than, those used by scuba divers; these smaller tanks held five pounds of compressed carbon dioxide. The system had potential, but it was a heavy load on a man's back and, in action, the hose connecting the tank to the gun often got caught in the underbrush. Next he tried a smaller canister containing a pound and a half of air that could be carried on the chest in an equipment vest. Finally, in March 1986, Gramps mounted his first 10-ounce canisters directly onto the paint gun; ten ounces of CO_2 was enough to shoot over 400 rounds at full power. The "constant-air" gun was born.

During the spring of 1986 the newly modified constant-air guns started showing up at all the major Southern California playing fields. That summer Gramps's home field, War Zone, announced that it would hold the world's largest paintball fight. Its two major playing fields would be combined to create a 350-acre battleground for a contest involving five hundred warriors from teams all across the region. On Saturday morning, August 23, the epic struggle began; by dusk the constant-air guns had proved their mettle. In November, War Zone scheduled Big Game II. This time twelve hundred gunners showed up, and two-thirds packed the big customized constant-air paint-pushers.[20] As word spread, the industry changed forever.

Delivering more firepower became the primary goal of air-gun technology. "Your Search for Better Close-Combat Equipment Stops and Ends Here!!!" is how Para-Ordnance Mfg. introduced its full-automatic paintball submachine gun, a literal copy of the famous Ingram MAC-10, the drug-dealer favorite.[21] The model 85 paint gun fired 1,100 rounds per minute, just like its real gun inspiration. A Tippman Pneumatics ad showed a player facing three adversaries. "Never Be Outgunned Again!" read the caption, and clearly this guy wasn't: his SMG-60 fired 600 rounds per minute and had "an authentic blow-back bolt system that duplicates the timing and feel of a real submachine gun."[22] By 1989 even NSG, Inc. was forced to develop and market its own semiautomatic constant-air guns. Retail list prices for these advanced weapons ranged from $250 to $450. Extended barrels, noise suppressors, high-capacity magazines, and scopes could easily add another few hundred dollars to the price.

Just as the weapons and accessories increasingly resembled their military equivalents, so the advertisements mimicked more and more directly the layouts and copy of ads in paramilitary magazines. In 1990 Brass Eagle introduced its Barracuda Semi-Automatic DMR Series with an ad showing an armed man in camouflage face paint wading waist deep in a swamp and carrying a coiled rappelling rope—a direct knockoff of Heckler and Koch's familiar promotions for their assault rifles on the back cover of *Soldier of Fortune*.[23] Adventure Game Supplies, Inc., in turn touted its new Landshark air gun by demonstrating its accuracy out at Sat Cong Village; the target was a standard B-2 human silhouette, the same one regularly used by gun writers testing combat weapons.[24]

A related advertising ploy was to link a paintball product as closely as possible to real military and police units. The "Products for Players" column in *Action Pursuit Games* proudly announced that T. G. Faust, Inc., a "respected manufacturer of body armor," many of whose "clients are government agencies," had now entered the paintball market with the "M-68 Tactical Vest" capable of holding 36 tubes (360 rounds).[25] Pursuit Marketing, Inc. claimed that more of its "Rough. Rugged. Reliable" line of air guns were used "by law enforcement and military for training than any other paintball gun."[26] When Corliss Delay, Inc. introduced its paintball *land mine*, the "Playmore P.D.S. Tripwire Activated Paintmine," it was clearly alluding to the U.S. military's "claymore" mine of Vietnam fame.[27]

Even leaving aside the paint grenades and land mines, paintball firepower dramatically escalated in the late 1980s. Whereas players armed with the original Nel-Spots might fire 20 rounds in a one-hour game, gunmen equipped with constant-air powered pumps and semiautomatics often fired over 100 rounds (and sometimes much more). The advanced guns also had a longer range of accuracy, upwards of 100 feet, and a maximum range well beyond that.

With so much paint flying around, the nature of the game was bound to change. In the beginning, the National Survival Game founders prided themselves on their woodsman-like abilities to hide and stalk silently. Indeed, in the opening game of June 1981 the victor was a professional forester named Ritchie White. Lionel Atwill, who also competed on that historic day, remembers that no one ever saw Ritchie, and he never fired a shot. "He crept through the woods from station to station, gathering flags as easily as a schoolgirl gathers flowers."[28]

But the high levels of firepower strongly favored a very different kind of tactical approach—the small-unit infantry practice known as "fire and maneuver." In fire and maneuver, one group of soldiers begins shooting either at a suspected enemy position or directly at enemy soldiers. Their objective is to make the enemy soldiers duck behind cover to protect themselves. While the enemy is thus blinded, part of the first unit then runs to a second position closer to the enemy. This second group then opens fire to cover the advance of the first group, who "leap-frog" past them to a third position. In this way an attacking force moves swiftly into a tactically favorable position.

Colonel Michael Duncan Wyle, vice president of Marine Corps University in Quantico, Virginia, was particularly impressed by the way paintball combat confirmed the military's own findings on how best to conduct fire and maneuver. Viewing the carnage generated during firefights at the Marine's Combat City training ground at Quantico in 1990, Colonel Wyle said: "One thing that I found particularly accurate was the fact that you need to get suppressive fire against the other guy in order to move . . . If you try it any other way, you get shot."[29] A second demonstration game was scheduled for viewing by the Marine Corps top brass; everyone was to be issued full-automatic paint guns and paint grenades. Colonel Wyle had been persuaded to host the exercise by a young private from California who, "despite his rigorous training schedule," had "continued to play the game he loved so well."[30]

Successful execution of fire and maneuver and the other infantry tactics described in game manuals and magazines required relatively high levels of social organization. Although paintball had always been a group-oriented sport that attracted teams of friends or coworkers, the militarization of the sport meant that disciplined units with a coherent leadership structure—from team captain down to lower fire-team leaders—had greater success than informal groups or makeshift collections of random individuals. Some teams became famous for both their ability on the field and their military aura. One motion-picture company even hired the famous Bushmasters to perform as soldiers in an action-adventure film—they showed up on the set with their own "cammies, weapons and a high degree of professionalism." The Bushmasters did so well that the producer promised he would "work with them again anytime and recommend them highly to any motion picture producer."[31]

All of these developments—the guns and especially the vast differences between novices and well-established teams—caused much worry and debate among paintballers. Many expressed concern that the constant-air guns had taken the basic woodsman skills out of the sport, leaving it to those who had the big money required to buy the advanced weapons. They also worried that first-time players were being slaughtered and so would never return. And indeed, industry analysts admit that turnover is something of a problem.

Playing-field operators developed some solutions to these problems. They began to schedule their playing fields for different kinds of games and different levels of ability. "Novices" were given their own games to be played with stock guns; constant-air gunmen got their own shootouts against similarly equipped foes; and "purists" who used sophisticated "tournament" style guns got their more sporting contests as well.

Still, despite this segmentation and stratification of the market, the overall direction throughout the 1980s was toward militarization and mock-combat, not woodsmanship. By 1986, there were over forty paramilitary playing fields in Southern California alone. A review of the sport in 1988 listed over a thousand playing fields throughout the country—from the green hills of upstate New York to the swamps of Louisiana to the indoor "urban warfare" ranges of Michigan. By that time well over two million highly armed men in camouflage and face masks had fought at least once in these mock wars and one million of them continued to play at least four times a year.[32] Even the National Survival Game had come around. Beginning in 1987, Worldwide Library, publishers of *Mack Bolan: The Executioner* and many other spin-off commando group sagas, became the official sponsor for the annual National Survival Game tournaments and awarded the "coveted Mack Bolan Trophy."[33]

The rise of paintball, however, cannot be explained merely by the invention of better toys or bigger and badder playgrounds. Its appeal was much more basic: some men, especially young men, wanted to get as close to combat as possible. Denis Bulowski, owner of Sat Cong Village, said, "There's such a thing as actual combat, and this is about as close as you can get to the real thing."[34] This, as one player put it, was "the dark side of the game."[35]

Perhaps it was this "dark side" that made paintball unattractive to most Vietnam veterans. Mike Jasperson thought that at most 10% of the California paintball players were military veterans, while in Illinois and Florida the percentage went up to perhaps 20%. Other estimates were much lower. Russell Maynard of *Action Pursuit Games* claimed that Vietnam veterans "wouldn't touch it with a ten-foot pole."[36] Out at Sat Cong Village one regular referee concluded that "maybe 5% of the players had seen action."[37] The owner of a large wholesale and retail store commented, "There's a lot of Vietnam veterans who come in here with their sons. They have no interest in putting on cammies and going out there."[38] Paintball businessmen thought that most combat veterans avoided the game because it threatened to bring back bad memories.

Indeed, most players of the game lacked any real combat experience; according to a Sat Cong employee, they were "people who wanted to be in a war; people who didn't get a chance."[39] Paintball was primarily played by men in their mid-twenties to their forties (playing fields do not allow players under sixteen). Most were white, except in California where Latinos and Asian-Americans also made very strong showings. Few black people ever played. No one knew why exactly, but one store salesman speculated that bad press coverage played a role, creating an impression among blacks that paintballers were "a bunch of Ku Klux Klan."[40] Nor was it a game for the very poor, as it required a significant outlay of cash. Beyond that, though, as one War Zone referee proudly explained, "all sorts of job types show up, blue collar and white collar. Everything from doctors, lawyers, down to the ditch digger. The field is an equalizer."[41]

Thus the two most commonly shared characteristics of players were that they were male, and that they had not fought in Vietnam. In the early 1980s, several books and magazine articles asserted that those American men who had missed the Vietnam War, either because of age or because they deliberately avoided the draft, were failures as men. Christopher Buckley published "Viet Guilt: Were the real prisoners of war the young Americans who never left home?" in *Esquire*'s September 1983 issue. Buckley (who did not go to Vietnam) stressed how the war had *confirmed* the veterans as men. They had the security of knowing "*I have been weighed on the scales and have not been found wanting*," whereas, poor Buckley confessed, "my sense at this point is that I will always feel the lack of it and will try to compensate for it, sometimes in good, other times in ludicrous, ways."[42]

The following November, *Esquire* published a sequel, William Broyles, Jr.'s essay "Why Men Love War." Broyles, like Buckley, emphasized the serene self-confidence that comes from having faced the enemy; he waxed lyrical about the brotherhood of war. "The enduring emotion of war," Broyles gushed, "when everything else has faded, is comradeship. A comrade in war is a man you can trust with anything, because you trust him with your life."[43] Like the New War movies and novels, articles such as these helped resurrect the warrior ideal for men.

These lessons were not lost on paintball publicists. Lionel Atwill begins one chapter of his 1987 manual with an epigram from Dr. Samuel Johnson: "Every man thinks meanly of himself for not having been a soldier."[44] Curiously enough, Christopher Buckley had quoted the same line in his 1983 essay. For those who felt cheated out of a war, paintball could serve as a test of manhood. Atwill writes: "A player might extrapolate Game performance to other stressful situations. Thus how you react in a Game may be an excellent clue to your behavior in the rest of your life."[45] Indeed, one corporation sponsored games during a corporate retreat and hired a psychologist to rate players on their aggressiveness.[46]

Atwill also promoted paintball as a means of creating comradeship. The NSG founders, he says, are men who "enjoy camaraderie," and the game as a whole is "so infused with a sense of honor, camaraderie, and fun that few players can walk away from it without feeling uplifted."[47] The idea that paintball encourages close friendships showed up again and again in players' accounts of the experience. One player told of how during his regular team meetings the goal was "for everyone to be tight with each other, both on and off the field."[48] Grubbs "Gramps" went further, declaring that when he played at War Zone, he didn't worry about watching his grandchildren because

"I've got 500 baby-sitters who will watch them."[49] Paintball, then, provided him a new, extended family.

Courage and comradeship are honorable values. But they cannot be separated from the essential truth of the game. At its core, paintball simulates killing. The fundamental sequence of play involves hunting other men, aiming a gun at them, pulling the trigger, and making the kill. That this sequence so closely resembles part of what is involved in real killing undoubtedly contributes to the high that many players experience. As the manager of Paint Pistol Express said: "I get an adrenaline rush out of this sport that I've never received from any other sport."[50] Military men speak of the "combat high." Time is experienced as moving very slowly—a few seconds can seem like minutes, minutes like hours. In focusing on the hunt and kill, sensory perceptions change. For example, peripheral vision usually disappears, leaving only a narrow "tunnel" straight down the barrel to the target. Players get so pumped up that oftentimes they don't even feel the sting when they themselves are hit—the pain and welts come later.

Moreover, despite its advertised good, clean fun, paintball in effect reproduces the notion that the only true men are those who have been tried in battle and become warriors, and that the highest form of friendship is the brotherhood of war. The simulated killings at the core of the game provide this magic touch of transcendence. A group of friends who play paintball are not just friends anymore, but "veterans." And at the end of a match, a player has not simply played a good game, but has proved his character under the stress of "combat."

At the same time, paintball puts men into contradictory relationships with basic social rules. On the one hand, the game allows men the fantasy of being soldiers legally and morally licensed to kill. On the other, since players are not really soldiers or police, the actions of aiming and firing a weapon at another person constitute a major *transgression* of law and morality. Only children can legitimately pretend to shoot other people during their play (legitimately, because children are not expected to know what real violence and death mean). Thus, paintball offers men the opportunity to act against the adult world in two ways: first, by approximating real violence, and second, by essentially playing a child's game.

Over and over the thrill of paintball is described by players in terms of returning to childhood. "Once you're on the field, you're five years old again," says paintball entrepreneur Russell Maynard.[51] One player exclaimed after his first game, "I can't remember having more fun. God! It's like being a kid again. The adrenaline rush alone—I mean, pretending I was in a war. When would I ever get a chance at that?"[52] Out at War Zone, Gramps said, "Cowboys and Indians have been popular for ages. This is being seven years old again and playing cowboys and Indians. I'm a toy maker. These are big kids' toys. That's what they are."[53]

Just like the New War movies and novels, then, paintball provides males a ritual transition to warrior adulthood through regression to childhood. All the posturing to create the aura of "badness"—the frightening face masks and elaborate military gear, the vicious-sounding team names and the various battle cries, the casual references to body counts, and the "toy" guns with a rate of fire found in real military weapons—all these elements are shouts of defiance against an imaginary frowning adult.

On fields full of children in camouflage equipped with rapid-fire big kids' toys and lots of ammunition, the line between play and violence gets awfully thin. The role of adult is passed on to completely different people—the referees. A referee *freezes* the game when he calls out "Paint check. Nobody shoot. Nobody move." If a player has indeed been splattered, the referee cries, "Man's hit! Do not shoot him again!"[54] "We are the order out here," said a Sat Cong Village referee. "Without the referee this would not be a game."[55] In stopping paintball's violent momentum for everyone on the field, the referee temporarily breaks the "combat high" experienced by players.

After players are hit and officially declared out they walk off the field and wait for the rest of their teammates at a staging area. As they leave the war zone, new players confront paintball's fundamental lesson. Everyone told a similar story, but Gramps was the most eloquent:

You find out very quickly that it's easy to die and as a result of that, you're just damn glad it isn't for real. They'd be putting you in a body bag. People realize that real fast. You ain't gonna get volunteers out of here for Nicaragua or anywhere else.

This is one of the biggest anti-war movements in existence. To be against war in a parade is one thing, but it takes a change of thinking and heart. In this country most guys are raised with a semi-macho image, the John Wayne, the Rambo. We glorify war, all that. War, as any good general will tell you, is absolutely insanity at its most vulgar. Being raised with that macho, pro-war image in our mind is what must be overcome. This game destroys the image I'm invincible when the first paintball hits.[56]

The problem is not that Gramps and his fellow enthusiasts are lying or even that they are providing rationalizations for violence. On the contrary, it is undeniably true that being hit by a fast-moving gelatin capsule in two or three out of every four games played (common averages) offers a crucial insight into the perils of real combat. But their testimonies are only a partial truth. As in *Casca: The Eternal Mercenary*, the paintball player dies only to walk off the battleground and be reborn a warrior half an hour later. Surviving players in regular games never even see the "corpses" of their fallen comrades. Instead, just as in the old war movies when the camera quickly cuts away from the fallen soldier with the red dot on his chest, casualties simply disappear from view. When Colonel Wyle ordered the "dead" paint-ball soldiers to lie where they had fallen for five minutes so that he could see the casualty pattern, author and player Jason Rein sheep-ishly acknowledged, "I must admit that it was a highly unusual sight to see individual 'bodies' (and in some cases, clusters) as I made my way off the field."[57] Both the New War mythology and the game obscure the fundamental reality that war creates death.

Indeed, what paintball does best of all is to fragment experience and thus allow men to embrace contradictory thoughts and feelings. The rapid changes from battle to game to battle create unusual op-portunities for the self to "float," suspended from ordinary identity. Men can play John Wayne or Sylvester Stallone when they posture with their guns and make successful kills, and simultaneously reject all fantasy warriors while nursing a stinging welt on the arm or leg. At one moment the game can be seen as a test of true grit. Minutes later a player can simply see himself as having become a kid again for an afternoon, with presumably no implications for his adult life.

In this shifting back and forth, the world blurs. Reality can be undone and reconfigured again and again. Even if the United States has problems winning military victories abroad, the Wolverines, Marauders, and Vigilantes can fight on indefinitely, with every man a hero and every hero a comrade for life. In this way good wars replace the bad one of the recent past. Yet it's all done, as Atwill says, tongue in cheek.[58] This is, after all, only a game.

8

To the average person at the newsstand, *Soldier of Fortune: The Journal for Professional Adventurers* seems to be a magazine version of *Rambo*. And in many ways, it is. But whereas Rambo is only a film character, *SOF*'s founder, its staff, many of its freelance writers, and frequently those who are interviewed in its pages as expert authorities actually do share a common background in U.S. government-sponsored "special" operations.

SOF, founded by Robert K. Brown in Boulder, Colorado, in the spring of 1975, was the culmination of a lifetime fascination with war. After graduating from the University of Colorado in 1954 Brown joined the Army (1954–1957) as a lieutenant in the Counterintelligence Corps, an elite branch of military intelligence that worked with the CIA. Later, as a graduate student in political science (again at Boulder), he became interested in the growing guerrilla movement against Batista in Cuba. In 1958 he traveled to Cuba, posing as a movement sympathizer, and tried to join Che Guevara and Camilio Cienfuegos in the Sierra Maestra. The guerrillas suspected he was an agent of some kind and sent him packing. Brown then helped train Cuban exile groups in the Florida Everglades (his holding corporation for *SOF* is called Omega Group, possibly named after the Cuban exile paramilitary group Omega Seven). In the mid-1960s, he rejoined the Army, this time as a captain in the Special Forces, and was sent to Vietnam in late 1968.[1]

There, Brown commanded a Green Beret unit near Pleiku, in the Central Highlands. His troops were part of MACVSOG, an acronym for Military Assistance Command Vietnam Studies and Observations Group. MACVSOG or SOG was the command and control organization for most covert reconnaissance patrols, commando raids, and other forms of special warfare conducted throughout Southeast Asia—including South Vietnam, Cambodia, Laos, North Vietnam, and perhaps southern China. Thus, "Studies and Observations Group" was but a light cover for its real name and function—"Special Operations Group." SOG drew its soldiers from Army Special Forces, Marine Force Recon, Air Force Air Commandos, Navy SEALs and their supporting patrol boats, select South Vietnamese units, and various Asian "indigenous forces" such as the Nungs, a Thai tribe of Chinese origin.

Most importantly, despite its formal listing as part of MACV, SOG was *not* subject to the normal military chain of command. In his memoir, *A Soldier Reports*, General William Westmoreland says that its operations were supervised instead by a special office in the U.S. Joint Chiefs of Staff and directly approved by the Secretary of State and the White House.[2] Another source stresses that the Central Intelligence Agency was heavily involved and often approved operations vetoed by others in the chain of command.[3] (The CIA financed and controlled or "coordinated" many operations in Vietnam, such as the Phoenix program to "neutralize" the Vietcong political infrastructure; the agency also ran its own war in Laos.)[4] Although Brown was not a high-level operative and sometimes ran afoul of his superiors, he got to know the world of special operations.

By 1970 Brown was out of the active duty Army (he stayed in the reserves) and was back in Boulder. There he worked with Peter Lund, another veteran of U.S. Army Special Forces, to establish Paladin Press, a publishing enterprise devoted to books on weapons and how to use them (often reprints of military publications). In 1974 Lund bought out Brown's share of the company and Brown went to Rhodesia to write a story on American mercenaries fighting in that country's civil war. When he tried to sell the piece to two men's adventure magazines, *Saga* and *Argosy*, however, he was rebuffed. One editor replied, "We're trying to get away from that hairy-chested stuff."[5] (*True* eventually bought the story but the magazine folded before it ran.)

Brown, however, was convinced that a market for "hairy-chested" men's adventure stories still existed. That year, he obtained a 40-page information packet from the Omani Defense Minister on how to become a mercenary in Oman. Brown then decided to sell this information to Americans by placing advertisements in the gun business's major wholesale advertising outlet, *Shotgun News*. According to Brown, "some of the responses came from recently discharged soldiers which made sense, but a lot came from lawyers, doctors, police, the too young and the too old. Now these people obviously were not going to go off to Oman, but it was clear to me that they wanted to read about going off to Oman as a soldier of fortune."[6]

Heartened by this success, in February 1975 Brown sent out promotional brochures for a new magazine he called *Soldier of Fortune*. The solicitation generated over 4,500 subscriptions. In July, a few months after the fall of Saigon, the first issue of *SOF* was published with a print run of 8,500 copies. Five years later the magazine was selling over 170,000 copies a month.[7]

Part of the magazine's success came from its appeal to the veterans of special operations and their supporters—both military and civilian. The American defeat in 1975 came as a particularly severe blow to these men; many had served several tours from the early 1960s right up to the end in 1975. To make matters worse, the CIA in particular and paramilitary warfare in general came under close public scrutiny in the 1970s. The various Congressional hearings on the Watergate affair had found traces of CIA involvement. For example, one of the burglars, Howard Hunt, had been involved in the Bay of Pigs disaster and the Cubans he recruited for the burglary all testified that they thought they were on an agency-sanctioned mission. In 1975 and 1976, both Congressman Otis Pike's Select Committee on Intelligence and Senator Frank Church's Select Committee to Study Government Operations with Respect to Intelligence Activities held extensive hearings on the previous twenty years of covert action. The CIA director in 1975, Richard Helms, was convicted of lying to Congress over the agency's role in the 1972 coup against Salvador Allende in Chile. In 1976 and 1977 both the Senate and the House of Representatives established new committees to review proposals for covert operations. Moreover, in the mid-1970s several former CIA agents such as Philip Agee, Victor Marchetti, and John Stockwell published highly critical books detailing the lies, killings, and corruption their operations had entailed.[8]

The Carter administration stepped up the attack against the clandestine services and their leaders. In June 1977 President Carter dismissed the chief of staff of United States forces in Korea, Major General John K. Singlaub, after Singlaub criticized Carter's Korean policy. Singlaub had spent most of his career in special operations. He worked first for the Office of Special Services in Indochina during World War II and later served in the CIA during the late 1940s and the Korean War—it's also worth noting that the years 1957–1966 have no listings on his résumé. He commanded MACVSOG from May 1966 to August 1969 and was well known to everyone in the paramilitary world (including Robert K. Brown, who served under him). Months later, in October 1977, Carter's newly appointed director of Central Intelligence, Admiral Stansfield Turner, laid off around two hundred operatives from the agency's Plans and Operations division—headquarters for running "live" agents in foreign countries and paramilitary operations—an action known as the "Halloween Massacre."[9]

Through the late 1970s and early 1980s Brown's *Soldier of Fortune* was an increasingly important clearinghouse for veterans of special operations and a public relations vehicle for their causes. For example, in repeated interviews, *SOF* gave Singlaub a platform for airing his right-wing political views and promoting the organizations with which he was affiliated—first the American Security Council and later the World Anti-Communist League (WACL). Two *SOF* correspondents were killed in foreign wars during this period. George Bacon, formerly with SOG in Vietnam and the CIA mission in Laos, died while fighting in Angola in 1976 (possibly as a CIA agent).[10] Mike Echanis, the martial-arts editor, was killed in a plane crash in Nicaragua in September 1978 while serving as an adviser to Brigadier General José Ivan Allegert, the Nicaragua National Guard commander in charge of combat forces for the Somoza regime. The deaths of these correspondents of course added to *SOF*'s mystique; *Soldier of Fortune* still had the guts to fight Communism, even if the Carter administration didn't. (That Carter approved a major CIA aid program to the Afghanistan mujahideen was never mentioned.)

Ronald Reagan and his director of Central Intelligence, former OSS officer William Casey, radically reversed Carter's policies. Covert action returned to favor and many special warfare units were expanded. Not surprisingly, the early 1980s also saw *Soldier of Fortune* expand in length, circulation, and foreign coverage. *SOF* correspondents frequently reported on the Nicaraguan contras; staff members actually trained some Salvadoran troops and reported favorably on many other Salvadoran units. Other reporters went in and out of Afghanistan, Angola, Mozambique, and South Africa. All of these journeys were described in great detail and came complete with several big color photographs; it was as if *National Geographic* had gone to war.

The United States government, both its armed forces and its intelligence agencies, were running major operations in many of the same areas *SOF* was visiting, certainly in Central America and Afghanistan. At the very least, U.S. military and intelligence agencies saw *SOF* as acting in the general interests of U.S. foreign policy—both *SOF*'s foreign reporting and its training operations were tacitly "sanctioned." Although the Neutrality Act forbids American citizens to enlist "in the service of any foreign prince, state, colony, district or people as a soldier or a marine," this law was never applied to people affiliated with *SOF*. The magazine could have been squeezed many ways if the government so desired; instead *SOF* writers continued to visit U.S. military units involved in commando operations and to write glowing reports—particularly about the arduous training necessary to become an elite warrior. And in the 1980s Robert K.

Brown was regularly invited to give lectures at the U.S. Army War College on "irregular forces." Brown was no longer on active duty, but he was a member of the reserves and during this period he was promoted twice, first to major and then to lieutenant colonel, before retiring in 1985.

But *SOF*'s appeal was not limited to special operations veterans. The magazine also had the look of a glamorous employment bulletin for freelance warriors. Each month, its classified advertisement section ran personal ads from men claiming to be highly experienced combat veterans who wanted to return to war. In reality, few such advertisers were actually recruited to work as mercenaries in foreign conflicts. By the late 1970s there simply wasn't a very large mercenary market for white infantrymen of any nationality. The largest market, Rhodesia, employed only 1,500 men, and did so only up until December 1979 when black revolutionaries won that country's civil war.[11] Nearly two years later, in November 1981, Mike Hoare, the legendary mercenary commander in the Belgian Congo during the 1960s, led over fifty men in a coup attempt in the Seychelles Islands off the East African coast. The attempt failed miserably. The Third World had changed; most countries had enough cohesive military and police forces to defeat the kinds of relatively small white units that had been effective in the 1950s and 1960s when newly independent Third World governments were still highly unstable and had poorly trained armies.[12] During the 1980s what mercenary jobs remained were mostly those for arms traders and technical specialists of one kind or another—electronic surveillance, aircraft mechanics, armorers, pilots, and military trainers. Many of the men who advertised in *SOF* were hired all right—but for domestic crimes. Still, regardless of how the advertisements were answered, their appearance in the magazine gave readers hope—somewhere out there, someone was really doing it.

Equally important was the fact that nearly every article appearing in *SOF* was written *as if* the reader was a soldier or mercenary who might go off to war *tomorrow*. The stories about weapon tests—with their step-by-step instructions on disassembly and reassembly—gave the impression that all these details were vitally important, that the reader's life might well depend upon his quick mastery of an alien firearm. The travelogues about El Salvador, Nicaragua, and Afghanistan also contributed to the sense of urgency: they read like intelligence reports addressed to soldiers on a mission, men who needed to know the deployment of enemy forces, their patrolling patterns, their armaments and morale. Robert K. Brown titled his editorials about the dangers of Communism abroad and liberalism at home "Command Guidance," as if every reader was a soldier in Brown's own elite special operations group, a new post-Vietnam SOG.

In the pages of *SOF* there was no need to debate politics and morality, because Communism, and, indeed, any kind of leftist movement or regime, was clearly the evil enemy. This enemy had to be defeated, and the only sure way to destroy him was through military force. If liberals and other assorted political cowards continued to restrain or prohibit the use of conventional forces, then irregular forces would have to do the job alone—and *SOF* was their magazine. The text represented a completely masculine society of heroic warriors operating in small groups, men whose muscled, painted, armed, and armored bodies appeared in the pictures that accompanied nearly every article. Death on the battlefield was tragic but noble, and carrying on the memory of the fallen was an important part of *SOF*'s agenda.

During the mid-1980s, the magazine's heyday, becoming a member of this society was especially appealing to young men between the ages of eighteen and thirty-four, who constituted *SOF*'s primary audience. Total sales numbered 250,000 and overall readership was four times that. More than half of the readers had at least some college education, and many were college graduates or held postgraduate degrees. About half were married. The vast majority took the magazine very seriously, reading each issue on average for over two hours before passing it on to three or more friends. And they liked guns, each spending over $1,000 a year on firearms and accessories.[13]

Although most magazines try to create a coherent world and personal image, such as *Cosmopolitan*'s "That Cosmo girl," *Soldier of Fortune* offered its fans something that other magazines didn't: a way to make its universe *real*. Since 1983 the magazine has sponsored a four-day convention every August or September in Las Vegas. In the years I

attended (1985–1987), about half of the thousand or so conventioneers who showed up each year had served in the military or were
currently in service, but of these only a few were combat veterans
who had fought in Vietnam. A great many were policemen; others
worked in the "security" business, ranging from professional security
agencies to guard-dog breeders. A good number of the people I met
were simply civilians who had neither military nor police experience.
Almost all of the conventioneers were white males in their twenties
to mid-forties. And to a man, they had all been reading *SOF* for
years. Going to the convention represented a further step into the
New War.

From the moment the conventioneer entered the lobby of the Sahara
Hotel and Casino, he was swept up into a paramilitary theme park
atmosphere and normal civilian life dropped away. *SOF* took great
pains to have everyone look more or less the same: some combination
of camouflage military fatigues and/or an *SOF* convention T-shirt were
the official uniform of the day and most men gladly complied. The
camouflage color scheme of the clothing matched the Sahara's brown,
black, and green decor. It was as if the hotel wasn't a hotel but an
imaginary, luxurious version of a French Foreign Legion fortress, a
lush desert oasis. And the conventioneers in turn were not ordinary
vacationers at play in Sin City, but active-duty military men who had
returned from battle to headquarters for briefings, training, rest, and
relaxation.

To heighten the fantasy, *SOF* abandoned the civilian way of measuring time by A.M. and P.M., preferring instead to list all events and
seminars in military time—1:00 A.M. is 0100 hours, midnight is
2400 hours. Moreover, immediately upon arrival, conventioneers
were required to sign a document releasing *SOF* from any legal
responsibility in the event of death or dismemberment. From Wednesday afternoon through late Saturday night, then, *Soldier of Fortune*
wasn't just a magazine. It was a living community whose members
were joined together against the outside world.

The convention was a grand festival, a multiring circus offering
countless activities. *SOF* scheduled seminars on global danger spots
and combat techniques. There were war games and training schools
of various kinds, ranging from knife-fighting classes on the grass by

the Sahara swimming pool to major shooting contests out in the desert. Up the escalator from the casino floor, a huge Combat Weapons Exposition, a trade fair for merchants to show their wares, dominated the mezzanine. And then there was Vegas itself, with its ubiquitous slot machines, cheap all-you-can-eat buffet dinners, drinking, girlie shows, and glowing marquees with blinking lights celebrating each and every thing the city has for sale. It's no wonder that these men attended; as one said, "It's better than Disneyland."

Still, the "studious" side of *SOF* caught my eye first. During each four-day convention, *SOF* sponsored from fifteen to nineteen seminars presented by the magazine's reporters and international experts. Seminars were scheduled consecutively from 9:30 A.M. (0930 hours) to 7:00 P.M. (1900 hours), with no more than one assigned to a given hour-long slot. Attendance ranged widely from thirty to over a hundred people, depending on the topic. Captain Ted E. Lawrence of the Israeli Defense Forces opened his seminar on "The Battle for Beaufort" with an admonition to his audience: "No pictures!" Several factions of the Palestine Liberation Organization were hunting him, he explained. Beaufort castle in southern Lebanon had been used by PLO forward observers to direct artillery and rocket attacks at Israel. After extensive training at another castle, Lawrence's commando unit hit Beaufort. They killed 27 PLO and one Yugoslavian; six Israelis were killed and 14 wounded. Lawrence described how his men killed three PLO members by burning them to death in a bunker with white phosphorous grenades. "They [the PLO] call them fighters," he said of the victims. "I call them terrorists."[14]

So popular was this speech that many in the audience stayed for the sequel, "Man Against Tank," conducted with the assistance of another Israeli, Captain Alan Wingate. "If you see a tank alone," Wingate said, "you know infantry is around."[15] But if there were lots of tanks, then that signified the presence of an armored unit. It was dangerous to attack a Soviet tank from the front, both men warned. They advised going around to the rear, where a man armed with a shaped-charge weapon like the RPG-7 had a chance of hitting exposed, unarmored fuel cells and setting the vehicle on fire. It was an attentive group; one middle-aged man asked where the tank commander normally rode so he would know where to take a shot at him—the man sounded as if he was expecting to see a Soviet tank appear in his back yard.

The next day a special agent from the Drug Enforcement Administration made his pitch in "Drug Busters." He wanted the *SOF*ers to become confidential informants for the DEA. After all, he said, "if you don't believe it's a war, check the body count in Miami." Becoming a confidential informant—in other words turning in anyone you suspect of either dealing or using drugs—was both a public service and a way to relive old times. The DEA man swore that being a c.i. "brings back everything in combat," an allusion to another drug rush, the adrenaline high. No one said a word. They waited politely until he finished his presentation, and then they all walked out. The special agent probably got the wrong audience—many were long-haired men who looked like they themselves had smoked a few joints not too long ago.

SOF firearms editor Peter G. Kokalis did much better with "Submachine Guns: Their History and Use." He walked into a packed room, raised a clenched fist salute, and shouted, "My name is Peter Kokalis! I am from Atlactal Battalion [the Salvadoran unit *SOF* trained]!" The crowd roared. When the cheering subsided, Kokalis got right to the point: submachine guns were dying. Assault rifles had replaced them in most armies. In Europe all the police still packed submachine guns every day—even the lowly traffic cops—but in the U.S., sadly, the weapon was associated with police brutality. "Remember," Kokalis said, "when it comes to police brutality, that's the fun part of police work!" Again the crowd exploded with glee. After reviewing a few obsolete guns, Kokalis finally came to one that still had promise, the Heckler and Koch MP5, the perfect choice for "shooting the scumbags in the car next to you." Time running out, he then held up the future in his hands for all to see: an Austrian-made Steyr Aug, a short-barrelled assault rifle that was unusually compact because of its advanced "bull-pup" design: "I'm going to take it down to El Salvador to try it out on a variety of targets."[16]

Not every presentation was a show-and-tell approach to killing. In 1985, Major General Ron Reid-Daly, formerly head of Rhodesia's Selous Scouts (a unit composed primarily of black soldiers who collaborated with the white government), gave a long talk on how the war against the revolutionaries had failed because the white Rhodesian government did not meet the needs of its black residents, and would not compromise by supporting any moderate, pro-Western Africans. Still, what got people's attention was the story of how his small 72-man unit equipped with heavily armed trucks masqueraded as part of the revolution and infiltrated a training camp in Pungwe, Mozambique, with plans to "capture the leaders and then simply machine gun the rest." The applause was so enthusiastic he had to stop for a moment before reaching the punch line, namely that the ruse worked, leaving about "a thousand chaps not very active" (1,026 killed, thousands more wounded).[17] When his presentation was over, Major General Reid-Daly received a standing ovation.

Conventioneers found these seminars vastly superior to the mainstream news media's coverage of world and national events. At the simplest level, the press was seen as just too biased. As a Minneapolis policeman said to me, "The newspapers are slightly weighed to the left."[18] Others used the word "liberal" rather than "left" in describing the news media, but the criticism was the same. This liberal bias was associated with a second complaint, namely that the news media didn't really go after the news. A former Navy helicopter pilot turned private detective gave one major example: "I just wish the press was going inside the Sandinista prisons."[19] Another man complained of inadequate coverage from inside Afghanistan. And a 36-year-old Houston private investigator observed, "A lot of time what I've seen in magazines and newspapers, why those reporters never went to the scene of the action. They sat in a hotel someplace."[20] The notion that the press did its reporting from hotel lobbies showed up time and time again. Indeed, on more than one occasion the people I interviewed noticed my press badge and offered me friendly advice: "Bill, no matter what you do, don't stay cooped up in a hotel somewhere."

In sharp contrast, the regular *Soldier of Fortune* reporters were seen as men of action. One 26-year-old security guard noted that "*SOF* has reporters in the field who go out into the field with the people."[21] A San Diego postman (who, at fifty years of age, was one of the oldest men in attendance) had been reading *SOF* for years because "it gives you a truer picture of what's going on in the world as far as conflict goes. I believe these guys."[22] "In seminars you get information from people who know what's going on," said a Palm Springs guard-dog breeder. "You're easily a year ahead on any kind of real information. Most of the news media is just too liberal."[23] A 33-year-old Washington, D.C., security director concurred: "I like the seminars. You get a different perspective. The media tends to be one-sided. I like to talk to people who have actually been in certain places, talk about what's happening."[24]

Although many *SOF* seminars conveyed information that was not readily available in the mainstream media, the information itself was secondary to the particular way it was presented: the smell of blood permeated the air of nearly every room. The guest lecturers were men who had either personally killed or commanded and trained others to kill. They had taken life and were, therefore, blessed with a special aura. By sharing the same space as the confirmed warriors, hearing their war stories, viewing their battlefield slides and videos, and asking them questions, the conventioneers seemed to absorb part of that aura as if by osmosis. Through a process described by anthropologist Sir James George Frazer as contagious magic, they too came closer to the brotherhood of war.[25]

Those conventioneers who wanted to become men of action themselves had an array of war games and training schools from which to choose. *Soldier of Fortune* hosted its own 3-gun match at the Desert Sportsman's Rifle and Pistol Club a few miles outside the Las Vegas city limits. In this type of match contestants must compete with three different weapons: an assault rifle, a combat shotgun, and a combat pistol. To maintain a "realistic" battlefield atmosphere, *SOF* put weight restrictions on every possible type of gun to prohibit shooters from trying to transform more or less stock combat weapons into special target guns. From two to three hundred people competed each year for thousands of dollars in prize money and various firearms and accessories donated by manufacturers. Although some of the contestants were actually federal officers sent by the Drug Enforcement Administration, the Department of Energy, the Customs Bureau, and other security agencies, most of the shooters were civilians.[26]

For those who chose to shoot in town, the contest at Vegas's The Survival Store was a real attraction. This store, specializing in the sale and rental of submachine guns and decorated with posters of nude women holding guns, was crowded with business every day. An old war surplus two-and-a-half ton truck driven by a showgirl dressed in shorts and a tank top saying "I do it automatically" picked up men at the Sahara Hotel and drove them to the store's indoor shooting range, where they paid $25 to enter the official *SOF* contest and rent a submachine gun. Ammo cost extra. The choice of paper targets included Arab terrorists, Russian paratroopers, Libya's Gadhafi, and of course Jane Fonda. According to the store's owner, in 1986 five hundred men participated in the competition and another thousand just showed up to shoot. In three days they fired 48,000 rounds.[27] A young guitar instructor from Redondo Beach told me that he chose to rent an old World War II Thompson submachine gun because "I wanted to feel what the guys in World War II felt. The gun was so heavy, it must have been one of their grievances."[28]

Parachute school awarded "jump wings" to those who paid the $125 to go airborne. Out on the grass near the swimming pool, Ernie Franco taught a knife-fighting class called The Defensive Edge for $30. Franco was president of Cold Steel, Inc., and designer of the Urban Pal push dagger and the famous Japanese-style Tanto fighting knife that promised to rip through bulletproof vests. Students were paired off in couples, given balsa-wood dowels about a foot long, and taught to dance with each other in quick cut, turn, and run movements (make your cut across the top of the opponent's hand—lots of blood vessels there). Of course graduates got a discount on the big $100 fighting knives.

Rappelling school wasn't just about learning how to climb down a mountain on a rope, but was instead a "martial art" requiring "balls." As the graduating students jumped off into the night for the long ride down from the tenth floor of the hotel to the poolside below, their instructor called out on a bullhorn, "This morning, these were normal, average people! Now they rappel 150 feet! You too can do this. Scare the hell out of your boss!"[29] Even paintball had a more vibrant paramilitary glow at the Sahara "Operations Area." Lieutenant Tim Oliver of Icon Training and Security required organized squads to sign up for "tactical live fire exercises" that included a "debriefing" by Icon staff when the game was over.[30]

Those who sought war games and training exercises beyond the convention itself could find many groups and businesses actively looking for recruits. Civilian Military Assistance showed up in force in 1985, eager for men to help send supplies to the Nicaraguan contras. The next year (after some of their members were shot down and killed while flying combat missions in Nicaragua) they shifted emphasis to Guatemala, seeking volunteers for the Guatemala '87 Freedom Jump, a three-day parachute school run by the Guatemalan Army. "Big Mike" Harvey operated closer to home with his Anti-Terrorist Analysis Command newsletter and his North American Defense Association for militia duty. He offered members an NADA uniform of sorts composed of black berets, cap and beret crests, cap and shoulder patches, and T-shirts—all with NADA lettering. Harvey's brochure explained that these NADA insignia would tell the world that *"You Are Always Ready to Defend!"*[31]

The Rocky Mountain Commando School offered a week of parachuting, martial arts, and survival instruction for about $1,100; by 1986, several hundred people, mainly from large cities, had taken the course. Executive Security International, Ltd. in Aspen wanted $3,480 plus $450 for room and board for their Executive Protection 14-day course. It was expensive, but the price included a videotape taken of the student during his final exercise which involved running through an obstacle course filled with old automobile tires and shooting at metal plates. The student even got to choose his own theme song for the tape; popular choices included Bruce Springsteen's "Born in the USA" and the sound track to Sergio Leone's first Clint Eastwood western, *A Fistful of Dollars*. (Years later ESI, Ltd. would advertise in paintball magazines with the query, "Are you ready for the real thing?")

Al Mar, a famous knife designer, sponsored guided seven-day trips down the Amazon for $1,540. Most popular of all were tours to Israeli and Taiwanese military centers. Special Veterans Excursions of Chicago offered separate Army, Navy, and Air Force tours to Israel, each group joining up with their Israeli Defense Forces counterpart for ten days and $1,760 worth of desert barbecues, briefings, parachute jumps, or skin diving. By taking trips to foreign countries near the "edge" where the enemy lived, the soldiers of fortune followed a path already taken by Hollywood film companies. As Larry Kubic, producer of *Death Before Dishonor* (1987), proudly told me, "Israeli security people worked undercover as extras in our picture. We didn't even know who they were. Security was with us all the time. The army was around a lot."[32] It was as if both film producers and paramilitary tourists thought they could absorb the aura of war and become more "authentic" in the process.

Complementing the paramilitary tourism booths were elaborate exhibits by gun and ammunition manufacturers, and distributors of all kinds of weapon accessories. These products also offered the conventioneers access to mythic battlefields. For example, several different firms selling black nylon "combat" or "SWAT team" equipment vests decorated their booths with the same movie poster showing Arnold Schwarzenegger wearing a black nylon vest over his huge bare chest; the caption read "Let's Party." For those warriors who wanted the ability to strike fast like New War commandos, several companies brought their special one-man planes and watercraft to examine. Air Command Mfg., Inc. presented an ultralight gyroplane (as seen in *The Road Warrior*) that was so small "it will even fold up to go through a standard door." The "swimmer entry vehicle" was a long camouflaged surfboard with a special recessed groove to hold an M16. The manufacturer assured me that the U.S. Navy SEALs were giving it a careful look.

Buying these guns, or going to paramilitary adventure schools, taking wild vacations, and participating in the more serious shooting matches like the 3-gun contest all required major expenditures. However, the *Soldier of Fortune* convention also offered trinkets. Vendors selling military insignia and jewelry, T-shirts, caps, how-to books, videos, and posters cluttered the gigantic exhibit hall. Most of these items, all priced under $20 (except the videos), made powerful statements about *Soldier of Fortune*'s world.

For a fist full of dollars anyone could buy the shoulder patches worn by virtually every elite military unit—Army Airborne, Rangers and Special Forces, Navy SEALs, Marine Force Recon, Air Force Commandos. For a few dollars more, lieutenant's and captain's bars, or even a colonel's eagles, could be had. *SOF* had its own insignia for sale, including shoulder patches in bright red for "dress," and the more subdued black on olive drab for basic "operational" wear. There were also red, silver, and gold badges for berets and epaulets.

For those who really wanted to make a liberal quiver, there were T-shirts proclaiming the wearer's death-defying fearlessness and limitless power. The biggest banger showed a Trident submarine cruising on the surface with a nuclear explosion in the background. Its caption read "24 Empty Missile Tubes, A Mushroom Cloud, and Now It's Miller Time." Snipers peering through telescopic sights came with a choice of slogans, such as "Reach Out and Touch Someone" or "I Was into Killing Before Killing Was Cool" (taken from the country-western hit, "I Was into Country Before Country Was Cool"). The classic T-shirt, though, showed a viciously smiling skull in a beret —the unofficial emblem for MACVSOG.[33] On a T-shirt, the most common version of this smiling death face added a dagger penetrating the skull and the words "Kill 'Em All, Let God Sort 'em Out."

The how-to books sold at the convention presented myriad ways to carry out this celebration of violence. At the low end of the spectrum were works like George Hayduke's *Getting Even: The Complete Book of Dirty Tricks*, which offered such advice as sending threatening letters to politicians under the name of someone you want to hurt.[34] In the middle came scores of books about how to convert semiautomatic weapons into full-auto machine guns, or how to build a noise suppressor, along with pamphlets such as L. Ranchero's *How to Fight Motorcycles* (with pits, trip wires, and spikes).[35] And then there were the straightforward killing manuals. Victor Santoro's *Vigilante Handbook* contains chapters on the tools needed for torture (fire, pliers, and stiff wire brushes), the advantages of using a car as a weapon (automobile accidents happen every day, and besides, it doubles as an escape vehicle), and the best methods of body disposal.[36] Although quite a few distributors offered these books, most of the more serious weapons conversion and killing books were published by either Desert Publications in Cornville, Arizona, or Paladin Press in Boulder.

Lastly, there was paramilitary culture's poster art. All the T-shirts had their poster equivalent, but much else was available, too. John Wayne showed up in poses ranging from his Western classics to *The*

Sands of Iwo Jima (1949) and *The Green Berets* (1968). *RoboCop* and Clint Eastwood's *Dirty Harry* decorated many a vendor's stall. An old Rhodesian Army recruiting poster with the invitation "Be a Man Among Men" hung alongside a "combat art" poster showing a helicopter door gunner whose wolf eyes stared out from under his helmet; heavy body armor and twin machine gun mounts hid his mortal flesh.

In contrast, the women featured in posters were all partially nude, but fully armed—black-widow women for sure. So popular had the genre begun by Chuck Traynor's picture of "Bo" become that many knife and holster and book suppliers offered their own versions, and even had the models there to autograph the posters. In 1987, though, Traynor upped the ante. He brought a huge plywood mock-up of an *SOF* magazine cover, with a big warrior's muscled physique dead center, and a hole in the plywood for a conventioneer's face. Two live models from The Survival Store curled in the plywood commando's arms. The headline cried, "Fearless Merc Rescues Damsels From Sandinista Terrorists." Ten dollars got you a picture and a chaste kiss on each cheek from the damsels.

Compared to the seminars, which, for all their appeal to blood lust, displayed some seriousness of purpose, the games, posters, and trinkets seemed silly and childish, more evidence of regressed bad boys at play in defiance of the adult world. (As two salespeople said, "The difference between men and boys is the price of their toys.") The conventioneers themselves saw things differently: they were getting ready for war. The world they saw was a very dangerous, threatening one: the enemy was everywhere and he was on the march. In Afghanistan, invading Soviet forces were fighting the indigenous mujahideen. On the African continent, Israel still faced hostile Arabs, while South Africa (a Western country) was under siege by the Communist-led African National Congress. And always, there was Vietnam, a bitter reminder of failure; its mere existence, together with the lingering question of unaccounted for missing-in-action U.S. soldiers, indicated that the old world order premised on American power was gone.

But the main worry of the conventioneers in the mid-eighties concerned a threat much closer to home: the Sandinista regime in Nicaragua and the revolutionary war in El Salvador. One young man described his fears: "I would support anybody that stands up and opposes Communist aggression. I hope this administration or the one coming up wakes up and realizes we're going to have severe problems with heavy concentrations of Communist troops in our backyard. *We're slowly being surrounded.*"[37] A Brooklyn, New York, librarian said, "I don't care what the Nicaraguans do to themselves, but I don't want them to *export it.* The countries around them have a right to protect themselves. I'm for anything that will guarantee the maximum freedom for the individual."[38] The San Diego postman sent a case of foot powder and equipment belts and packs to the Nicaraguan contras by way of *SOF*'s Nicaraguan Defense Fund. Like the librarian, he was deeply worried that Nicaragua would be "another Communist state like Cuba. If they [the Sandinistas] get established good enough, they will *export it* to other countries, like Mexico. We got to stop them someplace, somehow."[39] Otherwise, as a Colorado pharmacist and survivalist prophesied, "Eventually we're going to be a small island."[40]

This notion that social revolution was a thing that could be "imported" and "exported" across national boundaries came up repeatedly. In the opinion of most conventioneers, this "exported" revolution was inextricably connected to massive waves of Latin American (and other) refugees coming into the United States—and these refugees were the worst imaginable people. A 30-year-old businessman from Baltimore thought that Central American refugees would be *ordered* to go into affluent neighborhoods to commit crimes.[41] A Navy veteran who belonged to the paramilitary group called Civilian Military Assistance considered the impending refugee problem "a full-scale blow-up that's never been seen before." The "styrofoam" border of the United States would be crushed. "How many Latin refugees are actually Cuban agents?" he wondered.[42] The most terrifying scenario came from a 26-year-old security guard and Naval reserve member. The United States, he said, suffered from "moral laxity" and was thus "wide open" for terrorism. "It's just going to grow and grow. It will become a day-to-day thing like North Ireland." When asked who would commit these terrorist acts, he responded that foreigners, such as the Pakistanis running 7-Eleven convenience stores, were the most likely culprits. The climax would come when Daniel Ortega would take "ten million Mexicans, hand them rifles, and send them over the border to kill five Americans each."[43]

Not everyone thought that the combination of "exported" revolution and refugee waves would inevitably lead to terrorism and war on U.S. soil. Some expressed their worries in terms of how refugees would change politics and culture in their communities. One 38-year-old real estate agent from the San Francisco Bay area was sure that Honduras, Guatemala, and Mexico would all turn Communist. At that point, there would be so many refugees that Texas, New Mexico, Arizona, and California would simply "become Mexico."[44] A 35-year-old Dallas businessman, a member of the Texas State Guard, reported that "the same graffiti that was written on buildings in Managua now is written in Mexico. In Laredo, Texas, the Latin workers are unionizing. If Latins have voting power, then they are going to weaken normal politics."[45]

"Internally, the United States is going to have a problem with the Latins and other immigrants," said the 33-year-old director of a private security agency based in Washington, D.C. "American values and ethics are starting to deteriorate. Immigrants will impress their values, which may contradict our life style. I think they would be more leftist. Rights as we know it are going to change."[46]

The *SOF* conventioneers saw themselves as America's front line of defense against these foreign invaders. Above all, the conventioneers were *active* citizens. A 30-year-old Memphis dealer in explosives (for farm use) and machine guns (for police) thought the men he met at the convention were "people who do something, who don't just sit around drinking beer and watching TV" like some of his friends did back home. This man considered himself an adventurer, too, having previously helped Friends of the Earth as a scuba diver in Australia and just that day having completed his first parachute jump.[47] A Canadian collector of military arms also emphasized that "the great majority of Americans are very apathetic. They sit back, have a beer and a steak, too concerned about their own personal gains."[48]

Being *active*—in contrast to the passivity of the general populace—was a key value to the conventioneers. As active men, they considered themselves *responsible* for their own welfare and that of their families. A former U.S. Army Special Forces instructor who now ran a "Base Operational School" in Mesa, Arizona, praised his clients as "normal blue-collar and white-collar people who don't think the federal government is going to take care of them in a stressful time."[49] A Hawaiian aircraft mechanic and member of an Army National Guard unit spoke more personally: "We feel that it may come a time when it's up to the head of the household to take care of his family. On this planet, there are guys who are doers and guys who are watchers."[50]

But to be self-reliant was not necessarily to act alone. True, the individual could no longer trust federal and local governments to protect him and his family from criminals, terrorists, and waves of immigrants. But no individual was strong enough to do the job by himself. The world had become so dangerous—and gave every indication of becoming even more so—that simple home defense by a man with a pistol or shotgun was no longer enough. Instead, like the Minuteman at Concord in 1776, a good man needed the help of other good men who knew one another personally if the forces of chaos were to be kept at bay. He needed a private militia.

One former Navy SEAL from San Francisco came every year to the 3-gun match as a way of keeping in shape. "Only an armed citizenry can exercise power over government," he insisted, and that meant belonging to a "civilian militia." America had gone soft; most citizens would not be capable of coping with a limited nuclear war and the subsequent "mano-a-mano" struggle.[51] The Dallas businessman who was worried about Latin immigrants also competed in the 3-gun match because of what he called his militia mind-set. He saw himself as part of a growing movement: "People are becoming concerned and they don't want to be caught defenseless."[52]

From this perspective, the trinkets enabled men to buy membership into a paramilitary militia at a cheap price. With insignia and caps, posters and how-to books, you too belonged and were a bit more ready for the day when the enemy arrived on your doorstep. More than one guy told me he bought an AK47 manual, not because he owned an AK or even planned to buy one in the near future, but because if he studied how to use and clean one, he would know *what to do*. Not surprisingly, the favorite war film of most SOFers was not

Platoon or *Full Metal Jacket* but *Red Dawn*, John Milius's story of a Russian, Cuban, and Nicaraguan occupation of Colorado and the gang of high school boys and girls who form a militia unit, the Wolverines, and do some serious killing. In the film, the Wolverines start off fighting with hunting rifles, but later switch over to captured AKs. Even though few conventioneers still thought the Russians themselves were coming, Milius, they said, had the right concept.

With so many seminars to attend, war games to play, and shopping to do, one might think the *Soldier of Fortune* militiamen were a happy lot. Most did indeed seem to be having a very good time—the kind that energizes people—and spoke highly of the "camaraderie" they felt with others. As the Minneapolis policeman said, "It's like a club, like a VFW [Veterans of Foreign Wars] or an Elks convention."[53]

But there came a moment during interviews—after the news media had been debunked, the seminars praised, world dangers identified, movies discussed, and professions of camaraderie exchanged—when their major worry emerged. This problem had several names, all of them ugly: "Walter Mitty," "Rambo," and—worst of all epithets—"Wanna-be." With so many men in camouflage walking around wearing different military and paramilitary emblems, the question constantly arose: Who was a real warrior and who was not?

Nearly every man expressed some concern over this, and at one level, everyone had the same answer: *Walter Mitty or Rambo or Wanna-be was the other guy*. Each man said that he was "for real," and that his close friends were for real, but the status of casual acquaintances and strangers seen at the convention was a subject of great debate.

The one full-fledged mercenary I could find, a Belgian paratrooper on leave from his regiment who had just returned from six months of fighting with the Karen rebels in Burma, called most conventioneers "soldiers in the mind." He nodded his head and smiled slightly as he spoke, communicating that it was fine with him that people were interested in real soldiers like himself. A former Army Airborne officer who now worked as a security consultant for international corporations expressed the same basic idea. He saw himself as a "professional counter-terrorist," a member of a very elite fraternity that comprised no more than twenty firms. But he dismissed the majority of men at the convention: "There is always someone who would like to be more than they are," he said. "Insinuating yourself in a situation where you are with someone better than you is part of the American way of life."[54]

But as tough as this ex-paratrooper came on with his claims to having so much of the right stuff that it rubbed off onto anyone in his presence, his story had its own wanna-be complications. When he told me his name, it didn't register at first, but a few minutes later something clicked. I asked him if that wasn't the name of a character in Frederick Forsyth's 1974 novel (and subsequent movie) about mercenaries, *The Dogs of War*. The man looked genuinely startled when I said this. He pulled me over to a light (it was dark out by the pool) and took out a driver's license to prove to me that yes, it really was his name. Although the man undoubtedly was part of a security firm, it also seems likely that he had changed his name as a way of "insinuating himself with someone better," and thus getting closer to the status of a warrior-god.

A second group of men also held the wanna-be's in contempt. A San Jose narcotics officer and SWAT team member shook his head in despair and sighed, "Maybe five percent of the people here know what's going on." The previous year he'd seen a guy all decked out in tan and brown desert camouflage, a paratrooper's red beret with *SOF* badge, a gold *SOF* belt buckle, and assorted other jewelry. The wanna-be's "old lady was dressed up, too." "This guy was trying to identify with something," the policeman concluded.[55] The convention thus made him feel lonely, rather than uplifting him in a gathering of eagles. What was worse, another policeman thought, was that wanna-be's *discredited* the serious folks. "They give the people who are actually trying to give us a true view of what is happening in these Third World countries a bad name." The narcotics officer had earlier spotted a 21-year-old wearing a flight suit with a lieutenant colonel's silver eagles rank insignia. "He's not a vet; he doesn't know what the military is about. He probably thinks war is romantic, that it's a fantasy."

Ironically, in deriding other men as wanna-be's and Rambos, the *SOF* conventioneers were echoing a principal theme of the New

War—over the years it had become common practice for the paramilitary magazines, novels, and movies to criticize each other as being Rambo-like or "unrealistic." In explicitly denigrating someone else's war adventure as a childish fantasy, of interest only to armchair commandos, weekend warriors, and wanna-be's, each writer or producer made a tacit claim for the authenticity of his own story. At the same time, pointing out someone else's war romance served to obscure the mythological world in which the accuser stood.

For example, *Let's Get Harry* (1987), one of the many films modeled after *Rambo*, shows a teenager determined to rescue his kidnapped older brother in Colombia. He interviews mercenaries recruited from an ad in *Soldier of Fortune*. One candidate shows up in full camouflage, wearing dark glasses, and announces "You can call me Rambo." He doesn't get the job. The next guy (played by Robert Duvall) wears a sedate business suit and carries a Congressional Medal of Honor as his calling card. He's obviously the "real thing," and his presence lends credibility to the adventure. Duvall even showed up at the 1987 *SOF* convention to promote the film and emphasize the "realistic" training he received at a mercenary school in preparation for the part.

Although no one came out and said, "Yes, I am a wanna-be," quite a few men who were not combat veterans spoke about how disappointed they were to have missed out on war. Interestingly enough, like the paintball players, several had been physically hurt. For example, the Hawaiian aircraft mechanic had spent almost all of his active duty military service, from 1971 to 1973, in the hospital, victim of a head-on automobile collision. One 27-year-old was partially paralyzed in one leg; he could serve in a Naval reserve unit in a noncombat job, but that's all, and it grieved him.

Another young man had earned a top secret clearance in the Navy to work as an electronics technician on submarines. But he got tired of the job and volunteered for the SEALs. "That's where I felt I belonged," he said. Unfortunately, he didn't make it through Basic Underwater Demolitions. Doctors found a small bone spur on his knee that was nonetheless big enough to hurt him given the stress of training. He felt diminished for not having completed the course: "It would have made me a better rounded individual, better rounded physically and mentally. They teach you to take what is thrown in your face. That basic training would help you no matter what you did in life."[56]

Others got left out for different reasons. Many men in their twenties said they were just born too late. One SOFer had deliberately avoided the Vietnam War. He had successfully obtained a conscientious-objector deferment, then years later changed his mind about the ethics of not going to war. He regularly attended the convention, always dressed in full camouflage with *SOF* insignia. Another man, a 35-year-old real-estate appraiser from Gardnerville, Nevada, blamed the "politicians" at his draft board for disqualifying him for service. "I missed it. I would have loved fighting in Vietnam, fighting to keep everybody free, fighting to keep the Communists out. I wanted to be a sniper. I'm a pretty good shot when I want to be. I like to shoot and I own forty guns, including M16s. Guns stand for freedom. That's how our country was born."[57] He had come to the convention looking for a "civilian private army" to join.

All of these tensions about who is a warrior and who isn't are inherent in the *SOF* project, which both reclaims the warrior as the gender ideal for all men and opens up the boundaries of warriordom to include participation in war games, tourist vacations, and costume balls like the convention itself. Going to Las Vegas is after all the greatest adventure most SOFers will ever have, and for all the talk among conventioneers about "next year in Managua," or allusions to some other "real" adventure, everyone knew that it was more likely to be "next year in Las Vegas." This underlying sense of the severe limits to the convention experience, the tacit acknowledgment that what went on there wasn't real, fueled obsessive "wanna-be" worry. And the general youth of those in attendance—most were in their twenties and early thirties—compounded the tensions. Certainly young males were the group most anxious about their status as men. That they would deck themselves out in military insignia to which they were not entitled in order to make the ritual transition to warrior adulthood is not surprising.

Yet the fact that even the men who had military service of some kind or who were policemen or in the security business were so quick (and often anxious) to distinguish themselves from those whom they saw as lesser men points to a deeper problem at the core of the warrior ideal, namely: How much war does it take to make a warrior? For most men, there was no clear answer to this question. No matter where one stood in terms of combat experience, there was always someone who had seen more action, taken more risks, and killed more enemies.

From this perspective, any commitment to the warrior ideal carried with it an inevitable sense of lack or failure; every warrior was but a wanna-be in relation to someone else who was seen as more powerful and accomplished. When a conventioneer decried the kids who every night smacked each other with padded "pugil sticks" on a plank over the Sahara swimming pool, or when he rebuked a dandy in a gaudy uniform, he was, in part, trying to cast out his own insecurities. Still, these tensions did not destroy the convention. There were no fistfights, scuffles, or even heated arguments. The wanna-be problem was more like an atmospheric condition, a desert wind that charged the air and made everybody a bit on edge.

Whether deliberately or by just following a strong intuitive sense of the right thing to do, the *Soldier of Fortune* staff usually conjured up enough brotherhood to bridge the fissures among their followers. They were, after all, united in their struggles against Communists abroad and the liberal news media and politicians at home. *SOF* also stressed that everyone attending the convention shared a personal relation to the magazine. "Uncle Bob" was Robert K. Brown's nickname, and although most ordinary conventioneers spoke respectfully of Colonel Brown, it was not uncommon to hear Uncle Bob this, Uncle Bob that. Mario J. Calero, brother of Adolfo Calero (a leader of the FDN or Nicaraguan Democratic Resistance) and the contra seen most frequently at *SOF* affairs, was fond of calling himself "Uncle Bob's nephew." The *SOF* staff who ran the show were particularly adept at making everyone present feel that they were part of an extended family whose beloved tribal chief was Robert K. Brown.

The *Soldier of Fortune* convention was, then, a model of how to keep people enthralled by and permanently mobilized for war. Conventioneers were idealized as the vanguard of good Americans, men who would defend the traditional values of the Founding Fathers and the frontier creation myth. They were made to feel that they were members of an elite, privy to confidential information, alert to the machinations of the news media and liberals at home and of encroaching Communism and aliens from abroad, and charged with the responsibility of remaining perennially vigilant and ready for war against the evil ones at a moment's notice. Further, in providing an array of "militia" units to join, *SOF* channeled men of widely different financial resources and interests into real political activities, all the while providing entertainment and fellowship—and even religious transcendence.

On Saturday evening, the last night of the convention, the family gathered at 1830 hours for the annual *Soldier of Fortune* Sponsors' Banquet and Awards Presentation. The banquet followed more or less the same format every year. It was an outdoor affair, held on the huge roof of the Sahara Hotel parking garage to accommodate the hundreds who attended. An honor guard brought in the American flag for the Pledge of Allegiance, followed by a prayer honoring all who had fallen in past and present conflicts. In 1985 this included special mention of a man who had been killed in a parachuting accident at the school associated with the convention.

As dinner—a substantial buffet-style barbecue—was served, the awards ceremony began. Up on the speakers' podium sat a dozen men, representatives of various anti-Communist organizations. The cast didn't change much in the years I attended. Major General John W. Singlaub (U.S. Army, Retired) was often there. Mario J. Calero always made an appearance. And there was usually someone from Civilian Military Assistance (CMA), and someone from Afghanistan, and someone from Angola or Mozambique.

There was always a whole round of prizes, each organization affirming its ties to others by convoluted exchanges of introductions, walnut and bronze plaques, and acceptance speeches. Usually John Donovan—the demolitions expert who worked with Kokalis in fighting off the Communists out at the Desert Sportsman each year—introduced one of the prize winners, and he always said basically the same thing, "There's only one word that fits this man—warrior." Calero in his turn showed himself master of the five-minute acceptance speech as he pitched the cause of the FDN: "My brothers from

Afghanistan, Angola, and Mozambique . . . We are the dark horses, we are underdogs, but we will win . . . If you [the audience] don't help us today, you will be left alone, and we won't be there to help you tomorrow. America is the pot at the end of the rainbow. You are the target."[58] Calero received the CMA award in 1985, and his last words were "I'll return it to you guys and ladies next year in Managua."

After long affirmations of mutual respect and affection among the allies, the guest of honor spoke. Since 1983 this honor has gone to such men as General William Westmoreland, former commander of U.S. forces in Vietnam; G. Gordon Liddy, the Watergate burglar; and, in 1987, Dr. Lewis L. Tambs. Tambs had recently returned from Costa Rica as the Reagan administration's ambassador. He told the audience what they wanted to hear—that it was up to them to defeat the enemy: "The war in Vietnam was won four times on the River Mekong; it was lost on the River Potomac. We're still losing it on the River Potomac . . . San Antonio, Texas, is closer to Managua than to Washington, D.C., two hostile capitals . . . If you think the shootings on the L.A. freeways are terrible, just wait until we get the penetration agents with ten million refugees."[59]

Having worked up the crowd, *SOF* then moved on to an auction, the proceeds to be donated to the International Freedom Fighters Fund, an *SOF* offshoot similar to its more well-known El Salvador/ Nicaragua Defense Fund (ESNDF). Usually the prices were fixed— $10 for a signed poster of Brown standing in El Salvador ("Communism Stops Here!"), $100 to become an ESNDF Honorary Commando, or $500 to become an Honorary Colonel. But in 1987 the free market held sway.

A professional auctioneer and stand-up comedian helped move things along. He held up a flag from Surinam and said, "You can either hang it in your bathroom or use it." A Soviet 120mm mortar-round box captured in Afghanistan was said to be "a nice sandbox for your cat," while a Soviet gas mask was suitable for "wearing to the bathroom." A Chinese Communist Army cap had no special history, but was merely "just your garden variety commie pinko fag hat." Anything associated with the enemy had excremental overtones, even if, like a Sandinista uniform donated by CMA, it had been cleaned because "it was necessary to do that."

In contrast, several oil paintings and lithographs presented for sale took on a completely different aura. All of them were representations of the "Lady Ellen," a Vietnam war-surplus Huey helicopter bought by Mary Ellen Garwood of Austin, Texas, to send to the Nicaraguan contras. This helicopter had been featured in a film earlier in the week; according to the film, it was not a gunship, but the only medical evacuation helicopter available to the contras. While poster girls were typically naked, and Brown called all Washington politicians "whores," the Lady Ellen was a very different kind of woman; she was the good woman—just like Theweleit's "white nurse" serving the *Freikorps*.

Bidding on the first painting quickly reached $1,250, and in an inspiring moment, the buyer donated it back to be auctioned again; this time it sold for $750. The repentant conscientious objector turned SOFer bid $600 for another rendition, but lost. He didn't look unhappy, though; part of the magic of a charity auction is that it turns competition into cooperation for a common goal. Besides, he eventually did manage to acquire an oil version of Lady Ellen for $300, and was told to be careful, the oil was still damp. Vintage was not important; no one, possibly even himself, could ever again doubt his loyalty to the cause.

When all the prizes had been auctioned off, one last man came up to the podium to present an odd-looking gift to the Freedom Fighters Fund: a five-gallon water-cooler jug filled with cash and coins. He then pulled a prosthesis off his leg and held it high over his head so audience members could see it. He said that he collected the money during the convention by charging people five dollars to drink beer from his prosthesis. "Tet 1968! That's what it's all about!" he cried. In an unconscious repetition of the Christian Eucharist, the community of warriors had "eaten" his sacrificed leg and been renewed and strengthened in their primeval struggle against the evil ones. The banquet so ended; everyone rose and sang "God Bless America."

9

BECOMING THE ARMED MAN:

COMBAT PISTOL SHOOTING

AT GUNSITE RANCH

For all the glamour and comradeship found at the *Soldier of Fortune* conventions, going there was not the same thing as becoming a real warrior. To become a real warrior involved many things, but learning how to master combat weapons was absolutely essential—all who participated in paramilitary culture beyond a casual level agreed upon that. And while many were content to bang away at tin cans with pistols and semiautomatic rifles, others thought this amateurish approach was inadequate. They wanted professional training, but without having to become a soldier or police officer. During the 1970s and 1980s about five combat shooting schools open to civilians established national and international reputations. To attend one of these schools and earn a high grade for marksmanship was a source of great prestige in paramilitary culture. A man with such credentials would never be mistaken for a wanna-be.

Among the top five, one was preeminent: Jeff Cooper's American Pistol Institute (API) of Pauldin, Arizona. Cooper was internationally famous for developing combat shooting techniques. A former lieutenant colonel in the U.S. Marines who fought in both World War II and Korea, Cooper had spent most of his life preparing men for face-to-face armed confrontations. The universally used two-handed pistol grip that replaced the older one-handed position and cowboy fire-from-the-hip method had been developed by Jack Weaver in 1970 at Cooper's first shooting range in Big Bear, California. In the early 1970s Cooper founded the International Practical Shooting Confederation (IPSC), an organization of pistol clubs responsible for organizing "combat" style shooting matches featuring fast-draw firing against human silhouettes. The .45 semiautomatic craze that swept paramilitary culture in the 1970s and 1980s had its origin in his insistence that this weapon, once properly modified, was superior to any revolver or other semiautomatic. And Cooper was among the most intellectual of all the writers who published in gun magazines; a Stanford University honors graduate with a masters in history from the University of California, he wrote books, essays, and a two-page column of political and social commentary for *Guns and Ammo*, a mainstream gun magazine that reached over a half million men each month. He also served on the National Rifle Association board of directors.

In 1975 Cooper sold his Big Bear property and moved to the northwest Arizona high country near Prescott. There he founded API, better known as Gunsite Ranch—the first of the major-league schools. The ranch doesn't have any cattle, but it has nine pistol, six rifle, and six shotgun ranges scattered through its 853 acres. By 1992 over 9,000 would-be gunfighters had attended one or more of Cooper's combat-shooting courses for pistol, police shotgun, battle carbine (AR-15, Mini-14, or AK47 type semiautomatics), submachine gun, or long-range rifle training.

Part of API's mystique came from the mix of students who attended. It wasn't just civilians who enrolled in its courses. Men and women from local and state police units either paid their own way or were paid for by their employers. Federal agencies and military special

172 \ WARRIOR DREAMS

operations units also sent their employees to Gunsite to pick up new techniques and gain accreditation that would help enhance the prestige of both individual and agency.

Gunsite also had a unique reputation for making its students feel like they were part of something important. At one *SOF* convention a contestant in the combat shooting matches explained that he had first begun practicing with handguns because of an interest in self-defense. Then he went to Gunsite. When the man mentioned API his voice took on that soft, resonant tone people use when they are most earnest; the school was clearly one of the peak experiences of his life. He'd left feeling so close to his classmates, he said; all API graduates were "like family" to each other. To participate in the *SOF* matches was a way to sustain the excitement of shooting and to have a reunion with the people he had met at API. He had found the experience of combat shooting so spiritually uplifting that he too had become an instructor and now, in his leisure time, taught Ohio police how to shoot better. The man's business card even listed the API courses he had attended and the grade he had received in each one.

Clearly any study of paramilitary culture required investigation of this special place, for people who attended Gunsite seemed to experience some kind of personal transcendence. What was the thrill of mock-combat shooting? How did API create the "real" warrior identity in its students? It did not seem wise to approach Jeff Cooper directly since Cooper thinks that the great domestic enemies facing America are the CLAMs, an acronym for "Congressional Left, Academics, Media." Consequently, in the summer of 1988 I purchased a 9mm semiautomatic and applied for admission to API as an ordinary student. I enrolled in API's week-long, basic combat pistol course; all students were required to take this course before being considered for admission to more advanced classes. The prospect of going to Gunsite was intimidating, but I had owned guns as a teenager and was not a complete stranger to the firing line. In sociological terms, I had decided the only appropriate method of study was to "become the phenomenon." Like many other men, I would learn to shoot my way into warriordom.

———

Gunsite Ranch is at the end of a dirt road, eight miles from the state highway that runs from Prescott to Flagstaff. It is an impressive facility. The main compound consists of several buildings, including the Cooper home, called Sconce (an archaic word meaning a small fortress), a gunsmithy, and offices and barns named after the New Testament gospels—Matthew, Luke, Mark, and John (the latrine). Most of the buildings are decorated with a stylized black raven—the Gunsite Ranch logo and one of Cooper's totemic symbols. As his pamphlet, *Quoth the Raven*, explains, *"Odin*, the German *Wotan*, was the all-father of Norse mythology, and his familiars were the two ravens Jugin and Munin, who brought him news of both earth and heaven. Thus the raven may be termed *Wotansvogel*—God's bird."[1]

School began at 8:00 on Monday morning in a one-room cinder-block classroom with a galvanized steel roof. There was a front door for the students to use on their way to their assigned seats at long wooden tables, and a teacher's door at the side leading directly to the front of the class. A red school bell hung over the teacher's door. The building's official name, Revelation, was painted on the black raven logo outside; inside was a shrine to Cooper's life, four walls filled with plaques and awards from the West German Army, the South African Air Force, assorted U.S. military units, and scores of American police and sheriffs' departments. And then there were the epigrams:

> He shot at me, and missed. I shot back and did not. Neither of these acts was altogether unexpected, but both were—from my viewpoint—eminently satisfactory.
>
> —The Guru

The chatter among the forty-three students died down when Jeff Cooper rang the red school bell and walked in wearing a .45 automatic, his wrist dangling right over the handle. Even though he was now in his seventies he still looked tough. It was as if John Wayne had a twin brother, except this one was the real thing. He was a big man, broad-shouldered and well over six feet tall. His sharp, clear eyes searched the room carefully, judging whether the men and women in the class were strong enough to defeat "The Four Horsemen of the Aquarian Apocalypse—Vulgarity, Stupidity, Ignorance, Cowardice"—and instead make the dream on the wall come true:

A REACTIONARY MANIFESTO
LET US PUT:

Women back on a pedestal
Sex back in the bedroom
Obscenity back in the outhouse
Perversion back in the closet
Murderers back on the gallows
Education back in the schools
Gold back in the money
America back on top

Cooper paced back and forth, pointing to different individuals as he barked out: "You will never be surprised. You are in charge. You are in command of your weapon, your situation, your head. You follow what your instructors have to teach you here at Gunsite and you will finish this week stronger, safer, and more serene. You will have the ability to stay alive in a deadly confrontation. As General George Patton used to say, 'Courage is the product of competence and habit.' Competence and habit is what we teach here." He was preaching what he called a "philosophy of violence." Each man was morally obligated to defend himself, his family, and the larger society against criminal attack. And he was morally charged to repel any assault with all the force he could muster. Acceptance of that philosophy, together with mastery of the "martial art" of pistol shooting, would transform the students into men of courage, *armed men*.

The first objective was to make the pistol become part of the body—a comfortable part. "Many people have died because their gunbelts weren't comfortable," Cooper warned the class. A thick leather gun belt over two inches wide (threaded directly through the belt loops on the pants, not worn over them like cowboy or police gun belts), was to be put on in the morning and kept on until bedtime. The type of holster Cooper told his students to buy in his letters of acceptance was made by only three custom holster makers. It was not the full leather case used by police, but a small strip of leather called a "slide" that kept the pistol in place on the belt, but did not cover the barrel and so create unnecessary friction that would hinder a fast draw. "A pistol is only good if you can touch it," Cooper kept repeating. "A pistol not loaded is a waste. She doesn't shoot well with nothing in the chamber." It's legal to pack a side arm in Arizona as long as it's in plain view. Students could go everywhere armed if they so desired, and were explicitly told to arrive at the school each morning with their hardware loaded, in the holster, and ready to go.

At the end of this lecture, Cooper split the class into two gun-range sections, one with twenty-two students, the other with twenty-one. All those armed with Colt 1911-model .45 semiautomatics went to one range; everyone who had brought some other type of pistol went to another. Each range section had a mix of people from different occupational backgrounds. Over half of the forty-three students were from the military, federal agencies, or police forces. The U.S. Marine Corps had sent eight members of their new "security" or urban warfare battalions, units created to recapture buildings held by terrorists. They were to become the pistol instructors for the rest of the men in their battalions. Two other Marines, a team of machine gunners assigned to the elite Force Recon unit, were also there. (The Marines all carried .45s and so were all placed in the same range section).

The Department of Energy had sent three plainclothes security agents and weapons instructors to the class, men who guarded nuclear weapons and other radioactive materials as they were shipped across the United States in unmarked titanium-armored trucks. The Los Angeles Police Department was represented by a married couple. The woman (one of three in the class) was a member of their gang surveillance unit; he, a narcotics squad detective.

There were also plenty of civilians who had willingly paid $600 in tuition and $2,000 more for a state-of-the-art .45 or 9mm, a thousand rounds of ammunition, custom holster, transportation, and living expenses. A college student had come down from New York City to round out his education for his future career as a private detective. There were two physicians, one who practiced internal medicine in Cleveland, had spent years in an Army Reserve unit, and wanted finally to master the .45. The second, a cardiologist from Pasadena, California, had brought his son, a longhaired music student at UC San Diego, for a week of father-son bonding. Another man had just retired after thirty years as an elementary school teacher and librarian in Wyoming; he was thinking about starting a new career as a gun dealer and wanted the best instruction available before opening shop in his garage.

All of the civilians were white (the Marines had sent three blacks and a Latino, the only non-Anglos attending), educated, middle-class men between thirty-five and fifty-six. Not one was a survivalist who lived up in the hills in an arms-laden hideout. Some of the men had some shooting experience on target ranges. A few competed regularly in IPSC combat matches. All said they read *Soldier of Fortune* from time to time and everyone appeared to be politically conservative. Everyone was excited about training with the soldiers, federal agents, and police: this was the real thing. And although no one came right out and said, "I want to become more powerful through learning to kill," that was the unspoken subtext. When people smiled at each other, the exchange was only partly about common courtesy and the joy of sharing an adventure together far from the normal workaday world. It was also mutual recognition, an acknowledgment that when push came to shove, the people here were ready to go the distance. At Gunsite, the wimps and cowards of the world had been left behind, and that knowledge made the students feel good about each other.

Cooper lectured for an hour each morning and another hour after lunch on his philosophy of violence. Actual range instruction—about four hours twice a day—was conducted by a rotating cadre of the nation's top small-arms instructors. For example, Ed Stock, the range master of my class, was a DEA agent and a reserve officer in the U.S. Army Special Forces. He was teaching at Gunsite on his vacation time. He had two assistants, high-level shooters in their own right: one was normally in charge of construction at Gunsite; the other worked full-time for Arizona Power and Light and had this as a second job. Their responsibility, as they put it, was to "mold your bodies to fit the theory"—that is, to transform their students into well-honed weapons by correcting and perfecting each individual movement involved in drawing, aiming, and firing. Through intensive drills, these actions would become "conditioned reflexes" or "semiprogrammed responses"; the student would in time make the correct movements automatically and become progressively faster and more accurate.

Every firing technique at API was taught by the numbers. On the count of one, the right hand grabbed the pistol and the left hand moved in front of the body at waist level. On two, the gun was pulled straight up out of the holster and the gun hand moved toward the left hand positioned in front of the body. On three, the left hand grabbed the gun hand as it pushed forward to form a two-handed brace and the weapon was snapped up to eye level. On four, the shooter aligned the front sight on the target—this last step was Gunsite's major dictum: look at the front sight. Once on target, he pulled the trigger with a "squeeze press" that went off in what the instructors called a quick "surprise break." Every draw ended with two shots.

Half a range section, ten or eleven students, approached the firing line together, each facing a camouflaged human silhouette a few yards away. When the range master blew his whistle, the exercise began. The draw-and-fire sequence became rhythmic: one, two, three, four, boom! boom!; one, two, three, four, boom! boom! After three drills had been completed, Ed Stock yelled out, "Everybody in the leather! [Holster your guns.] Go forward and read your targets!" Over and over, for four hours every morning and four hours every afternoon, the beat went on. Everyone wore ear plugs to prevent damage to the ears. But the blasts were felt in the body, like shock waves rolling along.

The tempo never let up; every day the speed of the "killing stroke" (as the technique was called) got faster and faster. Each new session presupposed mastery of the preceding exercise. Sometimes the class moved in close to the target, to three or five yards, and fired so fast that the two shots merged into one. Other times the shooters pulled back to twenty yards and fired while kneeling or prone.

To compensate for the tunnel vision that shooters often develop from concentrating so intensely, the instructors taught the class to move their heads from left to right before putting their pistols back in their holsters. Failure to do so brought quick reprimands, but few people needed reminding to make these checks. The tunnel vision was so pronounced it was frightening; most students readily absorbed the lesson and began checking the men to the left and right of them.

After hundreds of draw-and-fire sequences, new drills began in which the class stood sideways to the targets. Students took a few steps, drew their guns, turned, and fired 90 degrees to the line of march. Later the class learned how to do a complete 180 degrees and so never get caught with backs to an adversary. Speed-reloading drills as methodical as the draw-and-fire sequences were taught so that gunmen could quickly "rejoin the war" after a fire fight.

By late Tuesday afternoon, the fourth training session, my normal experience of space and time—basic physical reality—had started to fade. Ed, the range master, announced that he was speeding up the draw-and-fire sequences. He stared deep into my eyes and said, "Buddy, the only two shots that count all week are the next two." This was one of his favorite expressions, his way of telling you to concentrate so hard that nothing else mattered.

I wanted to do well, to find out what the "inner experience" of combat shooting was all about, so I let go. I emptied my mind of everything from the outside world. All I could see was Gunsite, then all I could see was the range. Finally, all that was left was the target and the front sight of my weapon. It felt as though my face was only a couple of feet from the target. During the time it took to fire those two shots and wait for the closing whistle to blow (1.5 seconds after the command to draw) I felt like I was suspended in another dimension.

Indeed, that's exactly what was happening. The instructors at Gunsite were highly competent teachers who knew what they were doing. They were leading at least part of the class into what some athletes call "the zone," a state of altered sensory perception in which time is experienced as moving very slowly while eye-hand coordination dramatically increases. In recent years, a fair number of stories about the zone have surfaced. For example, baseball player Ted Williams has said that he could sometimes see the seams on a pitched ball headed toward him at over sixty miles an hour.[2] Chuck Yeager, the test pilot, has written of how time slowed down as he moved to escape a plane spiraling out of control.[3]

Psychologist Mihaly Csikszentmihalyi includes this phenomenon in his larger category of "flow experiences," those occasions when "self-consciousness is eliminated. Action and awareness are tightly and reflexively intertwined, merging together."[4] Said another way, the mind-body separation dissolves. Flow-experiences occur most often when the skills people possess match the challenges they face. Sociologist and mountain climber Richard Mitchell comments, "Flow emerges in circumstances which are perceived as both problematic and soluble."[5]

At Gunsite, the teachers encouraged students to have a heightened relationship to the most ordinary of exercises. Each drill came to feel like an imaginary gunfight—a life-and-death confrontation. In this problematic circumstance, killing the opponent was the solution; it created a unity between mind and body that was highly rewarding. By the end of the second day the instructors had "spun" part of the class far away from their usual perceptions. The firing range had become what anthropologist Victor Turner calls a "liminal" reality, a time and place in which the initiates of a ritual process have left their old selves behind, but have not yet graduated into a different identity and a new sense of the world.[6]

In this particular liminal space, the student initiates had a flow experience centered on killing. And like many initiation rites, it involved great physical pain: pain in the face from the hot sun, pain in the feet and legs from spending all day standing up, pain in the arms and shoulders from holding the pistol in that tight "Weaver position" two-handed brace, and, most of all, pain and swelling in the hands from gripping and regripping the automatic pistols hundreds of times. Many shooters also suffered from the recoil action of their .45's—one of the flaws in its 1911 design was that when the hammer kicked back, it often "bit" into the web of the hand, creating what in the trade is called "chopped meat." Some people bled almost every time they pulled the trigger. Taped hands became both war paint and battle scars at Gunsite.

By midweek the mental and physical pressures began to divide each range section. A few students seemed to thrive on the daily intensity and heat and pain, and went back to their hotels each night hungry for more. The biggest Marine, a man with a shaved head nicknamed Rambo by one range instructor, thought the school was the high point of his life. "It's all coming together for me. Everything I've ever done is coming together," he'd say every evening.

Other men were completely overwhelmed; the bang and kick of every round of gunfire seemed to push them down. Learning each new step in the gunfighter dance required far more coordination then they could summon, and they began to fall behind. The retired librarian started standing off by himself when not on the shooting line. He was shooting very poorly and had just about given up. All he could do was complain about how the long trigger pull on his brand-new $700 gun threw off his aim. Although the instructors were exceptionally friendly and patient with their students, they had limits. API preached an ethic of individual responsibility about guns called the "big boy" rule: "You're a big boy now. You bought that gun. You live with it."

The Pasadena doctor's body was so sore he could barely move. "I'm coming apart!" he cried at the end of a tough day. The would-be detective had great difficulty mastering the tightly controlled draw-and-fire sequence. He often jumped into the air when he drew his gun. "What's the matter with that man? He's doing it all wrong!" Cooper screamed one day when he showed up at the range (his wrist still dangling right over his .45). The critique didn't help the man calm down.

Even those who were doing pretty well showed signs of stress, and most people were physically exhausted at the end of each day. No one—not even the police or Department of Energy agents or the Marines—seemed to have anticipated how fast the pace of instruction would be, or how frightening the imaginary gunfights. Nothing seemed ordinary anymore. One man got so used to wearing his pistol all day at Gunsite that he forgot to take it off while entering a filling station minimarket and scared everyone to death. He was both embarrassed and worried that he could have provoked an incident.

Still, social life picked up by the middle of the week. Opening gambits in conversations often involved a glance at the other man's hardware: "Hey, how you like that Glock?" All of the federal agents, policemen, and policewomen soon found each other and began trading war stories about gunfights they'd been in or heard about. The L.A.

narcotics squad detective linked up with the head Department of Energy instructor when he learned that the DOE man had previously served in the Los Angeles Sheriff's Department. Both had been on duty in 1971 during an East Los Angeles antiwar protest. That day a *Los Angeles Times* reporter named Ruben Salazar was killed when officers fired a tear gas canister into the bar where he was having a drink. They joked endlessly about "The Ruben Salazar Memorial Tear Gas Round." The fate of Brian Willson, an antiwar protester who in the spring of 1988 had his legs amputated by a train carrying munitions at the Naval Weapons Station in Concord, California, became another object of amusement. "Poor Brian, he just couldn't get out of the way of a choo-choo," a Washington State policeman laughed. He had previously worked at the Concord station, and wore a logo cap every day reminding everyone of that fact, along with T-shirts sporting slogans like "The Ollie North Savings and Loan, Zurich, Switzerland."

On the lighter side, there was a little flirting. One Fresno policewoman, a rookie fresh from the academy, showed up Monday morning wearing a long-sleeved baseball shirt with "What part of 'no' don't you understand?" written on both front and back. By Wednesday she had changed to a clinging turquoise tank-top and hip-hugging black fatigue pants. The daughter of an Army Special Forces sergeant, she had shifted range sections to be with the Marines. The Marines loved to tease her and she relished their attention.

The Marines themselves were a mixed lot. Only Rambo seemed really fired up about Gunsite. Most were from poor families, and joining the service had been a way of getting out of a dead-end situation—either poverty, or a boring small town, or, in at least one instance, a jail sentence. They had stumbled into the urban warfare battalions because service in the unit offered them a pay raise. Few seemed to grasp how dangerous their assignment of "clearing" terrorists from buildings would be. The trip to Arizona was just a way to get away from the day-to-day grind in the Corps and an opportunity to meet people who weren't in the service. The two Force Recon Marines were decidedly unhappy. During their enlistments they had spent months away from home, and relationships with their girlfriends and families had been grievously strained. To make matters worse, since they were temporarily detached from their unit out in the Persian Gulf, their jump-pay and scuba-pay had been taken away. They felt the Corps didn't care about them at all.

The older men—and in the gunfighting world this meant forty to fifty—talked endlessly about pensions and what they would do when they retired. They'd all joined the Army or Marines when they were teenagers and had become federal agents or local police in part because their military-service time counted toward retirement. "For a man without a four-year degree, you just can't beat police work. Just make sure that you join a department with good benefits," one of the aging, forty-something Department of Energy men advised the young Marines.

Wednesday afternoon, the course shifted. "You people are in better command of your sidearms now than those who carry a pistol for a living," Cooper told the class. We had "refined our killing stroke" and it was now time to start thinking about how to respond in a real-life gunfight. In his pamphlet, *Principles of Personal Defense* (edited and published by *SOF*'s Robert K. Brown and Peter C. Lund of Paladin Press), Cooper had written that "anyone who is aware of his environment knows that the peril of physical assault does exist, and that it exists everywhere and at all times."[7] Students should expect that roughly one percent of the able-bodied male population are potentially violent.

"Why will people blow it when in a shootout?" he asked. "We live in an age of imitation adventure, so that when the flag goes up there's a fatal tendency to say, 'This isn't happening to me. This can't be real. Change the channel.' I want you to take a *vow*. Make a decision like at a revival meeting. Make a commitment in your everyday religious practice. I want you to be prepared for it [a lethal confrontation]. Say to yourself, 'I know it can come to me, and when it does, I will not be surprised. It can be today. I knew this was going to happen and I know what to do. I don't feel any excitement. I don't feel any pressure. If it happens to me, I am in command.' "

Once this religious principle had been accepted and internalized, the second task was to summon the psychological energy necessary to fight to the death. "Anger and fear are similar," Cooper emphasized.

"You need to flip a switch to transform your fear into rage. You should be angry at your adversary. After all, by attacking you he deserves no consideration." Of all the stories he told, the tales of summoning this spirit clearly moved Cooper the most.

He talked about a man he'd taught in Guatemala (Cooper teaches wealthy men and women throughout Mexico, Central America, and Latin America as part of his contribution to the war against Communism, what he calls World War III). This man was kidnapped in an urban parking structure by several men armed with submachine guns. He conjured up the spirit of righteous anger and took one of the submachine guns away from his kidnappers! Then, before they could react, he blasted a clip into three of them and escaped. "The attitude," Cooper whispered. "I admire the man's attitude."

To help summon the psychological will necessary to fight, Cooper taught us a battle code based on four colors. Condition White was the state of being relaxed and inattentive to the environment. The chances of surviving an attack while in Condition White were very small. Condition Yellow meant "relaxed alertness," the recognition that "this day, this time, I may have to use my weapon for blood," even though no specific potential threat had been identified. Condition Orange meant that a potential threat had been located, that someone was behaving very suspiciously. And last, in Condition Red, "you know you have a target. It's a fight." By moving quickly to get the drop on the bad guy, Cooper advised, "you can turn off the creeps of the world three times out of four."

Yet despite the power of Cooper's convictions, discussions of how best to conjure up rage and debates over whether one could really beat the reaction time of a terrorist armed with a machine gun faded late that afternoon. It rained and a beautiful rainbow arched across the sky. The rain dampened the dusty mesa and the air smelled fresh and sweet. Ed Stock, the range master, looked out at the beautiful Arizona desert and sighed, "At moments like this all I want is a baloney sandwich, a jug of wine, and a cheap woman." He laughed and winked—Ed was married and his entire salary for the week at Gunsite was going to buy new dining room furniture.

Then he got more serious. Ed spoke about how much he liked Gunsite. It was the only place on earth where the $25,000-a-year lumberjack from Oregon and the $250,000-a-year doctor from Texas could be buddies for a week and have something to say to each other. That kind of social transcendence was very important to him. He reminisced about the time the Navy SEALs were there to train, and how when it had rained, they decided to keep on shooting no matter how wet they got. Everyone else wanted to be like the SEALs, and they all got wet and muddy and what fun and friendship there had been that day.

As the rain ended, Ed asked, "Club Med, Pauldin! Is everybody having a good time? It's important to have a good time!" Of course we were. Where else could you learn to shoot from a man who had trapped drug dealers in the Philippines and Thailand for the DEA and now served as a reserve officer in a U.S. Army Special Forces intelligence unit, and was such a good guy to boot? He was a mentor beyond anyone's wildest dreams and this was a grand adventure.

On Thursday morning the training moved us closer to actual violence. From now on shooting exercises would take place in "simulators": narrow, craggy ravines filled with metal humanoid targets called "poppers" and houses stocked with human figures painted on plywood. No longer would the group stay together to share the rhythms of the firing line. Each student walked into a simulator accompanied only by a range officer.

My first "popper" looked like one of the Empire's troopers from *Star Wars*. It was a terrible shock. I'd spent three days on the firing line for *this*? Cooper's story of how a Vietnam veteran had once shouted "I'm not going in there!" and quit the course sounded like a tall tale. How could anyone be afraid of this ramshackle fantasy world?

My assigned range officer shouted at me, "Make ready!" "Make ready" was the command to make sure your weapon was loaded and your spare magazines of ammunition were in position on your belt. I did as I was told and walked into the ravine, with my 9mm drawn and ready to fire. I turned the corner and there he was! Boom! Boom! He went down and I walked on, breathing faster. Another. Boom! Boom! Another. Another. After a few more targets I was so nervous I fumbled a simple change of magazines. And then my range officer called out, "Bill, to your right!" I pivoted and there were three of them right there! Three I hadn't seen! *Three who could have killed me!*

Still shaking from the near-disaster, I moved inside the cinder-block "Fun House." All of the human targets were huge, with hideous ferocious faces (except for the few "hostage" targets, whom we were forbidden to shoot, of course). And they kept coming toward me! It was dark inside, and my fire echoed loudly off the walls, heightening the illusion that I was under attack. I knew the figures were not really moving, but stunned and frightened, I saw otherwise. I shot fast to keep them from reaching me. Boom! Boom! Boom! And then there were the corners to round and horrible, closed doorways that had to be opened and entered. I felt like I was living out a childhood nightmare in which I was a naked little boy, afraid and vulnerable, and *they* were waiting to kill me.

Back at the Revelation schoolroom that afternoon, shooters from both classes desperately sought consolation. "I blew it, I blew it," one of the policemen from Washington state cried. "I couldn't get it together. I kept missing."

"Bill, did you shoot the hostages?" one of the Marines asked me, terribly upset. "What about that guy with a knife wearing a motorcycle helmet? Did you shoot him? In the Marines we're taught to clear everything in the building." No one wanted to think he was the only one who had failed. And since so many students had a horrible time in the houses, there was plenty of embarrassment to go around. Still, the inability to meet this new challenge left almost everyone depressed. The sense of progressive mastery that had built over the previous days' instruction was shattered. The group as a whole was in deep crisis.

The range officers told the class the bad news in more systematic detail: we had all been too noisy; many of us had crossed our legs while moving (a violation—crossed legs can trip a person); some shooters had not looked at the front sights of their pistols (among the most serious of violations), but had instead looked over their guns at the target and fired. Worst of all, two-thirds of the shooters carrying Colt 1911-model .45s had shot their pistols dry and run out of ammunition *without knowing it*. Some had started missing and emptied their guns in panic, while others simply lost track of their shots under the pressure. Students had been operating under the Gunsite "Two Hits Per Gook" (THPG) rule. Every enemy was a "gook," and firing two shots into the chest assured that the gook in question would be stopped. In exceptionally threatening situations, gunfighters were advised to shift to the "Mozambique" variation of THPG—two in the chest and one in the head. Some students shifted to the three-shot rule in the darkness of the Fun House, thus increasing their rate of fire. But that was still no excuse. The school solution was to change clips whenever there was a lull in a gunfight, long before the pistol was empty. To run out of ammo while firing meant that the shooter was not in control of himself or of the situation. To run out of ammo in a firefight was fatal.

Having broken the class's confidence, Jeff Cooper and the range officers then built the students back up again. The range officer man in charge of the students with .45s got up and started teasing, "You're forbidden to watch *Miami Vice* for thirty days. Don't try to go faster than Crockett and Tubbs!" Cooper pursued the same line. He unloaded his gun and pulled it up close to his face. "Don't do this. This is a *Starsky and Hutch*-style movie frame so the camera can get the pistol and the face in the same shot. You can shoot yourself in the head. Keep your weapon out front, ready to snap onto target. And don't stand in the doorway like they do. Move through the door quickly."

As I sat there in the Revelation building I began to understand more thoroughly what was happening to the class. At Gunsite we were so deep inside the war romance that the movie heroes just looked like lightweights. Crockett and Tubbs and Starsky and Hutch and all the other war-western-detective movie gunmen were incompetent pretty boys. Crockett never knew when he was running low on ammo; he always shot his gun dry in a firefight before reloading. He was a loser. *We* were the real heroes. *We* knew how to really do it. *We* had the right stuff, not them. If we remembered to do things the Gunsite way, then *we* would become the true warriors.

A much older cultural process was going on as well. Gunsite was taking men through an initiation. The dark, horrifying journey through the Fun House and the ravines was an essential phase of that initiation, what Mircea Eliade calls the "passage through a *vagina dentata,* or the dangerous descent into a cave or crevice assimilated to the mouth or uterus of Mother Earth."[8] It was not by chance that I regressed into a naked little boy. The severe initiatory ordeals that usually precede symbolic rebirth are intended to promote fear and cause regression. In this state, the initiate surrenders his resistance to the tribal elders; their authority is confirmed by the rite: *Since the masters survived this same ordeal in the past, they must know what to do.* The initiate finally realizes that he must absorb their instructions in order to summon up the force necessary to defeat the remaining monsters and safely pass through the dark tunnel.

Thursday afternoon, then, the Gunsite elders reviewed all they had taught us about the martial art of pistol shooting and the mindset necessary to conjure up the power of righteous anger. Never had the class been so quiet, so attentive. We relearned, at a deeper level, everything that had been taught us earlier in the week. We were told to return to our hotel rooms and to spend that evening practicing the gunfighter motions of draw, aim, and fire over and over. "Dry-firing" without bullets was an old homework assignment. This time, though, much more was at stake. Hopefully, tomorrow morning, the conditioned reflexes would finally take hold in a more visceral, automatic way. Tomorrow, we would walk out of the ravines and dark cave-like houses alive, as victors, or else face the humiliation of failure, and the knowledge that failure meant loss of manhood and death.

Friday morning I stepped calmly into another creek bed, checked my gun and magazines, and waited for the shoot-out to begin. As I sucked that desert air deep into my lungs, the conditioned reflexes Gunsite had programmed into me during the week finally took over, flipping switches I didn't even know existed. Cooper's philosophy of violence had become part of me. Political ideas, shooting techniques, and flesh united to form a cold killing machine. It felt like massive whirls of energy came up from the ground, ran up my legs, raced through my torso, and grabbed my shoulders. It felt like the energy roared down my arms until it formed a tunnel that extended out to wherever I aimed my weapon.

The target had become everything. In the outdoor simulator I used the Cooper technique of scanning a narrow arc from close range to the horizon and started picking off the targets at a distance. "Don't shoot now. We can get closer," my instructor advised. "No, I can get him," I replied. I didn't want to wait. And I continued to take them, one after the other, each kill increasing the intensity of the experience. Sometimes the steel targets wouldn't fall down fast enough; I shot and I shot and I shot. "He's dead!" my range officer cried at one point.

Never had I reloaded magazines with more satisfaction than I did in that thirty-minute break between ending the outdoor run and entering the indoor simulator—the click, click, click of cartridges sliding into the magazine sounded really good. I was high on adrenaline. I was going to shoot the shit out of every jerk in a new house full of enemies, this one called the Play House. The first target was the one the Marine had agonized over, the guy wearing a motorcycle helmet and holding a knife. I remember thinking that anyone dumb enough to pull a knife on a man with a gun deserved to die. I shot him twice and moved on into the shadows. This time, the doors and corners were places for me to hide and decide when I would attack and where I would move next. Let *them* wait in fear, knowing that they were going to die. Today I was ready for them.

Soon the narrow hallways and small bedrooms gave way to a big open living room with a closet formed by an enclosed stairwell. I couldn't see anyone so I went for the closet door. There was a man inside with a revolver pointed at a woman's head! I "hammered" him (two shots fired in extremely fast succession) and then spun around, worried that my back had been vulnerable. Suddenly a target unhinged from the ceiling and dropped down in a long swinging arc. I didn't even wait for it to complete the first swing before firing another hammer. I knew I'd hit. I kept on hunting for more bad guys.

I was hungry for the unseen adversaries. I knew they were out there. I wanted to kill them. I wanted revenge for all the fear they'd caused me the day before. I wanted the thrill of a gunfight I knew I would win. I wanted to hear Boom! Boom! and to see my bullets go dead through the heart.

I kept moving through the large open room, scanning intensely for the smallest sign of a target. I knew they were out there. Where were they? *Where were they?*

The range officer with me that morning in the Play House started screaming at me. "Game over! Game over!"

No, no, no, I thought. It can't be over now!

"Game over! No more targets!"

I finally stopped. I was furious the hunt was over. Then it hit me—the week of intense training had created conditioned reflexes and an adrenaline rush strong enough to break through all the inhibitions that normally keep aggression under control. As a result, I'd loved the power of destruction. I'd loved the sensory distortions of time. I'd loved the adrenaline rush and that feeling of being so close to death, the "you're dead and I'm not" unspoken dialogue between shooter and target. I'd loved the way my mind and body worked together, remembering moves without consciously trying, dancing in one seamless flow. I had become the *armed man*—a reborn warrior.

The combat drills ended Friday afternoon. The next morning, even after a good night's sleep, we were all still high from Friday's mock combat. But gradually the rush subsided and it was easier to gain perspective on what had happened in the past week. The knowledge that in one important way we had become "real" warriors gave Gunsite's successful students a deep satisfaction beyond the excitement found on the range. In a world where most men have no real power or control over their lives, mastering a weapon is a kind of grand "compensation" prize: *I'm not rich. I'm not politically powerful. The news media doesn't call me up and ask me what I think about things. I don't have scores of beautiful women after me. But by God I can kill anything that moves within 35 yards of me and have a good time doing it. I have that much power, anyway. I may never use it, but I know I've got the power if anyone ever tries to mess with me.*

Moreover, this shared experience of newfound power created strong bonds among us; there had certainly been competition at the school, but there had been support, too. Everyone got a round of applause when he did well in an exercise, particularly underdogs like the would-be detective, who began to shoot well after a rocky start. People did not necessarily become good friends, but there was much mutual respect. Only those men who gave up were excluded from this comradeship.

The experience of Gunsite left a lasting imprint on the psyche as well. Indeed, although the high of combat shooting subsides after a while, it never quite vanishes. The memory of the shooting excitement is itself a pleasurable "buzz," and it can often be triggered by contact with New War culture. When the fantasy warriors attack with all their incredible rage, the shooter is instantaneously reminded of the moment when he, too, let go of all his constraints and attacked with full might. It's not a question of conscious recollection, a memory of shots fired a few days ago or a long time ago. The shooter is just there— *inside* the film or novel or magazine article. Put another way, the high that comes from mock-combat shooting helps men form a bridge from their lives to the imaginary worlds portrayed in the New War stories. John Wayne and his successors have undoubtedly seduced many boys and men who have never fired a real gun, but the shooting experience takes the seduction a step further, and makes the warrior identity a vital component of the self.

The Gunsite experience recapitulated the themes of New War mythology, but all the more forcefully for being "real." The power that grown men learned to express at Gunsite was at least in part the power of infantile rage. The constraints on aggression that the school taught shooters to overcome were old ones dating back to childhood. This regressive dynamic became clear in the very way power was experienced. The awful paradox of combat shooting was that the more powerful you got with a combat weapon, the more paranoid you became. At the very moment that men perceived that they could extend their boundaries to defeat enemies at five, ten, or twenty-five yards, those boundaries became extremely fragile.

Students could feel the power in their bodies as they learned to kill, but they also learned that an enemy was always out there, that "it" would come to them someday. Every moment of increasing physical and mental power was thus accompanied by increasing certainty that this power would be challenged in a lethal confrontation. That Jeff Cooper walked his own kingdom at Gunsite Ranch every day with his wrist frozen permanently over his 1911A1 .45 as if in anticipation of a gunfight was significant. Even in a private realm where everyone paid homage to him as the reigning deity of all paramilitary culture he projected an anxious need for self-protection.

Death stalked the warrior and it was never certain who would win. No matter how much one improved each day at gunfighter school, the escalating standards made each shooting exercise more and more difficult. The look of deep, brooding worry that appeared on nearly everyone's face after missing the target's kill zone, even just once or twice in a long series of shots, indicated that most, if not all, men experienced each and every miss as a sign of terrible failure, a fatal mistake.

In this psychological state, everyone and anyone was potentially the enemy. Just as in New War fictions, the enemy existed wherever there were other people. He could be walking down the street or waiting outside the bedroom or in a nearby car on the freeway. He could be Russian or Chinese or an Arab. Students learned to fear this enemy. Worse, they learned to hunger for him to come. Only then could warriors feel powerful and overcome their fears. Only then could they feel the wonderful release of being monsters who knew what to do.

Whoever fought the enemy was kin—an imaginary alter ego. Gunsite made its students feel themselves as part of a great chain of warriors. These men in Arizona felt validated by, even part of, struggles in Central America and Angola and America's inner cities. War was the way students learned to experience the world and themselves. The "military option" in foreign affairs was the *only* real option. Similarly, the only solution to mass drug abuse was "the war on drugs." Violent confrontation was the fundamental principle of existence, and it alone could make life meaningful. Only violent confrontation could provide the "moment of truth" and confirmation as a warrior.

On Saturday morning each class held a one-on-one speed shooting competition. Two shooters stood next to each other and fired at an identical series of targets laid out on separate sectors of the range. Whoever completed the course first won the round. Everyone got two chances to compete, and the survivors then faced each other in "sudden death" play-offs. In my group a Colorado policeman and competition shooter placed first; the leader of the DOE agents came in second, and I finished third.

When the contest was over, the students got into their cars and drove a couple of miles back to the Revelation building to receive their diplomas. The instructors announced that they had talked among themselves and evaluated each shooter. Cooper said that although he did not enjoy ranking students, it was his experience that most wanted a clear indication of where they stood. Consequently, to protect the reputation of the American Pistol Institute, the standards were necessarily high. "If we are not the best organization in the world of this nature, then we aren't in business." Only five of the forty-three students got a coveted "Expert" certificate, the degree Cooper said meant that API "wanted that man on our team."

The top half of the class were thought to be "in command of our environments" and received "Marksman First Class" certificates. (A small number of these men were told privately that they were good enough to join the experts and come back for the class offered to advanced shooters—I was in this group.) Many men, particularly those Marines and police who needed "Expert" certification to advance their careers, were disappointed. Those students who received a simple marksman ranking or a mere certificate of attendance looked crushed. But no one was cast out and left alone to despair. Once all the various certificates were handed out, Cooper opened his arms. "Welcome," he said. "You are now members of the Gunsite Family."

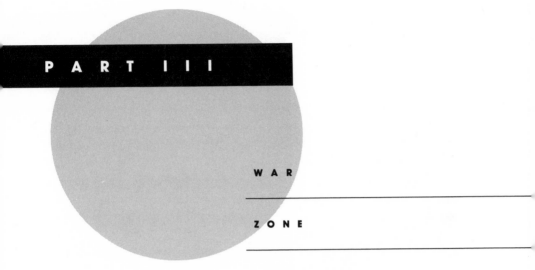

PART III

WAR

ZONE

AMERICA

10

HAVE GUN, WILL TRAVEL:

HIT MEN, MERCENARIES, AND

RACIST GROUPS JOIN

THE NEW WAR

As the New War heated up in the 1980s the line between doers and wanna-be's often blurred. Some men really did venture beyond the violent entertainment offered at paramilitary theme parks and playgrounds; they took the final step and became killers. Three different kinds of *organized* paramilitary activities developed in this period. First, some men who advertised their martial skills in the classified advertising section of *Soldier of Fortune* actually became hit men hired by husbands, wives, and business associates to murder their spouses and partners. Second, a few men abandoned their normal lives and, with the help of the *SOF* classified ads and organizations such as Civilian Military Assistance, found their way to Central America or Africa to fight as mercenaries. Finally, the old American racist right changed its character. Important new groups appeared, such as Aryan Nation, Silent Brotherhood, and Posse Comitatus. A newfound cooperation developed among most racist parties, including traditional organizations like the Klan, and the activities of these outfits accounted for extraordinary levels of brutality—between 1980 and 1986 alone nearly 3,000 violent racist incidents took place, including 138 attempted or successful bombings.[1]

The personality profile of the men who engaged in contract killing, mercenary work abroad, and race war (indeed, some men participated in all three) was remarkably consistent. First, they were deeply affected by the Vietnam War: their participation or their failure to make a personal appearance on the battlefield was a crucial event in their lives. Second, whether they fought in the war or not, these men drew the same conclusion from the defeat of the United States in Vietnam as did a certain part of the mass media: the white man's world was gone; dark forces of chaos had been unleashed and dangerous times made it not only permissible but morally imperative for them to take their personal battles far beyond the law. Paramilitary mythology offered men the fantastic possibility of escaping their present lives, being reborn as warriors, and then remaking the world. The material means for this self-transformation—the weapons, uniforms, and training schools—were all available for a price. Only through a New War could they redeem themselves and their country.

Starting in 1980, *SOF* published classified advertisements from would-be mercenaries in the back of every issue. A typical ad from 1984 read: "Ex-Marines, '67–'69 Nam vets, ex-Drill, weapons specialist, jungle warfare, pilot, multi-engine, high-risk assignments, U.S. overseas. 404/991-2684."[2] The ads cost one dollar per word or roughly $250 for twelve monthly issues. According to criminologist Park Elliot Dietz, *SOF* ran nearly 2,000 personal-service advertisements, ranging from around twenty per issue in the early 1980s down to around ten in the mid-1980s (*SOF* stopped publishing such advertisements in 1986).[3]

But mercenary ads played a more important role in *SOF* than mere revenue enhancement. The requests from men for "dirty work" or "anything, anywhere," or "all jobs considered" gave readers a sense that *SOF* was the real thing: *Real mercenaries read* Soldier of Fortune! Conversely, the memoirs by veterans of hitherto unknown battles fought in Southeast Asia and the lengthy feature articles from Afghanistan and Central America complete with large color pictures of men with guns hunting the enemy made the concise classifieds seem even more credible: since the heroes of the feature articles really did go just about anywhere, then undoubtedly the hired guns could too. In short, the features in the magazine and the ads mutually reinforced their respective warrior glamour or mystique; the unity of interests between advertising and editorial in *SOF* made for a very convincing package.

Apparently quite a few people, both would-be mercenaries and their clients, found *SOF*'s mystique extremely seductive. Major news media including UPI and AP wire services, *The New York Times*, and the *Los Angeles Times* reported crimes committed by over twenty different individuals or groups who were hired from *SOF* classified ads between 1980 and 1986.[4] These stories report only on the mercenaries who got caught; surely more crimes occurred.

The best-known case is that of John Wayne Hearn. Hearn was convicted of three contract murders: Cecil Batie on January 6, 1985; John Banister on February 2, 1985; and Sandra Black on February 21, 1985. In 1988, Mrs. Black's mother, Marjorie A. Eimann, filed a civil suit against Soldier of Fortune Magazine, Inc., and its holding company, Omega Group, Ltd., claiming that the magazine had been guilty of gross negligence (in legal terms, "conscious indifference") in running personal service ads.[5] Hearn's ad from the fall of 1984 is the one quoted above.

Hearn's personal history is particularly instructive. He volunteered for the Marine Corps and then for Vietnam, serving three tours from April 1966 to January 1969. He began in a tank unit, moved on to infantry, and ended the war as a helicopter door gunner. Although he planned to be a career service man, he was forced to retire after his knee was injured at a special drill instructor school. He then qualified as a pilot, experimented in aerial photography, and in the 1980s worked as a long-distance truck driver.

Hearn was also an avid anti-Communist and a devout reader of *Soldier of Fortune* from its opening issue in 1975.[6] He first entered the New War by engaging in small-scale international gun dealing. Hearn stockpiled over 600 rifles and some larger weapons such as mortars and machine guns in South African and Honduran ware-

houses. He began selling guns to the Nicaraguan contras in 1983—
a small part of the network orchestrated by Lieutenant Colonel Oliver
North at exactly the time that the first Boland Amendment prohibited
U.S. aid to them. [7]

In the spring of 1984 Hearn was separated from his fourth wife
and children and living with an unemployed roommate. The roommate
ran a job-wanted ad in the *Atlanta Journal* asking for work as a
warehouse supervisor; the roommate listed his experience as an ex-
Marine drill instructor as one of his qualifications. He then got a call
from a man who ran a school for mercenaries in the South, and who
promised that, for a few thousand dollars and some training courses,
he would be given overseas assignments.

Hearn and his roommate interpreted this mysterious call as a sign
that the market for mercenaries was ripe. They decided to place their
own advertisement in *SOF*, to continue their arms dealing, and to
make more contacts with the Nicaraguan contras. This strategy was
successful—the right calls arrived. Hearn reportedly delivered three
planeloads of weapons to Central America in the fall of 1984. [8]

But along with these "good" calls came some "bad" ones. In his
deposition for the Eimann-versus-*SOF* civil suit, Hearn says his *SOF*
advertisements, which ran from September 1984 through the winter
of 1985, brought in a minimum of ten to twenty calls *per day*. He
hired a message service to take the calls, and then returned them
from phone booths while on the road as a truck driver. Roughly ninety
percent of the callers were interested in hiring him for illegal activities. Between three and five callers per day wanted him to kill
someone. [9] Child-snatching was another popular request. His roommate moved out two weeks after these calls began.

With the roommate gone, Hearn modified the advertisement that
he ran in the January, February, and March 1985 issues of *SOF*. He
dropped the ex-drill instructor qualification and added that the advertisement was sponsored by an organization he'd invented called
the World Security Group. Callers heard a message in which Hearn,
who had held the rank of sergeant, called himself Colonel John
Hearn. [10] Hearn conducted numerous actions from this one *SOF* listing. Other would-be mercenaries called Hearn looking for work and
he in turn contacted people who advertised in *SOF*. One operation

he ran involved collecting DD-214 service forms (which summarize a soldier's military career up to the date of discharge) from applicants, removing their names from the forms, and then sending the résumés to a company looking for armed guards in Lebanon; for this service he charged the company $250 a man. For some of his own operations, he worked with four other men, all Vietnam veterans.

During the fall of 1984 Hearn had begun to prepare himself for committing acts of violence. He ordered a series of special books from Paladin Press, among them George Hayduke's *Get Even: The Complete Book of Dirty Tricks, Survival Escape and Evasion*, John Minnery's *How to Kill: CIA Methods for Explosives Preparation*, and at least three weapons manuals: *The AR-15/M-16: A Practical Guide, The Remington 1100 Exotic Weapons System*, and *The AR-7 Exotic Weapons System*.[11] Hearn never used any exotic weapons—the manuals served more to enhance his mercenary persona than as literal instructions for modifications.

In January and early February of 1985, Hearn killed Cecil Batie and John Banister. He believed that the murders had been a complete success, and on February 14, 1985, he agreed to kill Sandra Black. Her husband, Bob Black, had first called Hearn in 1984 looking for work as a mercenary, and, possibly, to sell some firearms. Hearn was interested in the guns for one of his upcoming deliveries to the contras.[12] When Hearn came to Bryan, Texas, in early January 1985 to examine the collection, Black requested his help in murdering his wife. Hearn refused. Weeks later Black asked Hearn to do the killing alone. By then the former Marine had killed two other people— killing a third was not such a big step.

After he murdered Sandra Black on February 21, 1985, Hearn's world began to fall apart. Georgia police investigators had determined that Hearn was the prime suspect in the Batie and Banister murders and that he had flown to Texas to do business with Bob Black. They notified Texas police and the Texans issued a warrant for his arrest. Hearn decided he would leave the country and make a fortune for himself at the same time. In March 1985, *Soldier of Fortune* announced that it would pay $100,000 to anyone who flew a Soviet-made Mi-24 Hind helicopter gunship out of Nicaragua.[13] When the notice first appeared, Oliver North of the National Security Council called Robert K. Brown at *SOF* and told him to up the reward to $1,000,000, saying that he would personally arrange payment if anyone succeeded in the mission.[14] Shortly after the increased reward notice was published, Hearn decided to drive to Boulder, Colorado, to meet Brown and learn more about what was involved in the theft of an Mi-24 and how to collect the $1,000,000. He got within sixty-five miles of Denver and then decided to go back and turn himself in to Texas authorities. It wasn't that he came to realize how extremely remote his chances of success were (he didn't even know how to fly a helicopter) but rather that he felt he would never see his family again if he left the United States. And his conscience was bothering him.[15]

Hearn confessed to all three murders and was given a life sentence for each. *Soldier of Fortune* lost the civil suit for negligence filed by Sandra Black's mother in 1988 and was fined ten million dollars in damages. A U.S. Court of Appeals later overturned the verdict, ruling that a publication could not be held liable for the actions of its advertisers. It was a fortunate ruling for *SOF*, both because of the financial implications, and also because it gave *SOF* a far more solid defense than its legal team had originally offered.

The magazine had defended itself in the original suit on very different grounds. First, staff members argued in court that they had never read any of the published accounts of crimes committed with the assistance of the personal-service ads and so had never thought to connect the two. *SOF* also claimed that the staff considered the readership to have a significant number of "Walter Mittys, the armchair warriors who don't really want to go out and participate but they want to be able to read in the magazine and live some of the adventure by reading the magazine."[16] The defense based much of its case on this characterization of *SOF*'s readership, and therefore on the contention that the classified ads were *not taken seriously* by any reasonable person.

Several defense witnesses put forth this position. For example, retired U.S. Army Colonel Charles Beckwith (the first commander of the U.S. military's secret "Delta" counterterrorist force and the man who lead the attempt to free U.S. hostages in Iran in 1979) testified that yes, he sometimes glanced at the personal-service ads, but no, he "didn't pay a lot of attention" to them. "You read one of these, it sounds so machoish, it just—it didn't make my heart beat fast so I'd go on to something else that did."[17]

Dr. Neil Livingstone, a Georgetown University professor, a consultant on terrorism to the Department of Defense and the National Security Council, and a frequent lecturer at the *SOF* conventions, thought that "at the time there were many, many ads in that magazine that looked to me like the work of posturers and Walter Mittys, people trying to impress their girlfriends."[18] In related testimony, some witnesses, such as Colorado's assistant district attorney, William Wise, simply could not believe that criminal solicitation could take place through an impersonal phone call: "I mean, people are stupid, but they're not that stupid. I just can't imagine off a cold ad there's going to be a telephone call: will you do this criminal activity?"[19]

Colonel Beckwith, Dr. Livingstone, and William Wise were not necessarily wrong in their interpretation of the personal-service ads. The defense introduced the story of "Swamp Rat," a man who in 1981 ran an ad in *SOF* reading: "Ex-Special Forces. V.I.P. Protection. Mercenary. Current Valid Passport. Only Serious Reply. Swamp Rat." When a television reporter called, Swamp Rat turned out to be a police chief in a small Texas town. Investigation revealed he'd served only in the National Guard and had been discharged because he deliberately shot himself with a staple gun.[20] In other words, Swamp Rat was a wanna-be. Many of the other *SOF* hit men similarly had only modest and, in many instances, highly flawed records as warriors. In 1986, a 28-year medical technician in the U.S. Army Reserves responded to an *SOF* ad run by "Sundance" because he thought this was the way one got recruited by the CIA—instead, the ad was intended to recruit men for a raid on an Indiana courthouse to rescue Sundance while he was on trial for murder.[21]

But if fantasy played a major role in the mental life of many *SOF* readers, that did not mean their aspirations were limited to daydreams. There was Richard Savage, for instance, who quit his career as a federal prison guard in 1980. A year later he opened a motel, which was a failure, then failed again when he tried to convert the motel into a nursing home. In the spring of 1985 he ended up running a dilapidated striptease bar near Knoxville, Tennessee. At the same time he began advertising his martial services in *SOF*.[22] Michael Wayne Jackson placed his own "'Nam Sniper" ad in *SOF* that same spring—Jackson had never served in Vietnam, but had been stationed in Guam as a Navy firefighter. He was also a former small-town policeman (he'd been fired after just three weeks; his treatment of prisoners and constant fast-draw practice struck his employers as crazy).[23] Savage and Jackson found each other through the pages of *SOF*, recruited more associates, and conducted a series of murders and bombings in the mid-1980s.

And then there was the three-time murderer John Wayne Hearn. Hearn's *SOF* ad, exotic-weapons manuals, gunrunning, and fantasy of stealing a Mi-24 helicopter gunship from Nicaragua point to an extraordinary infatuation with the heroic warrior figure. Hearn even helps to substantiate Dr. Livingstone's complaint that the men who ran ads were simply "trying to impress their girlfriends." In his trial, Hearn testified that he became a killer in the course of a relationship with Debbie Banister, who first called him asking his assistance in kidnapping her sister-in-law's children from her ex-husband, Cecil Batie. Hearn then began having an affair with Banister. In the course of the affair, Hearn said, she asked him to kill Batie and then kill her husband, John Banister. By that time, according to Hearn, Debbie Banister was handling his phone messages; she told him he "shouldn't have a conscience."[24] In his deposition, Hearn declared that his romantic involvement with Banister "was the only reason I did it [murdered]."[25] He planned to use the money from killing Sandra Black to open up a paintball war-game playing field in his hometown of Columbia, South Carolina.[26]

When the police were closing on Hearn, he even tried to use New War mythology to throw them off his track. He wrote a fake letter describing an operation he called Golden Eagle to Debbie Banister for the police to find. Hearn declared that he was leaving the country with World Security Group personnel: "WSG is an elite group of men, of whom I am the commander. We do things for Governments, including the good old US. If you ever ask they will deny it, of course. I can't and won't go into detail but we are in the final phase of Golden Eagle. I know you don't know what it is but it will hit national and international papers before long."[27] "Golden Eagle" is not a phrase Hearn created out of thin air—it is the special publishing imprint Worldwide Library uses for all of the *SOBs* (*Soldiers of Barrabas*), *Phoenix Force*, and *Able Team* volumes, together with all the *Mack Bolan: The Executioner* books after volume 38.

Finally, there is the issue of Hearn's name. Hearn's father was killed fighting in World War II, before Hearn was born. His mother named him after John Wayne, placing him under the mythic warrior's protection in the absence of a real father. In his 1986 book, sociologist Elliot Leyton reports that many serial and mass murderers were infatuated with John Wayne, including at least one, like Hearn, named after him—John Wayne Gacy.[28] Obviously, no case can be made that the murderers set out to imitate every one of John Wayne's characteristics or actions, but perhaps, at some level, they interpreted his films as messages about the necessity of killing people in order to become heroes.

As said earlier, "wanna-be" warrior and "real" warrior are not diametrically opposed identities. To identify oneself as a warrior, especially a warrior by the standards of New War mythology, is to be prey to persistent self-doubt, because there is always someone else—good guy or bad guy, real or mythological—who has killed more enemies and won more glory. Hearn, Savage, Jackson, and the other *SOF* hit men were clearly looking for a way to redeem their personal failures and take control of their lives by becoming paramilitary warriors. But as their battles continued, the redemption they sought inevitably eluded them. Most seem to have progressively lost any sense of the difference between the real world and the promises of the mythology.

The crimes of domestic hit men were not the only source of embarrassment to *Soldier of Fortune* in the mid-1980s. On January 23, 1985, 329 people died when an Air India flight from New York City to London exploded over the Atlantic. Investigations after the crash determined that the plane had been bombed by Sikh terrorists who had trained at Frank Camper's merc school near Birmingham, Alabama.[29] Although *SOF* was not directly involved in the affair, Robert

K. Brown decided to take a stand: "Since I'm the senior statesman of the popular paramilitary business in the United States, I figure it's time for me to set the record straight."[30]

In his column, Brown made it clear that he didn't care much for mercenary schools—Jeff Cooper's Gunsite Ranch was the only real exception to the rule. Quoting Jim Morris, a former staff member and at the time editor of *Eagle*, a competing paramilitary magazine, Brown warned his readers: "The only thing you can learn to be in a 10-day mercenary school is a corpse."[31] The Sikh graduates proved that this wasn't completely true, but Morris and Brown shared serious concerns: as warrior dreams progressively permeated American culture, the leadership was losing control of the fantasy world they had helped create. "Instant" mercs, graduates of what Brown called paramilitary McDonald's, dishonored *SOF*'s professional and political standards for correct warrior conduct. But there was little Brown could do and his complaints had little effect. The fact that men sought out such schools or simply decided to become mercenaries was an understandable development given the New War's consumer appeal and promise of mythical self-transformation. Frank Camper, Sam Hall, and John McClure were all drawn to the mercenary life in the 1980's. Interestingly enough, the tales they tell are pretty much the same.

For all three, the road to becoming a mercenary started with the Vietnam War. Frank Camper went to Vietnam in 1966, and served as a member of a long-range reconnaissance patrol. His missions into Cambodia and remote parts of Vietnam were under the command of the Studies and Observations Group. Soon after returning home to Birmingham, Alabama, in 1967, Camper first came down with malaria and then was hurt in an automobile accident. He was taken to an Air Force hospital, but the Air Force did not inform the Army that he had been hurt. Consequently, the Army declared Camper AWOL, and when he finally made it back to base weeks later they imprisoned him.

Finding himself in prison without apparent reason, Camper snapped: the Army became the enemy, and rather than trying to explain the situation, he escaped. He went to his sister, who saw that he was mentally disturbed and reported him. He escaped a second time from a military jail. This time, his parents turned him in to the authorities. Camper escaped yet again. Finally, months after his third escape, his wife left him for another man. Camper felt crushed: "My wife's admission she had begun to see another man had shattered me," he wrote in his memoir, "and she had done it just when I needed her most." She, too, reported him to the military. Camper's account compares her "disloyalty" to his military experience: "My country had not been loyal to those of us it had sent to Vietnam, with no definite idea of what we were to do once there."[32]

Although the Army finally discovered what had happened and permitted Camper to serve a bit longer as a ranger instructor, he was eventually discharged from the service, his file closed with a letter barring him from reenlistment. "Because of an Air Force clerical error and my reaction to it," Camper wrote, "at twenty-four years old, I was an outcast." Now his paramilitary activities began in earnest. He first traveled to Jamaica in hopes of infiltrating Cuban-led groups he thought were active there. He failed. Camper then infiltrated black activist groups in Alabama that he claimed were led by Communists. "In Asia," he wrote, "I would have called them the Vietcong." He became their military instructor. At the same time, Camper called the FBI and became an informant for them. He was trying, he wrote in his memoir, "to reestablish, on my own terms, some kind of relationship with my country."[33] He personified the New War warrior—going beyond the law in the name of justice. Years later, in 1981, he established his merc school (along with various liaisons with Army Counter-Intelligence, the FBI, and the Bureau of Alcohol, Firearms and Tobacco) for the same reason.

Unlike Frank Camper, Sam Hall never made it to Vietnam—much to his disappointment. By the time he was eleven, he was enrolled in special summer camps run by military officers and "had a dream of fighting for my country and having enough medals pinned to my chest to bow my back like Quasimodo's." After winning a Silver Medal for diving at the 1960 Rome Olympics, Hall enlisted in the Air Force. But he was given a medical discharge after damaging his right leg in pole vaulting. Like Camper, he was crushed: "After the discharge I felt empty with an ache that stayed with me long after the grief a death or a divorce or a lover's loss would have. It was impossible to shake the sadness and it tinged every joy that came later."[34]

Over the next decade or so, Hall's life was filled with alcoholism, drug addiction (steroids, uppers, downers), compulsive womanizing (and two divorces), two suicide attempts, lung cancer, a broken back from jumping off a 206-foot bridge, and a self-inflicted gunshot wound in the thigh suffered while practicing fast-draw in an elevator. However, after witnessing the televised account of the massacre of Israeli athletes at the 1972 Olympic games in Munich, and subsequently undergoing a "born-again" Christian experience, Hall changed. He got a job working for H. Ross Perot's Electronic Data Systems, providing logistic support for United Nations forces in the Sinai Desert. In Israel he decided to become a counterterrorist: "A terrorist seemed like an enemy you could relate to . . . There was a time when any kind of combat role was attractive to me, but no more. I longed for something more personal."[35]

First he was trained by Israeli paramilitary forces for cross-border operations. Delighted with the excitement of the patrols, especially his first kill, he nevertheless decided he would keep faith with his father, now dead, who had long worried about POWs and MIAs in Vietnam. Hall set out to organize his own rescue mission. With recommendations from his Israeli contacts, Hall was admitted to "instant" merc schools in England, Germany, and Holland. In all these educational endeavors, he was the oldest man attending by twenty years: "With sheepskins from this school and maybe a couple of other war colleges I could prove that a man in his mid-forties wasn't necessarily ready for the boneyard."[36] After graduating, Hall went to South Africa to find mercenaries for his POW mission and soon joined a group there to practice his new martial skills.

John D. McClure, a Florida clinical psychologist, also decided to become a mercenary while in his forties. According to McClure, in the early 1980s he was paying $1,500 a month for a luxurious office and driving a Corvette to give his patients confidence in his ability. Unfortunately, the director of his clinic thought that he must be dealing cocaine and having sex with his female patients. Although an examination by the state licensing board cleared him, McClure was now disgusted with his profession. An ardent reader of *Soldier of Fortune*, the owner of an AR-15 and other weapons, a martial-arts master, and a Vietnam veteran who regretted that the U.S. "didn't turn the place into a parking lot" (although in his completely self-serving memoir he never once mentions what he did there), McClure decided he was ready for a midlife change.[37]

First he joined some "outlaw bikers" for a mission in Mexico to collect a debt owed a South Florida drug dealer. Thrilled with the adventure and "a lot of cash in small U.S. bills," he moved to step two of his plan. He would travel to Nicaragua, make a decision about whether the Sandinistas or the contras were right, and offer his services to the winner. After a tour of duty in Central America, he would go into business for himself. When he told his wife to either help him pack his bags or get a divorce, he explained his future plan: "If I hook up with the Sandinistas or Pastora's group, my goal is going to be the formation of a private security company that can handle clandestine work for free-world governments. With my psychological training and experience, I can handle screening and interrogation, and with what I learned in the military, I can do everything from individual combat through training troops and even running operations."[38] After being arrested in Managua and questioned about photographing the Sandinista party headquarters, McClure made his way to Costa Rica and joined Pastora's group.

It seems clear that all three men fought their personal wars to establish a new heroic identity and a new relationship to society. At first, all three also found joy in the brotherhood of war. Camper contrasted his experience in Vietnam, where he "had fought beside men who would and did die to help save each other," to what he considered betrayal by his sister, parents, wife, and country.[39] After Hall watched his fellow mercs urinate on each other's wounds to clean them during his first mercenary mission in Mozambique to rescue kidnapped Canadian health workers, he exulted: "Right then I think I felt in touch with my own soul for the first time in my life. God how I loved this place and these men beside me. I hoped we would find the Canadians soon. I owed their rescue as another partial payment for all my useless years. But I didn't want this trip to end either."[40] And McClure, in turn, told his wife why he loved his work:

"Soldiering is what I live for—the camp life and the camaraderie with honest men. Fuck the wimpy civilians who smile at your face and stab you in the back for an advantage or promotion. No honey, I don't like killing. But this is worth killing for, and worth dying for."[41]

All three men, too, reveled in the journey back to the primordial chaos of war. Camper designed his school to be a "savage, regressive course, appealing to and developing the natural warrior in those who had it."[42] To develop this warrior, much of the course consisted of tear gas fights, of trainees beating each other with clubs and kidnapping and torturing each other.[43] As Camper says, "The medic was always busy with broken fingers, arms, legs, noses, and dislocations, freely applying splints and slings." No one was ever killed. "Few men, however, made it to graduation unscarred."[44] Sam Hall was so proud of a bayonet wound he received across his rib cage while fighting with the Miskito Indians in Nicaragua that he included in his memoir a photograph of himself stitching the wound.

McClure excitedly wrote about a food-gathering mission he went on with a contra group: "This was war as it had been ten thousand years ago. It was as if my tribe was raiding the gardens of another tribe. We might kill or be killed for a bag of roots." After all, he explained to his wife, "I'm in there with people who are more primitive than you can imagine. Some of them had never seen a white man until I came along." He got malaria, was wounded by grenade fragments, and most importantly, after one massive battle went to the Key Largo bar in San Juan, Costa Rica, looked into a mirror, and found that his "lines of vision didn't converge inside the building. Maybe they didn't meet at all."[45] In the bar mirror, McClure saw that he had finally obtained that prized invisible scar in the soul, the empty gaze war veterans call the thousand-yard stare.

At the same time that they were searching for a primordial reality, all three men looked to the mass media for inspiration on what to do, and validation that they had done things the warrior way. Camper himself wrote two pulp-novel commando books, in addition to memoirs about Vietnam and mercenary life.[46] At the end of the first year of the merc school in 1981, he reported that a group of graduates who called themselves the Death Merchants had started to violently harass new trainees at night. Although "death merchants" is a common name for gun dealers, it should be noted that a mercenary pulp-novel series, *The Death Merchant* by Joseph Rosenberger, had already been in print for several years by 1981 and was advertised in the back pages of at least one of Camper's books. Also, in the wake of the Air India bombings, Camper decided to turn his troubles into gold by taking his staff to Hollywood in search of a possible movie about his merc school. Nothing came of the trip, but in September Robert Duvall showed up at the school to prepare for his role in the mercenary-rescue movie *Let's Get Harry*. Camper proudly concluded: "He created his role as a mercenary in that movie largely by studying me."[47]

When Sam Hall went on his various "spy" missions to El Salvador and Nicaragua, he dressed like Clark Kent/Superman. Wearing civilian clothes on the outside, he often wore camouflage fatigues underneath for a quick change into jungle warrior. During his paramilitary travels, Hall formed a father-son relationship with Francis Douglas "Red Dog" Fane, who had once been commander of a U.S. Navy underwater demolition team. Hall writes that Fane was the model for the hero of the 1958 MGM movie *Underwater Warrior*. Fane supposedly introduced Hall, in 1984, to someone in the Special Warfare division of the Joint Chiefs of Staff who asked Hall to form an independent unit of counterterrorists for covert use by free-world forces. Hall devised a plan for a 540-man unit to carry out three operations at a total cost of nearly $20 million. Hall designated himself Warrior Leader, with the rank of lieutenant colonel in the U.S. Air Force, and called the unit the Phoenix Battalion.[48]

The plan was never carried out. Whether someone in the Special Warfare division was simply playing mind games with Hall or whether this entire story is Hall's fantasy is uncertain. But there is little doubt where Hall got the name Phoenix Battalion. When author Don Pendleton tired of Mack Bolan's 38-volume war against the Mafia, he switched publishers and changed the story. Mack Bolan was listed as officially dead and was then reborn in U.S. government computers as Colonel John Macklin Phoenix, U.S. Army, Retired. Bolan/Phoenix (both names are used) headed a secret counterterrorist organization based in the United States and made his debut in a novel called *The New War*.[49] Colonel Phoenix also commanded two other units composed of men from around the free world, each with its own series appearing four times a year, *Able Team* and *Phoenix Force*. The publisher, Worldwide Library (under the Golden Eagle imprint), regularly bought full-page advertisements in *Soldier of Fortune*.

As for McClure, when he left Miami for Nicaragua he had a layover in El Salvador. He was dressed, he writes, in a "khaki safari suit, and had my hair cropped close, G.I. style, and no doubt presented a somewhat military appearance." He was approached by a "rich" Canadian, apparently an intelligence operative. The man started talking shop with McClure, obviously assuming that the crew-cut American was a U.S. agent. McClure was beside himself with joy: "This was beyond my wildest dreams, and I certainly didn't want to blow it." Later, after having been detained by the Sandinistas for taking pictures, he first entertained himself with "a daydream in which I slap-kicked the pistols from their waistbands, spun around, and smashed double back-fists into their pimpled faces, then leapt across the room to put a flying side snap-kick into the receptionist's throat before she could reach the telephone."[50]

After he was released a couple of hours later, McClure quit fantasizing himself as Chuck Norris and instead became Christopher Walken, star of *The Dogs of War* (1981), a film he had seen while "pumping myself up for this career change." Like Walken's character, who was beaten by government agents during a reconnaissance mission to an African country, McClure dreamed of returning "at the head of an assault force" to exact "revenge." On another occasion McClure claimed that he followed James Bond's example and sealed the inside of his briefcase with "Scotch Tape indicators" before bedding a mysterious American freelance agent; later he'd know if she had examined it (she had).[51]

But, try as they might, these soldiers of fortune—unlike the New War heroes—could neither sustain their battles nor secure a relationship with the U.S. government. For all Camper's informing to federal agencies, not one came to his assistance after the Air India bombing; he was convicted on charges of criminal conspiracy, racketeering, and the possession of illegal weapons. He felt betrayed again: "My mistake had been in assuming, if not actual loyalty, at least an earned respect and debt for services rendered, from my government employers to me."[52] Hall fared slightly better. His contact on the Joint Chiefs of Staff, after telling him there was no money for the Phoenix Battalion, then instructed Hall to meet with Tom Posey, head of Civilian Military Assistance, and go to Nicaragua with them. He did so, and reportedly made contacts with and received some financial support from General John Singlaub and the United States Council for World Freedom, Lieutenant Colonel Oliver North, and Rob Owen, North's courier (money-man) to the FDN.[53] But the big money that Hall wanted from Singlaub and North for blowing up Nicaraguan bridges never came through, and instead he became a star furniture salesman in Florida. Before quitting the New War, though, he made one last mission to Nicaragua to photograph Mi-24 helicopters, during which he was captured, imprisoned for months, and interviewed at length by Sandinista psychiatrists. When his captors learned from U.S. press clippings that Tom Posey, Frank Camper, and Robert K. Brown also thought he was too much like Rambo, they released him. The fact that his brother, Tony Hall, was a U.S. Congressman probably helped. Like Camper, Hall thought he had performed vital services for the State and been rewarded with humiliation.

McClure saw his beloved group of contras led by Pastora first lose efficiency through factional fights, and then, after Pastora was hurt in an assassination attempt, disintegrate. He shifted his base of operations to Surinam, and persisted in thinking that the mysterious contacts he kept having with U.S. embassy officials in Costa Rica were actually CIA efforts to recruit him into the agency. Back in the States, he learned from another contact, a colonel in the Defense Intelligence Agency, that his record of mercenary missions was tainted by his association with the drug trade, and that although he might be used by the CIA, he would never really get inside. After a few more adventures, McClure returned to his wife in New York and became a computer programmer, and—like Hall—reported himself to be extremely successful.

What is to be learned here? At one level, these are all sad stories of troubled men. As people, they deserve some sympathy and compassion. But their stories are more than personal tragedies; they are testimonies to the way in which paramilitary culture helped form personal identities. The rapid oscillation between tremendous personal insecurity and extraordinary narcissism is a factor in all three memoirs. Each man knew he had reached a barrier of some kind in his life, and that realization contributed to his volatile, unstable character. Sensing his personal limitations, each thought he could transcend his problems by becoming a paramilitary warrior and contributing his own stories to the New War canon.

In these memoirs, it is frequently impossible to tell which stories are true, which are invented, and which—like Hall's Phoenix Battalion—are consciously and/or unconsciously lifted right off the pages of someone else's manuscript. It's doubtful the authors could make these distinctions, either. Like the hit men, they inhabited highly fluid personal worlds; at their narcissistic peaks, they imagined themselves living the lives of warrior-gods. Filled with delusions of power, they ended up pawns, toy soldiers who let themselves be used by military-intelligence authorities. They had desperately wanted to please these authorities as a way of reconnecting to society and securing their self-esteem as heroes. At least they finished their battles alive, but they were also left more alone than ever. Alone, they had to face another failure—the fact that their warrior dreams had not come true. Yet not one expressed any doubts about the New War myths they had tried to embody in their lives; only the government was at fault.

In the fall of 1981 the subscribers to *Soldier of Fortune* opened their mailboxes to find a surprise. William S. Pierce, the founder of a neo-Nazi party called The National Alliance and the publisher and editor of its magazine *The National Vanguard*, together with an accompanying mail-order book service, had bought *SOF*'s mailing list in search of recruits to his cause. Pierce's catalog specialized in works about Norse, German, and other "white" mythologies, racial "science," and stories about the "lie" of the Holocaust and the "crimes" of the Jews. Pierce also offered the second edition (1980) of his futuristic New War novel *The Turner Diaries*, written under the pen name Andrew Macdonald. *The Turner Diaries* told the story of white guerrilla warfare against ZOG, the Zionist Occupational Government—the coalition of Jews, nonwhite "mud people," and white liberal race traitors that ruled America in the 1980s.

That Pierce would try the *SOF* mailing list makes sense. A racist reader might well interpret the 1975 full-page photograph of a black Rhodesian with much of his forehead blown off and brains missing as a commentary on what should be done to unruly black people—rather than an example of what Communist terrorists do.[54] (Certainly the magazine never showed dead whites that way.) Indeed, *SOF*'s consistent support of white Rhodesians throughout that country's civil war might be construed as evidence of racist sympathies. And *SOF* regularly carried a fair number of ads for World War II German uniforms, helmets, knives, medals, and insignia—their presence didn't overwhelm the magazine, but it was evident.

Apparently, quite a few racist organizations tried to advertise in *SOF*. During the 1988 Eimann-versus-*SOF* civil suit, one of *SOF*'s former advertising managers, Dana Kim Drenkowski, testified that he routinely threw out potential ads with "KKK" and "Nazi" in them, along with other racist messages he could spot, such as one with "White Aryan Nation" in it.[55] With practice, Drenkowski learned that "Christian" was another bad sign: "Anything that said 'Christian,' I dumped. I got so I didn't even trust the Salvation Army anymore; but 'Christian Defense League,' 'The Arm of God,' 'The Sword of God,' various survivalist groups that initially appeared to be, you know, innocuous survival, basic—like Outward Bound-type training or whatever—some of these might turn out to be some sort of a strange organization. You never know. The names change constantly."[56] Pierce, then, just slipped by the advertising manager because *The National Vanguard* was one name that didn't sound an alarm.

Many readers, however, were quite perturbed, and complained. The *SOF* staff called the Anti-Defamation League of B'nai B'rith, learned what *The National Vanguard* was about, and tried to rectify the situation, both in a letter from Brown to all subscribers and in a magazine editorial. *SOF* was anti-Communist, Brown wrote, but it did not tolerate racism. At one level, the *Vanguard* incident, along with the many attempts by racist organizations to place advertisements, represented yet another instance of *SOF*'s inability to control the blossoming paramilitary culture: more people—and people of a different sort—wanted to become warriors than the editors of *SOF* thought appropriate.

Still, in the late 1970s and 1980s the men on the burgeoning racist right were reacting to the same American historical and cultural crises as those men whom *SOF* saw as legitimate—the defeat in Vietnam, and what many people perceived as the collapse of U.S. political, military, and economic power both at home and abroad. What the racist right did was simply stress that "non-whites," including Jews, were virtually the same as "Communists": the fight against Communism was also a fight for white supremacy. From this perspective, the defeat in Vietnam meant the defeat of all white men. The vast superiority of "white" Americans' war technology to what the "yellow" Asians had been using only made the defeat more mysterious and threatening. Events such as the 1971 conviction of U.S. Army Lieutenant William Calley for the murder of over 400 Vietnamese civilians at My Lai indicated to many white men that what they understood to be the fundamental and just American order was being destroyed— Calley had simply been doing his job. Undoubtedly many leaders of the far right were racists before the Vietnam War—the Ku Klux Klan, for example, dates back to the post-Civil War era—but defeat pushed their thinking to new extremes. There had to be a reason why the white man's world was in decline.

The search for a grand explanation led the racist right in much the same direction as Hollywood, the pulp novels, and paramilitary magazines. The racist right came to embrace two cosmogonic myths. One was a theology called "Christian Identity." The second was embodied in Pierce's novel *The Turner Diaries*, which he saw as a doctrinal statement of the church he founded, "The Cosmotheist Church." A shared belief that the sacred order could only be restored through fighting a New War unified the movement to an unprecedented degree.

The opening shots of the far right's New War were fired on November 3, 1979, in Greensboro, North Carolina. For that day, the Communist Workers Party (CWP), a radical descendant of the New Left and the antiwar movement of the 1960s, had organized a demonstration provocatively advertised as "Death to the Klan." The summer before, the CWP had interrupted a Klan rally in a neighboring town, burning the Klan's Confederate flag and preventing a screening of D. W. Griffith's *Birth of a Nation*. The CWP then challenged the

Klan to attend their November 3 demonstration. And they did: ten carloads of heavily armed men poured into Greensboro to confront the CWP. The demonstrators surrounded the cars; some of the Klansmen jumped out, retrieved their weapons from car trunks, and opened fire. Five CWP activists were killed before police arrived and arrested twelve Klansmen and National Socialist Party (Nazi) members.

Months later, the North Carolina Advisory Committee to the United States Commission on Civil Rights held public hearings on the Greensboro killings. Virgil Griffin, a Grand Dragon (state leader) of the Invisible Empire of the National Ku Klux Klan, testified that at Greensboro the "enemy was the Communist Party . . . the same enemy whom thousands of soldiers lost their lives fighting in the Viet Nam and Korean Wars."[57] Harold Covington, a leader of the National Socialist Party, told the committee that he had served in the U.S. Army in Vietnam and in the 1970s had also fought as a mercenary in the Rhodesian Army. The war at home was part of this same struggle.

Glen Miller, Jr., one of the racist activists present in the caravan, had previously been a sergeant in the U.S. Army Special Forces. In his assessment, "I was more proud to have been in Greensboro for eighty-eight seconds in 1979 than twenty years in the U.S. Army. It was the only armed victory over communism in this country."[58] Miller was active in the National Socialist Party and later founded his own branch of the KKK in North Carolina. He was one of the first Klansmen to abandon the traditional Klan uniform of old white sheets for camouflage military fatigues. He also established paramilitary training camps for new recruits.

In neighboring Alabama, Bill Wilkinson, leader of the largest KKK organization in the late 1970s, opened a paramilitary training center in 1980 and named it Camp My Lai, in honor of Lieutenant William Calley. Louis Beam, Grand Dragon of the Texas KKK, reformed his group as the Texas Emergency Reserve (TER) and refashioned it as a paramilitary army. Beam told his followers to emulate their comrades in North Carolina. "When the shooting starts, we're going to win it just like we did in Greensboro," he said.[59] TER's first major armed action occurred in March 1981: an intimidation campaign against Vietnamese refugees who were fishing for shrimp in Galveston Bay and thus competing with white fishermen. TER also formed a paramilitary training camp and initiated some "patrols" along the Texas-Mexico border in search of Mexican immigrants. Beam had served eighteen months as a helicopter door gunner in Vietnam. When he returned to the United States in 1968, his disgust with antiwar protesters convinced him that he had a war to fight at home as well: "That's where my struggle started. If they can do that in this country, then I still have a mission."[60] Antiwar protesters, Viet Cong, Vietnamese refugees, and Mexican immigrants—all coalesced to form one common enemy.

A fourth major leader of the far right in the 1980s, Robert Matthews, had wanted to go to Vietnam, but changed his mind after Lieutenant Calley was court-martialed and sentenced to prison. At the time, Matthews was a Phoenix teenager who had decided that colleges were hotbeds of Communism and that only West Point could provide him a satisfactory education and possible career. His father arranged for him to take the entrance exam, but after Calley's conviction Matthews decided the Army was corrupt. To appease his father, he took the exam anyway, but—perhaps deliberately—failed the math section. In 1972, Matthews formed a paramilitary group called the Sons of Liberty that trained in the Arizona desert. He said to a reporter at the time: "The way this country is headed, there must be changes or people will die. Can't they see? The people of Arizona, of the whole country, are woefully unprepared for this chaos. We must return to the constitutional law of the land."[61] Over a decade later he founded the Silent Brotherhood, also called The Order, a group responsible for several major robberies of armored cars during the mid-1980s that netted over four million dollars. The members of the Order also committed multiple murders.

Most of these men—and many more—soon found their way to Christian Identity, to help make sense of the world. This new religion was put forth by an Englishman, Edward Hine, in his 1871 book, *Identification of the British Nation with Lost Israel.* Hine's teachings, which spread to the U.S. in the late 19th century, begin with a reinterpretation of Genesis. Although Adam was the father of Abel, it seems that Eve also slept with Satan, who fathered Cain. Cain, the first Jew, killed Abel and fled the Garden of Eden. Adam, however, had other children, and God (Yahweh) chose one of them, Abraham, to receive the Covenant and found the non-Jewish nation of Israel. Abraham's grandson Jacob in turn took two wives and two concubines and fathered twelve sons, the leaders of the twelve tribes of Israel.

In 721 B.C. the Assyrian leader Sennacherib took the ten northern tribes captive, and they disappeared from Biblical stories. Hines contends that these tribes became the settlers of Europe, including Great Britain, and that one tribe, the Manasseh, eventually crossed the Atlantic on the *Mayflower*, where God gave them a new covenant: the Declaration of Independence, the Constitution, and the Bill of Rights.

Meanwhile, in 586 B.C. Nebuchadnezzar seized the southern tribe of Judah and took them to Babylonia. Babylonia was where Cain had fled after killing Abel; it was there he mated with wild animals and created nonwhite races, known in Identity Christianity as mud people. Consistent with tradition, Nebuchadnezzar converted the tribe of Judah to Satanism, and thus formed the so-called Jewry—the people who killed Christ, gave birth to Karl Marx and Communism, and took over the Federal Reserve Bank in the United States.

From Christian Identity's perspective, white Anglo-Saxons are the true Jews. They are God's chosen people, and they will be redeemed if they follow God's will. As Satan, and his children (the imposter Jews) and their children (the mud people), gain power, the world approaches its end. Good Christians, the true Jews, must be prepared, both for the Apocalypse and to help bring the Apocalypse on through their battles against Satan's secular respresentatives—the Zionist Occupational Government that runs the United States.

It is a bizarre scenario, but as myth it has two highly attractive elements. First, Christian Identity presents a view in which all threats to the white man are connected, and ultimately collapse into one enemy—Satan. It's a simple, economical explanation of a complex world. Second, it offers the highly reassuring promise to desperate whites that they are the true people of the covenant. Despite their worst fears, God has not abandoned them after all. He will keep his promise of redemption if they abide by his will, as revealed by Christian Identity preachers, and make the necessary sacrifices.

Kerry Noble, a preacher for a paramilitary organization called The Covenant, the Sword, and the Arm of the Lord (CSA), described the coming chaos in words remarkably similar to those of pulp novels such as *Phoenix #1: Dark Messiah, C.A.D.S.*, and *The Survivalist* series:

> Russia and possibly China and Japan will attack America, probably with some limited nuclear warfare. Communists will kill white Christians and mutilate them; witches and satanic Jews will offer people up as sacrifices to their gods, openly and proudly; blacks will rape and kill white women, and will torture and kill white men; homosexuals will sodomize whoever they can. Prisoners from Federal and State prisons will be set free to terrorize, while Cuban refugees will do the same. Nowhere will be safe without the grace of God. The coming war is a step towards God's government.[62]

The acronym CSA also stands for the Confederate States of America, and in truth, the sacred order to which the Covenant aspired was a mythical version of the pre-Civil War South—except that this time all the mud people would be eliminated in the race war. To prepare for this war, CSA established a 224-acre compound in the Ozark Mountains of Arkansas near the Missouri border. There they stockpiled food and ammunition, built a gunsmith works for full-automatic conversions and production of noise suppressors, and established a paramilitary training course called Endtime Overcomer Survival Training School. Charging $500 in tuition, the school had a series of indoor target ranges (like those at Gunsite) called Silhouette City, featuring targets with pictures of famous Jewish leaders.

Ku Klux Klan leader Louis Beam articulated the need for a sacrifice to reestablish the sacred covenant: "We will have a national racial state. We shall have it at whatever price is necessary. Just as our forefathers purchased their freedom in blood, so must we. There can no more be a peaceful birth of our nation in the 1980s than there was for our ancestors in 1776. We will have to kill the bastards."[63]

In the Midwest, the language of Christian Identity was adopted by another right-wing organization, the Posse Comitatus. The group took its name from an Act of Congress passed after the Civil War that barred President Grant from using federal troops to safeguard ballot boxes in the South during Reconstruction. The law said, in effect, that military forces could not be used to enforce domestic laws. In the 1980s, Posse Comitatus claimed that the only legitimate level of government was the county and that, furthermore, the law-enforcement powers of the county ultimately resided in the posse, a local militia of armed men. Posse Comitatus members refused to pay income taxes, declared their homes and farms separate nations, and sometimes threatened government officials with execution if they did not comply with Posse Comitatus demands.

Gordan Kahl, a North Dakota tax protester, became the Posse's greatest hero. Imprisoned in 1981 for failure to file his federal income tax form (and his efforts to promote tax resistance), Kahl still refused to cooperate with the government when released on parole. Moreover, he vowed that he would never again allow himself to be arrested, and frequently carried a Ruger Mini-14 semiautomatic rifle. Although both federal and local law-enforcement officials were highly divided on the best way to apprehend Kahl for not meeting his parole officer (a misdemeanor), in February 1983 six U.S. marshals and a local sheriff's deputy tried to arrest Kahl near his hometown in Medina, North Dakota. They failed; two were killed and four wounded.

Kahl escaped, and later wrote two letters explaining his position. The influence of Christian Identity (whose churches Kahl had encountered years earlier during annual winter trips with his family to Southern California) is evident in both documents. In the first, he outlines his version of the shoot-out at Medina, and concludes: "I realize that being an enemy of the Jewish-Masonic-Communist-Synogogue [sic] of Satan is not conducive to a long life, so I am writing this while I still can."[64] As Kahl had earlier explained to his friends, all U.S. government law-enforcement agencies, and all local police, were under the control of the Mossad, Israel's secret intelligence agency. The Mossad also had informants in every town in America. Thus, it was only a matter of time before he would be discovered.

Three weeks later Kahl mailed the second letter, providing both a more detailed version of the Medina fight and a summation of his theological and political position. "We are a conquered and occupied nation," Kahl wrote:

> conquered and occupied by the Jews . . . [who] have two objectives in their goal of ruling the world. Destroy Christianity and the white race. Neither can be accomplished by itself. They stand or fall together.
>
> We are engaged in a struggle to the death between the people of the Kingdom of God, and the Kingdom of Satan. It started long ago, and is now best described as a struggle between Jacob and Esau [Abraham's sons].

In conceiving of his personal battle as but a moment in a struggle that began in the Garden of Eden, Kahl saw himself as an agent of God, whose "prophecy will be fulfilled."[65] Months later, on June 3, 1983, federal agents tracked Kahl to a house near Smithville, Arkansas. The local sheriff, Gene Matthews, entered the house by himself (contrary to plan) and was shot by Kahl. He stumbled out, mortally wounded. After a prolonged rifle and tear-gas barrage, two SWAT team members poured diesel fuel into the house's air vent on the roof. The house caught fire and burned for over two hours as agents renewed their gunfire. Kahl's completely charred body was later found inside.

Although Christian Identity provided the most comprehensive mythology for the far right's New War in the 1980s, William S. Pierce's *The Turner Diaries* offered a second, more succinct formulation of how warriors could achieve a sacred order. First published in 1979 by Pierce's own company, National Vanguard Books, it became an incredibly influential book—and for very particular reasons. Whereas Christian Identity basically told a story about the fall of the white man and foretells the end of the world, Pierce's novel is built on the premise of a white government looking back on its successful rise to power. *The Diaries* are presented as an archeological find, the recently recovered records of Earl Turner, an early foot soldier and war hero. The author presents himself as an academic who annotates and corrects Earl Turner's diary entries. His notes are necessary because the "Great Revolution" was fought between 1989 and 1999, a century ago.

Turner's diary entries begin in November 1989, when the white resistance against ZOG moves underground after federal officers confiscate all firearms, according to the provisions of the "Cohen Act." The whites have buried their guns to conceal them from the feds, but although they have access to the guns they fear that they may have waited too long to act. The FBI, in conjunction with Israeli hit men, is now hunting them down. Soon, the Supreme Court rules that rape laws are unconstitutional since they discriminate against men (who cannot be raped). Thousands of white women are immediately raped by blacks. Since white men are now disarmed and are no longer capable of defending their women, the future of the race is in doubt. ZOG is elated at this prospect, since its goal is universal miscegenation, meaning the end of the white race, and the definitive victory of Satan.

By the fall of 1991, though, the Organization, as the white underground calls itself, regroups. First, the leadership finally recognizes that many members of the white underground are Vietnam veterans who have learned vital martial skills useful for guerrilla war. Second, the white leadership, having concluded that the Vietnamese revolutionaries won because they were terrorists who intimidated the larger population into supporting them under threat of death, decides to adopt a similar strategy.

The white underground is reorganized into secret groups—constructed, ironically, along the lines of Leninist cells—and begins guerrilla assaults against ZOG, both to cripple the "System" and to provoke the "liberal" authorities into highly oppressive measures against the white population. At the same time, the Organization will treat uncommitted whites who have been corrupted by materialism "like a herd of cattle. Since they are no longer capable of responding to an idealistic appeal, we began appealing to things they can understand: fear and hunger."[66]

At first, Earl Turner's cell engages in relatively minor affairs, such as robbing and murdering a Jewish couple who run the local liquor store and deli, and killing a group of young black men and white women who stumble upon their hideout. But Turner, a fit, disciplined man in his mid-thirties, makes progress as a leader. His group blows up the FBI's new computer complex in Washington, D.C. (thus saving the Organization) and soon launches a mortar attack against the U.S. Congress. Turner's diary entry describes the glory of war in language very similar to that of his ancestors in the *Freikorps*: "We saw beautiful blossoms of flame and steel sprouting everywhere, dancing across the asphalt, thundering in the midst of splintered masonry and burning vehicles, erupting now inside and outside the Capitol, wrecking [sic] their bloody toll in the ranks of tyranny and treason."[67]

These heroic actions come to the attention of the Organization's secret leadership cadre, an all-male religious fellowship known as The Order. Turner is first drugged and given special lie-detector tests to see if he meets the Order's standards. Passing this first test, he is given access to The Book, a secret history of the white race and its place in the cosmos. In fact, he is given access to the *very first typescript of The Book*, a document lost in the revolution. Turner then learns the secret "sign" of the Order—so that he can recognize other leaders. He also vows never to be captured and is given a pendant containing a poison pill with which he can kill himself. Finally, dressed in a gray monk's robe, he and the other initiates swear "a mighty Oath, a moving Oath that shook me to my bones and raised the hair on the back of my neck." He concludes, *"Now our lives belong to the Order. Today I was, in a sense, born again."*[68]

Not long afterwards Turner's hideout is attacked by ZOG. Although his group escapes, an explosion in the escape tunnel knocks Turner unconscious. He is captured and his pendant removed. Drugged and sodomized with a thick metal rod by two black men and the Israeli agent Rubin, he eventually breaks down during the ZOG interrogation. He is then sent to a special prison for white revolutionaries, but is rescued in a daring raid by the Organization that saves four hundred white men (a clear contrast to the failed POW raids during the Vietnam War).

Once rescued, Turner is tried by the Order for breaking his oath and allowing himself to be captured. He is sentenced to death. But since he had not taken the full "rite of Union" with the Order before he was captured, he is allowed the honor of undertaking a suicide mission for the group when the cause requires it. As the Order's judge explains, this will give him *everlasting life*: "If you complete it successfully, the act of completion will remove the condition from your Union. Then, even though you die, you will continue to live in us and in our successors for as long as our Order endures, just as with any other member who achieves Union and then loses his life."[69] Turner's blood sacrifice will thus allow his spirit to be reborn in the brotherhood of war known as the Order. Knowing that his eventual death will lead to everlasting life makes Turner happy.

While waiting to be called, he takes part in a massive counterfeiting operation that pours tons of bogus dollars into the economy. He is then sent to Southern California for the whites' first area-wide attack. The battle succeeds. On August 1, 1993, the "Day of the Rope," thousands of white news-media people, academics, and other liberal professionals are hung from street lamps bearing signs that say "I betrayed my race." Thousands of white women known to have slept with men of other races are also hung bearing signs that read "I defiled my race." Jews are herded into canyons and shot. Blacks, Asians, and Latinos are exiled.

The race war intensifies. Using captured nuclear missiles, the Organization blows up New York and Israel and attacks the Soviet Union to provoke nuclear retaliation. The Soviets launch a limited nuclear attack, sparing Washington, D.C. and a few other cities. Tens of millions die; ZOG is crippled. And to give ZOG the death blow, the Order asks Turner to fly a plane equipped with a 60-kiloton nuclear warhead into the Pentagon. Turner gladly offers his life and his comrades respond: "Brother! We accept your life. In return we offer you everlasting life in us. Your deed shall not be in vain, nor shall it be forgotten, until the end of time. To this commitment we pledge our lives."[70] On November 9, 1993, Turner's cleansing nuclear fire destroys the System's Jewish nerve center, after which the black and brown arms and legs of the beast atrophy.

In his 1986 National Vanguard book catalog, William S. Pierce printed a "Guide for Readers" listing thirty books as *must* reading for white supremacists. The very last book on the list was *The Turner Diaries*. Only those who had previously read Hitler's *Mein Kampf* and several other titles in the "solution" category of race relations were advised to tackle *Turner*—"which will be too strong a dish for any reader who has not thoroughly prepared himself for it."[71]

But by 1986 many people had already found that *The Turner Diaries* tasted just right. Pierce offered readers a vision in which the sacred order had already been created. Consequently, at least some white activists reading the novel in the 1980s interpreted it as prophecy. Their battles could not fail since the book was itself evidence that the revolution had already been won in the future. Their victory in a race war was *predestined*—as one believer said, "You gotta read it. Everything that's gonna happen is in there."[72] All that was required to make the book's plot reality was for some good white men to accept the divine call and follow the path laid out in the *Diaries*.

In early September 1983, Robert Matthews, the former guerrilla organizer of the Sons of Liberty in Phoenix, Arizona, attended William S. Pierce's National Alliance convention in Arlington, Virginia. Many years before, Matthews had moved to Metaline Falls, Washington, as part of what the racist right called the "Ten Per Cent Solution." This plan called for whites to form a "White American Bastion" in the Pacific Northwest—an area thought to be roughly ten percent of the country—and live as members of a "family of families." By 1983, though, Matthews thought whites simply could not settle for ten percent of the country. Deeply influenced by *The Turner Diaries*, he attended the convention in search of additional recruits for an "action" group he was forming back home. His speech to the delegates stressed the ascension of whites over the mud people: "Ten hearts, one beat! One hundred hearts, one beat! Ten thousand hearts, one beat! We are born to fight and die and to continue the flow, the flow of our people. Onward we will go, onward to the stars, high above the mud, the mud of yellow, black, and brown! Kinsmen, duty calls! The future is now!"[73]

A few weeks later, Matthews gathered together his first eight recruits for the New War. He told them, "Before we go on, if all of you are willing to join with me, we first must bond to one another as blood brothers." Standing hand in hand in a circle, the men repeated after Matthews:

I, as a free Aryan man, hereby swear an unrelenting oath upon the green graves of our sires, upon the children in the wombs of our wives, upon the throne of God almighty, sacred in His name, to join together in holy union with those brothers in this circle and to declare forthright that from this moment on I have no fear of death, no fear of foe; that I have a sacred duty to do whatever is necessary to deliver our people from the Jew and bring total victory to the Aryan race.

I, as an Aryan warrior, swear myself to complete secrecy to the Order and total loyalty to my comrades.

Let me bear witness to you, my brothers, that should one of you fall in battle, I will see to the welfare and well-being of your family.

Let me bear witness to you, my brothers, that should one of you be taken prisoner, I will do whatever is necessary to regain your freedom.

Let me bear witness to you, my brothers, that should an enemy agent hurt you, I will chase him to the ends of the earth and remove his head from his body.

And furthermore, let me bear witness to you, my brothers, that if I break this oath, let me be forever cursed upon the lips of our people as a coward and an oath breaker.

My brothers, let us be His [God's] battle ax and weapons of war. Let us go forth by ones and twos, by scores and by legions, and as true Aryan men with pure hearts and strong minds face the enemies of our faith and our race with courage and determination.

We hereby invoke the blood covenant and declare that we are in a full state of war and will not lay down our weapons until we have driven the enemy into the sea and reclaimed the land which was promised to our fathers of old, and through our blood and His will, becomes the land of our children to be.[74]

This new Order, or Bruder Schweigen (Silent Brotherhood, a name for the Nazi SS storm troopers in World War II, who were in turn descended from the post-World War I *Freikorps*), then began to act out the plot of the *Diaries*. Getting money was top priority. Just as Earl Turner's cell first robbed a Jewish-owned deli and liquor store,

Matthews's group decided to steal from an equally "depraved" source, in this case a Spokane, Washington, pornography shop. But the October 28, 1983, heist netted only $369.

They soon escalated their efforts. The Order began a large-scale counterfeiting operation, distributing fake bills in both the West and, through a Philadelphia recruit named Thomas Martinez, the East as well. On December 20, Matthews robbed a Citibank branch in Seattle and made away with $25,900.

The next year the Order switched to robbing armored cars. They appear to have gotten this idea during a July 1983 convocation of loosely affiliated racist groups at George Butler's Aryan Nation compound in Hayden Lake, Idaho. Reverend Robert Miles, a Christian Identity preacher, had been impressed by the Black Liberation Army and Weather Underground's holdup of a Brinks armored car in 1981. During a ceremony in which he blessed their guns, he told one of the assemblies: "If we were half the men the leftists were, we'd be hitting armored cars too."[75] On April 23, 1984, Matthews's group stole $500,000 from an armored car in a Seattle shopping center. That July they attacked another armored car on a highway near Ukiah, California; this time the take was $3,600,000. (According to a confession later made to the FBI by one of the robbers, Bruce Carroll Pierce—no relation to William S. Pierce—part of this money was distributed to other racist organizations: Tom Metzer, founder of the White Aryan Resistance (WAR) near San Diego, California, received between $250,000 and $300,000; Louis Beam, the Texas Emergency Reserve leader and an "ambassador at large" for the Aryan Nations in Idaho, received $100,000; Glen Miller, Jr., the North Carolina paramilitary organizer, got $300,000; William S. Pierce received $50,000; a few other men received smaller sums. Pierce later recanted the confession and all of the alleged recipients denied receiving any money from Matthews's group.[76])

By now the Order had over twenty active members and a recruiting list for nearly another twenty. Anyone who hadn't read *The Turner Diaries* was given a copy by Matthews before his initiation. Each initiate also received a silver medallion inscribed with a shield, a Roman cross, the words Bruder Schweigen, and "Ye be my battle axe and my weapons of war" written in Gaelic.[77] As the money poured in from counterfeiting and robberies, the Order moved on to another phase of *The Diaries*, the Day of the Rope. At first the list of candidates for assassination included the names of such men as Henry Kissinger, David Rockefeller, TV producer Norman Lear, the heads of the major television networks, and anti-Klan activist Morris Dees. This list was nearly identical to the one Louis Beam of TER had placed on his national computer network in 1983—each had a rating on a point scale to motivate would-be warriors to win "Aryan Warrior" status.[78]

But all these men were too difficult to attack, so the Order settled for Alan Berg, a Denver radio-show personality who loved to bait the right wing. Berg, a Jew, had at one time deeply offended David Lane, a member of the Silent Brotherhood, when Lane spoke with Berg on his call-in talk show. Lane had never forgotten the humiliation. Jean Craig, the one female member of the Order—though she was never allowed to take the full oath—first went to Denver to investigate Berg's routines and then "threw the runes," special stones used by the medieval Norse as a way of divining the future. The runes determined that Berg should be assassinated at his home. On June 18, 1984, Bruce Pierce shot Berg with a .45 MAC-10 submachine gun, equipped with a noise suppressor, that been bought from the head armorer at the CSA compound in the Arkansas Ozarks. David Lane drove the getaway car while Matthews supervised the operation.

Though the murder of Alan Berg could be interpreted as a minor assassination by a fringe group, it was in fact emblematic of the way the New War obliterated its victims. Extremist groups like the Order had declared "full and unrelenting war" against the evil ones. And this made for extraordinarily savage crimes: When the Order went after Alan Berg, they shot him twelve times. The only reason he wasn't shot even more times was that the submachine gun jammed on the thirteenth or fourteenth shot—the plan was to empty the entire thirty-round magazine into him. Still, those twelve bullets made thirty-four different wounds in Berg's body; he was pulverized.[79]

In at least two other instances during the 1980s, extremists ripped their victims to shreds. Michael Ryan, or General Ryan as he called himself, ran a Christian Identity compound near Rulo, Nebraska, in the mid-1980s. His group of over thirty people was shown Christian

Identity videotapes along with *Red Dawn* as they waited for the Apocalypse to occur right outside their farm (beginning with a tank battle between the United States and the USSR.). At one point, Ryan disciplined a dissenter by having him sodomized with a shovel handle, shooting his fingers off, partially skinning him, and then jumping up and down on his chest until his internal organs ruptured and he died.[80]

In Washington State, Charles Chat Ng and Leonard Lake formed a two-man group waiting for the coming nuclear war. Lake had previously run a paintball playing field that specialized in postnuclear war fantasies and published a magazine called *War Games Magazine*. Ng, who believed himself to be a reincarnated Ninja warrior from medieval Japan, had stolen $11,000 worth of machine guns while he was a Marine. After he was released from prison, he and Lake established a rural fortress. An untold number of women were brutally tortured to death there as the men "tested" candidates to be "warriors' wives." These torture sessions were all videotaped; the victims' bodies were dismembered and then burned. Lake habitually wore camouflage fatigues; he killed himself with a poison pill when caught by police.[81]

It was not only these acts of violence that revealed the interplay of "real world" actions and New War fictions. Matthews in particular seems to have been strongly influenced by the more mainstream mass-media versions of New War mythology. When he visited Thomas Martinez in Philadelphia to recruit him for the counterfeiting operation, Matthews specially requested to see Clint Eastwood movies on Martinez's VCR. As Martinez explains, "Racists, I've found, are great fans of Eastwood's vengeful cop stories."[82] Instead, Martinez showed him *Fighting Back*, a 1982 action-adventure about a delicatessen owner who forms a vigilante group to go after a black gang after his wife and mother are injured. Martinez reports that Matthews wanted to see several scenes over and over. Matthews himself chose to show Charles Bronson's *Death Wish 2* (1982) to his mistress, Zillah Craig. "This is what's wrong with society today," he told her as Bronson killed a villain. "We have to do that because the government won't. Our police state doesn't do that. We have to cleanse the land ourselves."[83] Matthews said that he personally was doing a lot, just like Bronson, but wasn't appreciated very much.

On another occasion Matthews wrote Zillah Craig a letter about his forthcoming rescue mission to free a true Mexican, "a white Spaniard," from a Mexican prison because the man was an enemy of Jews and "non-white Mexicans who are pouring into our country."[84] Actually he was going to rob the bank in Seattle, but the story bears some resemblance to the various heroic rescues from Vietnamese prisons that appeared in pulp novels, comics, and films of the early and middle 1980s.

There were several other instances in which Order members appeared to be looking toward the commercial New War for help in planning their battles. When the FBI broke into Order member Gary Yarbrough's house in October 1984 they found a copy of Kenneth Goddard's *Balefire*, a novel about a terrorist assault against the 1984 Summer Olympics in Los Angeles. Several passages were underlined in red. Bruce Pierce, the murderer of Alan Berg, bought a gyroplane like the one in *The Road Warrior* with his share of the money from the armed robberies.

Most importantly, the Silent Brotherhood shared paramilitary culture's fascination with the newest in weaponry. If they had been willing to buy older guns on the used market, Order members could have drastically reduced their presence in government records. Instead, their paper trails grew longer week by week. One Order member bought a brand-new 9mm automatic in his own name, thus leaving a record with the Bureau of Alcohol, Firearms and Tobacco. Robert Matthews borrowed this gun for the Ukiah, California, armored car robbery and dropped it in the armored car. The FBI traced the registration to a P.O. box from which they obtained vital names and addresses of Order members. To take another example, by any reasonable criminal standards, the MAC-10 used to kill Alan Berg should have been destroyed immediately. But Order members were simply too smitten with it; they couldn't let it go and the gun was found at Gary Yarbrough's house.

This carelessness about weapons—and Thomas Martinez's work as an FBI informer after his arrest on counterfeiting charges—led to the demise of the Order. In November 1984, the FBI raided a Portland, Oregon, motel where Matthews and other members of the Order were staying. Several members were captured but Matthews, though wounded, escaped and made his way to a safe house on Whidbey Island in Puget Sound across from Seattle. There other gang members joined him to sign yet another declaration of "full and unrelenting war" against the Zionist Occupational Government. In one section called "Open Letter to Congress" the document warned that the Day of the Rope would come to them soon for their "atrocities," particularly the "betrayal of 55,000 Americans" killed during the Vietnam War.[85] Matthews wanted to send the declaration of war to the three largest newspapers in every state.

Preparations for this mailing were well under way when more than 150 FBI agents closed in on the Order's island hideout in early December. Several members of the Order surrendered; Matthews refused. FBI agents finally fired three magnesium Starburst flares from an M79 grenade launcher into the house. It caught fire, exploding ammunition caches inside in a cleansing conflagration worthy of any New War spectacle. Matthew's charred body was found the next morning with his gold Bruder Schweigen medallion melted into his chest cavity. The note he left could have been written by Casca, the eternal warrior: "I have been a good soldier, a fearless warrior. I will die with honor and join my brothers in Valhalla . . . For the future of my children. For the green graves of my sires."[86] In Valhalla, immortal warriors fight forever.

Many, if not all, of the other Order members were captured in 1985 and tried for crimes ranging from the Alan Berg murder to the various robberies and violations of federal gun laws. Most received long prison terms. In 1987, the federal government prosecuted Louis Beam, Robert E. Miles, Richard Butler, and several other men for seditious conspiracy to overthrow the United States government. A Fort Smith, Arkansas, jury acquitted all defendants on April 7, 1988. Louis Beam reportedly walked out of the federal courthouse, stood before a statute of Confederate soldiers, and said, "Praise Yahweh."[87]

11

On March 30, 1981, newly elected President Ronald Reagan attended a luncheon with supporters at the Washington Hilton to celebrate his victory over Walter Mondale. Outside the hotel, Reagan fans gathered to catch a glimpse of the new leader. A former Hollywood film star, Reagan knew how to please a crowd. As he left the hotel and prepared to step into his limo, he turned and waved. Among those cheering him on was a 25-year-old Denver man. To him, Reagan's wave was a secret message. Reagan was signalling "Now is the time," thought John Hinckley.[1] He drew two small .22 revolvers from his pocket and opened fire. President Reagan was seriously wounded in the lung, while his press secretary, James Brady, took a nearly fatal shot in the head. A Secret Service agent was also wounded.

In the days immediately following the assassination attempt, many in the news media speculated that Hinckley was a paramilitary warrior of some sort. One *Washington Post* story showed a photograph of four neo-Nazi youths, one of whom was blond like Hinckley. The story said that Hinckley had invented an imaginary white supremacist group in his diaries. A guest on "Good Morning America" wondered aloud if Hinckley was a member of the Libyan hit squads, assassins that had supposedly been sent to the U.S. by Mu'ammar Gadhafi to attack the Reagan administration.[2] (Years later it was revealed that the rumors of Libyan hit squads were part of a Reagan administration campaign against Libya.)[3] Both speculations were indicative of widespread fears that the New War had started for real and that the most evil of enemies, namely Nazis and Libyan terrorists, had fired the first shots.

Over the next three years, press stories and testimony given during Hinckley's trial for attempted murder and assault revealed a different story. Hinckley was a paramilitary warrior, but his role model had come from Hollywood, not the Middle East. In 1976, Hinckley had dropped out of Texas Technical University in Lubbock and moved to Los Angeles in the hope of launching a career as a songwriter. Like most would-be songwriters, he was ignored by the music industry. But in Hinckley's case, this was one rejection too many; a deep-seated mental illness—later diagnosed as "process schizophrenia," or the inability to form an ego or self—finally took over. In a few short months, Hinckley watched *Taxi Driver* (1976), a film in which Robert De Niro played a seriously disturbed Vietnam veteran named Travis Bickle, at least sixteen times. According to one of his attorneys, Hinckley "became Travis Bickle; he *was* Travis."[4]

Taxi Driver is the story of Travis's mental breakdown. What happened to him in Vietnam is never mentioned, but even while working as a New York City taxi driver he always wears a uniform of olive-drab fatigue jacket, black boots, and dark glasses. He has neither family nor friends. At first Travis tries to form a relationship with a beautiful, well-educated woman who is working in a Presidential campaign; she rejects him. Travis also tries to befriend a young prostitute and steer her away from street life. She also rejects him. In his desperate isolation, Travis decides that the only way he can reestablish both a personal identity and a new relationship to society is by becoming a warrior again and committing a spectacular killing. He works out, buys several pistols, and shaves his head, leaving only a warrior's Mohawk. After his efforts to assassinate the Presidential candidate fail, he attacks the young prostitute's pimp and clients. The news media subsequently portray him as a hero. Yet the end of the movie takes away this sense of redemption. When Travis picks up the beautiful Presidential campaign worker in his taxi she looks at him as if nothing happened—because *nothing did happen*; all the killing was merely Travis's sad fantasy.

Hinckley, though, saw *Taxi Driver* as a success story. He bought the same kind of clothes that Travis wore; he started drinking peach brandy like Travis. And he started hunting Presidents. His first target was Jimmy Carter. The first three pistols he bought (confiscated at the Nashville airport on a day that Carter was in the city) were the same model handguns Travis used. Hinckley also decided to save the same woman Travis did, Jodie Foster, the actress who played the prostitute in *Taxi Driver*. In a letter to the *New York Times*, Hinckley wrote, "The shooting outside the Washington Hilton hotel was the greatest love offering in the history of the world. I sacrificed myself and committed the ultimate crime in hopes of winning the heart of a girl."[5] At other times Hinckley subtly changed his story to one in which Reagan was being sacrificed for the sins of the nation. Hinckley apparently thought that by killing Reagan, he would then become President, Foster would marry him, and together they would live happily ever after as king and queen ruling over a restored American kingdom. In 1984, Hinckley was found not guilty by reason of insanity on all the many charges filed against him. He was committed to a mental hospital.

Unfortunately, Hinckley's story was not unique. As it turned out, he was a harbinger, the first of many psychotic 1980s killers who saw themselves as warriors. Year after year, Hinckley's successors shot their way across the country with extraordinary regularity and pretty good aim. Throughout the decade, the body count in war-zone America kept getting higher.

In 1981, a Ohio steel worker named James Oliver Huberty bought one of the first Israeli Uzi 9mm carbines imported into the United States for his growing gun collection. A relative of Huberty had helped design the Lewis machine gun of WW I fame, and as a boy, Huberty had been fascinated with it—the gun was clearly a source of power for a boy left lame after a childhood illness. Huberty also had a long record of mental illness. After he lost his job as a steel worker in 1982 and suffered further losses on real-estate transactions, his precarious mental health deteriorated further. He developed an interest in survivalism and studied gun magazines. Huberty also railed against the Federal Reserve and in an act that seems at least partially aimed at defying the Fed moved his family to San Ysidro, California (south of San Diego, not far from the Mexican border), in the hope of getting rich by taking advantage of Mexico's fluctuating peso.

On July 19, 1984, 41-year-old Huberty dressed in black T-shirt, camouflage pants, and dark glasses. To complete the look, he carried his Uzi, his Winchester 12-gauge shotgun, his Browning 9mm pistol, and a bag of ammunition magazines. He told his wife and daughter, "I'm going hunting humans."[6] That afternoon he walked into a McDonald's restaurant near his home and shouted at the mostly Latino crowd, "I killed thousands in Vietnam and I want to kill more."[7] Huberty had never been in the military at all, but that day he fought his own personal war, firing a hundred and forty rounds, killing twenty-one and wounding nineteen before a San Diego police sniper finally shot him.

After Huberty, the frequency of paramilitary murder incidents increased. In early February 1985, a Los Angeles man who apparently was an ardent paintball player donned his cammies and went after his neighbor, wounding him with a shotgun. A few months later, in June, 18-year-old Robert M. Rosenberg, also of Los Angeles, got into a fight at his own graduation party and was thrown out of the house by his parents. At first despondent, he tried to rent a handgun at a local gun range with which to kill himself. The clerk said that he was too young to rent a handgun, and instead offered him an Uzi. Rosenberg decided to buy one—California did not have a waiting period for "long guns." His despondency or self-hate was soon transformed into rage against others, and within days Rosenberg settled an argument with an old friend by shooting him eleven times. And in the fall of that year, a Pennsylvania woman wearing military fatigues and black boots and carrying a semiautomatic military-style rifle opened fire in a shopping center, killing two and wounding eight.

In April 1986, two FBI agents in Miami were killed and five critically wounded in a shoot-out with a pair of camouflage-wearing bank robbers, Vietnam veterans armed with a Ruger Mini-14, shotguns, and pistols. This incident received national attention because it seemed to indicate that many "ordinary" criminals were arming themselves with advanced combat weapons. In August, an Edmonton, Oklahoma, postal worker threatened with dismissal counterattacked by killing fourteen of his co-workers with two .45-caliber semiautomatic pistols. To end the year, a fired utility-service crew member at the University of Kentucky returned to campus wearing a black ninja suit and carrying a rifle and samurai sword with ammo belts crisscrossing his chest. Fortunately, only one man was slightly wounded before the ninja was disarmed with a fire department water hose.

The killings continued in 1987. A Florida gunman killed six people with a Ruger Mini-14, while a camouflage-wearing Texan—nicknamed Rambo—committed three murders in Missouri before shooting his boss, his estranged wife, and her boyfriend in Corsicana, Texas. But the big news in 1987 concerned a new development—the appearance in Australia and Great Britain of mass murderers following the same pathological pattern. On August 13, a Melbourne, Australia, man killed several people with a military-style semiautomatic rifle. A few days later, on the 19th, Michael Ryan killed sixteen people (including his mother, a widow with whom he lived) and wounded fourteen others in Hungerford, England. Ryan used a semiautomatic version of an AK47. He was dressed in military-style clothing. Police later found in his car trunk a set of body armor, a gas mask, bandages, a Swiss Army knife, and brandy. The story Ryan told his family before the killing spree was that he was secretly working for a wealthy man and father-figure named Colonel Ash, who was paying for his flying lessons and preparing him for a mission on his tea plantation in India, where he would be given a Porsche, Ferrari, or Rolls-Royce.[8] By December, the action returned to Melbourne again, where another man killed eight and wounded three with a sawed-off .30-caliber M1 carbine.

1989 was the biggest year of them all. The most famous incident occurred in January, when a young man in Stockton, California, took a semiautomatic version of an AK47 to a local schoolyard. Dressed in an Army fatigue jacket, Patrick Purdy killed five Southeast Asian children and wounded twenty-nine others, along with one teacher, before shooting himself with a 9mm pistol. Two months later, a 16-year-old boy in Poughkeepsie, New York, murdered his parents and his brother. When police arrested him, he gave his name as Rambo; a search of his bedroom revealed "dozens of Rambo posters and magazines, army packs, smoke grenades and ammunition pouches."[9] In September, a printer in Louisville, Kentucky, who had been put on long-term disability by his employer, returned to work with an AK47, two 9mm MAC-11s, a SIG-Sauer 9mm semiautomatic pistol, and a .38 revolver. He murdered eight and wounded twelve before killing himself. A former co-worker said that the killer, Joseph Wesbecker, had been reading *Soldier of Fortune* for years.[10] Finally, in December, Marc Lepine, a Montreal man who blamed feminism for his failure to succeed in college, dressed in hunting clothes and entered the École Polytechnique of the University of Montreal with a Ruger Mini-14. He ignored the male students, and instead screamed "I want women." Lepine ultimately shot twenty-seven women, killing fourteen.[11] The *Los Angeles Times* reported that "he seemed to seek refuge from his personal troubles in war movies, which police said he watched as if 'obsessed.' "[12]

American history is full of serial murderers—meaning individuals who kill their victims one or two at a time over a long period. However, mass murder—the killing of many people at once—did not become widespread until the 1980s.[13] Although the list of multiple murders provided here is by no means exhaustive, it does display a distinct cultural pattern. In many of these cases, the murderer was deeply fascinated by the movies and magazines of the New War. Most of the men (and one woman) committed their crimes while wearing some kind of paramilitary uniform—be it camouflage shirt and pants, khaki clothes, or a fatigue jacket. Changing into warrior clothes apparently helped these people abandon their previous selves and appropriate a new self-image—that of a powerful person with a mission.

The murderers' choice of weapons—primarily semiautomatic rifles based on military designs—suggests the same fascination with New

War myths. The AK47 has long been famous as the quintessential "bad" gun used by Communists and terrorists to wreak havoc on the world. The Israeli-made Uzi is another glamorous "bad" weapon with an aura of great power—after all, the Israelis, unlike the Americans, both won their wars and took revenge for every act of violence committed against them. In contrast, "ordinary" guns are just that—ordinary; they are not imbued with symbolic powers or associated with modern mythic warriors. Like the *SOF* hit men, many of these mass murderers very much wanted that association; they needed "bad" guns to become "bad" men.

Although several of these paramilitary killers went after former co-workers and bosses, and some even killed their families, most targeted a distinct social group, an enemy already familiar from New War fictions. Thus, Huberty seems to have considered the Latinos at the San Ysidro McDonald's to be Vietnamese. Patrick Purdy was found to have been a white supremacist; his choice of Asian schoolchildren was not an accident. Canadian Marc Lepine shot only women.

Throughout the 1980s, most of these murders received widespread attention in print and television news; even stories about the foreign killings, particularly Michael Ryan's rampage in Hungerford, England, were extensively covered. Details about the clothes the killers wore, the guns they carried, the characteristics of the people they shot were always reported. In short, paramilitary killings became a *known*, well-established, codified type of action. It was not necessary for each prospective murderer to invent his crime from scratch. He could readily learn how to do it by following the news media—and easily imagine the spectacular effects of his crime. For example, in the 1989 Louisville incident, when police entered Joseph Wesbecker's home, they found not only copies of *SOF*, but also the February 6, 1989, issue of *Time* magazine, which had the cover headline "Armed America: More guns, more shootings, more massacres." When Wesbecker left his home to attack the people working at the Standard Gravure printing plant, he left the magazine open to the article.[14]

It's also important to note the way most of these killing sprees ended. The one woman in this list of killers told the Springfield, Pennsylvania, policeman who found her: "Hurry up, man, you know

I'm guilty. Kill me on the spot."[15] In contrast, most of the males killed themselves after finishing their personal wars. Self-destruction was a final act of defiance and separation from society. By killing themselves, the mass murderers made certain that society could not punish them or exact payment for their crimes. Suicide (or repeatedly providing a clear shot for the police, as Huberty did in San Diego) also meant that the role of demonic mass murderer was opened up for someone else.

The paramilitary mass murderer thus became a kind of impersonal cultural "role" or figure in the 1980s, a special breed of devil for the decade. And though no one would seriously argue that the mythology of the New War drove these people insane, it did activate existing pathologies and suggest a way of expressing them. Like the mercenaries, hit men, and race warriors, the paramilitary mass murderers *directly* lived out the modern warrior mythology that permeated much of American culture.

For Americans to have understood these killers and the significance of their acts would have required understanding the social significance of paramilitary culture. But the genuine horror of these crimes so frightened and angered people that there was no space for critical reflection on what America had become. Instead, from the time of Hinckley's assassination attempt in 1981 on, the debate on how to stop paramilitary killings became exclusively framed in terms of the need for stricter gun control legislation. The two R.G. Industries .22 revolvers John Hinckley used had been bought over the counter at a Dallas pawnshop for less than $45 apiece. They were the legendary Saturday Night Specials, whose importation had supposedly been banned by the Gun Control Act of 1968. By a glitch in the law, importing the *parts* for such guns was not illegal; consequently, importers had simply begun assembling them in the U.S.

Nor did Texas have a waiting period for purchasing guns. Gun-control advocates insisted that had a federally mandated waiting period been in effect, authorities would have learned that Hinckley did not live at the Texas address he gave. Hinckley also told his father that, while the death penalty would not have stopped him from his quest, gun control would have been a deterrent: "Maybe if I'd had to wait a while to buy a gun. Had to fill out forms, or get a permit first, or sign with the police, or anything complicated. I probably wouldn't have done it."[16] It's hard to believe that filling out a few more forms than current gun laws require would have proved an insurmountable task for a man who crisscrossed the nation several times by plane and bus over many months while maneuvering to get within range of first Carter and then Reagan. Moreover, at the time of purchase, whatever his street address, Hinckley was a legal Texas resident, had a valid I.D., and had no criminal record—it seems most unlikely that a routine check conducted during a waiting period would have revealed anything amiss. Still, Hinckley did blame the lax gun laws both for the assassination of his hero, John Lennon, and for his own attempt to murder Reagan.

So did a lot of other people. Pete Shields, at the time president of Handgun Control, Inc. (HCI) a small organization devoted to requiring more stringent regulations on handguns, reported that in the weeks after the attack, HCI received over 250,000 letters of support and gained many new members and contributors. President Ronald Reagan was not among them. In his first press conference after the March 30 attack, Reagan was asked if he had changed his position on gun control. He replied:

> There are, today, more than 20,000 gun-control laws in effect—federal, state, and local—in the United States. Indeed, some of the stiffest gun-control laws in the nation are right here in the district and they didn't seem to prevent a fellow, a few weeks ago, from carrying one down by the Hilton Hotel. In other words, they are virtually unenforceable. So I would like to see us directing our attention to what has caused us to have the crime that continues to increase as it has and is one of our major problems in the country today. And that's it."[17]

During much of the 1980s, the Reagan administration and its Congressional supporters successfully maintained their resistance to federal gun control—indeed, some previous Congressional acts regulating the gun business were overturned and funding for the Bureau of Alcohol, Tobacco and Firearms was reduced.

But the January 17, 1989, attack on the Asian schoolchildren in

Stockton, California, shocked the country. If little children playing in a school yard—a sacred space even in the eyes of the most secular Americans—were not safe, then no one was. Chaos and evil were obviously spreading faster and faster, and many people felt the need to do *something*. Gun control immediately became the chosen venue for trying to push back the disorder: the "bad" guns used by mass murderers, drug dealers, gangs, and other desperados would be banished.

Almost immediately after the Stockton shooting, Californians realized that legislation banning certain military-style rifles was both inevitable and imminent. This extraordinary overnight consensus among people of vastly different social backgrounds and political orientations in turn led to two very different mass movements. The first consisted of people desperate to *buy* assault rifles before they were banned or otherwise stringently regulated. Within a week of the Stockton killings, gun stores in California were inundated with customers. Even the privately owned gun store at the Los Angeles Police Academy found its assault-rifle sales increasing from one a month to four a day. "The demand for the weapons has skyrocketed," one policeman said.[18]

For the next few months, gun dealers were searching frantically for wholesale distributors who could supply them with hundreds or thousands of high-tech rifles. Prices on many firearms doubled or tripled. Variants of semiautomatic AK47s like the one Patrick Purdy fired in the school yard had formerly cost from less than $300 to $400; by late spring the price went up to between $600 and $900. When on March 15, 1989, Colt Industries announced that it was voluntarily suspending sales of all its Model AR-15 variants, those guns, which had formerly cost around $600–$800, jumped into the $1,000–$1,800 range. Uzis doubled to $1,200–$1,500; MAC-10s tripled to $1,250–$1,500. The really exotic weapons that had typically sold for at least $900—such as the Heckler and Koch rifles, the Israeli Galil rifle, and the Steyr-AUG carbine—soon brought between $1,500 and $2,500. Both press reports and personal interviews revealed that a few buyers saw their purchases as straight investments—they fully intended to sell the dreaded weapons in the future (after over-the-counter sales of new guns were banned) at far higher prices. For the most part, though, the stampede to purchase assault rifles was impelled by mass fear—people sought firepower to ease their anxieties over what the future might bring. Working people bought the "cheaper" AKs. The more affluent had more elegant tastes. One dealer told me that the customers for the really expensive guns that he was selling at the rate of 500 to 600 a week were "yuppies to the max."[19]

Of course, depriving yuppies of their newest toys was not what the gun-control advocates had in mind. They were worried about the psychopaths like Purdy and the use of semiautomatic rifles by gangs and drug dealers. A new gang practice of drive-by shootings, in which gang members sprayed a house or a busy street corner with anywhere from ten to fifty rounds, often involved the use of military-style weapons. Somehow politicians began to hope that if the semiautos were banned, then mass murder, gang violence, and drug dealing would disappear with them. In Los Angeles, City Councilman Nat Holden held a press conference on January 24, 1989—a week after the Stockton killings and before the inflation of gun prices began—to announce his underdog candidacy against Mayor Tom Bradley. Suddenly, acting on impulse, Councilman Holden declared that he would pay cash for each AK47 that was turned in to law-enforcement officials. To buy back these weapons of destruction, Holden gallantly volunteered $50,000 from his own campaign funds. He set a price of $300 for the AK47s.[20]

Not to be outdone in citizenship, a Los Angeles radio station announced that it would pay $1,000 to the first person who showed up at the station with a receipt from the police indicating that he or she had surrendered an AK47; everyone else would be paid $300. The race was on. One woman bought thirteen and turned them over to the police. In the grand excitement some people seem to have gotten a bit confused about how many rewards were out there. One policeman told a *Los Angeles Times* reporter, "Some of these people seem to think they may get paid for them from more than one source . . . Some come in and ask if they can get their guns back if they can't get money from more than one source. We tell them no, because, once we get them, we are going to destroy them."[21]

To make matters worse for good citizens, Councilman Holden changed his mind once the guns started showing up at his office. He paid for them all right, but decided that only Yugoslavian and Hungarian AK47s—both fairly rare firearms in the United States (only 11,000 of these guns had been imported)—were really worth $300.[22] The common Chinese-made AKs, similar to the one Purdy used, were only worth $150. On the bright side, someone who just happened to own an Uzi or AK47 and had been storing it, unused, in the closet or under the bed could turn it in and get some money. The first two people to respond to Holden were in this category—not gang members.[23] Indeed, there never was a report of any gang member or drug dealer turning in his weapon. The rush to buy up AK47s, though, did help to drive up their market price.

While Councilman Holden got the first glory for his quick moves in January, by February he had disappeared from the papers and other advocates of gun control had taken his place. City councils in Stockton, Compton (a poor, largely black city of 90,000 in Los Angeles County), San Diego, Santa Monica, Los Angeles, and many other municipalities passed ordinances banning the future sale, and in most cases the current possession, of guns designated as semiautomatic assault rifles. Like Holden, most California politicians made a connection between mass murderers such as Purdy and the gang members and drug dealers in their cities. For example, Diane Watson, a state senator from a section of Los Angeles with serious gang problems, proposed a 10% gun tax whose revenue would be allocated to finance "gang abatement and drug-trafficking programs."[24] Watson also warned her fellow legislators that banning semiautomatic weapons was necessary because "the gangs are branching out and if they are not in your district right now, they soon will be. The gangs are rolling."[25] Los Angeles police chief Daryl Gates in turn testified before the state senate that "there's a domestic arms race in this country right now. Do you want us to be like Colombia where everybody has automatic weapons? Everybody gets shot down there."[26]

In early March 1989, both the California state senate and the assembly were preparing to vote on different bills banning some semiautomatic firearms. During the days of testimonies by witnesses for and against the gun-control measures, increased security measures were taken as a precaution against feared attacks by those who were opposed to the proposed restrictions.[27] One legislator, Jackie Speier of South San Francisco, even declared that the progun forces were so dangerous that "I hope to God that we don't have to wait for the press to be reporting on this building being riddled with bullets before we take some action."[28] Presumably, people against the proposed legislation would simply drive by the capitol building and shoot it up, much like gang members making a hit or marking their turf.

By April, both the California assembly and senate passed versions of a bill sponsored by Assemblyman Mike Roos of Los Angeles. Governor George Deukmejian signed the legislation on May 24—slightly less than four months after Purdy's attack. The Roos bill prohibited the sale of over forty types of semiautomatic rifles, pistols, and shotguns thought to be especially dangerous. Individuals who already owned such guns were required to register them with the California Attorney General's office before January 1, 1991.

The list of official "bad" guns warrants close examination. The legislature intended to ban all rifles derived from Avtomat Kalashnikov's original design, the AK series. Colt's AR-15 and CAR-15, the semiautomatic versions of the gun it made for the U.S. military, were listed. The MAC-10 and MAC-11, the favorite submachine guns of bad guys on *Miami Vice* in the late 1980s, got a spot as well, along with their Israeli cousin the Uzi. That all these glamour guns of paramilitary culture got banned should come as no surprise.

What is surprising is that the list includes many guns that had not gained a reputation as either movie star or criminal favorites. Belgium's Fabrique Nationale military-style rifles, which weighed 9½ pounds unloaded and cost from $1,325 to $1,860, were included, even though there were only 25,000 in the United States. Also on the list were rifles made by a Swiss firm named SIG—only 1,000 of which had been sold in the United States.[29] Another company, Weaver Arms, which had briefly manufactured a 9mm semiautomatic carbine like the Uzi, had already gone bankrupt by 1989 after selling very few guns. Because there were so few of them, these guns had no impact on crime. But their pistol grips, flash hiders, bayonet lugs (mounts), folding stocks, and metal parts with dull, parkerized finishes that didn't reflect light made them look "bad."

Conversely, several military-style weapons were not classified as deadly "assault" guns and thus were *omitted* from the list. At one point, the *Los Angeles Times* reported how it happened that Assemblyman Charles W. Quackenbush, a Republican initially opposed to the proposed legislation, changed his mind and decided to support it. After thumbing through a gun catalogue that showed pictures of all vaguely military-looking guns, he asked that a Beneilli M121-M1 shotgun be removed from the list since to him it looked like a sporting firearm. To which Assemblyman Mike Roos replied, "To get your vote, Mr. Quackenbush, I would be glad to give up one Beneilli M121-M1."[30]

Although only tiny numbers of Beneilli combat shotguns had been imported by 1989, the California list had some glaring omissions of important military guns widely available on the American market. The Institute for Research on Small Arms in International Security in 1989 calculated that Americans owned around 3,707,000 military-style rifles and carbines (small rifles). Of these, over 2,200,000 were M1 carbines, a gun used in World War II which fires a .30-caliber, 115-grain bullet at around 2,000 feet per second. In contrast, the banned Uzi carbine fires a 9mm (.36-caliber), 115-grain bullet at about 1,250 feet per second, and the AK47—also banned—fires a 7.62mm (.30-caliber), 122-grain bullet at 2,350 feet per second. Magazines holding fifteen or thirty rounds were routinely used in the M1 carbine. Ruger's Mini-14s (firing either 5.56mm ammunition like the AR-15 or 7.62 × 39mm ammunition like the AK47) had by 1989 sold over 500,000 guns. Twenty-round magazines are most commonly used in these guns. The M1 carbines and Mini-14s comprise about 73 percent of all the semiautomatic military-style rifles in the United States. Yet the Ruger models were not listed as assault guns, and only a very old commercial model of the M1 carbine made by a company that no longer existed was listed in the California legislation. Both the M1 carbine and the Ruger were normally sold with brown wooden stocks that lack pistol grips—thus they did not convey the same lethal aura, even though as real, functioning weapons, both the power of the bullets they fired and their large magazine capacities were comparable to the banned guns.

Finally, in its haste, the bill passed by the California legislature inadvertently omitted the version of the AK47 used by Patrick Purdy at Stockton. Since the legislation was written in such a way that any gun not explicitly forbidden was legal to buy and own, this particular piece of devil's hardware remained legal firepower even as gun-control advocates celebrated its presumed banishment from the community of "good" guns.[31]

Meanwhile, back in Washington, in March of 1989 the Bush administration finally reacted to the Purdy killings and the rapidly growing gun-control movement. The administration announced its alarm that in the first ten weeks of 1989 gun dealers had sought permission to import over 110,000 military-style semiautomatic rifles. Although in the 1988 Presidential campaign Bush had explicitly rejected the strict gun-control agenda put forth by his opponent, Michael Dukakis, things now looked different to administration officials.

William J. Bennett, director of the White House Office of National Drug Control Policy, ordered the Bureau of Alcohol, Tobacco and Firearms to institute what he called a temporary suspension prohibiting further importation of over twenty types of foreign-made military-style rifles. He acted under a provision of a 1968 federal law that allowed firearms to be imported only if they are "particularly suitable for, or readily adaptable to sporting purposes."[32]

Originally the law had been passed to stop the importation of cheap pistols firing small cartridges—the Saturday Night Specials. The military-style rifles chambered for fairly powerful cartridges, with long barrels and adjustable sights, had been judged to have enough favorable "points" on the Bureau of Alcohol, Tobacco and Firearms Form 4590 to meet this sporting-purposes criterion. Now the ATF was instructed to revise its criteria and conduct a study of imported assault guns to see if they really were sporting arms.

The ATF Working Group subsequently came up with a new list of negative features—detachable magazines, bayonet lugs, pistol grips, luminous night sights, flash suppressors, folding stocks, and similar "bad gun" elements so esteemed by paramilitary culture. ATF staffers filled their report with lines such as "it is generally illegal to hunt at night," and "we are not aware of any particular sporting use for grenade launchers."[33] The bureau even waded through scores of mag-

azines like *Guns and Ammo, Firepower,* and the *American Rifleman*
to note how each rifle was both advertised and reviewed; any references to a weapon's firepower or suitability for home defense, combat,
or serious law-enforcement work were included in the study. Ironically, then, paramilitary culture wrote its own indictment.

The ATF also sent questionnaires to state game commissions,
target-shooting associations, hunting/shooting editors, and several
hundred men who led hunting trips asking them to evaluate the
sporting use of each imported military-style weapon. Although the
target-shooting associations noted that such firearms qualified for "any
rifle" or "unlimited class" shooting competitions, virtually none of
the hunting guides or target-shooting leaders who responded to the
ATF survey knew of anyone actually using an Uzi, Fabrique Nationale
(FN), or AK47 in their sports.[34] Politically speaking, then, the assault
rifles at that time did not seem to have any easily definable or significant constituency.

On July 7, the day after the ATF study was officially released, the
Bush administration announced that forty-three types of military-style
firearms would henceforth be permanently banned from importation.
The list included the obvious bad guns like the AK and Uzi, and,
like the California list compiled a few months earlier, many obscure,
expensive firearms that had previously been imported in only tiny
numbers. More than anything, the ban served to underline just how
many foreign guns were on their way to American borders; new audits
of import-license requests at the ATF showed that in 1989 importers
had already received authorization for bringing in over 640,000 rifles
and were close to getting approval for 136,000 more. All those permits
were to be rescinded and the Customs Service was directed to impound
any shipments it discovered.[35]

The Bush administration's reaction to the shootings in Stockton
and its subsequent decision to ban foreign-made military weapons
created a framework that strongly influenced the discussion of gun
control for the next few years. It was significant that William J.
Bennett, often referred to as the nation's drug czar, made the initial
announcement concerning the ban of foreign guns. Thanks to this,
psychotic killers like Purdy were symbolically linked with drug
dealers—as if they were two faces of one devil figure. Presumably

they shared "madness," pleasure in killing, and a taste for "foreign" substances such as drugs made in Colombia or assault rifles made in China; vicious and intoxicated, they were destroying American children and thus America's future.

The Bush administration's actions also challenged the traditional liberal–conservative split on gun-control legislation. By making a dramatic effort to stop all the bad foreign guns, the administration sought to take the pro–gun-control stance away from the Democrats and expand the Republican Party's appeal to moderates and liberals. At the same time, since the ban did not affect American-made guns—like the Ruger Mini-14 and the M1 carbine—the action could be viewed by its more conservative supporters, such as the members of the National Rifle Association, as the best possible compromise given the political climate. After all, Bush had also called for a mandatory ten-year prison sentence for anyone committing a crime with a banned gun—the kind of blame-the-man-rather-than-the-gun approach favored by the NRA.

However, the gun-control issue could not be so neatly contained and packaged for a deft political maneuver: the intoxicating symbolism of guns and drugs, life and death, madmen and order, freedom and totalitarianism was much too alluring and explosive. At the very moment the import ban was announced, liberal critics decried what to them was its gross limitation, namely that it did not affect American guns. As Representative Pete Stark, a Democrat from California, exclaimed, "If you're a cop on the street and some guy is spraying you with a Street Sweeper or an Uzi, it's not time to fuss about buy-American."[36]

Stark and many of his Democratic colleagues in both the House and Senate favored banning many America-made military semi-automatic rifles and pistols as well. In 1989 both Senator Howard Metzenbaum of Ohio and Senator Dennis DeConcini of Arizona initiated separate legislative proposals that sought to ban the sale and ownership of various models of American-made semiautomatic firearms. Identical versions of the two bills were also introduced in the House. The two proposals differed only in the number of guns banned. Metzenbaum's more expansive measure called for outlawing future sales of two popular American-made semiautomatics, the Colt

AR-15 and Ruger Mini-14; his bill also prohibited sales of many foreign-made guns and made it illegal for any gun owner either to transport a rifle outside his home (making it impossible to actually shoot the gun) or to sell it.

DeConcini had more limited ambitions. He wanted to outlaw several of the same bad foreign guns, but on the domestic side his bill did not list the popular Ruger rifles with their ordinary wooden stocks. Instead, it targeted Colt's black plastic gun, the AR-15, along with the MAC-10 and MAC-11, a pistol called the Intratec TEC-9 that resembled a submachine gun, and two shotguns designed in South Africa but made in America called the Street Sweeper and Striker 12. (The prototype for these lovely items—an experimental 25mm grenade launcher—first appeared as actor Christopher Walken's weapon of choice in the 1981 film version of Frederick Forsyth's classic novel about mercenaries, *The Dogs of War*.) DeConcini's bill was named the Anti-Drug Assault Weapon Limitation Act.

One other vitally important piece of national gun-control legislation, known as the Brady Bill, also came under serious consideration and debate in the aftermath of the Stockton killings: the proposed institution of a federally mandated waiting period which would require prospective handgun buyers to wait seven days after they purchased a pistol or revolver before taking it out of the store. This delay presumably would help people who were temporarily enraged and bent on committing violence to cool off and regain their sanity. The waiting period would also provide a stretch of time long enough for police to determine whether a potential buyer was legally qualified to own a gun.

Although federal legislation creating a waiting period for the purchase of handguns would not affect the purchase of military-style semiautomatic rifles like the one Purdy used in Stockton, the gun-control movement used the Stockton killings to revitalize interest in all forms of gun control. At the same time, Handgun Control, Inc. expanded its political agenda to include the banning of military-style semiautomatic rifles.

The Brady Bill was named after James Brady, who had narrowly escaped death after being shot in the head when John Hinckley attempted to assassinate President Reagan and who was now, partially paralyzed, confined to a wheelchair. Jim Brady had felt obliged to maintain a discreet silence on gun control while Reagan was in office. His wife Sarah Brady, however, was under no such constraint and in 1986 she began lecturing and writing opinion-page essays in support of the agenda of Handgun Control, Inc.

By the time of the Stockton killings, Reagan was no longer President, and Jim Brady lost his reticence. He took advantage of the national concern over assault rifles to mobilize support for the Brady Bill. His first advertisement in print for HCI read in part: "Ever since I was shot, I have watched from my wheelchair as the gun lobby blocked one sane handgun control bill after another. But I'm not just watching anymore. I'm calling on Congress to pass a common-sense law—the Brady bill requiring a 'cooling off' period before the purchase of a handgun. So police have time to check if the buyer has a criminal record . . . It seems that the only people against the Brady bill are psychopaths, criminals, drug dealers, and the gun lobby."[37]

Brady's charge signified another important moment in the symbolic framing of the gun-control issue. While Bennett as White House drug czar had officially linked guns, drugs, and madmen, HCI now expanded the association much further: the "gun lobby," too, was contaminated with the same fundamental evil as dealers and madmen. But the "gun lobby"—or, more accurately, the National Rifle Association—differed in one basic way from psychopaths, criminals, and drug dealers. Whereas these marginal groups and individuals spent most of their time hiding in the shadows and thus could only rarely be located and confronted by the forces of good, the National Rifle Association, a public organization with around 2,800,000 members, had a known address, published magazines and newsletters, and employed a staff of some 350, including many full-time lobbyists. The NRA was thus a target that could be found. And if it could be defeated in debates over gun control, then perhaps all the other forces of evil—the madmen and drug dealers who were so difficult to find and stop—could be defeated as well.

Both in its exhortations to faithful members and in its public advertisements, HCI set out to beat the NRA devils back into Hades. In early 1989 at least one of the form letters sent to new HCI members came in an envelope emblazoned with the battle cry: "Your first real chance to tell the National Rifle Association to go to hell!" In the enclosed letter Sarah Brady warned new members that the NRA was "working feverishly to block all attempts to ban plastic, *undetectable handguns that could easily be smuggled onto airplanes.*" When not helping terrorists onto airplanes, the NRA was busy trying to keep "cop killer" bullets in circulation. Not only did the NRA support unspeakably foul deeds, Brady implied, but they wanted to contaminate all Americans with their evil: "Some [NRA] leaders believe *you should be required by law* to keep a gun in your home."[38]

In the fall of 1989 HCI launched "OPERATION SPOTLIGHT," an effort to break "the *stranglehold* the NRA has long held on state legislatures throughout the nation." SPOTLIGHT, Sarah Brady wrote, "will be the most aggressive *gloves-off* campaign we have ever launched."[39] In the spring of 1990 this rhetoric of personal combat changed to the language of strategic bombing. A letter to HCI members, with "Confidential" stamped on the envelope, broke the war news: "It now appears we are within striking distance of winning passage of the 'Brady Bill.' Consequently, *we have put our entire Washington lobby staff and our entire grassroots operations on full alert* . . . Victory is within our grasp."[40]

And just to make sure no one forgot who the enemy was, in July 1990 HCI ran a series of nearly full-page newspaper advertisements featuring a Ku Klux Klansman wearing white robes decorated with a cross and the stars and bars of the Confederate flag. In his hands he held an AR-15 with a 30-round magazine. The caption read: "Why is the NRA allowing *Him* Easy Access to Assault Weapons?" The first paragraph of the text listed all the evil weapons that the NRA wanted to preserve and protect: "The AK-47s used in Stockton and Louisville . . . the Colt AR-15s used by Los Angeles gang members . . . the UZI assault pistols used by crack peddlers . . . the military-style guns used by white supremacists—the Skinheads, the Nationalist Movement, the Order, the Ku Klux Klan, and other paramilitary hate groups."[41]

Although Speaker of the House Thomas S. Foley postponed consideration of the Brady Bill in the fall of 1990, by the next spring it was back on the legislative docket.[42] As the Brady Bill approached its appearance before the House Judiciary Committee in mid-April,

HCI sounded confident of victory. After all, just weeks earlier, former President Ronald Reagan had reversed his previous opposition to more gun-control laws and had publicly endorsed the Brady Bill. In her communiqué to HCI members Sarah Brady proudly noted that "the National Rifle Association will hold its annual meeting in San Antonio, Texas, against the backdrop of the Alamo where Texas heroes fought to death against the siege by the Mexican Army. Ironically, Texas is the state where John Hinckley purchased the Saturday Night Special he used to shoot my husband and President Reagan. The NRA believes itself, like Jim Bowie and Davy Crockett, to be under siege."[43]

Brady's underlying message to HCI members is not difficult to decipher—but it is a bit bizarre. The leaders and ideologues of the National Rifle Association had for years viewed the Alamo as an important example of citizen soldiers using their personal weapons to defend freedom. And now, over 150 years after the Mexican Army decimated the defenders of the Alamo, the HCI would symbolically kill the NRA. Ironically, with its visions of hand-to-hand combat, strategic bombing campaigns, and battlefield charges against demons who enjoyed the pleasures of drugs, guns, and mayhem, HCI's "war" against gun violence extended paramilitary culture's reach into new social strata. The language and imagery of war and warriors became the preferred discourse also of those who saw themselves as fundamentally opposed to paramilitary culture's most infamous material artifact—the "assault" weapon.

The National Rifle Association and other members of the progun fraternity conducted their own massive campaigns to stop the passage of all the proposed state and federal legislation regulating the sale and possession of firearms. The basis of their opposition was a particular reading of the Second Amendment to the Constitution: "A well-regulated Militia, being necessary to the security of a free State, the right of the people to keep and bear Arms, shall not be infringed." Progun advocates contended that legally the term "people" in the Second Amendment was the same "people" that also appears in the First, Fourth, Ninth, and Tenth Amendments; the "people" means every individual. The Second Amendment, then, does not apply only to government militia units such as the National Guard.[44] Each adult citizen has a constitutionally protected individual right to keep and bear arms.

Moreover, from the perspective of NRA members and other ardent foes of gun control, the Second Amendment—by entitling each citizen to own firearms—provides the basis for all the other amendments in the Bill of Rights and the Constitution as a whole. This was often explicitly stated by both NRA officers and rank-and-file members. In a letter to the editor of the *American Rifleman*, the NRA's main magazine, David Gregg writes: "The First Amendment is our highest expression of democracy of the intellect and the spirit. The Second Amendment is the highest material expression of the physical and material foundation of our democracy. The First without the Second would restore democracy to little more than a ghost haunting reality and praying that it will not be exorcised by the natural forces of bureaucracy, greed, power and corruption. History gives that little hope."[45]

If the Second Amendment is the "material foundation of democracy" it necessarily follows that armed men must be ready at a moment's notice to defend democratic rights. The NRA could find ample historical evidence for this need in the American Revolution with all its citizen soldiers. For the NRA, these heroic stories of armed men rising to defeat the foes of liberty were a key part of an American creation myth. NRA pamphlets and magazine accounts of American history imply that the militiamen of the Revolution in effect persuaded God to form a kind of covenant with the American people. America was destined to be a great nation under God's special protection because the Founding Fathers had been willing to fight for their freedom. Moreover, the Founding Fathers bequeathed to their heirs the right to continue the fight for freedom by passing the Second Amendment of the Bill of Rights. And their action was thoroughly validated by succeeding generations of brave freedom fighters, the frontier scouts, cowboys, army cavalry, and lawmen who fought all the Indians, Mexicans, and outlaws and so "won the West."

Each year the National Rifle Association convention features an awards banquet to honor its "Man of the Year." The ceremony culminates in the presentation of an exquisitely handcrafted (four hundred hours of labor) remake of a "Pennsylvania" or "Kentucky" flintlock rifle.[46] "Kentucky" rifles were used by the Founding Fathers and by frontier scouts like Daniel Boone. Thus the recipient of the precious rifle—the sign of the covenant—is being anointed, so to speak, and publicly confirmed as a direct descendant of the Founding Fathers. For example, in 1990 NRA President Joe Foss—a white Republican and former World War II ace fighter pilot—presented a rifle to Congressman Mike Espy of Mississippi. Espy, a Democrat who is black, said in his acceptance speech, "The firearm is a part of our past and will remain a part of the future . . . In the face of technological advance, the Constitution still endures."[47] Espy's personal commitment to the creation myth illustrates its transcendent appeal across political and racial lines. NRA Executive Vice President J. Warren Cassidy once commented to a *Time* magazine reporter, "You would get a far better understanding if you approached us as if you were approaching one of the great religions of the world."[48]

As a religion, the NRA must sustain the covenant between God and the American people by protecting the Second Amendment and everything it symbolizes. The NRA must also reach out to large numbers of "ordinary" Americans, persuade them that the right to bear arms links them to the Founding Fathers, and honor those who are armed and prepared for personal combat in defense of their person, family, and property.

And the organization does meet its religious obligations. Each month the *American Rifleman* features "The Armed Citizen," a page-long compendium of newspaper accounts (sent by members) detailing how armed citizens defended themselves against would-be robbers, muggers, rapists, and murderers. These cases apparently represent only a tiny fraction of the citizens who act in armed self-defense. Sociologist Gary Kleck has determined that in the 1980s nearly 950,000 Americans used guns to protect themselves against criminals each year, and citizens killed between 1,500 and 2,800 felons and wounded another 8,000 to 16,000 annually.[49] The NRA interprets these numbers to mean that their religion is not just alive and well, but absolutely necessary for the survival of the nation: the forces of chaos will win unless every citizen is armed and ready to resist. It's a matter of "good" versus "evil," and whichever side has the most guns wins.

From their perspective, then, the lobbying efforts of Handgun Control, Inc. and other groups at local, state, and national levels represented perilous threats to the fundamental covenant and all the good values it symbolized. At the most basic level, progun supporters began to insist that military-style semiautomatic rifles were not "bad" guns at all, but rather the very embodiments of patriotism. In Texas and California, advocates held shooting contests for semiautomatic rifle owners. In interviews with journalists, many shooters talked about their military guns in reverent and civic terms such as "It's a little piece of history" or "Soldiers died so we'd have the right to shoot all we want—it's a tribute."[50] Others declared that they would simply not abide by the new assault rifle legislation; one California man protested that "the Revolution wasn't fought over taxes; it was fought over the British trying to take away people's arms."[51]

Meanwhile, NRA leaders and magazine editors did their best to exorcise the evil symbolism of military semiautomatics. Given that *bad* looks are often intrinsic to a weapon's functional design and are sometimes even exaggerated as part of a power-death aesthetic, ritually purifying them to make them clean and wholesome presented a truly awesome task. But the NRAers did what had to be done. President Joe Foss declared at the June 1990 convention in Anaheim, California, that "all guns are good guns . . . If you're an honest, hardworking citizen, you should be able to own any gun you want."[52] Congressman Mike Espy backed him up during the convention, arguing that the issue is not one of "good guns and bad guns," but rather, "good guys and bad guys."[53] Bruce Herschensohn, a noted conservative television and radio editorialist in Los Angeles (and Republican candidate for the Senate in 1992), reminded the assembled conventioneers that when Eve ate the forbidden fruit in the Garden of Eden, "God blamed Adam and Eve. He didn't blame the apple. He didn't say that it would be forbidden."[54] Movie actor Charlton Heston, who has played both Moses and God in his career, served as the narrator for the NRA's video promoting the Golden Bear Campaign, the organization's effort to register voters in California and defeat pro–gun-control legislators. Heston solemnly reminded viewers (with luscious imagery) that originally California was the new Eden, but that eventually the Golden Bear—the state symbol—was exterminated. "Today gun owners are the endangered species," Heston warned.[55]

Back in Washington, D.C., NRA publicists did their best to make assault rifles respectable to the public. One widely distributed brochure, called "Semi-Auto Firearms: The Citizens Choice," showed four popular semiautomatic hunting rifles lined up against a hitching post in front of a log cabin with deer and moose antlers hanging from the wall. The caption read, "Targeted for extinction are . . ." with the clear implication being that these "good" guns—and the traditional American way of life they symbolized—were the blood brothers of the "bad" guns and would be banished along with them if misguided gun-control legislation was passed. The next two pages showed a drawing of a Revolutionary War soldier wearing a buckskin jacket and holding a flintlock rifle. It was captioned with the message, "Military and civilian rifles looked alike in the 18th century just as they do today—and helped establish and preserve the American way of life."[56]

Over at the *American Rifleman*, other NRA writers addressed themselves to persuading the general membership that saving military-style semiautomatic rifles from the gun controllers was worth a good fight. Although both *Soldier of Fortune*'s Robert K. Brown and Gunsite Ranch's Jeff Cooper had been elected to the NRA's board of directors during the 1980s, the membership as a whole seemed to have mixed feelings about contemporary combat weapons. Finn Aagaard, the *American Rifleman*'s principal writer on hunting rifles, was certainly of the "Old Guard," as he put it, concerning gun aesthetics—he liked bolt-action rifles with deep-blue gun barrels and hand-checkered, finely grained walnut stocks, not the military rifles' black plastic stocks with gray or black matte finish. But once the military rifles came under attack in early 1989, Aagaard contributed a feature article entitled "The Semi-Auto Rifle Afield." He joined a hunt for wild boar sponsored by Springfield Armory, an American manufacturer and importer of military-style semiautomatics. Aagaard was not very happy with the gun he was loaned for testing (one on the ATF banned list), a Fabrique Nationale SAR-48: "It weighed 11 lbs. with the scope, which is 1½ lbs. heavier than the heaviest rifle I have in my battery . . . The separate pistol grip felt strange, and the long magazine got in the way of my arm sometimes. And it was simply ugly."[57] Nor was it a very accurate rifle, shooting at best three-inch-wide groups (of five shots) at a hundred yards, in comparison to the one-inch groups many bolt-action guns deliver. Still, Aagaard shot a 250-lb. boar that day and later took the same rifle on a successful wild sheep hunt. In this way he "proved" that the SAR-48 was a perfectly adequate hunting rifle.

In the same issue, another writer briefly reviewed the Intratec TEC-22 Scorpion. The TEC-22 was a semiautomatic .22 pistol that looked like the Czechoslovakian machine pistol of the same name— the one Peter G. Kokalis of *SOF* described as an ideal weapon for close-range assassination. The ads for the pistol in earlier issues of *American Rifleman* had not been subtle: the gun was shown amidst raging flames. And the first two sentences of an unnamed staff reviewer's review of the gun read: " 'I can't define pornography,' a U.S. Supreme Court justice once said, 'but I know it when I see it.' The Intratec TEC-22 is one of those guns that arouses an analogous emotion in the breast of the anti-gunner—he knows it has 'no redeeming social value,' but he can't say why." The author then proceeded to take the pistol apart, just as *American Rifleman* gun testers disassemble and reassemble every gun they test. He next described how he fired it with various brands of ammo to test its accuracy. And when all was said and done, he concluded that despite its wicked grin, the TEC-22 "is an accurate, reliable, well-made plinking gun that needs no apology for it."[58]

In issue after issue from 1989 on, the *American Rifleman* reviewed military weapons. In effect, their tests and articles about those tests were efforts to *redeem* military-style rifles and pistols, to "normalize" them, make them guns like any other guns. Even the cartridge fired by the AK47 was salvageable. As C. E. Harris wrote, "The evil connotation the 7.62 'Russian short' has acquired should not prevent practical target shooters and hunters from exploring its genuine utility."[59] Once all the evil connotations of a rifle or pistol had been removed by the "normalizing" gun tests and articles, then surely all NRA members—and hopefully the general public—would see military-style firearms as worthy of protecting from those eager to ban them.

At the same time, the redemption of the "bad" guns and their symbolic transformation into "good" guns necessarily implied that those who wanted to control guns through more stringent legal regulation had highly questionable motives. The April 1989 issue of the *American Rifleman* had a fold-out cover filled with drawings of all kinds of semiauto rifles, pistols, and shotguns and a headline screaming, "Stop the Semi-Auto Gun Ban!" The accompanying inside-cover text complained that "anti-gunners and lawmakers need to face the facts: it's time for a ban on criminals, not semi-autos. *Outlaws behind bars don't commit crimes.*" The article also warned readers not to "let the criminals get away with your rights."—The "criminals" here are all those who seek to "get away with" or *steal* gun rights, i.e., the gun-control movement, but who, interestingly enough, "won't lift a finger to keep repeat offenders like Purdy in jail."[60] The implication is that at some level the controllers are soft liberals, just like the liberals who crippled American war efforts in Vietnam, condoned drug use, and refused to retaliate against terrorists.

Even worse, HCI advocates were compared to the Nazis. J. Warren Cassidy, executive vice president of the NRA, entitled his April 1989 column in the *American Rifleman* "And Then There Were None?" He began with Pastor Martin Niemöller's famous statement when he was arrested by the German Gestapo in 1937: "In Germany, they came first for the communists, and I didn't speak up because I wasn't a communist. Then, they came for the Jews, and I didn't speak up because I wasn't a Jew . . . Then, they came for me, and by that time no one was left to speak up."[61] In Cassidy's paraphrase, the gun grabbers first came after the machine guns, then the handguns, then the semiautos, and would ultimately go after every hunting rifle and shotgun in the country.

In the summer of 1990, after HCI ran its advertising campaign associating the NRA with the Ku Klux Klan, NRA president Dick Riley shot back, labelling HCI founder Pete Shields's 1981 book, *Guns Don't Die, People Die*—a call for stricter firearms regulation—the *Mein Kampf* sequel for the gun-control movement. In his column for the *American Rifleman* Riley warned that Shields had a "final solution" for guns, namely outlawing all private possession.[62] As a result, the covenant of the Second Amendment would no longer be broken only in part; it would be completely shattered. Hence the gun-control movement was the true heir to totalitarianism and a threat to all American values.

In the winter of 1991 this morality play escalated to yet another level. The NRA's lobby arm, the Institute for Legislative Action, solicited the membership for more financial donations with the question, "Have you ever wondered just what our troops in the Middle East were thinking just before the advance began?" Twenty-two Desert Storm Marines of the 1st Battalion, 1st Marine Division "who led the breakthrough to Kuwait City in the battle to free Kuwait" had written to the NRA and asked "that while they protect freedom abroad, the NRA and its members continue to fight to protect the Second Amendment freedoms right here at home."[63] Saddam Hussein's American allies were none other than Sarah and Jim Brady.

Given the evil they attributed to gun-control advocates, it is not surprising that the NRA and its allies came to the conclusion that gun control was not only ineffective but in truth would cause more crime. Waiting periods would cause crime because police resources would be diverted into background checks on law-abiding citizens who wanted to buy guns.[64] Waiting periods would also hurt women who were being battered by their husbands or boyfriends and needed a weapon—immediately—to defend themselves against further assaults.[65]

Finally, more gun-control legislation would cause crime because it would create a whole new class of criminals. All of the proposed federal legislation and most of the state bills aimed at banning military-style semiautomatics in effect banned only future sales of such weapons. People who already owned these guns would be required to register them. Hence, according to the NRA's reasoning, otherwise law-abiding citizens who refused to register their military-style semiautomatic rifles would become criminals.[66] Just as *Red Dawn* and *The Turner Diaries* prophesied that in the future new legislation would make owning guns a crime, the lobbying group, California Gun Owners, Inc., distributed a facsimile of a newspaper at the June 1990

NRA convention showing a row of men being stood up against a wall about to be shot for violating gun laws!

Hence, in the great gun-control debate of the late 1980s and early 1990s, both sides—Handgun Control, Inc. and the National Rifle Association, together with their respective supporters—came to mirror each other in their accusations. In the process, any real discussion of why America suffered from so much crime and drug abuse and so many random madmen vanished from serious public debate. Instead, these serious problems became reframed at the level of symbolic politics. To HCI, stopping the NRA became the same thing as solving all these other problems, while to the NRA stopping the gun controllers was a way of restoring America's covenant with God after the long period of American decline since defeat in Vietnam. Both sides fought this holy war in the name of national rejuvenation. Yet, for all the talk about reestablishing order in America, the gun-control debate was but another arena for the mythic replaying of regeneration through violence.

Slightly different versions of the Brady Bill requiring a federally mandated waiting period for handgun purchases were passed by both the House and Senate in the summer of 1991, and a conference committee came up with a compromise. But in 1992 the Brady Bill was attached to the Bush administration's omnibus crime bill; that legislative package never left committee for a vote by Congress. The Senate passed the DeConcini bill regulating the sale of some foreign and domestic assault rifles in May 1989, but the House of Representatives failed to pass similar legislation in October 1991.

However, the Bush administration's ban of many imported military-style semiautomatic rifles continued. In light of these federal actions, and the increased regulation on the state level in the late 1980s and early 1990s, the gun-control movement can be said to have won the struggle for public opinion even though much of the legislation they lobbied for did not become the law of the land. Surely they won it at the level of what sociologist Harold Garfinkel calls "degradation ceremonies"—political struggles which serve to publicly affirm certain groups as virtuous and "degrade" others as immoral.[67] The NRA was successfully defamed as being against laws that banned armor-piercing bullets and prohibited the manufacture of detection-proof plastic guns—charges the NRA vehemently denied as misrepresenting its opposition to what it termed vaguely written early drafts of proposed legislation. Nor was the NRA able to defend its adamant anti–gun-control position in the face of testimony by men like Baltimore police chief Leonard Supenski who said in 1989, "We're tired of passing out flags to widows of officers killed by drug dealers with Uzis." The NRA asked the Federal Bureau of Investigation how many police officers had been killed by desperados packing Uzis. In the summer of 1990 the FBI responded: only one officer (in Puerto Rico, not Baltimore) out of 828 killed between 1980 and 1989 had been murdered by someone armed with such a weapon, but by then it was too late—the Uzi's evil symbolism had already carried the day and the gun was banned.[68]

The bad-gun symbolism was so persuasive that the NRA was never able to communicate to the wider public outside its membership ranks any of the statistics that might have cast doubt on the efficacy of the proposed semiauto bans. Each year the Federal Bureau of Investigation publishes its *Uniform Crime Statistics* report. One of its regular features is a table entitled "Murder Victims, Type of Weapon Used." From 1983 to 1989, rifles of *all types* accounted for around 4 to 4.5 percent of all murder weapons. Although the FBI did not distinguish between military-style semiautomatic rifles and other kinds, military-style rifles in general comprise a small percentage of all rifles and the models that most gun-controllers wanted to ban made up only a minuscule number. Even if such weapons are statistically over-represented in rifle homicides, the number of people killed with such weapons is tiny. (For example, New Jersey outlawed possession of assault rifles in May 1991; by 1993 state records showed that only about 2,000 citizens—at most 5 percent of the estimated number of people who owned banned firearms—had turned in their guns. Still, the illegal rifles still in circulation were used in only .026 percent of all felony offenses committed since the ban went into effect.[69]) Knives, in contrast, were used in over 20 percent of all murders in the United States during the 1980s.[70] Unfortunately, then, banning a few assault rifles could not seriously affect the crime rate.

Indeed, what the gun-control debate about military rifles accomplished was simply to make these "bad" guns *badder than ever*, just as the one forbidden fruit growing in the Garden of Eden was the tastiest of all. For those who wanted them, Uzi-apples simply went up in price. Even if the cost per gun on the used market escalated to several thousand dollars, this price was not at all prohibitive for those most evil of badmen: in 1989 the drug trade was doing $160 billion a year in business.

Ironically, if prospective buyers had waited until 1991, they wouldn't have had to pay a premium at all for many models. For example, the Chinese manufacturer of AK47s—a firm called Norinco—removed the bayonet lug, flash hider, and some of the other goodies, and redesigned the stock, eliminating the bad-looking pistol grip. By ATF standards, it was now legal to import. Discreetly advertised, this new version of the AK, called a sporter, cost less than $300. Norinco also started exporting the predecessor of the AK47, a rifle called the SKS that fired the same cartridge but had only a 10-shot clip built into the gun (as opposed to the 30-shot removable magazines available for the AK47). These rifles sold for under $130. Domestically, Colt Firearms—which had taken its AR-15 off the market in the spring of 1989—also introduced a sporter version without bayonet lug or grenade launcher in late 1990. Cobray offered a new version of the banned MAC-10, and Ruger just kept on pumping out the Mini-14 and Mini-30 without missing a beat.

Still, the question must be asked: Would increased gun control, such as banning future sales of assault rifles and imposing a federally mandated waiting period for all guns—not just handguns as the Brady Bill proposed—have stopped any of the paramilitary mass murderers of the 1980s?

It's hard to believe that the simple gun-control legislation would have done much good. Consider how each mass murderer obtained his weapons. The English, Australian, and Canadian killers had no previous criminal records and had gone through far more complex legal processes—including lengthy waiting periods—to obtain their weapons than any of the Americans. Hinckley's claim that gun control would have stopped him is, as previously discussed, not entirely persuasive given the way in which he relentlessly pursued first Carter and then Reagan. Huberty had no criminal record—indeed, he had finished a course as an armed security guard in the spring of 1984 and was licensed to carry a pistol for work.

Patrick Purdy had had several previous run-ins with the police for violating gun laws, soliciting, armed robbery, and other crimes. However, the armed robbery case (a felony) was plea-bargained down to a misdemeanor. Consequently, he could legally buy guns over the counter and did so. Purdy got his AK47 rifle without waiting (that was the law), but he didn't take possession of the 9mm he used to kill himself until the fifteen-day waiting period mandated by California law was over. And both the AK47 and the 9mm were bought months in advance of his attack on Asian-American children in a Stockton school yard—plenty of time to buy weapons on the used market or steal them. There are, after all, an estimated two hundred million guns in the United States. Over-the-counter purchases are but one means of acquiring firearms.

A Florida gunman who killed eight people and wounded six others in 1990 was a convicted felon and thus could not legally own any guns. He simply lied about his criminal record on the ATF form when he bought the .38 revolver with which he shot himself. Quite possibly a law like the Brady Bill would have stopped this purchase. But no one knows where he got the .30-caliber M1 carbine he used to kill his victims.

A more responsive mental-health establishment might well have had a greater impact in stopping these rampages than gun-control legislation would. John Hinckley's parents had sent him to a Denver psychiatrist years before he tried to kill Reagan, but the psychiatrist diagnosed him as simply immature, if slightly depressive. While living in Ohio, James Huberty had once put a gun to his head and threatened suicide. Although he was taken into police custody after the episode, Huberty was soon released—and the Browning 9mm he later carried to McDonald's was returned to his wife (and thus to him) by a local judge. After he moved to San Ysidro, just days before his McDonald's rampage, Huberty twice called a local mental-health clinic for help, but was informed he would have to wait a week for an appointment. Huberty reportedly told his wife, "Society had its chance."[71] Patrick Purdy, the Stockton killer, was receiving disability payments for mental illness at the time he committed his murders. The Louisville man had been put on medical leave by his employer because of emotional problems. Local police already knew the Pennsylvania woman to be disturbed. Thus, there is some evidence that a mental-health system more acutely attuned to the signs of possible breakdown might have done some good. Ironically, funding for mental-health agencies and institutions declined during the 1980s.

Most of all, stopping the madmen would have required understanding that they were not isolated "deviants" who simply invented their mayhem out of thin air and looked and acted completely different from the "ordinary" people in the mainstream of American culture. On the contrary, in their killings they gave expression to some of the most basic cultural dynamics of the decade—in the face of either real or imaginary problems, declare an enemy responsible and go to war. Sometimes they even learned their killing *techniques* from the fictional heroes of the New War: when George Hennard drove his pickup truck through the plate-glass window of a Killeen, Texas, cafeteria and then killed twenty-two people with 9mm Glock and Ruger semiauto pistols, almost all of the press attention focused on his guns. What no one seems to have wondered is just where does a man get the idea of driving a truck through a window before attacking his "enemies"? The answer is not hard to find. The scene was fairly common in New War movies. To name two prominent examples: Arnold Schwarzenegger drove into a police station and then shot seventeen officers to death in *The Terminator* (1984); a few years later Mel Gibson drove his police car into a building to get closer to the bad guys in *Lethal Weapon 2* (1989). Although the press did not report on Hennard's movie preferences, one article did say that "he often went shirtless, showing off his muscles and a tattoo," and that he thought of most women as "vipers" except for a few whom he fantasized to be his "groupies."[72]

To argue, then, that many of these murderers could have been stopped solely by increased gun control is to pretend that the social and political crises of post-Vietnam America never occurred and that the New War did not develop as the major way of overcoming those disasters. Paramilitary culture made military-style rifles desirable, and legislation cannot ban a culture. The gun-control debate was but the worst kind of fetishism, in which focusing on a part of the dreadful reality of the decade—combat weapons—became a substitute for confronting what America had become.

12

Ronald Reagan seemed to make the world move during his very first day as President. On January 20, 1981, at 12:05 P.M., a mere five minutes after he had been inaugurated, the Iranians released fifty-two American hostages who had been held prisoner since November 4, 1979. The long dark nights of ABC's television news show, "America Held Hostage," were over. It was as if a Hollywood movie had suddenly come alive, or, more accurately, as if a film production team had suddenly come to power to stage a presidency. Indeed, that's very close to what did happen. Although Ronald Reagan served as governor of California from 1967 to 1974, he spent most of his adult life as a film and television actor. That experience had vast formative impact upon him, and he treasured it. Even as President, the stories he told friends and staff members, journalists, domestic politicians, and visiting heads of state all had to do with Hollywood figures he had known or films he had seen.

In his eight years as President, Reagan spent 183 weekends at the Presidential retreat at Camp David, Maryland. Each time he saw at least two movies per weekend. Even when he was not at Camp David, the film projectors rolled. Early in Reagan's presidency, Treasury Secretary James Baker brought him an important briefing book to prepare for an appearance the next day at an international summit meeting of West European leaders. The next morning Baker found that the book had never been opened. When asked what happened, Reagan replied, "Well, Jim, *The Sound of Music* was on last night."[1]

Reagan normally worked a roughly nine-to-five day when he was in the White House. Two to three hours each day were always blocked out as "personal staff time." During this period he handled correspondence—not political or governmental correspondence, but replies to personal letters. Reagan thus spent one-third of his working days as President answering his fan mail; there was no disjunction between his Hollywood career and his political performances. Those many film critics who characterize him as only a B-grade movie actor miss the point. As journalist Lou Cannon so aptly subtitles his book on the man, to Reagan being President was *The Role of a Lifetime*.

Reagan took seriously the fantasies created by Hollywood. Westerns and war movies were particular favorites; they both provided ways of understanding the world and possible guides to how he should act on the political stage. During much of the 1950s Reagan had served as host to the Western television series, *Death Valley Days*, which featured a new tale of pioneer courage in the wilderness each week. During the Vietnam War, Reagan often remarked in his political speeches that it was unthinkable that the descendants of the pioneers who had so resoundingly defeated the Indians could not defeat the Indian-like Vietcong. After all, the United States had the technological capacity to "pave the whole country [Vietnam] and put parking strips on it and still be at home by Christmas."[2] During his first Presidential primary campaign in 1976, Reagan frequently repeated the applause-winning line, "Let us tell those who fought in that war that we will never again ask young men to fight and possibly die in a war our government is afraid to win."[3] This idea—that the U.S. deliberately refused to win the Vietnam War—became part of the rationale for the massive military expenditures, amounting to two trillion dollars, during his administration. The next war would be fought with everything money could buy.

One of the weapons systems envisioned by the Reagan administration was the complicated network of antimissile missiles and space-based laser guns (powered by nuclear explosions) called the Strategic Defense Initiative. Its proponents prophesied that the completed system would stop most, if not all, incoming Soviet missiles during a nuclear attack. Its opponents decried the SDI as a deadly illusion, an extraordinary boondoggle for the aerospace industry that would at best create a false sense of invulnerability and at worst scare the Soviets into launching a first-strike attack. (In mid-1993 the Pentagon revealed that the successful tests of SDI in the 1980s had been faked.)

Even though the SDI soon got the nickname Star Wars, an obvious allusion to George Lucas's *Star Wars* movies, news coverage and public debate centered almost exclusively on the practical merits and faults of the proposed system. The debt that the SDI notion owed to fantasy—to those science-fiction novels and movies in which laser weapons had supplanted conventional ones—was not seen as pertinent.[4] But President Reagan's mind worked in a different way. In 1985 he even offered to share the SDI technology with Soviet Premier Gorbachev, a move straight out of *The Day the Earth Stood Still* (1951).[5] In this sci-fi classic, a wise alien comes to earth to warn the earthlings that unless they abandon their bloody squabbles (the Cold War) earth will be destroyed by the aliens to protect the rest of the galaxy from human aggression. Instead of listening to the alien, the U.S. Army kills him. But as the movie ends, the alien is miraculously resurrected and again warns earthlings that "the universe is getting smaller every day. There must be security for all, or no one is secure." Apparently Reagan frequently talked about the film and his hope that space invaders might be able to prompt American–Soviet cooperation. By sharing SDI technology with the Soviets, he hoped to make *The Day the Earth Stood Still*'s vision of world peace come true.

The Western movie served as a large part of Reagan's cognitive framework for understanding the Vietnam War, and science fiction helped to inspire the SDI. Nor are these the only instances of his deriving policy from myth. The mythic world was Reagan's primary source of information and inspiration—and he knew that myth sometimes differed from what actually happened. At one of the Washington Press Club's Gridiron dinners, newspaper columnist Charles Mc-Dowell told Reagan how thrilled he had been one day in the late 1930s to walk into his hometown drugstore in Lexington, Virginia, and see Reagan and Eddie Albert in a booth. In McDowell's mind, Reagan had been there filming the 1938 comedy, *Brother Rat*. But the President insisted McDowell was mistaken: "I have something serious to tell you. I remember the others coming back from Lexington and telling me what it was like, but I simply wasn't there." McDowell protested, proclaiming that he had been telling people this story all his life. Reagan then inquired about how many times McDowell had seen *Brother Rat*. Five or six, the newspaperman replied. In response the President commented that seeing the movie so many times "implanted in your head that I was there. You believed it because you wanted to believe it. There's nothing wrong with that. I do it all the time."[6] Reagan thus understood that he sometimes confused what happened in movies with what happened in real life, but he did not think such confusion necessarily caused problems. To the contrary, mythic truth was a higher order of truth to him. As he explained on another occasion, "My actor's instinct simply told me to speak the truth as I saw it and felt it."[7]

After he retired from the Presidency Reagan reflected on the role of movies in shaping his military and foreign policy: "Maybe I had seen too many war movies, the heroics of which I sometimes confused with real life, but common sense told me something very essential —you can't have a fighting force without an esprit de corps. So one of my first priorities was to rebuild our military and, just as important, our military's morale."[8] Creating this esprit de corps, both in the military and among civilians, was Reagan's mission. Nothing else mattered. He was a shaman of sorts who wanted to restore and build upon America's fundamental creation myths through Presidential performances.

But despite these ambitions, Reagan remained aloof and disengaged from the day-to-day tasks of governing. During many meetings he is reported to have fallen asleep or, more commonly, to have doodled and told stories not germane to the subjects at hand. Memorandums on important policy matters requiring his decision were frequently reduced to one-page mini-memos, with policy options presented in a short, multiple-choice format. He had neither the analytical ability nor the interest to read and reflect more deeply.

Many cabinet members and White House staff soon learned how to play to Reagan's mythic mentality, or what General Colin Powell termed his hidden transistors. Secretary of Defense Caspar Weinberger was a particularly astute player, routinely showing up at White House meetings with animated cartoons or vivid graphics to make his points. In an effort to slow down those playing to Reagan's predilections, his old California crew—Attorney General Edwin Meese, White House Chief of Staff James Baker, and Michael K. Deaver, the man in charge of scheduling (and staging) all of Reagan's activities and meetings—adopted a policy in which at least one of them was required to be present during every Presidential meeting. According to Kenneth Duberstein, chief of staff following the public exposure of the Iran–Contra affair in 1987, for the Reagan White House to function effectively there had to be "a very strong stage manager-producer-director" and "very good technical men and sound men" at all times.[9] The White House was a movie set, a sound stage.

But it is a mistake to reduce the political culture of the 1980s to the story of one magic mythmaker and his retinue who seduced the innocent and trusting American public. The dreams of redeeming Vietnam and recovering from all the other disappointments and traumas of the late 1960s and 1970s were not Reagan's alone, but a widespread, collective response among the American people. Reagan astutely tapped into these dreams; his candidacy and Presidency provided a formal channel to translate them into practice.

In some ways Reagan's public performances resembled those of Stallone's Rambo. Both were so extreme that they often fell into humorous self-caricature. For example, in a moment of self-recognition after *Rambo: First Blood, Part 2* was released in 1985 Reagan announced that he would send Rambo abroad to handle the next foreign emergency. Such Presidential antics tended to *deflect* attention away from other, less obvious forms of post-Vietnam warrior mythology that animated Reagan's officials and guided their actions.

Nowhere is this process of hidden myth finding its way into policy more evident than in the first major debate concerning the nature of terrorism and what the Reagan administration's approach toward terrorism should be. The debate centered on journalist Claire Sterling's book *The Terror Network*, published in 1981. Sometime in the summer or fall of 1980, Sterling's publisher gave a copy of the galleys to General Alexander M. Haig, Jr. Haig had both a professional and personal interest in European and Middle Eastern terrorism. In June 1976, while Haig was serving as the commander of NATO forces, terrorists had tried to blow up his limousine near Mons, Belgium.

Haig was particularly impressed with Sterling's charge that most and perhaps all of the major European and Middle Eastern terrorists—from the Irish Republican Army to the German Red Army Faction to groups run by Abu Nidal and "Carlos"—were all part of one vast terror network or "family."[10] Moreover, all of them were funded, trained, and controlled by either a "surrogate" or "satellite" of the Soviet KGB—meaning the intelligence service of virtually any Communist country. These countries were simply henchmen carrying out policies formulated and ordered by the top echelons of the KGB. Moreover, the Soviets and their surrogates were so successful that terrorists were said to be "mass-produced." The terror network itself was so efficient that "the machinery practically runs itself, and anybody who wants to be a terrorist can get to be one."[11] The terrorist goal was nothing less than "the destruction of Western democracy." One group, the Italian Red Brigades, had even published a *timetable* for this coming debacle.

For Haig, Sterling's book made the world fall into place. The people who had tried to kill him in Mons were but the offspring of those whom he had fought his entire professional life; the old Cold War and the new war against terrorism were joined in one continuous struggle against monolithic Communism in all its evil forms. After Reagan was elected in November 1980, Haig was made secretary of state. On January 27, 1981, during his very first official press conference, Haig announced that international terrorism had become "rampant" and that the Soviet Union deliberately wanted to "foster, support, and expand" terrorist attacks against the West.[12] Haig's speech was the first by a U.S. government official to accuse the Soviet Union of being the hidden force behind terrorism.

On March 1, 1981 *The New York Times Magazine* published as its cover story Claire Sterling's "Terrorism: Tracing the International Network." Secretary of State Haig's speech was quoted extensively and referred to as outside support for Sterling's thesis that all the West European left-wing political groups (and intellectuals) were fronts for violent terrorists and that the Soviets themselves were ultimately behind the terror network.

Sterling's article, in turn, very much impressed the new director of the Central Intelligence Agency, William C. Casey. Casey had spent most of his life as a financier; he invented the concept of the tax shelter. But as a young man in World War II, Casey had joined the predecessor to the CIA, the Office of Strategic Services, and had parachuted into France to help the non-Communist French Resistance fight both the Germans and their other foe, the French Communist Party. For Casey, too, Sterling's book helped explain the war against terrorism as an extension of his World War II combat experience and of Cold War anti-Communism.

The week after the *New York Times Magazine* article appeared, Casey ordered the CIA staff to search their files in an effort to confirm or reject Sterling's thesis. Although Sterling had claimed that South Yemen was the site of "a kind of postgraduate school in international terrorism," regularly attended by members of all terrorist groups, one analyst noted that there was only one known case of an Italian Red Brigade member attending a training camp there. The analysts concluded that Sterling practiced rhetorical "linkmanship." She had used the KGB's presence in South Yemen to assert a connection between the KGB and the Red Brigades when empirical evidence of the presence of many Red Brigade members, much less their control by the KGB, simply was not there.[13]

Later the national intelligence officer responsible for the Soviet Union reported that Sterling's thesis about the KGB's crucial role in promoting and controlling terrorist groups also did not match the evidence. Although it was clear that in the name of supporting "liberation struggles" Eastern Europe provided safe havens for many terrorists and sold them arms, there was no evidence that the KGB or East European intelligence agencies controlled them. By this time, though, Casey had the book version of *The Terror Network* and said to his analysts: "Read Claire Sterling's book and forget this mush. I paid $13.95 for this and it told me more than you bastards whom I pay $50,000 a year."[14]

What *The Terror Network* gave Haig, Casey, and its other readers inside and outside the Reagan administration was actually something more than a descriptive account of the rise of terrorist groups and a political analysis of their objectives in attacking the entire Western world: for $13.95 a reader bought a ticket to a titillating freak show. The biography of one Italian terrorist reads like a potboiler: "Born to one of the nation's great families and endowed with a bottomless bank account, condemned to a frozen childhood under a succession of Teutonic governesses, sexually impotent, intelligent but untalented, evidently driven by social guilt and God knows what private furies besides." Warped by his harsh frozen nannies, the perverse terrorist could only get an erection "when he turned up a phonograph to recordings of gunfire and martial music."[15] Another terrorist began life with an equally cold mother who imposed "harshly unbending ethical standards" that tormented him and "cut him off from other people his own age." But Sterling reports that "judging from the number of girls who jumped into bed with him during his few grown-up years of freedom, he overcame his childhood inhibitions."[16]

According to Sterling, the terrorists all have lots of women who want them. Poor "Norbert," yet another terrorist pervert, even made "lists of the girls he slept with and prescriptions he renewed for recurrent bouts of gonorrhea."[17] The famous "Carlos," the man who held the oil ministers of the Organization of Petroleum Producing States hostage in Vienna in 1974, was said to be "keeping at least two Paris flats and four Venezuelan girls, several if not all taking turns in his bed."[18] Not to be outdone, IRA members routinely went to brothels and massage parlors to collect money and who knows what other kinds of donations.

The collective portrait of terrorists Sterling creates is thus a familiar one—they are the very same enemies that Mack Bolan and his allies fight in *The Executioner* series and all the other pulps. In language very similar to that used by the German *Freikorps* in describing the left, Sterling even wrote about an Italian "mother cell whose proliferating offspring" are responsible "for a terrorist attack somewhere in the country once every three hours and four minutes."[19] Terrorism is thus at once a cancer, a crime, and a sexual passion so powerful that it threatens to destroy all social, moral, and psychological boundaries: *everything* will dissolve into complete chaos. Sterling's "real" terrorists are identical to the New War fictional villains; they are the living embodiment of the "evil infinite of human desire."

The psychological hook in Sterling's work is first this voyeuristic access to the terrorist life of pleasure unburdened by moral restraint—a fantasy land of infantile regression. Yet, just like the better pulp writers, Sterling creates a second "hook" by allowing the reader to simultaneously just say no to this seductive portrait and maintain self-control. And the message is clear: social order *can* triumph over the threatening chaos caused by uncontrolled desire, and good *can* triumph over evil—but only if the Soviet KGB is recognized as the origin of evil, and a holy war is unleashed against it.

Once the problem was redefined this way, readers such as Alexander Haig, William Casey, and Oliver North could readily "judge" *The Terror Network* as basically correct, in spite of problems in empirical evidence or the CIA analysts' criticisms of Sterling's "linkmanship." Lincoln Gordan, a past president of Johns Hopkins University hired by the CIA as an outside consultant to study Sterling's thesis, even found that part of her evidence on the Italian Red Brigades had come from a CIA-sponsored "disinformation" campaign in the Italian news media.[20] His report did not matter either.

John Hinckley's assassination attempt against Reagan in 1981 was experienced by many members of the Reagan administration as confirmation of Sterling's assessment that the forces of chaos were becoming more powerful every day. After all, in the words Sterling attributed to the Italian Red Brigades in her *New York Times* article, the ultimate objective of terrorists worldwide was "the supreme symbol of multinational imperialism, the United States."[21] And if the United States was the symbol of imperialism, then surely President Ronald Reagan was the symbol of the United States. An attack on his body was an attack on everybody. *Washington Post* reporter Bob Woodward concluded that after the assassination attempt, "the Reagan presidency, from the inside, would never be the same. That sense of peril, that anyone or anything might strike—terrorists, a quick move by the Soviets, other adversaries—became a permanent, ingrained maxim of Administration policy."²²

The New War against this sense of peril began almost immediately. European terrorists were one target, but they were by no means the main adversary. That honor was reserved for the Third World as Reagan carried through on his 1980 campaign promise to radically increase the level of U.S. intervention. The days of "self-imposed restraint" were now officially over. Central America—where the leftist Sandinista movement had come to power in Nicaragua, and where a civil war raged in El Salvador—drew the immediate attention of the Reagan administration.

In the spring of 1981, President Reagan signed a national security decision directive authorizing U.S. intelligence agencies to intervene in the forthcoming Salvadoran elections on behalf of Napoleon Duarte's Christian Democratic Party. Once the decision to intervene was made, the National Security Agency was told by the director of the Central Intelligence Agency to use electronic surveillance to spy on both the far right-wing opposition party led by Roberto D'Aubuisson and on the leftist guerrillas fighting in the Farabundo Martí National Liberation Front (FMLN). NSA officials responded that they had no such monitoring devices in place, so instead a new U.S. Army command structure called the Special Operations Division got the assignment. Formally established in February 1981, SOD was responsible for coordinating and financing most of the Army's growing number of counterterrorist and covert-action units. These secret groups had come into existence in 1980 after the rescue mission that attempted to free American hostages in Iran failed. The units were established because of the Army's dissatisfaction with the raid and what the Army saw as chronic CIA incompetence and Congressionally mandated restrictions that destroyed the agency's ability to conduct operations secretly.

One of these units, the Intelligence Support Activity (ISA), carried out covert reconnaissance, together with intelligence collecting and analysis, and provided logistic support for Delta Force and other commando outfits; ISA had its own hit teams as well. SOD further created two air-support units: the relatively overt Task Force 160, a helicopter squadron at Fort Campbell, Kentucky, and a "black" group which operated as a commercial air-transport company called Sea-spray. Yellow Fruit—another SOD outfit—established commercial covers and covert financial channels for these operational units and also provided electronic security services to the SOD's shadow warriors.

For the intelligence mission in El Salvador, SOD leased a Beech King Air twin-engine prop plane and modified it with sophisticated electronic monitoring systems. The spy plane was sent to Honduras on a supposed commercial geological mapping operation. In January 1982, it began flights along the Honduras, El Salvador, and Nicaragua border areas. The Salvadoran government was given information on the location of FMLN guerrillas, while the Nicaraguan contras opposed to the Sandinistas got the take on the locations of Sandinista military units.

The success of this mission in turn prompted further SOD involvement in Central America. In 1982 the ISA and Yellow Fruit opened up scores of businesses, bank accounts, and safe houses and essentially created a secret infrastructure to support large-scale paramilitary operations. And these covert activities were bolstered by new official policies. Reagan signed a National Security directive (called a "finding") authorizing the CIA to spend $19 million organizing and training the contras. His own National Security Council staff became increasingly active in organizing the campaign against Nicaragua.

But in the fall of 1982 an obstacle developed. Congress passed the first Boland Amendment, prohibiting both the U.S. military and the CIA from spending tax dollars "for the purpose of overthrowing the Government of Nicaragua." The Reagan administration's response to this Congressional challenge was twofold. First, in March 1983 Reagan escalated his rhetorical attacks on Communism, calling the Soviet Union an "evil empire." Early on in his speech to the National Association of Evangelicals in Orlando, Florida, Reagan said, "We know that living in this world means dealing with what philosophers would call the phenomenology of evil or, as theologians would put it, the doctrine of sin."[23] Reagan, a professed believer in the coming of Armageddon in our time, meant what he said: "Communist" countries such as Nicaragua were, to his mind, literally the minions of the devil.

Second, the Reagan administration further mobilized its covert action groups. Robert McFarlane of the National Security Council helped organize Operation Tea Kettle, in which Israel shipped thousands of tons of weapons and ammunition captured from PLO bases in Lebanon to the contras in Honduras, Guatemala, and Costa Rica. Yellow Fruit operatives trained Nicaraguans in California and Florida to fly light planes for future bombing attacks. The Air Force in turn declared three planes belonging to the New York Air National Guard that were suitable for these missions to be surplus and therefore of no financial value. They were then transferred to the CIA and the CIA gave them to the contras. SOD even bought a huge ship, a Norwegian grain hauler, to use as a floating base for launching commando attacks.

In September 1983 Reagan signed a new finding, this time declaring that U.S. covert operations were not intended to overthrow the Sandinistas but only to make them negotiate a settlement with their contra opponents. Congress did not renew the Boland Amendment; instead, it appropriated $24 million to fund the contras in 1984. With this legal backing, the CIA then asked the military for $12 million in armaments for the war against Nicaragua; Secretary of Defense Caspar Weinberger issued a directive to the armed services ordering them to assist the CIA "in accordance with the law."[24] The future looked good.

But then, yet another major problem emerged. It had begun in the U.S. Army's Yellow Fruit unit. Millions had been spent with little accountability. Planes, boats, and luxury cars had been bought. There had been European junkets, first-class hotels and gourmet meals, and even plain bags full of cash handed out for who knew what. It also emerged that Yellow Fruit had been asked by the head of SOD to bug the hotel rooms and bathrooms at a forthcoming reunion and convention of CIA and Army paramilitary operatives. This information was to be used to give the commander of SOD leverage in future bureaucratic quarrels.

In late 1982 an Army officer assigned to approve all Yellow Fruit expenses reported these violations to higher authorities. The vice chief of staff of the Army, General Maxwell Thurman, pulled the plug on Yellow Fruit. Soon the mainstream Army leadership declared a halt to most SOD covert operations. Thus by the end of 1983, just as the Reagan administration was getting Congressional approval for increased covert action against Nicaragua, the principal component of its paramilitary apparatus was shut down.

The autumn of 1983 also saw a dramatic escalation of the Reagan administration's New War against international peril. The catalytic event occurred on October 23, when a Mercedes cargo truck loaded with twelve tons of explosives crashed into the U.S. Marine compound in Beirut, Lebanon. Two hundred and forty-one soldiers died in the explosion. Subsequent investigations revealed that the attack was sponsored by Hezbollah, a fundamentalist Shiite Muslim organization. Hezbollah had several factions, including the Islamic Jihad and the Islamic Amal, two groups that had been responsible for the bombing of the U.S. embassy in Beirut in April 1983.[25]

Surely the "defeat" in Lebanon triggered the invasion of Grenada two days later, on October 25, 1983. President Reagan claimed that the invasion was necessary to rescue U.S. medical students supposedly endangered by the recent coup, even though coup leaders had met with U.S. embassy officials and medical school officials and guaranteed the safety of the students and the chancellor of the medical school. In both private communications to the White House and in public announcements the leaders had confirmed that the students were not in danger.[26] Nevertheless, Grenada was invaded. Interestingly, many medical students were not "rescued" until the second, third, and fourth days of the invasion—more than enough time for them to have been executed if the Grenada regime had had hostile intentions. American military maps did not even show the locations of many medical school dorms and facilities.[27]

But this contradiction did not matter to most Americans. Public opinion polls showed enormous support (71%) for the invasion, and gave Reagan his highest overall approval ratings (63%) since April 1981, when he was recovering from Hinckley's bullet.[28] Victory in Grenada immediately displaced the pain and bad symbolism of the catastrophe in Lebanon: the news media could agree with the President's statement that "America is back." A leftist government was overthrown, stopping both the completion of "runways for Soviet bombers" and potential "training camps for terrorists." As Reagan explained in his October 28 address to the nation: "The events in Lebanon and Grenada, though oceans apart, are closely related. Not only has Moscow assisted and encouraged the violence in both countries, but it provides direct support through a network of surrogates and terrorists."[29] Thus the invasion was justified as a war against Moscow and its minions; Communism was still the ultimate source of evil in the world. The struggle against this evil would continue despite the Marine casualties in Lebanon.

Indeed, in late 1983 and 1984 counterterrorism and other forms of warfare against America's enemies became an obsession of sorts dominating government and media discussion. A new interdepartmental coordinating body was formed called the Terrorist Incident Working Group. At the White House, a young Marine lieutenant colonel named Oliver North was assigned to the National Security Council. North, a man of prodigious energy, soon became responsible for most counterterrorist efforts; he played a major role drafting National Security Decision Directive 138, issued in 1984, which declared that "states that use or support terrorism cannot be allowed to do so without consequences."[30]

In this martial atmosphere, the Central Intelligence Agency stepped up the pace of its attacks against Nicaragua. The agency had begun bombing and strafing attacks from light planes and fast gunboats armed with 25mm cannons during the fall of 1983.[31] (By March 1984, over forty such missions had been conducted.) In January the CIA seriously escalated the level of violence by having its contract operatives mine three Nicaraguan harbors with seventy-five "firecracker" mines containing charges of up to three hundred pounds of C-4 plastic explosives. Nicaraguan trade, both importing and exporting, came to a halt.

Several prominent senators, among them Republican Barry Goldwater of Arizona and Democrat Samuel Cohen of Maine, expressed outrage at the CIA's actions. Planting mines, in their assessment, was an overt act of war, and Congress subsequently refused to appropriate an additional $21 million for the contras. President Reagan delivered a national address on Central America on May 9 in an effort to rally support for the contras. He declared that they were "the moral equal of our Founding Fathers," modern "freedom fighters" struggling against "a Communist reign of terror."[32] But despite this invocation of the American creation myth, public opinion remained divided. In October 1984, the House and the Senate passed a new, more restrictive version of the Boland Amendment prohibiting *any* direct or indirect expenditure of funds for assistance to the contras or attacks on Nicaragua by the "CIA, Department of Defense or any other agency or entity involved in intelligence activities."[33]

The Reagan administration had earlier begun preparations to deal with the possibility of a Congressional shutdown of funding. In March, National Security Advisor Robert McFarlane and CIA Director William Casey began asking other countries to secretly fund the contras. Israel—McFarlane's first choice—refused. On the other hand, Prince Bandar, the Saudi ambassador to the United States, agreed to transfer $1 million a month (later increased to $2 million a month) to a secret bank account in the Grand Cayman Islands set up by Yellow Fruit operatives. The Sultan of Brunei gave $10 million. The Honduran government agreed to pass along millions in military equipment to the contras, in exchange for increased U.S. military and economic assistance.[34]

Retired Major General John Singlaub, the former head of the Studies and Observation Group in Vietnam and at the time a leader of the World Anti-Communist League (WACL), made overtures to both Taiwan and South Korea for $5 million apiece.[35] These two countries were the primary backers of WACL.[36] Singlaub first cleared his plan for soliciting with Lieutenant Colonel Oliver North, the National Security Council staff member in charge of the secret aid program to keep the contras together "body and soul," as President Reagan said.[37] Eventually Singlaub's requests generated millions. The retired general also worked his own domestic network for contributions. The contras' Lady Ellen helicopter (the star of the 1985 *Soldier of Fortune* convention) was bought with $65,000 raised by Singlaub from Mary Ellen Garwood of Austin, Texas.[38] Similarly, *Soldier of Fortune* solicited money and supplies, such as packs and uniforms, from its middle- and working-class subscribers.

Outright donations, however, were only one source of funding for the contras. They also received millions of dollars from profits made by paramilitary operatives conducting other covert operations. According to the version of events that would become most widely accepted in the late 1980s, National Security Council operatives began to sell weapons to Iran in 1985. It was secret business. The return of the U.S. embassy hostages upon Reagan's inauguration had not brought peace with Iran and the two countries still did not have diplomatic relations. Moreover, in the spring of 1983, the United States had launched Operation Staunch, a program to persuade all nations to refuse to sell arms to Iran on the grounds that it sponsored terrorism abroad.

Nevertheless, in the early winter months of 1986 Reagan administration officials approved plans for shipping 4,000 TOW missiles and other munitions and spare parts to Iran. North and his associates decided to price these munitions far above their actual replacement costs, providing a considerable profit to be used in buying weapons for the Nicaraguan contras.[39] The diversion plan was approved by officials at least as high as North's new boss, Admiral John Poindexter (who had replaced McFarlane as National Security Advisor), and CIA Director Casey.

Some investigative reporters contend that there were other covert business deals that funded the contras. There is some evidence that American government officials made deals with cocaine smugglers in exchange for financial aid to the contras. For example, in November 1991 Carlos Lehder Rivas, a former leader of the Medellín drug cartel, testified as a U.S. government witness in the trial of Panama's former dictator, General Manuel Antonio Noriega. Lehder, already serving a sentence in a U.S. federal prison, said during cross-examination that to the best of his recollection "there was some contribution to the contra anti-Communist movement." Upon further questioning from Noriega's chief counsel, Frank Rubino, Lehder said that the Medellín cartel donated about $10 million to the contras. When asked if this money could have been payment for use of the air strips owned by a man named John Hull in northern Costa Rica, Lehder said that cocaine shipments "could have been, yes" sent to Hull's ranch before moving further northward.[40]

Hull's 5,000-acre ranch with its six runways was a staging base for the contras. Hull was a CIA contract agent paid to provide security to the contra supply operation from 1982 to 1986. Oliver North paid him an additional $10,000 a month in 1984 and 1985, the years when the most stringent Boland Amendment was in effect. From 1986 to 1989, Senator John Kerry's subcommittee on terrorism and narcotics investigated reports of a connection between the contra resupply network and drug smuggling. Five witnesses testified that John Hull was involved in the narcotics traffic. [41]

Although questions remain about the role of the drug trade in funding the contras, much is known about the resupply operation. Oliver North's network was staffed at the higher levels with "retired" career-soldier agents. At the top was former Major General Richard Secord, who had a long career in U.S. Air Force special operations. In the spring of 1980, after the first attempt to rescue American hostages in Iran (Operation Ricebowl) failed, Secord became executive officer for planning and managing a much larger second mission code-named Snow Bird. But President Jimmy Carter never gave the order for the mission and Snow Bird personnel became the cadre for the units in the Army's SOD as well as for covert-action groups in the other armed services. In 1982, Secord became commander of Operation Tea Kettle, the secret shipment of weapons from Lebanon to the contras. That same year Secord was investigated by the Justice Department for his role in awarding contracts to an air freight firm involved in shipping arms to Egypt that had bilked the U.S. government out of $8 million in overcharges—the firm had been owned by former CIA agents. Although Secord was not charged with any crime, he chose to retire in May 1983, and he soon went into business with several recent retirees from special operations.

In time Secord came to Oliver North's attention and was awarded a near monopoly for resupplying the contras. [42] The operation became known as the Enterprise. According to a Congressional investigation, the firm took in at least $48 million in revenues and over $6.6 million in profits in the mid-1980s. [43] There seems to have been a tacit quid-pro-quo in this lucrative arrangement. At one point when the Enterprise was being set up, Secord said to CIA Director William Casey, "Mr. Director, if and when you get your hunting license back, whatever assets we are creating right now are yours." [44]

Thus at one level the Enterprise was a privately run, privately funded business venture, while at another it functioned as an arm of the U.S. government that operated outside the laws and regulations that supposedly regulate government action in a constitutional democracy. This duality characterizes the fundamental structure of paramilitary operations, a synthesis of privateers' tactics and politicians' agendas.

While the Enterprise served as the primary means for funding and supplying the contras, other organizations were also involved. In addition to John Singlaub's WACL, there was the southern-based Civilian Military Assistance (CMA) led by Tom Posey, which recruited volunteers for missions against Nicaragua. In the promotional literature distributed at the *Soldier of Fortune* conventions, CMA said it was better to fight Communism in Nicaragua than in Mexico or inside the United States; they felt strongly that American interests were being especially threatened in Central America. In September 1984, CMA received considerable national press coverage when one of its helicopters was shot down during a raid against Nicaragua and two "volunteer" pilots killed. Although CMA did sometimes send people on ground patrols inside Nicaragua, in this instance CMA was only a cover for the CIA. The agency had borrowed a Hughes 500MD helicopter from the U.S. Army and hired two contract pilots for the mission.[45]

Aside from these organized efforts, there were also some off-the-street contract operatives and volunteers working to support the contras. Sam Hall and Dr. John McClure were not isolated cases; as political scientist Neil Livingstone reports, Central America at the time was overrun by "flakes purporting to be assassins or counterterrorist specialists."[46] The narcissistic fantasies and real limitations of such men have been previously noted. But ironically, these men's emotional instability made them particularly *useful* to the Enterprise, the CIA, and other major players. Sam Hall and Dr. John McClure belong to a category of operatives the former CIA agent David MacMichael calls "disposable assets." As author Gary Sick, a former NSC officer, learned when he interviewed MacMichael, the recruiting of such "assets" was conscious CIA policy: "The agency looks for these freelancers at small community airports and gun ranges—places where men go to escape the boredom of everyday life. Looking for adventure, these men are fascinated by the imagined glamour and excitement of the world of espionage."[47] Both paramilitary romanticism and emotional instability are useful to those who manage covert action because these qualities *discredit* the operatives if they ever go public and tell their tales. As another former case officer explains, "The agency likes things that way . . . The wilder and crazier and sillier the story, the more they like it. The agency indulges people to come up with that. It's the best defense."[48]

On October 5, 1986, the Sandinistas shot down a C-123 cargo plane belonging to the Enterprise. Only one crew member, Eugene Hasenfus, survived the attack. Hasenfus was captured and confessed that he thought he was working on a CIA operation, just as he had over a decade before in Laos. After all, he was flying in the very same type of aircraft and was working with many of the same men (Secord had run the covert air war over Laos). The Enterprise ended their contra resupply program immediately. Seven aircraft were ritually destroyed by the CIA in a remarkable ceremony: "First they had the little air force flown to a remote airfield. Then an enormous crater was dug with bulldozers. The planes were pushed into the pit, covered with explosives, and blown up. The remaining wreckage was saturated with fuel and then cremated. The fire burned for days."[49]

Unlike such rituals in New War movies and novels, the consecration of the planes through cleansing fire did not completely erase the "stain" of the Enterprise. Back in Washington, Oliver North began shredding documents and preparing his own personal blood sacrifice: "William Casey, the director of the CIA, had told me to 'shut it down and clean it up.' It was clear that somebody's head would have to roll, and I was prepared to be the victim. Offering me up as a *political* scapegoat was part of the plan, although Casey believed there would be others."[50]

In July 1987 the Senate and House of Representatives began televised hearings on the Iran-Contra affair. Oliver North testified for one week, during which he received 150,000 telegrams of support. By July 23, his defense fund had received $1,276,000 in contributions—a figure that grew to $3.1 million by early December. When the *National Enquirer* ran a "900" number telephone poll asking readers, "Would you vote for Oliver North for President?," they answered yes by a 15-to-1 margin.[51] Although at the peak of his popularity North got only a 45% approval rating for his actions —the same percentage disapproved of him—his supporters were fervent.[52] "Ollie-mania" ruled the day.

It was as if a mythical hero of New War fiction had stepped off the screen into real life. By the time of the hearings, the images and stories of the fictional New War had been circulating for several years. And North appeared to be on trial for being a man who, like Rambo and Dirty Harry and their whole band of brothers, pointed the way out of defeat in Vietnam toward a healing victory in Central America. Moreover, he seemed unfairly accused, even ahead of his time; after all, in October 1986 Congress had appropriated $100 million for the contras, the highest sum yet. In New War terms, North was a man of action whose only crime was that he ignored the "self-imposed restraints" created by politicians and government bureaucrats. In fact, North publicly accounted for his 1973 clinical depression and hospitalization by blaming the political leaders who "kept putting restraints on how we could respond."[53]

Like the fictional New War heroes, North became known as a man who personally fought duels with the evil ones. One former colleague at the National Security Council said, "Ollie took an oath to hunt and bring to trial the Shiite terrorist who was responsible for the bombing of the Marine Headquarters."[54] At one point during his televised testimony, the Congressional panel inquired about the Enterprise's installation of a security system in North's home. In response, North claimed that he had been threatened by Abu Nidal, whom he described as the "principal, foremost assassin in the world today" and simply wanted to protect his family. But as for himself, North said, "I'll be glad to meet Abu Nidal on equal terms anywhere in the world. There's an even deal for him."[55]

North also shared one other important characteristic with the mythical heroes of the 1980s—an obsessive concern with boundaries. As a young officer, he had asked to be "assigned to a forward-deployed unit at the edge of the empire."[56] In the mid-1980s North feared that the empire was shrinking. As Patrick Buchanan recalls, "Late one night when Ollie and I were laboring away on an address for the President on Central America, he mused that if we lose this war, 'I may one day be leading young Marines into battle at Gila Bend (Arizona).' "[57]

The Sandinistas even threatened the boundaries of his body. In his autobiography, North writes about Nora Astorga, a Sandinista revolutionary who lured a Somoza-regime general to her bedroom where commandos killed him. Later she became the Nicaraguan ambassador to the United States. The Reagan administration, however, refused to accept her. North gleefully notes that several liberal senators nervously laughed about her role in the revolution, since "Nora Astorga was said to be on very close terms" with them.[58]

This tremendous fear of "enemies" who threatened to penetrate national, cultural, and even bodily boundaries motivated much of American foreign and domestic policy during the 1980s. The notion that the Sandinistas or the FMLN guerrillas in El Salvador would somehow march north and *invade* the United States was not just an idea peculiar to John Milius's film *Red Dawn*. Reagan first popularized the idea in his 1983 address to Congress on Central America: "El Salvador is nearer to Texas than Texas is to Massachusetts. Nicaragua is just as close to Miami, San Antonio, San Diego, and Tucson as those cities are to Washington, where we're gathered tonight."[59]

Over at the Immigration and Naturalization Service, Harold W. Ezell, the commissioner for the western United States, similarly emphasized the necessity of maintaining boundaries against dangerous, polluting foreign elements. In his interview with *Soldier of Fortune* Ezell sounded the alarm: "I believe it is the borders that are out of control. The borders that are allowing the drugs, the illegal aliens, terrorists, whatever, to come in . . . and most of them are illiterate and most of them are bringing diseases with them and they're bringing all of the problems found in a Third World country."[60] Disease, terrorism, drug abuse, and illiteracy were thus condensed into Ezell's nightmare vision of alien forces on the attack. Only if American boundaries were maintained could all these evils be controlled.

North was only the most visible symbol of a whole pyramid of warriors dedicated to maintaining these cultural and national boundaries. At the top were the men of Navy SEAL Team 6, a counterterror team who called themselves The Jedi, after the spiritual fighters in George Lucas's *Star Wars* films. Neil Livingstone, in his *The Cult of Counterterrorism*, speaks of the men of SEAL Team 6 as "gods come to earth in the likeness of men." In a world full of terrorists, Livingstone wrote, SEAL Team 6 and the other elite counterterror units "may be all that stands between us and the abyss."[61]

Below the SEALs and their immediate kin in the pyramid came paramilitary units such as police Special Weapon and Tactics teams. Originally formed in response to such events as the Watts riots in 1965 and the Symbionese Liberation Army attacks in 1974, by the mid-1980s SWAT teams had been established in virtually every local police, sheriff's department, and state police organization in the country. Even small towns had squads equipped with M16s and H&K 9mm submachine guns fitted with noise suppressors, along with sniper rifles and other military hardware. Magazines such as *S.W.A.T.* and *Police Marksman* made large-scale combat on American soil seem imminent while at the same time showing how the police could equip themselves to fight this war and win.

Moreover, many local police units had been integrated into state, regional, and national command-and-control "counterterror" networks. For example, in the 1980s the Federal Emergency Management Agency (FEMA)—formally responsible for civil defense projects like bomb shelters—became an intelligence organization that coordinated local police departments in war games which involved sweeping arrests, mass imprisonment, and/or combat against political dissidents, potential terrorists (such as environmentalists), and illegal aliens.[62]

The National Guard formed the third tier of the pyramid. By 1985 National Guard units that had formerly trained at military bases for one weekend a month and a couple of weeks in the summer were being redeployed for actual paramilitary operations like the "war on drugs." In some states, National Guard helicopters transported joint Guard and police teams into marijuana-growing areas first identified by photographs taken from U-2 spy planes.[63] On other occasions, National Guard construction brigades built roads and buildings for use by Border Patrol agents. And sometimes they patrolled border areas themselves in search of drug smugglers and illegal aliens.[64]

The National Guard became such an integral part of both the Pentagon's plans for war abroad and for what the Reagan administration called domestic defense that a new kind of guard unit called the state reserve militia or state guard was invented. In theory these state guards would perform the functions of National Guard units in the event that the National Guard was mobilized and sent abroad. But whereas National Guard units were organized in a variety of ways to fulfill different tasks, almost all state guard units were organized as "military police" units, with each county having its own battalion or company. Part of a FEMA plan to enforce martial law, the state guard units were in charge of organizing and training an even larger paramilitary force once a domestic "emergency" had been declared.[65] Open to anyone of "good moral character" between the ages of eighteen and sixty, these state guards frequently recruited new members at gun shows and the annual *Soldier of Fortune* convention.

Several *private* militia units (in addition to the ultraright groups discussed earlier) made up the fourth tier. These units also recruited at gun shows. Civilian Military Assistance led its own patrols along the Arizona border. In Texas, a veteran of two tours in Vietnam and mercenary service in the Rhodesian Light Infantry formed the Texas Reserve Militia—and even equipped it with assault rifles of his own design and manufacture.[66] Although both the CMA and TRM border patrols were halted under government pressure in the mid-eighties, the existence of such private groups indicates the great appeal of paramilitary culture's redemptive warrior hero and the extreme sense of American vulnerability. It should be stressed that the number of terrorist incidents on American soil in the early and mid 1980s was *tiny*. A citizen was 124 times more likely to choke to death while eating than to be killed in a terrorist attack—a mere sandwich was a far more perilous foe than the evil ones.[67]

Thus, when Oliver North testified in July 1987 he was speaking to a nation saturated with New War fantasies and actual political-military programs, both of which made war and the warrior essential to America's salvation and survival. New War myths had already framed political leaders' view of the world, and "real" world events —like the Marines' deaths in Lebanon and the invasion of Grenada—had already become departure points for action-adventure movies such as *Death Before Dishonor* (1987) and *Heartbreak Ridge* (1986) that had happy endings with clear American victories. North's great popularity was a public celebration of this merger between myth and policy—the New War's dream come true. And the public excitement over North was sufficient to dissuade both the Senate and the news media from a more rigorous investigation of U.S. covert action in Iran and Central America. It was not even an issue in the 1988 election campaign between Vice President George Bush and Massachusetts governor Michael Dukakis.

George Bush won the Presidency, to a large extent, on the strength of popular support for the Reagan administration's military revival. Unfortunately for Bush, however, 1989, the year he entered office, saw the approaching end of the Cold War. Confrontations between the Soviet Union and the United States in Third World countries began to diminish radically. Soviet troops began withdrawing from Afghanistan after ten years of counterinsurgency warfare. Although fighting continued between the Communist Afghan government and Islamic fundamentalist mujahideen, and both the Soviets and the United States continued to provide financial aid to their respective allies (over \$2 billion by the United States since 1980), the withdrawal of Soviet soldiers marked the end of an era.[68] In March the Bush administration finally acknowledged that the Nicaraguan contras had been militarily—if not politically—defeated. Consequently, the United States announced that it would no longer provide military assistance to the contras, thus ending a seven-year war that had caused the deaths of 20,000 to 30,000 people and cost the United States an estimated \$433 million.[69] Now the contras were told to demobilize and return home to Nicaragua to participate in the forthcoming national elections.[70] In September the United States and the Soviet Union held a conference on how the two nations could work together against terrorists.[71] And in December, the Soviet Union proposed that both countries stop all arms shipments to Central America, implying that the repressive governments in El Salvador and Guatemala as well as their guerrilla opponents would in time be compelled to negotiate.[72]

The prospect of impending peace created yet another cultural and political crisis. If the Soviets had previously been seen as literal incarnations of human evil (the devil)—as both Ronald Reagan and New War mythology insisted—they were now at least morally neutral and perhaps even "good." Americans, then, could no longer cast themselves as the righteous heroes of a morality play performed on world history's stage. The disappearance of the "enemy" meant that the play was over, and that a vital "mirror" had been irreparably shattered. Americans would no longer find it so easy to project their own aggressions and desires upon an imagined foe or to blame the enemy for their social problems. The rest of the world could no longer be easily divided between "our" side and "their" side, "good" guys versus "bad."

President Bush—once the director of the CIA under Gerald Ford—and other seasoned U.S. political and military leaders had spent their entire careers fighting the Cold War. Without a devil figure and the powerful mobilizing dynamics of war, they were completely disoriented. To provide the missing purpose, terrorists and drug traffickers were now magnified into greater threats than ever. On September 18, 1989, Secretary of Defense Dick Cheney ordered his military commanders to develop new plans for a drug war. At the time, some fifty U.S. Army Green Berets and a paramilitary force of over a hundred Drug Enforcement Administration agents were already conducting operations in the principal coca-growing regions of Bolivia and Peru.[73] After Cheney's order, the armed services escalated their efforts. A new military command, Joint Task Force 6 at Fort Bliss, Texas, was established to organize military surveillance of the Mexican border. As one general explained the military's new enthusiasm for the war against drugs, "With peace breaking out all over, it might give us something to do."[74] Antiterrorism also got a boost: the U.S. Air Force proudly announced that its Tomahawk cruise missile, originally designed to give aging B-52 bombers a "stand-off" capacity to fire nuclear-equipped missiles at the Soviet Union, was a perfect weapon for fighting terrorists—along with the new B-2, the stealth bomber that cost $850 million per plane.

Indeed, all of a sudden many people began complaining that the war on drugs wasn't being fought hard enough. Congressman Joseph I. Lieberman argued that Executive Order 12333, a 1975 regulation forbidding U.S. government officials from ordering assassinations against specific individuals, was a serious hindrance.[75] An article in *Soldier of Fortune* contended that the drug war suffered from *exactly* the same flaws as did the Vietnam War:

> It's a war with such a negative image that politicians want to deny it exists in their communities. A war in which the enemy is better armed than the police and knows no rules of fair play. A war in which Bleeding Hearts pity the drug dealers and gang members. A war of frustration and futility for cops who haul offenders off to jail, only to see them back on the street in less time than it takes to book them. A war that was ignored while it seemed to be a problem of the black and poor. A war not backed by legislation with teeth. It's a war where the police, as the soldiers of the streets, aren't given the opportunity to win.[76]

Once again, "defeat" was cast as the result of self-imposed restraints—and thus a New War was needed to achieve victory and make the world right again. In late December 1989, President George Bush ordered 24,000 U.S. troops to invade Panama and drive General Manuel Noriega from power, on the grounds that he engaged in international drug smuggling. Within days Noriega was captured, placed under arrest by U.S. marshals, and flown to the United States for trial. Back in Panama, the news media excitedly ran stories about how U.S. soldiers searching Noriega's headquarters found fifty-five pounds of cocaine and an extensive pornography collection. One month after the invasion, the cocaine was revealed to be a flour used in making tamales, but by then Noriega's image as an acne-scarred devil figure (nicknamed "pineapple face") was well established.[77] Other troubling aspects of the war, such as Latin American anger over the invasion, the controversy over just how many Panamanians were actually killed given the extensive air bombardment and ground combat in the densely populated neighborhoods of Chorillo and San Miguelito, and Noriega's decades-long record as a paid informant for the CIA and the Drug Enforcement Administration did not get much attention.[78] Nor, for that matter, was there serious discussion of whether getting rid of one drug trafficker would affect the estimated $160 billion U.S. market.

Instead, the invasion of Panama was celebrated as a sign that Bush would follow Reagan's record of military intervention. Lee Atwater, chairman of the Republican National Committee, claimed that with the invasion President Bush "knocked the question about being timid and a wimp out of the stadium."[79] Public opinion polls showed that the military action had an approval rating of over eighty percent. The columnist David Broder concluded that "the static on the left should not obscure the fact that Panama represents the best evidence yet that, 15 years after the Vietnam War ended, Americans really have come together in recognition of the circumstances in which military intervention makes sense. The elements of agreement have been in place for some time. President Bush's contribution is to demonstrate that the new national consensus will survive when tested."[80]

Aglow with the political success of the invasion, the Bush administration immediately *escalated* its drug war and announced that a U.S. Navy task force equipped with an aircraft carrier or helicopter assault ships (depending on availability) would henceforth be stationed off Colombia to interdict drug smugglers. Ardent protest by Colombia and Peru forced the administration to abandon the plan. Still, in the spring of 1990 the administration announced that it would spend $676 million to support antidrug efforts by the national armies of Peru, Bolivia, and Colombia over the next five years. Spending for U.S. military involvement in the war against drugs would also be dramatically increased. As General Maxwell D. Thurman, the U.S. Army Southern Command leader who planned the Panama invasion, said, the Latin American drug war "is the only war we've got."[81]

That was true until August 2, 1990, when Saddam Hussein ordered Iraqi forces to invade Kuwait. By August 5, President Bush had already decided to send U.S. military forces to Saudi Arabia in Operation Desert Shield—even before he met with Saudi King Fahd to discuss a possible joint U.S.–Saudi Arabian response to the invasion. Although Bush's decision to send troops to Saudi Arabia reversed his earlier policy of support for Iraq—and was not supported by CIA and Defense Intelligence Agency reports that an Iraqi invasion of Saudi Arabia was highly unlikely—such a reversal makes perfect sense given the culture of the New War.[82] With Communism in rapid decline and Noriega out of commission in a Miami jail, American political culture needed a new demon against which to mobilize. And Bush undoubtedly needed to exorcise his own guilt over supporting Iraq for ten years. A holy war against "Saddam," as Bush called him, could provide both Bush's personal redemption and a national renewal.

Bush got the holy war he needed. By October 30, he had secretly agreed to military plans for an air war in mid-January 1991 to be followed by a ground invasion of Kuwait and Iraq in February.[83] In mid-November, the United Nations Security Council passed a resolution authorizing President Bush to go to war if Iraq did not leave Kuwait by January 15, 1991. In December, Congress passed a resolution authorizing President Bush to go to war. Bush now had what he wanted. As he explained to White House staff after spending the Christmas holidays at his Camp David mountain retreat, "I have resolved all moral questions in my mind. This is black and white, good versus evil."[84]

And on January 16 at 7:00 P.M., American fighter-bombers hit Baghdad; Cable News Network broadcast the bombing live from their correspondents' hotel-room balcony. Two hours after the bombing began, President Bush addressed the nation on television. In that speech, he promised that the new Persian Gulf War would not be like the war in Vietnam. This time, he said, American forces "will not be asked to fight with one hand tied behind their back."[85] As he later said in his State of the Union speech, the "dark chaos of dictators" would be vanquished and a "New World Order" would be founded.[86]

During the war strict military censorship controlled the information presented to the American people. For the most part, the limited stock of stories and images repeated a number of themes. The old Western imagery of two gunfighters squaring off showed up again and again; *Newsweek*'s February 11 cover announced the "Showdown in the Sand." Another favorite topic concerned stories about Hussein's evilness—he was sometimes compared to Hitler. In contrast, American soldiers were wholesome men and women who wanted to get the job done and go home. And certainly it seemed that the Americans had the technological brilliance to achieve victory. On television, the Patriot missile's flame and subsequent detonation projected an image of near-total success. Another typical videotape broadcast during the war consisted of military footage showing a tank or bunker get larger and larger as a "smart bomb" closed in on its target; in essence, the television viewer was put in the same position as the crew member of the fighter-bomber who was using the live transmissions to *guide* the bomb to its target. From this perspective, the War in the Gulf looked very sharp and clean. And clearly the United States had several advanced weapons systems (such as targeting devices for tank guns and rockets) that worked well.

But for all the firepower and all the gunfighter language, there wasn't much of a fight. The United States and its United Nations allies won in a hurry all right—though largely because the Iraqi troops did not want to pursue the war. But what did it mean to win? Despite all the killing in Kuwait, Saddam Hussein remained in control of Iraq after the war ended. Bombing had destroyed much of the country's infrastructure—its electrical generating capacity, its sewage and water systems, and its industrial production. The first United Nations survey of civilian damage in March 1991 called the toll "near apocalyptic," indicating that Iraq had been reduced to a "pre-industrial" age.[87] An estimated 5,000 to 13,000 civilians were killed in these attacks.[88] In the months after the war, investigations showed that malnutrition, cholera, and other life-threatening diseases were reaching epidemic proportions, particularly among children.[89]

But neither the destruction of Iraq nor the fate of its people mattered all that much in comparison to the symbolic importance a New War victory had for American political culture. As early as January 28, before the ground war had been launched, pundits such as *New Republic* editor Charles Krauthammer prophesied about just what victory would mean in his essay "How the War Can Change America," which appeared in *Time* magazine. "If the war in the gulf ends the way it began—with a dazzling display of American technological superiority, individual grit and, most unexpectedly for Saddam, national resolve—we will no longer speak of post-Vietnam America. A new, post-gulf America will emerge, its self-image, sense of history, even its political discourse transformed." To Krauthammer, victory over Iraq would mean a return to the golden age, for America would regain "the legacy of the last good war, World War II, a legacy lost in the jungles of Vietnam."[90]

After the ground war ended so quickly and so decisively, the celebratory exorcisms of the Vietnam demon permeated the political world. "It's almost like the whole burden of Vietnam has been lifted off everyone's shoulders," said Clayton Yeuter, Lee Atwater's successor as chairman of the Republican National Committee. "Americans have pride again."[91] Or as George Bush exclaimed, "By God, we've kicked the Vietnam syndrome once and for all."[92] Leslie Gelb—a policymaker during the Vietnam War and in 1991 a columnist at *The New York Times*—stated the mythic logic of the New War even more directly. One new blood sacrifice had redeemed another: "U.S. servicemen and women who fought and died in the Persian Gulf earned back honor for those who served and fell in Vietnam. Don't ask me exactly how. There is no real link of honor between the two wars. Nor should there be. Yet there is."[93] The Bush administration felt so good about its redemption of America that it even announced a $1 million donation to Vietnam for purchasing artificial limbs, the first U.S. aid since the old regime fell in 1975.[94]

Throughout America, people over and over celebrated victory in the Gulf as a kind of ritual redoing of Vietnam. The returning Vietnam veterans had never had a proper parade, but this time the mother of all parades would be held in New York City. Joseph H. Flom, cochair of Operation Welcome Home, announced that "it's going to be the largest tickertape parade in history," with 30,000 expected marchers being showered with 1,000 tons of paper.[95]

Within months of the March victory, hundreds of new products hit the market to commemorate the war. Model airplane manufacturers had a banner year—one company even advertised a functional rocket called the "Patriot."[96] For the bigger kids, Beretta came out with its limited edition (10,000) Desert Storm Commemorative 92F 9mm pistol at $499.99. Springfield Armory countered with a .45 automatic engraved with tanks, a camel, Patriot missiles, and a scene of Baghdad being bombed—all for only $799.[97] Desert Storm knives of all sorts were created, such as Cold Steel's Recon Scout model, "one of the first blades into Kuwait in the hands of an elite Special Forces group!"[98] *Soldier of Fortune* presented a line of "Operation Desert Storm T-Shirts," featuring scenes such as an Arab riding a camel centered in a fighter-bomber gun site with the caption, "We Flew 10,000 Miles To Smoke A Camel!"[99] In California, the Supply Sergeant chain of military surplus gear and uniforms reported that sales had never been higher in forty years of business.[100]

Even firms whose products were normally far removed from paramilitary culture did their best to ride the wave. Outboard Motor Corporation (OMC), manufacturer of Evinrude and Johnson outboard motors, replaced their normal wholesome advertisements with a full-page ensemble of five U.S. Navy SEAL commandos, dressed in camouflage clothes and face paint, pointing their guns over the edges of their inflatable boat. "Not everyone uses our outboards to go fishing on weekends," said OMC.[101] One condom manufacturer even came out with Desert Shield Condoms, "lubricated and electronically tested condoms designed with the hardened veteran in mind."[102] Undoubtedly some were used at the famous Mustang Ranch brothel in Nevada—the manager gave all single Desert Storm veterans a free night with "their pick of the litter," as *Soldier of Fortune* described the offer.[103]

Celebrities scrambled to join the New War. *Vanity Fair*'s June 1991 cover featured Annie Leibovitz's photo of Dolly Parton in a low-cut, sand-colored sequin evening dress sitting on the shoulders of sand-camouflaged GIs standing next to their sand-colored tank. Inside, Ms. Parton announced, "I've got an all-American heart."[104] And comedian Jonathan Winters found employment with America West airlines imitating General Norman Schwarzkopf, "announcing Air Superiority for Civilians," complete with uniform, podium, briefing book, and pointed finger.[105]

Schwarzkopf emerged as the star of Desert Storm—his briefings had deeply impressed the television-news media and through them much of the public. He became canonized as America's newest folk hero, "Stormin' Norman," or "the Bear." Commercial videocassette recordings of Schwarzkopf's briefings and war footage were sold (and reviewed in newspapers) right alongside video versions of paramilitary movies such as *Predator 2*.[106] A good half-dozen paperback biographies also hit the drugstore and supermarket racks within a couple of months after the war ended in March. Zebra Publishing Co., responsible for *Saigon Commandos*, *C.A.D.S.*, and *The Survivalist*, remained true to the genre when they released Jack Anderson and Dale Van Atta's *Stormin' Norman: An American Hero*. Inside the cover the "teaser" began: "The Apache helicopters of the 101st Airborne Brigade crossed the border into Iraq on the dark but clear night, with a newly-arrived moon giving advantage to their night-vision capability. Like the courageous Indian tribe after whom they were named, they were both scouts and killers against overwhelming forces."

The authors describe Schwarzkopf as "the personification of the American spirit—tall, burly, big shouldered." He is a "Renaissance man," who speaks French and German, listens to music from operas to country and western, reads books ranging from military memoirs to philosophy, and most of all, has a "granite-like assurance" that "was forged in fire and in the blood of many past battles."[107] Even Queen Elizabeth II of England got caught up in the canonization of Schwarzkopf—on May 20, 1991, she knighted him.[108] Like the old jokes that rhetorically asked what a 2,000-pound grizzly bear ate, in the spring and summer of 1991 the response to "What is General Schwarzkopf going to do after he retires?" was "Anything he wants."

Part of what Schwarzkopf wanted to do was fish, and hunt, and resume his lifelong hobby of shotgun games such as trap and skeet. The National Rifle Association learned of his interest and they asked him to host the first annual Schwarzkopf Cup, a celebrity "sporting clays" shooting contest to help raise money for the U.S. shooting team. The event was also a potential publicity vehicle to give shooting a good image and thus curtail the radical fringe of the gun-control movement. In Schwarzkopf's assessment, "We can turn the American people around on gun ownership with games like sporting clays if we don't let it become a game for the elite."[109]

At this particular event, though, the presence of Hollywood stars and sports heroes made for a fairly glamorous competition. Gerald McRaney, who played Rick, the Marine Vietnam veteran turned redneck detective on *Simon and Simon* and, later, Major Dad, was there. Robert Stack, the original FBI agent Elliot Ness on television's *The Untouchables*, hit 76 out of 100 targets, a respectable score. But John Milius, producer of *Uncommon Valor* and director of *Red Dawn*, carried the day with 86 hits. The *American Rifleman* article noted that it was his second win of the year.

CONCLUSION:

WAKING UP FROM

WARRIOR DREAMS

President Bush and many other politicians and news commentators saw the 1991 Persian Gulf War as a way to realize America's warrior dreams on a grand scale. Yet despite the crushing defeat of the Iraqi military, the New World Order that was supposed to be created from the chaos of Desert Storm never came to be. Iraq lay in ruins, but Saddam Hussein remained in power. Further, the peace conferences held among Israel, the Palestinians, and the Arab states failed to reach any substantive agreements. And even after the Soviet Union dissolved in January 1992, thus marking the definitive end of the Evil Empire, America's victory in the forty-five-year Cold War did not bring any great sense of renewal and hope for the future.

Instead, in 1991 and 1992 the Reagan and Bush administrations came under increasing attack for their dealings with Iran in the 1980s.[1] Former Defense Secretary Caspar W. Weinberger was even charged with five felony offenses surrounding the Iran-Contra scandal.[2] Evidence also emerged that the Bush administration had altered official documents to obscure just how much aid was going to Iraq before the Gulf War.[3] The prospect of another Watergate crisis lingered in the air.

Nor did the Gulf War and Cold War victories rejuvenate the domestic economy. Accounts of prolonged mass unemployment, increasing crime, homelessness, and assorted other ills made it clear that the very fabric of American society was coming undone. In May 1992, Los Angeles burned: the riots that followed the first Rodney King verdict resulted in fifty-eight deaths and hundreds wounded, and cost hundreds of millions of dollars. Most Americans seemed finally to acknowledge that their society had profound problems that could no longer be ignored.

By the summer, less than a year and a half after his duel in the Kuwaiti sun, President Bush was floundering, with a less than 50% approval rating in the polls. Both the War in the Gulf and the Cold War were so far removed from the day-to-day realities of American life that they seemed like old TV shows or ancient history—interesting, perhaps, but not really relevant.

Bill Clinton's victory in that year's Presidential election appeared to indicate a clear repudiation of the old Cold War warrior. During the campaign, he had refused to fall for Bush's constant efforts to portray him as a draft dodger and antiwar activist who might even be connected to the Soviet KGB.[4] Clinton seemed like a different kind of man in other ways, too. When he was nominated, he'd hugged the candidate for Vice President, Al Gore. He also emphasized repeatedly that his wife, Hillary, would remain his most important adviser.

After Clinton's election, events conspired to make it seem as if the whole New War era had come to a close. In his last week in office, President Bush ordered new air raids against Iraq. But no one talked about societal renewal through Desert Storm II. No one even talked about the raids forcing Hussein out of power. It was evident that they were primarily a personal issue for Bush, a way for him to show that during his Presidency he had stood for something.

Around the same time, the Supreme Court read a request from SOF's lawyers, who sought a review of the decision of the 11th Circuit of the United States Court of Appeals. In that decision, in contrast to the 1988 Hearn case, *SOF* was fined $4.3 million for publishing a classified ad from a mercenary who was later hired to kill a man. *SOF*'s lawyers pleaded that the fine was so high that the magazine would quickly be forced out of business. The Supreme Court declined the defendant's request, and the fine was levied.[5] (As of mid-1993, SOF remained in print.)

At first glance, then, the changes of 1991 and 1992 seemed to signal that the claims to power, honor, and glory that had been central tenets of post-Vietnam warrior culture were being challenged, or at least deflated. The warrior had lost his charm in a world where most of America's old enemies had been defeated or crippled—but things at home still weren't right. Deep-seated cultural mythologies, however, are not at all equivalent to scientific theories that can be tested and refuted by the facts. That victory in the Gulf did not bring America's national renewal and that *Soldier of Fortune* received a near-mortal wound does not imply that the warrior mythology of the 1980s was destroyed or universally discredited.

Texas billionaire H. Ross Perot's great popularity as an independent candidate for President in 1992 was largely based on his self-cultivated image as a man who was outside the normal political system. Perot had always seen himself as a kind of unofficial commanding general. Electronic Data Systems, the company which made his fortune, was almost exclusively staffed at management levels by retired U.S. military officers. During the Vietnam War Perot chartered jet planes and attempted to send supplies to American prisoners of war in North Vietnam (he was refused landing rights in Hanoi). After 1975, he became one of the leaders of the POW–MIA movement to locate and if possible rescue men who were believed to be still captive in Vietnam. In 1979, when employees of Electronic Data Systems working in Iran were taken prisoner during the overthrow of the Shah, Perot financed and organized a successful rescue mission. This tale was subsequently told in Ken Follett's book, *On the Wings of Eagles*, and in a made-for-TV movie by the same name. During the spring of 1992, the book was rereleased and stayed on the best-seller list for more than five months.

The Los Angeles riots also revitalized some aspects of paramilitary culture. The failure of the Los Angeles Police Department and the

National Guard to deploy their forces effectively led some small business owners (of all races) to take up arms to defend their property. Although a few were shot and at least one was killed, these people saved their businesses while all around them the unprotected stores and warehouses burned. California gun sales soon increased to a twenty-year high.[6] Buying a firearm for self-defense does not necessarily imply a full embrace of the New War. But neither are combat weapons just neutral, inert things: they are connected to a wider culture. When prospective gun owners thumb through the pages of gun magazines and make their way around gun shops, shooting ranges, and instructional courses, they are exposed to the culture of the experts from whom they seek advice. Given both America's racial polarization, and the mythologies in which combat weapons are so deeply embedded, it can be difficult to retain a perspective in which guns are to be used solely for self-defense—a last resort—rather than as a solution to social problems. The power of the gun to stop an intruder can be felt in the hand; the benefits of peace that comes from social reconstruction seem far away.

In the early 1990s both the book-publishing industry and Hollywood continued to recycle commando-cop sagas of men who act outside the establishment. *Rogue Warrior*, the autobiography of Richard Marcinco, a former Navy SEAL veteran in Vietnam, who later organized and commanded SEAL Team 6, the Navy's counterterrorist unit, stayed on the *New York Times* best-seller list through the spring and summer of 1992.[7] As for Hollywood, *Lethal Weapon 3* was released shortly after the L.A. riots and became a box office hit of historic proportions, bringing in $27.5 million during its first weekend. The next year Chuck Norris, of *Missing in Action* fame, got his own television series in which he plays a modern-day Texas ranger.

Other incidents also testified to the continuing appeal and power of paramilitary culture. Massachusetts college student Wayne Lo had a reputation as a "tough guy," and he chose a "tough gun," a Chinese SKS rifle—the kind that was imported after the original AK47s were banned—for his December 1992 rampage on the campus of Simon's Rock College. Lo killed two people and wounded four others.[8]

The sight of a bad man holding a bad man's gun sparked another shooting that fall. When an off-duty Los Angeles County deputy sheriff answered his door at ten o'clock at night and saw a figure dressed in an all-black ninja suit and pointing an Uzi submachine gun at him, the deputy opened fire with his service pistol. He then slammed the door shut, got his wife, and together they took cover. Only when he recognized the cries of pain coming from the doorway did he realize what had happened. He had shot a friend—an eleven-year-old boy who'd painted over the red stripe on his plastic Uzi (a stripe indicating that it was a toy gun) with black paint to make it more realistic looking.[9]

Self-proclaimed religious prophets also continued to arm themselves with advanced weapons, explosives, and camouflage uniforms to defend their cults against the satanic forces of the modern world. When agents from the Bureau of Alcohol, Tobacco and Firearms assaulted the Branch Davidian center near Waco, Texas, on February 28, 1993, four officers were killed. Cult leader David Koresh had for years seen himself as a militant prophet and paramilitary warrior (in 1987, armed with Ruger Mini-14 semiautomatic rifles, he led seven of his followers in a battle against another cult leader).[10] By late April his self-conception had changed to that of a supreme deity—the vengeful Yahweh Koresh. In phone calls and letters to federal officials, Koresh proclaimed his group ready for war and warned that the compound would explode if agents tried to enter.[11] When the agents made the attempt, on April 22, the building complex turned into an inferno. It burned to the ground within half an hour, incinerating eighty-six people in a hot, cleansing fire.

Lastly, despite what was being called the liberal tilt of the Clinton administration, warrior myths continued to influence public policy. In mid-April 1993, an Australian researcher claimed to have found an old 1972 Russian translation of a North Vietnamese document indicating that the Vietnamese never returned several hundred American POWs. Although analysts soon uncovered many discrepancies between this document and previously verified intelligence, and the Vietnamese government offered strong evidence that the document was a fake, most Americans wanted to believe the report was authentic. After all, the Vietnamese Communists had been a symbol of evil in New War mythology for nearly twenty years. President Clinton subsequently refused to lift the eighteen-year-old trade embargo against Vietnam, and U.S. representatives serving in international development agencies were told to continue voting against financial assistance.[12] (Some months later, after the POW issue faded from the news, Clinton dropped his opposition to international loans for Vietnam).

Thus, it would be wrong to conclude that the New War ended in 1993. Certainly once the Iraqi Army was routed in 1991, some of the burden of defeat in Vietnam was lifted. For a moment, the military victory gave Americans confidence that at least they could win a war—if nothing else. But through the 1980s Vietnam became more than a symbol of humiliating military defeat. Rather it stood for everything that had gone wrong—from the cowardly, corrupt politicians to unruly women to a deteriorating economy. Originally, all New War sagas—no matter where the battle took place—featured heroes or villains somehow connected to the Vietnam War. But by the late 1980s and early 1990s the New War was an established genre and its conventions were taken for granted. Movies and pulp novels no longer necessarily mentioned Vietnam or had Vietnam veterans as their heroes. The message remained the same, though: the warrior identity was the essence of masculinity; battle was the way to right any imagined wrong. The black-widow succubuses of the New War still appealed in the 1990s to men's worst fears about women. Its male villains still excited them with scenes of the violent murder of loved ones. The infantile rage of vengeance still seemed like the purest form of justice.

This cultural continuity carries with it a great danger. Even if today's warrior myths are not as charged and overtly political as they were at their peak, it is quite possible that at some later date the mythology will be reworked and reinvigorated to mobilize support for some other war effort, regardless of the rights and wrongs at issue. After all, this is exactly what happened the last time around when the paramilitary heroes of the New War arose to replace the discredited exploits of John Wayne.

How can we avoid this danger and break the chain of mythic warrior heroes? How can we create conditions in which warrior mythology and the acts of war they render so alluring will lose their appeal? How can we wake up from warrior dreams? A full discussion of these questions is obviously not within the scope of this book, but it is possible to sketch out, briefly, several important directions for change.

First and foremost, masculinity needs to be redefined in a way that will reduce the pull of the warrior on the masculine unconscious. This in turn requires changing the structure of the family, particularly the role of fathers. In patriarchal societies, fathers have not been involved in the care of infants and young children. Consequently, the child experiences himself or herself as dependent solely upon the mother. Over the years this nurturing relationship creates both utter reliance on the mother and resentment toward her for the humiliations that reliance entails.

The father, on the other hand, is not associated with the male child's memories of humiliation, dependency, and emotional vulnerability. Psychologist Dorothy Dinnerstein and other analysts conclude that as a consequence, men grow up devaluing women and spurning and degrading all nurturing activities and emotional expressiveness as unwelcome reminders of past dependency.[13] As the beginning of New War stories indicates, the death of the family often serves as the prelude to the birth of the warrior. Who can be more of a man than the warrior whose childhood ended at an early age when his parents were killed by the evil ones? Who can be more of a man than the warrior who lives outside normal society and is not contaminated by the mundane (and thus feminized) chores of domestic life and children?

If the all-powerful mother is replaced by equal parenting—if men, too, become child-rearers—then perhaps adult masculinity will no longer be defined in terms that are the complete opposite of "feminine" characteristics. Men might become more emotionally expressive and less psychologically distant. They might grow to approach erotic relations without fear of black-widow women or "the evil infinite of human desire" carrying them away and ruining their lives. Indeed, they might experience eroticism as a connecting force, not a destructive, devouring hunger that must be rigidly controlled or rejected. And this new connection to erotic life and nurturance—to sexuality and child-rearing—might finally devalue the idea that killing in combat is the highest expression of masculinity.

But redefining manhood will also require new relationships among boys and men that stretch far beyond the years of childhood, as well as new images of bravery and new coming-of-age narratives. In tribal societies, initiation ceremonies for young men often lasted months. During this period adolescent boys were removed from their homes, introduced to secret male-only versions of creation myths, and frequently required to undergo ordeals of various sorts. For example, in several American Plains Indian tribes, youths were sent into the wilderness on vision quests, journeys in which, through isolation and hunger, initiates prepared themselves to receive the tribal deities in visions and dreams. The elders then helped the youths understand their dreams and visions when they returned. Once the meaning of the experiences was interpreted and publicly acknowledged by the tribe in a ceremony, the boys were born again and renamed. They had passed an important threshold toward manhood.

Today, only one kind of male initiation ceremony is broadly accepted and practiced in the United States—military/police training and the ordeal of combat. The bitter truth is that the infantile regression that often occurs in the permissive lawlessness of real combat zones and almost always occurs in warrior myths has become the principal culturally certified path toward manhood.

Nowhere is this more evident than in the growth of gangs. In 1991, Los Angeles County alone had an estimated 100,000 gang members organized in around 1,000 groups. Over 700 gang-related homicides occurred in L.A. County that year, about one-third of all murders.[14] Gangs are clearly warrior societies, extended families in which weapons are key emblems of manhood and drive-by shootings or gunfights serve as important initiation rites.[15] The death of a gang member reaffirms the bonds among surviving brothers, and perpetuates an endless war of vengeance.

Middle-class secret societies and fraternities are also gangs of sorts—with their own rites of initiation, designed to create group cohesion. During the mid-1980s, for example, a high-school gang in Fort Worth called the Legion of Doom (originally part of a group authorized by the school principal to patrol the halls) became famous for vigilante assaults on students it considered undesirable. A few years later in Long Beach, California, a group called the Ace of

Spades (originally part of a local high school's Army ROTC program) killed one of its members for talking to the police about car thefts group members had committed. In 1990, members of another ROTC unit in San Diego's Mar Vista High School played war games along the border between Mexico and the United States in which they stalked and shot—with paintball guns—illegal immigrants crossing the border.[16] A number of college fraternity members were prosecuted for gang rapes in the 1980s. All of these crimes are variants of the same process of initiation through violence.[17]

Rethinking parenting and recasting initiation rites will no doubt move us toward a new masculine ideal but they will not break the spell of warrior dreams unless we recognize something even more basic. At the broadest level, paramilitary culture shows the continuing need for myth and ritual even in the heart of the modern secular world. Over the last two hundred years, the spread of Enlightenment ideas, together with a wealth of material goods produced by technologically advanced economies, have taught that the myths that ruled our ancestors have no power over our lives, no value but as entertainment. But through most of human history people have understood themselves and their world through myths. They are not mere fictions to be replaced by reason.

Critical analysis of warrior mythology certainly contributes to the process of waking-up or disenchantment. But disenchantment alone is not enough. One of the most serious problems advocates of a peaceful world have always faced is that while peace means an end to the horrors of war, it also means an end to the travels, challenges, stories, and male initiation that war has traditionally provided. If paramilitary culture is to be abolished, then other areas of social life will have to be reenchanted. Without enchantment—without access to a magical kingdom of some kind—the responsibilities of adulthood are simply too much: people break down and flee in one direction or another.

The men's movement has promoted one version of enchantment, the "wildman" weekends proposed by Robert Bly. At these gatherings, men talk about their relationships with their fathers in a "pre-industrial" atmosphere: they beat drums, wear face paint, and practice old masculine rites.[18] Despite the movement's good intentions, these weekends resemble the *Soldier of Fortune* conventions in Las Vegas: both are visits to theme parks, places in which experiences and their larger meanings come in packages clearly labeled in big print.

Such failures are inevitable. Creating a culture of myths and rituals that offers a mix of well-defined and open-ended experiences and does not appear ridiculous to sophisticated urban American sensibilities is not easy. On the other hand, it's not necessarily impossible, either. Much can be learned from paramilitary culture. For example, when one looks past the culture's violence, two important elements come into view: the extraordinary level of adventure and the experience of community. All paramilitary heroes leave the normal world behind and embark on important journeys, sometimes to distant countries and different cultures, other times to remote wilderness areas. They frequently travel in exotic vehicles, virtual chariots of the gods such as helicopters, motorcycles, and cigarette-style powerboats: their very form of transport transcends the ordinary world. On their adventures, the heroes must be continually alert. They are either considering how to meet the challenges ahead or else are so completely absorbed in the experience that they move with an uncommon unity of mind and body. Both their intellects and their bodies are pushed beyond previous limits; they become more powerful as the adventure unfolds.

Except for the occasional lone warrior, most of the time the warrior heroes work in pairs or small groups. To survive their adventure, they must cooperate and learn to respect one another. As they do so, they leave behind the mundane world of competition, envy, and feelings of inadequacy. Unfortunately, in paramilitary culture the positive qualities of mythical adventure are tied to a single objective: killing the enemy. My week at Gunsite Ranch is a good example. Indeed, it is the shooting and implied killing that make the Gunsite Ranch adventure, like the paintball battles, seem serious—a worthy project for grown men. War or combat has had a near-monopoly in American culture as the major socially legitimate form of adult adventure.

One possible way, then, to reduce the appeal of warrior mythologies is to treat the concept of adventure seriously and make actual adventures available to millions, not just a few. People need to experience a break in the constant routines and often burdensome responsibilities of work and family. The typical suburban menu of small pleasures like going out for dinner or working in the yard only provides relief within the familiar world of everyday life. Adventure implies a more fundamental break in the rhythms of life, an opportunity for recreation that at least sometimes and perhaps often offers a re-creation of the self in the context of an unfamiliar world.

Wilderness areas provide just this opportunity for re-creation. For example, mountaineers and scuba divers journey into a natural environment immensely different from that of urban life; simply being in the high mountains or under water requires totally different skills and sensibilities. These sports make the adventurer feel empowered—his or her actions count. Some enthusiasts make more radical claims for their sports—claims to transcendent experience. Mountaineers speak of becoming one with the mountain: the boundaries between themselves and the world change.

At the end of their climbs or dives, the adventurers return to urban life and their families and co-workers. They have stories—like war stories—to tell of their adventures. In these stories, they describe not only the world they visited, but their inner transformations and their experiences of comradeship with fellow adventurers. The grand adventuring sports offer practioners some kind of rebirth.

Still, can adventure deflect the appeals of warrior mythology when it lacks war's seriousness, its high purpose in defending the moral boundaries of society against the evil ones? No definitive answer is possible. But it is interesting to note that what begins as adventure or sport often turns into a crusade. Many outdoor sports enthusiasts have become ecological activists. Captain Jacques Cousteau began his voyages on the *Calypso* in the 1950s with the intention of exploring the undersea world and making films. By the early 1970s, he had reoriented his research trips and documentary films toward protecting the environment. Similarly, in the past decade America's climbers, hikers, and campers have been active in creating and revitalizing scores of environmental organizations.

Adventure sports and ecological movements are only two examples of how to rework, for worthwhile ends, those aspects of warrior mythology that speak to real human needs. Undoubtedly, other kinds of activities and other myths that move men forward toward maturity and transcendent experience can be developed. To assert that myths meet human needs and that we need new myths does not imply that the Age of Enlightenment is over, just that rationalism has limits: it can take the world apart, but not put it back together. Only stories and visions do that.

For most of America's history, our guiding stories and visions have glorified war and the warrior. Yet the way of the warrior is a lonely, tragic path. For all the power that the warrior seems to have, he is left stunted and diminished inside his hardened boundaries. And for all his supposed autonomy, he remains vulnerable to manipulation. In the end, the paramilitary warriors of the 1980s were not much different from other men who went to Vietnam and, in their experiences of war, found that they had been seduced by warrior myths and used by the state.

Nietzsche once prophesied that war would end when the men of a nation felt so powerful and so positive about themselves and the prospects of life offered them that they declared, "I break the sword." The warrior as we know him can never break the sword or chains of war; without war, he would not know who he was or what the world was about. But a different kind of man might. To do so, he would not have to renounce the pleasures of physical power and the risks of danger, or shun the comradeship of male groups, but instead find ways to use them to grow, rather than regress. Transforming warrior culture is not about men becoming something less than they are, but rather, something more.

NOTES

INTRODUCTION

1. Peter G. Kokalis, speaking at the *Soldier of Fortune* firepower demonstration at the Desert Sportsman Rifle and Pistol Club, Las Vegas, Nev., September 20, 1986.

2. Gar Wilson, *The Fury Bombs*, vol. 5 of *Phoenix Force* (Toronto: Worldwide Library, 1983), 30.

3. *SOF* regularly hired the firm of Starch, Inra, Hopper to study their readership. A condensed version of their 1986 report, from which these figures were taken, was made available to the press at the September 1986 *SOF* convention in Las Vegas.

4. Lionel Atwill, *Survival Game: Airgun National Manual* (New London, N.H.: The National Survival Game, Inc., 1987), 22–30.

5. Richard Slotkin, *Regeneration through Violence: The Mythology of the American Frontier, 1660–1860*. (Middletown, Conn.: Wesleyan University Press, 1973).

6. Mircea Eliade, *Myth and Reality*, trans. Willard R. Trask (New York: Harper and Row, 1963).

7. Richard Stivers, *Evil in Modern Myth and Ritual* (Athens: University of Georgia Press, 1982).

8. Will Wright, *Sixguns and Society: A Structural Study of the Western* (Berkeley: University of California Press, 1975), 20.

1

1. Henry Nash Smith, *Virgin Land: The American West as Symbol and Myth* (New York: Vintage, 1950), 120.

2. Edmund Morris, *The Rise of Theodore Roosevelt* (New York: Coward, McCann and Geoghegan, 1979), 613.

3. Ibid.

4. Kevin Brownlow, *The War, the West, and the Wilderness* (New York: Knopf, 1979), xvi.

5. Morris, *Rise of Theodore Roosevelt*, 629.

6. Raymond Fielding, *The American Newsreel, 1911–1967* (Norman, Okla.: University of Oklahoma Press, 1972), 30.

7. Brownlow, *The War, the West, and the Wilderness*, 32.

8. Bruce W. Oris, *When Hollywood Ruled the Skies: Aviation Films of WW II* (Los Angeles, Calif.: Aero Associates, 1984), 5–6.

9. Clayton R. Koppes and Gregory D. Black, *Hollywood Goes to War: How Politics, Profits, and Propaganda Shaped World War II Movies* (New York: The Free Press, 1987), 36–37.

10. Emmanuel Levy, *John Wayne: Prophet of the American Way of Life* (Metuchen, N. J.: The Scarecrow Press, 1988), 24.

11. Don Graham, *No Name on the Bullet: A Biography of Audie Murphy* (New York: Viking, 1989), 20.

12. Koppes and Black, *Hollywood Goes to War*, 64–65.

13. David A. Cook. *A History of Narrative Film* (New York: Norton, 1981), 396–97.

14. For accounts of the relationships between Hollywood and the Defense Department after WW II, see Lawrence H. Suid, *Guts and Glory: Great American War Movies* (Reading, Mass: Addison-Wesley, 1977) and Julian Smith, *Looking Away: Hollywood and Vietnam* (New York: Scribner's, 1978).

15. Ron Kovic, *Born on the Fourth of July* (New York: McGraw-Hill, 1976), 42–43.

16. Philip Caputo, *Rumor of War* (New York: Holt, Rinehart and Winston, 1971), 32.

17. John Sack, *Lieutenant Calley: His Own Story* (New York: Viking, 1974), 32.
18. Michael A. Kubkler, *Operation Baroom* (Gastonia, N.C.: TCP Publishers, 1980), 124–25.
19. Michael Herr, *Dispatches* (New York: Avon, 1978), 223.
20. Tom Suddick, *A Few Good Men* (New York: Avon, 1978), 23–24.
21. Kovic, *Born on the Fourth of July*, 181.
22. Robert Jay Lifton, *Home from the War* (New York: Simon and Schuster, 1973), 97.
23. Levy, *John Wayne*, 218.
24. Gustav Hasford, *The Short-timers* (New York: Harper and Row, 1979), 32.
25. Charles Anderson, *The Grunts* (San Rafael, Calif.: Presidio, 1976), 100.
26. Ibid., 145.
27. James Webb, *Fields of Fire* (Englewood Cliffs, N. J.: Prentice-Hall, 1978).
28. Robert Evans and Richard D. Novak, *Nixon in the White House* (New York: Summit, 1983), 506.
29. Sir James George Frazer, *The Golden Bough: A Study in Magic and Religion*, abridged edition (New York: Collier, 1922), 14–43.
30. Seymour M. Hersh, *The Price of Power: Kissinger in the White House* (New York: Summit, 1983), 506.
31. James William Gibson, *The Perfect War: Technowar in Vietnam* (New York: Atlantic Monthly Press, 1986).
32. Alexander M. S. McColl, "Requiem for Three Nations," *Soldier of Fortune*, Summer 1975, 6.
33. Interview with Menahem Golan, Los Angeles, February 13, 1987.
34. Interview with Joseph Zito, Los Angeles, October 21, 1986.
35. Interview with Lionel Chetwynd, Los Angeles, February 17, 1987.
36. Interview with John Milius, Los Angeles, May 20, 1987.
37. Mike McCray, *Cold Vengeance*, vol. 2 of *The Black Berets* (New York: Dell, 1984), 21.
38. Robert Warshow, "The Westerner," in *Awake in the Dark: An Anthology of American Film Criticism, 1915 to the Present*. Edited by David Denby (New York: Vintage, 1977), 431.
39. Larry Heinemann, *Close Quarters* (New York: Penguin, 1977), 111.
40. Klaus Theweleit, *Male Bodies: Psychoanalyzing the White Terror*, vol. 2 of *Male Fantasies*, trans. Erica Carter and Chris Turner (Minneapolis: University of Minnesota Press, 1977), 353.

2

1. Jack Hild, *Firestorm U.S.A.*, vol. 16 of *SOBs: Soldiers of Barrabas* (Toronto: Worldwide, 1987), 43.
2. Don Pendleton, *War Against the Mafia*, vol. 1 of *The Executioner* (New York: Pinnacle, 1969), xviii.
3. Paul Kupperber, "A Life!," *Vigilante* no. 50, (February 1988), 7.
4. Tom Clancy, *Patriot Games* (New York: Putnam, 1987), 427.
5. Ibid.
6. Jonathan Cain, *Cherry Boy Body Bag*, vol. 4 of *Saigon Commandos* (New York: Zebra, 1984), 62.
7. Stephen Coonts, *Final Flight* (New York: Doubleday, 1988), 153–54.
8. Mark Warman, "Afghan Elite Forces," *Soldier of Fortune*, December 1983, 66.
9. Mike McCray, *Louisiana Firestorm*, vol. 5 of *The Black Berets* (New York: Dell, 1985), 19.
10. Ibid., 32.
11. Tom Clancy, *Red Storm Rising* (New York: Berkeley, 1987), 690–91.
12. Clancy, *Patriot Games*, 53.
13. Bruno Bettelheim, *Symbolic Wounds* (Glencoe, Ill.: The Free Press, 1954).
14. "The man with no name" was actor Clint Eastwood's name in Leone's Westerns: *A Fistful of Dollars* (1964); *For a Few Dollars More* (1965); *The Good, the Bad, and the Ugly* (1966). This role was Eastwood's birth as a star warrior. Previously he had played the scout Rowdy Yates in the 1950s television series *Rawhide*.
15. In *Lethal Weapon 3* (1992) Roger (Danny Glover) and Riggs (Mel Gibson) finally do exchange "I love you"s. Riggs says that Roger, his wife, and two children *are* his family.
16. Hild, *Firestorm U.S.A.*, 58.
17. Gar Wilson, *Weep, Moscow, Weep*, vol. 27 of *Phoenix Force* (Toronto: Worldwide, 1987), 39.
18. Gar Wilson, *The Fury Bombs*, vol. 5 of *Phoenix Force* (Toronto: Worldwide, 1983), 187–88.
19. Mike McCray, *Cold Vengeance*, vol. 2 of *The Black Berets* (New York: Dell, 1984), 148.
20. Charles M. Simpson III, *Inside the Green Berets: The First Thirty Years* (Novato, Calif.: Presidio, 1983).

21. Alexander M. S. McColl, "Requiem for Three Nations," *Soldier of Fortune*, Summer 1975, 6.

22. William Broyles, Jr., *Brothers in Arms: A Journey from War to Peace* (New York: Avon, 1986), 192.

23. Ibid., 190.

24. E. O. James, *Origins of Sacrifice* (Port Washington, N.Y.: Kennikat Press, 1953; reissued 1971).

25. Pendleton, *War Against the Mafia*, 170.

26. Gayle Rivers, *The Specialist: Revelations of a Counterterrorist* (New York: Stein and Day, 1985), 165.

27. Barry Sadler, *Casca: The Eternal Mercenary* (New York: Charter, 1979), 24.

28. Bruno Bettelheim, *The Uses of Enchantment: The Meaning and Importance of Fairy Tales* (New York: Knopf, 1976), 36 and 63.

29. René Girard, *Violence and the Sacred*, trans. Patrick Gregory (Baltimore: Johns Hopkins, 1972), 14–15.

30. Dorothy Dinnerstein, *The Mermaid and the Minotaur: Sexual Arrangements and Human Malaise* (New York: Harper and Row, 1977).

31. Nancy Chodorow, *The Reproduction of Mothering: Psychoanalysis and the Sociology of Gender* (Berkeley: University of California Press, 1978).

32. Franco Fornari, *The Psychoanalysis of War*, trans. Alenka Pfeiffer (Bloomington, Ind.: University of Indiana Press, 1975), 55.

33. Daryl Jones, *The Dime Western Novel* (Bowling Green, Ohio: Bowling Green State University, 1978), 78–82.

34. Will Wright, *Sixguns and Society: A Structural Study of the Western* (Berkeley: University of California Press, 1975), 59–74.

3

1. Jerry Ahern, *The Quest*, vol. 3 of *The Survivalist* (New York: Zebra, 1981), 42–43.

2. Ibid., 44.

3. Richard Stivers, *Scorched Earth*, vol. 13 of *Able Team* (Toronto: Worldwide, 1984), 38.

4. Richard Stivers, *Ghost Train*, vol. 31 of *Able Team* (Toronto: Worldwide, 1987), 43.

5. Tania Modleski, *Losing with a Vengeance: Mass-Produced Fantasies for Women* (Hamden, Conn.: Archon, 1982), 16.

6. Mike McCray, *Louisiana Firestorm*, vol. 5 of *The Black Berets* (New York: Dell, 1985), 56–57.

7. Jonathan Cain, *Cherry Boy Body Bag*, vol. 4 of *Saigon Commandos* (New York: Zebra, 1984), 149.

8. Jack Hild, *Alaska Deception: Red Star Over Alaska*, vol. 20 of *SOBs: Soldiers of Barrabas* (Toronto: Worldwide, 1987), 94.

9. Don Pendleton and staff writers, *War Born*, vol. 123 of *The Executioner* (Toronto: Worldwide, 1989), 110.

10. Jerry Ahern, *The Nightmare Begins*, vol. 2 of *The Survivalist* (New York: Zebra, 1981), 85–88.

11. Jonathan Cain, *Torturers of Tet*, vol. 10 of *Saigon Commandos* (New York: Zebra, 1986), 70–74.

12. Wilbur Smith, *The Delta Decision* (New York: Doubleday, 1979; Signet, 1982), 1.

13. Ibid., 5.

14. Ibid., 51.

15. Stephen Coonts, *Final Flight* (New York: Doubleday, 1988), 219.

16. Stivers, *Ghost Train*, 13–14.

17. Ibid., 211.

18. Gayle Rivers, *The Specialist: Revelations of a Counterterrorist* (New York: Stein and Day, 1985); *The War Against the Terrorists: How to Win It* (New York: Stein and Day, 1986).

19. Rivers, *War Against the Terrorists*, 18–19.

20. Peter G. Kokalis, "Atlacatal Assault: *SOF* in Combat with Salvador's Elite Immediate Reaction Battalion," *Soldier of Fortune*, June 1984, 57.

21. Ibid., 58.

22. Klaus Theweleit, *Women, Floods, Bodies, History*, vol. 1 of *Male Fantasies*, trans. Stephen Conway with Erica Carter and Chris Turner (Minneapolis: University of Minnesota Press, 1987), 68.

23. Ibid., 74.

24. Ibid., 125.

25. Jerry Ahern, *The Nightmare Begins*, vol. 2 of *The Survivalist* (New York: Zebra, 1981), 185.

26. Don Pendleton and staff writers, *Hell's Gate*, vol. 86 of *The Executioner* (Toronto: Worldwide, 1986), 17–18.

27. Ibid., 62.

28. Ibid., 69.

29. Ibid., 134.

30. Mike Barron, "Sacrifice Play," *The Punisher*, vol. 11, no. 13 (November 1988), 13.

31. Stivers, *Ghost Train*, 80–81.

32. Hild, *Alaska Deception*, 64–65.

33. Ibid., 45, 68.

34. Interview with Andy Ettinger, the first editor of *The Executioner*, October 17, 1986, in Los Angeles.

4

1. Kai T. Erikson, *Wayward Puritans: A Study in the Sociology of Deviance* (New York: Wiley, 1968), 12.

2. Don Pendleton and staff writers, *War Born*, vol. 123 of *The Executioner* (Toronto: Worldwide 1989), 128.

3. Jeff Cooper, "Cooper on Rhodesia: An Alternative View to the State Department Position," *Soldier of Fortune*, Summer 1975, 28.

4. "Beirut: Christian Soldiers Man the Green Line," *Soldier of Fortune*, November 1986, 55.

5. "The War on Our Doorstep: *SOF*'s Front-Line Report from Central America," *Soldier of Fortune*, July 1983, 48.

6. Wilbur Smith, *The Delta Decision* (New York: Doubleday, 1979; Signet, 1982), 93.

7. Don Pendleton, *War Against the Mafia*, vol. 1 of *The Executioner* (New York: Pinnacle, 1969), 32, 36–37.

8. John Sievert, *C.A.D.S. #1: Computerized Attack Defense System* (New York: Zebra, 1985), 71; Gayle Rivers, *The Specialist: Revelations of a Counterterrorist* (New York: Stein and Day, 1985), 80–81.

9. Carl H. Yaeger, *A Hunger for Heroes* (New York: Tom Doherty Associates, A *Soldier of Fortune* Magazine book, 1988), 66.

10. John Sievert, *C.A.D.S.*, 326.

11. Pendleton et al., *War Born*, 238.

12. Smith, *The Delta Decision*, 226, 203, 67.

13. Sievert, *C.A.D.S.*, 365.

14. David Alexander, *Dark Messiah*, vol. 1 of *Phoenix* (New York: Leisure Books, 1987), 61.

15. Jack Hild, *Firestorm U.S.A.*, vol. 16 of *SOBs: Soldiers of Barrabas* (Toronto: Worldwide, 1987), 186.

16. Robert Moss and Arnaud De Borchgrave, *Monimbo* (New York: Pocket Books, 1983), 1.

17. Paul Ricoeur, *The Symbolism of Evil*, trans. Emerson Buchanan (Boston: Beacon, 1969), 254.

18. Alexander, *Dark Messiah*, 61.

19. Major L. H. "Mike" Williams, "The Cavalry Rides Again," *Soldier of Fortune*, June 1984, 55.

20. Peter G. Kokalis, "Atlacatal Assault: *SOF* in Combat with El Salvador's Elite Immediate Reaction Battalion," *Soldier of Fortune*, June 1984, 55.

21. Sara Diamond, *Spiritual Warfare: The Politics of the Christian Right* (Boston: South End Press, 1989).

22. William S. Pierce (under the pseudonym Andrew Macdonald), *The Turner Diaries* (Arlington, Va.: The National Alliance, 1978; second edition, 1980).

23. Gar Wilson, *The Fury Bombs*, vol. 5 of *Phoenix Force* (Toronto: Worldwide, 1983), 7.

24. Ibid., 5.

25. Cartoon drawn by Asay, Copley News Service. Reprinted in *Soldier of Fortune*, October 1983, 6.

26. Brian Garfield, *Death Wish* (New York: McKay, 1972), 68.

27. Jack Hild, *Vultures of the Horn*, vol. 10 of *SOBs: Soldiers of Barrabas* (Toronto: Worldwide, 1986), 31–32.

28. Don Pendleton, supplement to *The Executioner Series Style Guide*. No date or page number on document. Delivered to me in August 1988.

29. Ibid.

30. Paul Kupperberg, "A Life!", *Vigilante*, no. 50 (February 1988), 7, 23.

31. Roland Barthes, *Mythologies*, trans. Annette Lavers (New York: Hill and Wang, 1987), 143.

32. Bruno Bettelheim, *The Uses of Enchantment: The Meaning and Importance of Fairy Tales* (New York: Knopf, 1976), 63.

33. Quoted by Elizabeth Mehren, "Some Dare Call It Romance," *Los Angeles Times*, July 29, 1988, V:2.

34. Angela Carter, *The Sadeian Woman: An Exercise in Cultural History* (London: Virago, 1979), 146–47.

35. Ibid., 147.

5

1. Adrian Forty, *Objects of Desire: Design and Society from Wedgwood to IBM* (New York: Pantheon, 1987), 9.

2. Rick Hacker, "Meet the Father of Dirty Harry," *American Rifleman*, April 1992, 30.
3. Interview with Dale Dye, October 18, 1986, in Northridge, Calif.
4. Interview with Mark Lester, February 1987, in Los Angeles.
5. Mircea Eliade, *Myth and Reality*. trans. Williard R. Trask (New York: Harper and Row, 1963), 141.
6. Jeff Cooper, *Fighting Handguns* (Los Angeles: Trend Books, 1958), 3.
7. American Historical Foundation advertisement, *Soldier of Fortune*, September 1988, 13.
8. Glock, Inc., "Aiming for the 21st Century" advertisement, *American Rifleman*, April 1989, 2.
9. Advertisement, *Soldier of Fortune*, April 1982, inside cover.
10. John Berger, *Ways of Seeing* (New York: Penguin, 1977), 148.
11. Bill Bagwell, "Battle of Blades," *Soldier of Fortune*, September 1987, 22.
12. Klaus Theweleit, *Male Bodies: Psychoanalyzing the White Terror*, vol. 2 of *Male Fantasies*, trans. Erica Carter and Chris Turner with Stephen Conway (Minneapolis: University of Minnesota Press, 1989), 206–25.
13. Mark Moritz, "Counter-Ambush Tactics: It's When You Need . . . Speed, Power, Accuracy," *Combat Handguns*, April 1984, 44.
14. Peter G. Kokalis, "Mac Attack," *Soldier of Fortune*, January 1986, 54.
15. Peter G. Kokalis, "Skorpian," *Soldier of Fortune*, November 1986, 38.
16. Ibid., 41.
17. Advertisement, *Soldier of Fortune*, July 1982, 77.
18. Mark Moritz, "Gunsite Service Pistol," *American Handgunner*, October 1987, 76–77.
19. Phil Engeldrum, *Handgun Tests*, May 1986, 9–11.
20. Gustove Zamora, Jr., and *Gung-Ho* staff, "Special Operations Training," *Gung-Ho*, August 1985, 12–13.
21. Paris Theodore, "Birth of the Pocket 9," *Combat Handguns*, October 1986, 12–13.
22. Interview with novel editor working at a major paperback publishing house who asked to remain anonymous, October 1986, in New York City.
23. Jay Mallin, "Heating Up Honduras: U.S. Troops Train for Nicaragua Threat," *Soldier of Fortune*, November 1983, 51.

24. J. B. Woods, "Custom .45 Revolver," *Combat Handguns*, April 1983, 38–39.

25. Robert Lange, "The Single Action Stars," *Special Weapons and Tactics*, March 1988, 24–26.

26. Linda Lovelace claims that Traynor could not reach orgasm without first being aroused by hitting her or else seeing her sexually abused by others. See her autobiography, *Ordeal*, written with Mark Grady (Secaucus, N.J.: Citadel, 1980).

27. Interview with Chuck Traynor, Las Vegas, August 1987.

28. Peter G. Kokalis, "Fusil Automatique Legere," *Soldier of Fortune*, June 1982, 80.

29. Don Pendleton and staff writers, *War Born*, vol. 123 of *The Executioner* (Toronto: Worldwide, 1989), 167.

30. Jerry Ahern, *The Quest*, vol. 3 of *The Survivalist* (New York: Zebra, 1981), 53–54.

6

1. E. O. James, *Origins of Sacrifice* (Port Washington, N.Y.: Kennikat Press, 1933; reissued 1971), 184.

2. Tom Clancy, *Red Storm Rising* (New York: Berkeley, 1983), 324.

3. Brian Garfield, *Death Wish* (New York: McKay, 1972), 144.

4. Joseph Campbell, *The Hero with a Thousand Faces* (Princeton, N.J.: Princeton University Press, 1968), 88, n. 51.

5. Mickey Spillane, *I, The Jury* (New York: Dutton, 1974; Signet, 1975), 246.

6. Interview with Dale Dye in Northridge, Calif., September 1986.

7. Don Pendleton and staff writers, *War Born*, vol. 123 of *The Executioner* (Toronto: Worldwide, 1989), 166, 43.

8. Gar Wilson, *The Fury Bombs*, vol. 5 of *Phoenix Force* (Toronto: Worldwide, 1983), 140.

9. Harold Coyle, *Team Yankee: A Novel of WW III* (Novato, Calif.: Presidio, 1987), 270.

10. John Sievert, *C.A.D.S. #1: Computerized Attack Defense System* (New York: Zebra, 1985), 7.

11. Arnold Schwarzenegger apparently learned this trick from Rambo, since years later, in *Predator* (1987), he too covers himself with mud to avoid the special ultraviolet eyes of the space monster.

12. Sievert, *C.A.D.S.*, 175.

13. Pendleton et al., *War Born*, 82.

14. Don Pendleton and staff writers, *The New War*, vol. 39 of *The Executioner* (Toronto: Worldwide, 1981), 30.

15. David Alexander, *Dark Messiah*, vol. 1 of *Phoenix* (New York: Leisure Books, 1987), 86.

16. Jerry Ahern, *The Battle Begins*, vol. 1 of *The Defenders* (New York: Dell, 1988), 165.

17. Ibid., 243.

18. Mike McCray, *Cold Vengeance*, vol. 2 of *The Black Berets* (New York: Dell, 1985), 108–9.

19. Tom Clancy, *Red Storm Rising* (New York: Berkeley, 1986), 320.

20. Interview, New York City, October 1986.

21. Interview with Walter Zachereis, New York City, April 23, 1986.

22. Interview, New York City, October 1986.

23. Don Pendleton, *The Executioner Series Style Guide*, no date or page number. Pendleton gave the guide to me in August 1988.

24. Interview, New York City, October 1986.

25. Ibid.

26. Klaus Theweleit, *Male Bodies: Psychoanalyzing the White Terror*, vol. 2 of *Male Fantasies*, trans. Erica Carter and Chris Turner (Minneapolis: University of Minnesota Press, 1989), 191.

27. Ibid., 276.

28. General Sir John Hackett, *The Third World War: The Untold Story* (New York: Macmillan, 1982), 311–12.

29. John Sievert, *C.A.D.S.*, 244–48.

30. Mircea Eliade, *The Sacred and the Profane: The Nature of Religion*, trans. Willard R. Trask. (New York: Harcourt Brace Jovanovich, 1959), 76.

31. Henri Hubert and Marcel Mauss, *Sacrifice: Its Nature and Function*, trans. W. D. Halls (Chicago: University of Chicago Press, 1964), 38.

32. Jack Hild, *Vulture of the Horn*, vol. 10 of *SOBs: Soldiers of Barrabas* (Toronto: Worldwide, 1986), 209.

33. Clinton Sanders, *Customizing the Body: The Art and Culture of Tattooing* (Philadelphia: Temple University Press, 1989), 30.

34. Bruno Bettelheim, *Symbolic Wounds* (Glencoe, Ill.: The Free Press, 1954), 88.

35. Don Pendleton and staff writers, *War Born*, vol. 123 of *The Executioner* (Toronto: Worldwide, 1989), 23.

36. Barry Sadler, *Casca: The Eternal Mercenary* (New York: Charter, 1979), 7.

37. Joe Guinto, "Childhood's End," unpublished paper, Southern Methodist University, 1988, 5.

7

1. Quoted from *Architectural Design*, September–October 1982, 10.
2. Advertisement for Conquest playing field, *Action Pursuit Games*, June 1988, 74.
3. All quotations from personal interviews at Conquest playing field, Malibu, Calif., August 12, 1988.
4. Brian Sutton-Smith, *Toys as Culture* (New York: Gardner, 1986), 64.
5. Lionel Atwill, *The New, Official Survival Game Manual* (New London, N.H.: The National Survival Game, Inc., 1987), 155.
6. Interview with Mike Jasperson, publisher and editor of *Front Line* magazine, Huntington Beach, Calif., May 16, 1987.
7. Interview with Denis Bulowski, Sat Cong Village paintball field, Corona, Calif., July 22, 1987.
8. Advertisement for War Zone playing field, *Front Line* magazine, February 1987, 31.
9. Interview with Mike Jasperson, publisher and editor of *Front Line* magazine, Huntington Beach, Calif., May 21, 1987.
10. Frank Hughes, "Picking Your Paintball Persona," *Action Pursuit Games*, April 1988, 27.
11. Gary Alan Fine, *Shared Fantasy* (Chicago: University of Chicago Press, 1983), 3, 182.
12. Hughes, "Picking Your Paintball Persona," 27, 72.
13. J. C. Crocker, "Ceremonial Masks," in *Celebration: Studies in Festivity and Ritual*, ed. Victor Turner (Washington, D.C.: Smithsonian Institution, 1982), 80.
14. The concept that individuals "conjure up the spirit" and so change their subjectivity comes from Jack Katz, *Seductions of Crime: Moral and Sensual Attractions of Doing Evil* (New York: Basic Books, 1988), 7.
15. Interviews with two managers working at Adventure Game Supply, Bellflower, Calif., August 10, 1988.
16. Interview with Mike Jasperson, publisher and editor of *Front Line* magazine, Huntington Beach, Calif., May 21, 1987.
17. Sutton-Smith, *Toys as Culture*, 252.
18. Atwill, *Survival Game Manual*, 11.
19. Ibid., 31.

20. Interview with Lou Grubbs, War Zone playing field, Fountain Valley, Calif., August 1, 1987. Grubbs's account of how he invented constant air appears to be universally accepted. I've never heard a story that contradicted or even slightly differed from his history.

21. Advertisement by Par-Ordnance Manufacturing, Inc., "Your Search for Better Close-Combat Equipment Stops and Ends Here!!!," *Front Line* magazine, December 1986, 36.

22. Advertisement by Tippman Pneumatics, Inc., "Never Be Outgunned Again!," *Action Pursuit Games*, January 1988, inside back cover.

23. Advertisement by Brass Eagle Paint Ball Air Guns, "Barracuda Semi-Automatic DMR Series," *Action Pursuit Games*, November 1990, 32.

24. Advertisement by Adventure Game Supplies, Inc., "Test," *Paintball Sports International*, November 1990, inside back cover.

25. "Products for Players," *Action Pursuit Games*, April 1988, 14.

26. Advertisement by Pursuit Marketing, Inc., "The New PMI-3 Semi-Automatic," *Action Pursuit Games*, November 1990, inside front cover.

27. Advertisement by Corliss Delay Inc., *Paintball International Sports*, November 1990, 85.

28. Atwill, *Survival Game Manual*, 27.

29. Jason Rein, "Paintball Meets the Marines," *Action Pursuit Games*, November 1990, 63–64.

30. Ibid., 62.

31. *"Front Line* Mail Call," *Front Line* magazine, February 1987, 2.

32. Interview with Russell Maynard, publisher and editor of *Action Pursuit Games*, Burbank, Calif., August 17, 1988.

33. Atwill, *Survival Game Manual*, 155.

34. Interview with Denis Bulowski, Sat Cong Village, Corona, Calif., July 22, 1987.

35. Interview with one of the employees at Adventure Game Supply, Bellflower, Calif., August 10, 1988.

36. Interview with Russell Maynard, publisher and editor of *Action Pursuit Games*, Burbank, Calif., August 17, 1988.

37. Interview with Ken S., Sat Cong Village, Corona, Calif., July 22, 1987.

38. Interview with the owner of The Annihilator, a wholesale paintball company, Diamondbar, Calif., August 16, 1988.

39. Interviews with Denis Bulowski and one of his employees, Sat Cong Village, Corona, Calif., July 22, 1987.

40. Interview with an employee, Adventure Game Supply, Bellflower, Calif., August 10, 1988.
41. Interview with a paramedic and part-time referee, War Zone, Fountain Valley, Calif., August 1, 1987.
42. Christopher Buckley, "Viet Guilt: Were the Real Prisoners of War the Young Americans Who Never Left Home?" *Esquire*, September 1983, 72.
43. Ibid., 58.
44. Atwill, *Survival Game Manual*, 15.
45. Ibid., 153.
46. Ibid., 152.
47. Ibid., 23 and 153.
48. Interview with one of the Vigilantes, Malibu, Calif., August 12, 1988.
49. Interview with Lou Grubbs, War Zone, Fountain Valley, Calif., August 1, 1987.
50. Interview with the manager of Paint Pistol Express, Anaheim, Calif., August 15, 1988.
51. Ibid.
52. Rick Soll, "War Game: Adults Play Cowboys, Indians," *Los Angeles Times*, November 18, 1983, A1, 8.
53. Interview with Lou Grubbs, War Zone, Fountain Valley, Calif., August 1, 1987.
54. Referee, War Zone, Fountain Valley, Calif., August 1, 1987.
55. Interview with referee, Sat Cong Village, Corona, Calif., July 22, 1987.
56. Interview with Lou Grubbs, War Zone, Fountain Valley, Calif., August 1, 1987.
57. Jason Rein, "Tell It to the Marines," *Paintball Sports*, November 1990, 66.
58. Atwill, *Survival Game Manual*, 17.

8

1. Ward Churchill, "*Soldier of Fortune*'s Robert K. Brown," *Covert Action Information Bulletin* 22 (Fall 1984), 12–21.
2. General William C. Westmoreland (USA, Retired), *A Soldier Reports* (Garden City, N.Y.: Doubleday, 1976), 107.
3. Jim Graves, "SOG's Secret War," *Soldier of Fortune*, June 1981, 42.
4. Charles M. Simpson III, *Inside the Green Berets: The First Thirty Years* (Novato, Calif.: Presidio, 1983).

5. Page 8 of *Soldier of Fortune* press release, "Robert K. Brown: Editor/ Publisher Biography," 1986 *SOF* convention, Las Vegas, Nev.

6. Ibid., 9.

7. Starch, Inra, Hooper, "1981 Subscriber Survey of *Soldier of Fortune* magazine," September 1981, 3.

8. Philip Agee, *Inside the Company: CIA Diary* (New York: Stonehill, 1975); Victor Marchetti and John D. Marks, *The CIA and the Cult of Intelligence* (New York: Knopf, 1974); John Stockwell, *In Search of Enemies* (New York: Norton, 1978).

9. Stephen Emerson, *Secret Warriors: Inside the Covert Military Operations of the Reagan Era* (New York: Putnam, 1988), 34.

10. Jay Mallin and Robert K. Brown, *Merc: American Soldiers of Fortune* (New York: Macmillan, 1979), 144–45. See also Stockwell, *In Search of Enemies*.

11. Ibid., 353.

12. See Gerry S. Thomas, *Mercenary Troops in Modern Africa* (Boulder, Col.: Westview Press, 1984).

13. "The *Soldier of Fortune* Story: A March to Success," press release distributed at the 1986 convention. The magazine's readership studies were done by an outside auditing firm, Starch, Inra, Hooper.

14. Captain Ted E. Lawrence, "The Battle for Beaufort," *SOF* convention, September 19, 1985.

15. Captain Alan Wingate, "Man against Tank," *SOF* convention, September 19, 1985.

16. Peter G. Kokalis, "Submachine Guns: Their History and Use," *SOF* convention, September 20, 1985.

17. Major General Ron Reid-Daly, "Counterinsurgency Warfare," *SOF* convention, September 19, 1985. Many in the audience had undoubtedly read about the Mozambique adventure in an earlier issue of *SOF* or at least seen the advertisements for Reid-Daly's book *Selous Scouts: Top Secret War* (Boulder, Col.: Phoenix Associates, 1983). Phoenix Associates was the name of Brown's very first publishing effort, the predecessor of both Paladin Press and *SOF*. The inside-cover advertisement for the book in the February 1983 issue of *SOF* stressed the body count.

18. Interview, *SOF* convention, August 28, 1987.

19. Interview, *SOF* convention, August 28, 1987.

20. Interview, *SOF* convention, August 27, 1987.

21. Interview, *SOF* convention, August 26, 1987.

22. Interview, *SOF* convention, August 27, 1987.

23. Interview, *SOF* convention, August 28, 1987.
24. Interview with Larry Lawrence, *SOF* convention, August 28, 1987.
25. Sir James George Frazer, *The Golden Bough: A Study in Magic and Religion* (New York: Collier, 1922), 43–52.
26. A former Bureau of Alcohol, Tobacco and Firearms agent and a renowned pistol smith from Los Angeles told me about federal-agent participation at the *SOF* 3-gun match. It's a form of training. *SOF* convention, August 27, 1987.
27. Interview with Robert W. Irwin, part owner of The Survival Store, Las Vegas, Nev., August 26, 1987.
28. Interview, *SOF* convention, August 27, 1987.
29. Rappelling instructor, *SOF* convention, August 28, 1987.
30. Lieutenant Tim Oliver, "The Icon Challenge" (advertising flier), *SOF* convention, September 20, 1986.
31. Big Mike Harvey, director, North American Defense Association, "Application Form," distributed at 1985 *SOF* convention.
32. Interview with Lawrence Kubic, Los Angeles, May 17, 1987.
33. One of the first MACVSOG patches is shown on the front cover of *Soldier of Fortune*, June 1981.
34. George Hayuduke, *Getting Even: The Complete Book of Dirty Tricks* (Secaucus, N.J.: Lyle Stuart, 1980).
35. L. Ranchero, *How to Fight Motorcycles* (Weatherford, Tex.: Dagger Press, 1981).
36. Victor Santoro, *Vigilante Handbook* (Cornville, Ariz.: Desert Publications, 1981).
37. Interview, *SOF* convention, August 26, 1987.
38. Interview, *SOF* convention, August 27, 1987.
39. Interview, *SOF* convention, August 26, 1987.
40. Interview, *SOF* convention, August 26, 1987.
41. Interview, *SOF* convention, August 26, 1987.
42. Interview, *SOF* convention, September 20, 1986.
43. Interview, *SOF* convention, September 20, 1986.
44. Interview, *SOF* convention, September 19, 1986.
45. Interview, *SOF* convention, August 26, 1987.
46. Interview, *SOF* convention, August 29, 1987.
47. Interview, *SOF* convention, August 27, 1987.
48. Interview, *SOF* convention, September 21, 1986.
49. Interview, *SOF* convention, August 29, 1987.
50. Interview, *SOF* convention, August 27, 1987.
51. Interview, *SOF* convention, September 19, 1986.

52. Interview, *SOF* convention, August 26, 1987.
53. Interview, *SOF* convention, August 27, 1987.
54. Interview, *SOF* convention, August 27, 1987.
55. Interview, *SOF* convention, September 20, 1986.
56. Interview, *SOF* convention, August 26, 1987.
57. Interview, *SOF* convention, August 28, 1987.
58. Mario J. Calero, *SOF* convention, September 21, 1985.
59. Dr. Lewis L. Tambs, *SOF* convention, August 29, 1987.

9

1. Jeff Cooper, *Quoth the Raven: Seventeen Points to Ponder* (Paulden, Ariz.: American Pistol Institute, 1981), 3.
2. Lawrence Shainberg, "Finding 'The Zone,' " *New York Times Magazine*, April 9, 1989, 35–39.
3. Chuck Yeager and Leo Janos, *Yeager: An Autobiography* (New York: Bantam, 1985), 147–48, 66–67, 150–51, 200–2.
4. Quoted in Richard G. Mitchell, Jr., *Mountain Experience: The Psychology and Sociology of Adventure* (Chicago: University of Chicago Press, 1983), 219.
5. Ibid., 170.
6. Victor Turner, *The Ritual Process: Structure and Anti-Structure* (Ithaca, N.Y.: Cornell University Press, 1969).
7. Jeff Cooper, "Principles of Personal Defense," ed. Robert K. Brown and Peter C. Lund (Boulder, Col.: Paladin, 1972), 5.
8. Mircea Eliade, *Myth and Reality*, trans. William R. Trask (New York: Harper and Row, 1963), 81.

10

1. James Ridgeway, *Blood in the Face* (New York: Thunder Mouth Press, 1990), 24.
2. John Wayne Hearn deposition transcript at 5, Eimann *v.* Soldier of Fortune Magazine, Inc. 680 F.Supp.863 (S.D.Tex.1988).
3. Trial transcript at vol. III, 194, Eimann *v.* SOF.
4. Unpublished study by Professor Park Elliot Dietz as an expert witness for the plaintiffs in Eimann *v.* SOF.
5. Judge David Hittner of the U.S. District Court for the Southern District of Texas instructed the jury that gross negligence means "such an

entire want of care as to show that the act or omission in question was a result of the conscious indifference to the rights, welfare, or safety of the persons affected by it." Trial transcript at vol. IX, 54, Eimann *v.* SOF.

6. Ben Green, *The Soldier of Fortune Murders: A True Story of Obsessive Love and Murder-for-Hire* (New York: Dell, 1992), 140.

7. Ibid., 14. Author Ben Green notes that some of the detectives who investigated Hearn doubted his claims to have been part of North's network of gunrunners.

8. John Wayne Hearn deposition transcript at 62–63, Eimann *v.* SOF.

9. Ibid., 14.

10. Green, *The Soldier of Fortune Murders*, 171.

11. John Wayne Hearn deposition transcript, 8–9.

12. Ibid., 27–28.

13. "Wanted: Soviet Mi-24 'Hind D' Attack Helicopter—Intact and Functional," *Soldier of Fortune*, March 1985, 101.

14. Robert K. Brown, press conference on August 28, 1987, at the *Soldier of Fortune* convention in Las Vegas, Nev. Brown claimed that the $1,000,000 reward offer "kept the Nicaragua Air Force grounded for about six months."

15. John Wayne Hearn deposition transcript, 34, Eimann *v.* SOF.

16. Trial transcript at vol. II, 40, Eimann *v.* SOF.

17. Trial transcript at vol. V, 210, Eimann *v.* SOF.

18. Trial transcript at vol. VI, 69, Eimann *v.* SOF.

19. Trial transcript at vol. VI, 176, Eimann *v.* SOF.

20. Trial transcript at vol. IX, 119, Eimann *v.* SOF.

21. James Barron, "Commando-Style Raid Is Prevented in Indiana," *New York Times*, March 10, 1986, A15.

22. Ken Geiger, "Trail of Terror," *Dallas Life Magazine*, Sunday supplement to the *Dallas Morning News*, June 21, 1987, 14.

23. J. Michael Kennedy, "Soldier of Fortune Ads Helped Spark Network of Hired Killers," *Los Angeles Times*, September 6, 1987, A6.

24. Trial transcript at vol. II, 100, Eimann *v.* SOF.

25. John Wayne Hearn deposition transcript at 90, Eimann *v.* SOF.

26. Green, *The Soldier of Fortune Murders*, 342.

27. Ibid., 399.

28. Elliot Leyton, *Compulsive Killers* (New York: New York University Press, 1986). Republished in paperback as *Hunting Humans: Inside the Minds of Mass Murderers* (New York: Pocket Books, 1988), 36.

29. Frank Camper, *Merc: The Professional* (New York: Dell, 1989), 220–27, 282–86.
30. Robert K. Brown, "Command Guidance," *Soldier of Fortune*, October 1985, 2.
31. Ibid.
32. Camper, *Merc*, 27–28.
33. Ibid., 50, 53, 51.
34. Sam Hall with Larry Hussman and Felicia Lewis, *Counter-Terrorist* (New York: Donald I. Fine, 1987), 31, 35.
35. Ibid., 73.
36. Ibid, 110.
37. John D. McClure, *Soldier without Fortune* (New York: Dell, 1987), 46.
38. Ibid, 22.
39. Camper, *Merc*, 27.
40. Hall, *Counter-Terrorist*, 143.
41. McClure, *Soldier without Fortune*, 150.
42. Camper, *Merc*, 114.
43. Timothy K. Smith, "In Alabama's Woods, Frank Camper Trains Men to Repel Invaders," *Wall Street Journal*, August 19, 1985, 1, 9.
44. Camper, *Merc*, 116.
45. McClure, *Soldier without Fortune*, 120, 151, 147.
46. Smith, "In Alabama's Woods," 9.
47. Camper, *Merc*, 292.
48. Hall, *Counter-Terrorist*, 252–63.
49. Don Pendleton, *The New War*, vol. 39 of *Mack Bolan: The Executioner* (Toronto: Worldwide, 1981).
50. McClure, *Soldier without Fortune*, 26–27, 32, 42.
51. Ibid., 44, 189.
52. Camper, *Merc*, 299.
53. Hall, *Counter-Terrorist*, 267–79.
54. Major Robert K. Brown (U.S. Army Reserves), "American Mercenaries in Africa," *Soldier of Fortune*, Summer 1975, 23.
55. Trial transcript at vol. VII, 236 and 214, Eimann *v.* SOF.
56. Ibid., 214–15.
57. *Black–White Perceptions: Race Relations in Greensboro.* A report of the North Carolina Advisory Committee to the United States Commission on Civil Rights prepared for the information and consideration of the Commission. (Washington, D.C.: U.S. Commission on Civil Rights, November 1980), 10.

58. Kevin Flynn and Gary Gerhardt, *The Silent Brotherhood: Inside America's Racist Underground* (New York: The Free Press, 1989), 165.

59. Bill Minutaglio, "Biography of a Hatemonger," *Dallas Life Magazine*, Sunday supplement to the *Dallas Morning News*, May 22, 1988, 14.

60. Geiger, "Trail of Terror," 14.

61. Flynn and Gerhardt, *The Silent Brotherhood*, 30.

62. Quoted in Anti-Defamation League of B'nai B'rith, *Hate Groups in America: A Record of Bigotry and Violence* (New York: Anti-Defamation League of B'nai B'rith, 1982), 51.

63. Minutaglio, "Biography of a Hatemonger," 11.

64. James Corcoran, *Bitter Harvest: Gordon Kahl and the Posse Comitatus: Murder in the Heartland* (New York: Viking, 1990), 137.

65. Ibid., 152–53.

66. Andrew Macdonald (pseudonym for William S. Pierce), *The Turner Diaries* (Arlington, Va.: The National Alliance, National Vanguard Books, second edition, 1980), 101.

67. Ibid., 61.

68. Ibid., 73–74.

69. Ibid., 99.

70. Ibid., 204.

71. William S. Pierce, National Vanguard Books, Catalogue No. 10, March 1986, 21.

72. James Coates, *Armed and Dangerous: The Rise of the Survivalist Right* (New York: Hill and Wang, 1987), 50.

73. Flynn and Gerhardt, *The Silent Brotherhood*, 95.

74. Ibid., 97–98.

75. Ibid., 90–91.

76. Coates, *Armed and Dangerous*, 57.

77. Flynn and Gerhardt, 294.

78. Ibid, 64–65.

79. Ibid., 67.

80. Ibid., 124–33.

81. Ibid., 183–91.

82. Thomas Martinez with John Gunther, *Brotherhood of Murder* (New York: McGraw-Hill, 1988), 55.

83. Flynn and Gerhardt, *The Silent Brotherhood*, 265–66.

84. Ibid., 266.

85. Ibid., 361.

86. Ibid., 376.
87. Jeff Collins, "Jury Clears Extremists of Sedition," *Dallas Times Herald*, April 8, 1988, A13.

11

1. Jack and Jo Ann Hinckley, with Elizabeth Sherrill, *Breaking Points* (Grand Rapids, Mich.: Chosen Books, 1985), 303.
2. Ibid., 251.
3. Bob Woodward, *Veil: The Secret Wars of the CIA, 1981–1987* (New York: Pocket Books, 1987), 196–201.
4. Hinckley, *Breaking Points*, 237.
5. Ibid., 341.
6. Christopher Reed, "The Day Huberty Went 'Hunting Humans,' " *The Melbourne Age*, September 22, 1984, A9.
7. David Freed, "21 Die in San Diego Massacre," *Los Angeles Times*, July 19, 1981, 1A.
8. Sarah Boseley, "Fantasy Life of a Hungerford Killer," *The Guardian* (Manchester, England), September 25, 1987, A1.
9. Lisa W. Foderaro, "Parents and a Brother Slain by a Self-Styled 'Rambo,' " *New York Times*, March 23, 1989, A16.
10. Eric Harrison, "Gunman Kills 7 and Himself at Kentucky Plant," *Los Angeles Times*, September 15, 1989, A1, 22.
11. Mary Williams Walsh, "Canadian Killer Sulked When Things Went Wrong," *Los Angeles Times*, December 8, 1989, 24A.
12. Mary Williams Walsh, "Montreal Looks within Itself in Wake of Mass Killings," *Los Angeles Times*, December 9, 1989, A6.
13. Jack Levin and James Alan Fox, *Mass Murder: America's Growing Menace* (New York: Plenum Press, 1985).
14. *Louisvillle Courier-Journal*, September 16, 1989.
15. Associated Press, "Woman Dressed in Army Fatigues Opens Fire at Shopping Center; Two Killed, Eight Wounded," *Los Angeles Times*, October 31, 1985.
16. Hinckley, *Breaking Points*, 203.
17. Pete Shields, *Guns Don't Die—People Do* (New York: Arbor House, 1981), 163–64.
18. John Crust, "Police Academy Gun Store May Halt Assault Rifle Sales," *Los Angeles Herald Examiner*, January 26, 1989, A7.
19. Interview with the manager of B and B Guns, Westminister, Calif., March 1989. See also John Kendall, "Rapid-Fire Buying of Assault

Guns Marks Deadline of New Law," *Los Angeles Times*, June 1, 1989, B1.

20. Dolores Wood, "Gangs Get Offer for Their Uzis," *Santa Monica Evening Outlook*, January 25, 1989, D1.

21. Hector Tobar and Nieson Himmel, "Inspired by Holden's Buy-Back Offer, AK-47 Assault Weapons Come Rolling In," *Los Angeles Times*, January 27, 1989, A19.

22. "Assault Rifle Fact Sheet #2: Quantities of Semi-Automatic 'Assault Rifles' Owned in the United States," The Institute for Research on Small Arms in International Security (Washington, D.C., 1989).

23. John Crust, "Citizens Surrender AK-47s, Uzi to Cops," *Los Angeles Herald Examiner*, January 26, 1989, A1, 7.

24. Carl Ingram, "Broad Gun Restrictions Proposed," *Los Angeles Times*, January 27, 1989, 18.

25. Carl Ingram, "State Senate Votes to Ban Assault Guns," *Los Angeles Times*, March 10, 1989, A1, 38.

26. Josh Getlin, "Senators Hear Gates Assail Assault Rifles," *Los Angeles Times*, February 11, 1989, A1, 27.

27. Daniel M. Weintraub, "Gun Hearings Bring Threats: Senate Tightens Security," *Los Angeles Times*, March 9, 1989, A1, 31.

28. Carl Ingram and Jerry Gillam, "Assembly Passes Assault Gun Ban," *Los Angeles Times*, March 14, 1991, A1, 23. Jackie Speier was wounded in 1978 when she was an aide to Congressman Leo Ryan investigating Jim Jones and the Peoples Temple cult in Jonestown in Guyana.

29. "Assault Rifle Fact Sheet #2."

30. Carl Ingram and Jerry Gillam, "Assault Gun Ban Gains in Legislature," *Los Angeles Times*, March 1, 1989, A1, 22.

31. This story first surfaced in the "NRA—California News," newsletter of the NRA's Institute for Legislative Action: "Roberti/Roos Act Misses Purdy Gun," vol. 1, no. 4, August 1, 1989, 7. The story did not appear in the mainstream press until two years later when the California bill banning certain assault rifles was reported to be in the process of being rewritten. See Carl Ingram, "Lungren, Roberti OK Rewriting of '89 Gun Law," *Los Angeles Times*, August 29, 1991, A1, 29.

32. Douglas Jehl and Cathleen Decker, "U.S. Bars Import of Assault Guns," *Los Angeles Times*, March 15, 1989, A1, 12.

33. "Report and Recommendation of the ATF Working Group on the Importability of Certain Semiautomatic Rifles," Bureau of Alcohol, Tobacco and Firearms, Department of the Treasury, July 6, 1989, 8.

34. "Report and Recommendation of the ATF Working Group on the Importability of Certain Semiautomatic Rifles," Attachment 11.
35. Douglas Jehl, "Assault Gun Ban Made Permanent," *Los Angeles Times*, July 8, 1989, A1, 26.
36. Ibid., A25.
37. Wayne King, "Target: The Gun Lobby," *New York Times Magazine*, December 9, 1990, 45, 76.
38. Sarah Brady and Handgun Control Inc., letter to new members, February 1989.
39. Sarah Brady and Handgun Control, Inc., letter to members, November 28, 1989.
40. Sarah Brady and Handgun Control, Inc., letter to members, May 15, 1990.
41. Advertisement by Handgun Control, Inc., "Why Is the NRA Allowing *Him* Easy Access to Assault Weapons?," *New York Times*, July 24, 1990, A7.
42. HCI blamed the NRA for this delay. See also Nathaniel C. Nash, "Law-Enforcement Groups Accuse Foley of Thwarting Gun Control," *New York Times*, September 26, 1990.
43. Sarah Brady and Handgun Control, Inc., letter to members, March 29, 1991.
44. The work most often cited in NRA publications on the history and legal meaning of the Second Amendment is Dr. Stephen P. Halbrook's *That Every Man Be Armed: The Evolution of a Constitutional Right* (Albuquerque, N.M.: University of New Mexico Press, 1984).
45. David Gregg, letter to the editor, "Readers Write" column, *American Rifleman*, June 1991, 15. For a similar perspective by a NRA leader, see executive vice-president J. Warren Cassidy's essay, "The Case for Firearms" in *Time* magazine's special feature, "Who Is the NRA?" January 29, 1990, 22.
46. Joe Foss, president of the National Rifle Association, speech to the 1990 awards banquet, NRA annual convention, Anaheim, Calif., June 9, 1990.
47. Congressman Mike Espy, acceptance speech, NRA convention awards banquet, June 9, 1990.
48. Richard Lacayo, "Under Fire," *Time*, January 29, 1990, 16.
49. Gary Kleck, "Crime Control through the Use of Armed Force," *Social Problems*, vol. 35, no. 1 (1988).

50. Patrick Mott, "In Defense of the AK-47," *Los Angeles Times*, February 24, 1989, V:1; Lisa Belkin, "Bored with the Usual Fireworks? Try This," *New York Times*, May 28, 1990, A1.

51. Seth Mydans, "California Gun Control Law Runs into Rebellion," *New York Times*, December 24, 1990, A24.

52. Joe Foss, speech to membership, NRA annual convention, June 9, 1990.

53. Congressman Mike Espy, acceptance speech, NRA annual convention, June 9, 1990.

54. Bruce Herschensohn, speech to conventioneers, NRA annual convention, June 9, 1990.

55. Charlton Heston, narrator, Golden Bear Campaign Video, produced for the NRA, exhibited at their annual convention, Anaheim, Calif., June 8–10, 1990.

56. National Rifle Association Institute for Legislative Action, "Semi-Auto Firearms: The Citizen's Choice" (Washington, D.C., 1989), 4–5.

57. Finn Aagaard, "The Semi-Auto Afield," *American Rifleman*, September 1989, 82.

58. "Intratec TEC-22," Dope BAG feature, *American Rifleman*, September 1989, 67–68.

59. C. E. Harris, "The 7.62mm as a Sporting Round," *American Rifleman*, April 1990, 28.

60. Cover and inside cover, *American Rifleman*, April 1989.

61. J. Warren Cassidy, "And Then There Were None?," *American Rifleman*, April 1989, 9.

62. Dick Riley, "When Rights Are Wronged," *American Rifleman*, September 1990, 62.

63. Fund-raising letter, National Rifle Association Institute for Legislative Action, Winter 1981.

64. "Waiting Periods *Threaten* Public Safety," NRA Official Journal feature, *American Rifleman*, July 1991, 59.

65. Peter Alan Kasler, "A Victim of Gun Control," *New York Times*, July 13, 1991, A21.

66. "Senate Semi-Auto Showdown Looms," Official Journal feature, *American Rifleman*, June 1989, 48.

67. Harold Garfinkel, "Degradation Ceremonies," *American Journal of Sociology* 61 (March 1958), 420–24.

68. "FBI Facts Flay Anti-Gun Myths," NRA Journal feature, *American Rifleman*, September 1990, 64.

69. Iver Peterson, "New Jersey's Ban on Assault Guns Has Little Effect on Violence," *New York Times*, June 20, 1993, A11.

70. Federal Bureau of Investigation, U.S. Department of Justice, *Uniform Crime Statistics, 1983–1989.*

71. Reed, "The Day Huberty Went 'Hunting Humans,' " A14.

72. Don Terry, "Portrait of Texas Killer: Impatient and Troubled," *New York Times*, October 18, 1991, A13.

12

1. Lou Cannon, *President Reagan: The Role of a Lifetime* (New York: Simon and Schuster, 1991), 57.

2. *Fresno Bee*, Oct. 1965. Cited by Mark Green and Gail MacColl, *There He Goes Again: Ronald Reagan's Reign of Error* (New York: Pantheon Books, 1983), 33.

3. Lou Cannon, *Reagan* (New York: Putnam, 1982), 217.

4. H. Bruce Franklin, *War Stars* (New York: Oxford University Press, 1989).

5. Cannon, *President Reagan*, 61–63.

6. Ibid., 39.

7. Ronald Reagan, *Speaking My Mind: Selected Speeches* (New York: Simon and Schuster, 1989), 14.

8. Ibid., 127.

9. Cannon, *President Reagan*, 56.

10. Claire Sterling, *The Terror Network* (New York: Holt/Reader's Digest, 1981; New York: Berkeley, 1982), 15.

11. Ibid.

12. Claire Sterling, "Terrorism: Tracing the International Network," *New York Times Magazine*. March 1, 1981, 16.

13. Bob Woodward, *Veil: The Secret Wars of the CIA, 1981–1987* (New York: Pocket Books, 1987), 126.

14. Ibid., 127.

15. Sterling, *The Terror Network*, 28–29.

16. Ibid., 82.

17. Ibid., 94.

18. Ibid., 140.

19. Ibid., 187.

20. Woodward, *Veil*, 127–31.

21. Sterling, "Terrorism: Tracing the International Network," 24.

22. Woodward, *Veil*, 124.

23. Reagan, *Speaking My Mind*, 175.

24. Stephen Emerson, *Secret Warriors: Inside the Covert Military Operations of the Reagan Era* (New York: Putnam, 1988), 134.

25. Ibid., 191.

26. See Peter G. Bourne, "Was the U.S. Invasion Necessary?" *Los Angeles Times*, November 10, 1983, IV:1, 3, and John T. McQuiston, "School's Chancellor Says Invasion Was Not Necessary to Save Lives," *New York Times*, October 26, 1983, Y8. The chancellor, Charles R. Modica, reported that he subsequently changed his mind after talking to State Dept. officials. See Doyle McManus, "Chancellor Changes Mind: U.S. Students Were in Peril," *Los Angeles Times*, October 27, 1983.

27. Public Broadcasting Service's television documentary series, *Frontline*, June 5, 1990.

28. Jack Nelson, "Reagan's Popularity Boosted by Grenada," *Los Angeles Times*, November 10, 1983, I:1, 8.

29. Ronald Reagan, "Text of President's Speech on Lebanon, Caribbean Crises," *Los Angeles Times*, October 28, 1983, I:16.

30. Neil C. Livingstone, *The Cult of Counterterrorism: The "Weird World" of Spooks, Counterterrorists, Adventurers, and the Not-Quite Professionals* (Lexington, Mass.: Lexington Books, 1990), 234.

31. Woodward, *Veil*, 314.

32. Cannon, *President Reagan*, 365–66.

33. Theodore Draper, *A Very Thin Line: The Iran-Contra Affairs* (New York: Hill and Wang, 1991), 24.

34. Doyle McManus, "Secret Reagan Iran-Contra File Located," *Los Angeles Times*, June 24, 1989, I:2.

35. Major General John K. Singlaub, U.S. Army (Ret.), with Malcolm McConnell, *Hazardous Duty: An American Soldier in the Twentieth Century* (New York: Summit, 1991), 463–66.

36. Joe Conason and Murray Waas, "The Old Right's New Crusade," *Village Voice*, October 22, 1985, 19.

37. President Reagan first gave this order to his National Security Advisor, Robert McFarlane, in 1984. McFarlane in turn passed it along to his deputy, Oliver North. See Cannon, *President Reagan*, 385.

38. Singlaub, *Hazardous Duty*, 477.

39. Oliver L. North with William Novak, *Under Fire: An American Story* (New York: HarperCollins, 1991), 19–20.

40. Larry Rohter, "Drug Ring Gave up to $10 million to Contras, Noriega Jury Is Told," *New York Times* November 26, 1991, A8.

41. Joel Bleifuss, "The First Stone," *In These Times*, May 8–14, 1991, 4.

42. Singlaub, *Hazardous Duty*, 476.

43. Emerson, *Secret Warriors*, 217.

44. Woodward, *Veil*, 496.

45. Emerson, *Secret Warriors*, 135.

46. Livingstone, *The Cult of Counterterrorism*, 58.

47. Gary Sick, *October Surprise: America's Hostages in Iran and the Election of Ronald Reagan* (New York: Times Books, 1991), 214.

48. Ibid.

49. North, *Under Fire*, 272.

50. Ibid., 9.

51. Livingstone, *The Cult of Counterterrorism*, 284–85.

52. Louis Harris, "North's Support Fading, Harris Survey Indicates," *Dallas Morning News*, August 31, 1987, A1, 9.

53. North, *Under Fire*, 139.

54. Livingstone, *The Cult of Counterterrorism*, 243.

55. Lt. Col. Oliver North, *Taking the Stand: The Testimony of Lieutenant Colonel Oliver L. North* (New York: Pocket Books, 1987), 187.

56. North, *Under Fire*, 385.

57. Patrick J. Buchanan, "Whom Will History Indict?," *Newsweek*, July 13, 1987, 21.

58. North, *Under Fire*, 230.

59. Reagan, *Speaking My Mind*, 147.

60. Jeffrey Junkins, "Harold W. Ezell: Immigration's Man with a Mission," *Soldier of Fortune*, September 1987, 30–31.

61. Livingstone, *The Cult of Counterterrorism*, xvii and 395.

62. Keenen Peck, "The Take-Charge Gang," *The Progressive*, May 1985, 18–24.

63. "U-2s Said Used to Find Pot," *Fort Worth Star Telegram*, June 10, 1983, A2.

64. John Gonzales, "National Guard Enlisted in War on Smuggling," *Dallas Morning News*, September 17, 1987: A1, 18, H2.

65. James Ridgeway, "From Garden Plot to STARCS," *L.A. Weekly*, March 8–15, 1985, 31–32.

66. James L. Pate, "Citizen Soldiers: Fighting for the Right to Defend America," *Soldier of Fortune*, May 1987, 59.

67. *Newsweek*, June 2, 1986.

68. Elaine Sciolino, "U.S. May Be Ready to End Assistance to Afghan Rebels," *New York Times*, May 12, 1991, A1, 11.

69. Cannon, *President Reagan*, 356.

70. David Lauter, "New U.S. Policy on Contras Told," *Los Angeles Times*, March 25, 1989, A1, 10.

71. Robin Wright, "U.S. and Soviets Seek Joint War on Terrorism," *Los Angeles Times*, September 29, 1989, I:1, 9.

72. Michael Parks, "Soviets Ask U.S. to Join in Central America Arms Ban," *Los Angeles Times*, December 9, 1989, A14.

73. Michael T. Klare, "Fighting Drugs with the Military," *Nation*, January 1, 1990, 8–12.

74. Douglas Jehl and Melissa Healy, "In Reversal, Military Seeks Drug Role War," *Los Angeles Times*, December 15, 1989, A1, 36.

75. Joseph I. Lieberman, "Reissue a License to Kill," *Los Angeles Times*, September 18, 1989, II:5.

76. Morgan Tanner, "Crack in America: L.A. Drug Gangs Create Depraved New World," *Soldier of Fortune*, June 1989, 40.

77. Douglas Jehl and John M. Broder, "Accuracy a Casualty in Panama," *Los Angeles Times*, April 24, 1990, A1, 16, 17.

78. For discussions about Panamanian casualties see David E. Pit, "The Invasion's Civilian Toll: Still No Official Count," *New York Times*, January 10, 1990, A9. A report of Noriega's history of involvement with U.S. intelligence agencies is provided by Joel Bleifuss, "In Short," *In These Times*, January 10–16, 1990, 4.

79. Jack Nelson, "For Bush, Panama Seen as Major 'Political Bonanza," *Los Angeles Times*, January 6, 1990, A4.

80. David Broder, "New Consensus Survives a Test," *Los Angeles Times*, January 6, 1990, Metro section, 5.

81. Douglas Jehl, "Anti-Drug Role of GIs Expanded in S. America," *Los Angeles Times*, July 2, 1990, A1, 11, 12, 13.

82. Judith Miller and Laurie Myrolie, *Saddam Hussein and the Crisis in the Gulf* (New York: Times Books, 1990), 192.

83. Thomas L. Friedman and Patrick E. Tyler, "From the First, U.S. Resolve to Fight," *New York Times*, March 3, 1991, 1, 18.

84. Hugh Sidey, "The Presidency," *Time*, January 28, 1991, 33.

85. "Transcript of the Comments by Bush on the Air Strikes Against the Iraqis," *New York Times*, January 30, 1991, A14.

86. "Text of President Bush's State of the Union Message to Nation," *New York Times*, January 30, 1991, A14.

87. Paul Lewis, "U.N. Survey Calls Iraq's War Damage Near-Apocalyptic," *New York Times*, March 22, 1991, A1, 9.

88. Edmund L. Andrews, "Agency to Dismiss Analyst Who Estimated Iraqi Dead," *New York Times*, March 7, 1992, Y5.

89. Patrick E. Tyler, "Health Crisis Said to Grip Iraq in Wake of War's Destruction," *New York Times*, May 22, 1991, A16; Patrick E. Tyler, "Disease Spirals in Iraq as Embargo Takes Its Toll," *New York Times*, June 24, 1991, A1, 6.

90. Charles Krauthammer, "How the War Can Change America," *Time*, January 28, 1991, 100.

91. Quoted by Bruce Anderson, *Anderson Valley Advertiser*, February 20, 1991, 7.

92. Maureen Dowd, "A Different Bush Conforms to a Nation's Mood," *New York Times*, March 2, 1991, A7.

93. Leslie H. Gelb, "Best and Brightest," *New York Times*, May 26, 1991, E11.

94. Clifford Kraus, "U.S. Gives Vietnam $1 million; Assistance Is First since the War," *New York Times*, April 26, 1991, A7.

95. Robert D. McFadden, "Fund-Raising on Target for Whopping Victory Parade," *New York Times*, May 13, 1991, B1, 4.

96. North Coast Rocketry, "Patriot" advertisement, American Airlines *American Way* magazine, December 15, 1991, 145.

97. David Freed, "Spoils of War Surface on U.S. Shelves," *Los Angeles Times*, October 25, 1991, A1, 26.

98. "Lynn Thompson's Special Products," *Soldier of Fortune*, August 1991, back cover.

99. "The Official *SOF* Operation Desert Storm T-Shirts," *Soldier of Fortune*, August 1991, 114.

100. Freed, "Spoils of War Surface on U.S. Shelves," A1, 26.

101. Outboard Motor Corporation advertisement, "Not everyone uses our outboards to go fishing on weekends," *Trailer Boats*, June 1991, 2–3.

102. "Stop Naked Aggression with Desert Shield Condoms," advertisement in *Soldier of Fortune*, August 1991, 115.

103. "Bulletin Board" department, *Soldier of Fortune*, August 1991, 4.

104. Kevin Sessums, "Good Golly, Miss Dolly!," *Vanity Fair*, June 1991, 110.

105. America West advertisement, "Announcing Air Superiority for Civilians," *New York Times*, May 9, 1991, B5.

106. "New Video Releases," *New York Times*, May 16, 1991, C22.
107. Jack Anderson and Dale Van Atta, *Stormin' Norman: An American Hero* (New York: Zebra, 1991), 10–11.
108. Karen De Witt, "No Kneeling, but Schwarzkopf Is an Honorary Knight," *New York Times*, May 21, 1991.
109. Robert W. Hunnicutt, "Four Star Shooting Clays," *American Rifleman*, January 1992, 82.

CONCLUSION

1. Gary Sick, *October Surprise: America's Hostages in Iran and the Election of Ronald Reagan* (New York: Times Books, 1991). See also the many reports by Joel Bleifuss in his column, "The First Stone," published in *In These Times* during the late 1980s and early 1990s.
2. Ronald J. Ostrow, "Weinberger Indicted in Iran-Contra Affair," *Los Angeles Times*, June 17, 1992, A1, 14; David Johnston, "Walsh Implies Bush Used Pardons to Avoid Testifying," *New York Times*, February 9, 1993, A9.
3. Martin Tolchin, "Cover-Up on Iraq Is Charged to U.S.," *New York Times*, June 24, 1992, A5, 7.
4. Michael Kelly with David Johnston, "Campaign Renews Disputes of the Vietnam War Years," *New York Times*, October 1992, A1, 13.
5. Linda Greenhouse, "High Court Shuns Two Free-Press Cases," *New York Times*, January 12, 1993, A11.
6. Timothy Egan, "Los Angeles Riots Spurring Big Rise in Sales of Guns," *New York Times*, May 14, 1992, A1, 11.
7. Richard Marcinko with John Weisman, *Rouge Warrior* (New York: Pocket Books, 1992).
8. "College Student Sprays Campus with an Assault Rifle, Killing 2," *New York Times*, December 16, 1992, A9.
9. Mathis Chazanov, "Deputy Wounds Ninja Warrior—Who Turns Out to Be Neighborhood Boy," *Los Angeles Times*, September 14, 1992, B1, 6.
10. Sam Howe Verhovek, " 'Messiah' Fond of Rock, Women, and Bible," *New York Times*, March 3, 1993, A1, 11.
11. Louis Sahagun, " 'Ready for War,' Defiant Leader of Cult Tells FBI," *Los Angeles Times*, March 9, 1993, A1, 22.
12. Michael Ross, "Clinton Says He's Not Satisfied on POWs," *Los Angeles Times*, April 24, 1993, A5.

13. Dorothy Dinnerstein, *The Mermaid and the Minotaur* (New York: Harper and Row, 1977), 126.

14. Jesse Katz, "Gang Killings in L.A. County Top a Record 700," *Los Angeles Times*, December 8, 1991, A1, 24, 26.

15. David Freed, "L.A. County Found Armed, Dangerous," *Los Angeles Times*, May 17, 1992, A1, 26.

16. Martin Salvador Rocha, "Human Rights Abuse in the United States: Border Violence in the Hands of the INS," unpublished paper, Department of Chicano Studies, California State University, Long Beach, 1992.

17. The Legion of Doom story was made into a movie, *Dangerously Close*, in 1986. See also Dean E. Murphy et al., "Ace of Spades—Unlikely Clique of Militaristic Teens," *Los Angeles Times*, June 22, 1992, A1, 18.

18. Robert Bly, *Iron John: A Book about Men* (Reading, Mass.: Addison-Wesley, 1990). For an account of the men's gatherings see Jerry Adler et al., "Drums, Sweat, and Tears," *Newsweek*, June 24, 1991, 46–53.